Lecture Notes in Computer

Edited by G. Goos, J. Hartmanis, and

Springer
Berlin
Heidelberg
New York
Barcelona
Hong Kong
London
Milan
Paris
Tokyo

Gary J. Chastek (Ed.)

Software
Product Lines

Second International Conference, SPLC 2
San Diego, CA, USA, August 19-22, 2002
Proceedings

 Springer

Series Editors

Gerhard Goos, Karlsruhe University, Germany
Juris Hartmanis, Cornell University, NY, USA
Jan van Leeuwen, Utrecht University, The Netherlands

Volume Editor

Gary J. Chastek
Carnegie Mellon University
Software Engineering Institute
4500 Fifth Avenue
Pittsburgh, PA 15213, USA
E-mail: gjc@sei.cmu.edu

Cataloging-in-Publication Data applied for

Die Deutsche Bibliothek - CIP-Einheitsaufnahme

Software product lines : second international conference ; proceedings /
SPLC 2, San Diego, CA, USA, August 19 - 22, 2002. Gary J. Chastek (ed.). -
Berlin ; Heidelberg ; New York ; Barcelona ; Hong Kong ; London ; Milan ;
Paris ; Tokyo : Springer, 2002
    (Lecture notes in computer science ; Vol. 2379)
    ISBN 3-540-43985-4

CR Subject Classification (1998): D.2, K.4.3, K.6

ISSN 0302-9743
ISBN 3-540-43985-4 Springer-Verlag Berlin Heidelberg New York

Springer-Verlag Berlin Heidelberg New York
a member of BertelsmannSpringer Science+Business Media GmbH

http://www.springer.de

© Springer-Verlag Berlin Heidelberg 2002
Printed in Germany

Typesetting: Camera-ready by author, data conversion by Steingräber Satztechnik GmbH, Heidelberg
Printed on acid-free paper   SPIN: 10870457   06/3142   5 4 3 2 1 0

Foreword

Software product lines are emerging as an important new paradigm for software development. Product lines are enabling organizations to achieve impressive time-to-market gains and cost reductions. In 1997, we at the Software Engineering Institute (SEI) launched a Product Line Practice Initiative. Our vision was that product line development would be a low-risk, high-return proposition for the entire software engineering community. It was our hope from the beginning that there would eventually be sufficient interest to hold a conference. The First Software Product Line Conference (SPLC1) was the realization of that hope.

Since SPLC1, we have seen a growing interest in software product lines. Companies are launching their own software product line initiatives, product line technical and business practices are maturing, product line tool vendors are emerging, and books on product lines are being published. Motivated by the enthusiastic response to SPLC1 and the increasing number of software product lines and product line researchers and practitioners, the SEI is proud to sponsor this second conference dedicated to software product lines.

We were gratified by the submissions to SPLC2 from all parts of the globe, from government and commercial organizations. From these submissions we were able to assemble a rich and varied conference program with unique opportunities for software product line novices, experts, and those in between. This collection represents the papers selected from that response and includes research and experience reports.

I would like to take this opportunity to thank the authors of all submitted papers, and the members of the program committee who donated their time and energy to the review process. I offer my special appreciation to Len Bass and Henk Obbink, the program co-chairs, to Gary Chastek, the tireless editor of these proceedings, and to Pennie Walters who assisted in the editing process. We hope you will enjoy the fruits of our labor. Together we are pushing the frontier of software product lines.

August 2002   Linda M. Northrop

Preface

SPLC2 continues to demonstrate the maturation of the field of product lines of software. By their nature, product lines cut across many other areas of software engineering. What we see in the papers presented at this conference is the sharpening of the distinction between software engineering for single system development and software engineering for product lines. The distinction exists not only during the software life cycle (requirements gathering, design, development, and evolution) but also in the business considerations that enter into which systems to build and how to manage the construction of these systems.

We have papers that cover the introduction of product lines and the dynamics of organizations attempting to introduce product lines. We have papers that discuss how to choose which products to produce and how to model the features of those products. All of these topics are essential to the success or failure of a product line within an organization and contribute to the uniqueness of the discipline.

We have several sessions that deal with the discovery, management, and implementation of variability. Variability is perhaps the single most important distinguishing element of product lines as compared to single system development. Identification of variation among products is essential to discover the scope of a set of core development assets and identification of variations within a design is essential to manage the production of products from these core assets.

We also cover specialized topics within normal software engineering and their relationship to product line development. Topics such as necessary tool support, validation of aspects of a system's behavior, and the relationship between product lines and component-based software engineering are also covered within the program.

In short, we have selected a collection of papers that cover a broad spectrum of the areas within product lines of software and are excited about the continued development of the field.

August 2002   Len Bass and Henk Obbink

Organizing Committee

Conference Chair: Linda M. Northrop
                            (Software Engineering Institute, USA)

Program Co-chair: Len Bass
                            (Software Engineering Institute, USA)
                            Henk Obbink
                            (Philips, The Netherlands)

Tutorial Chair: Patrick Donohoe
                            (Software Engineering Institute, USA)

Workshop Chair: Sholom Cohen
                            (Software Engineering Institute, USA)

Panel Chair: Paul Clements
                            (Software Engineering Institute, USA)

Demonstration Chair: Felix Bachmann
                            (Software Engineering Institute, USA)

Proceedings Editor: Gary Chastek
                            (Software Engineering Institute, USA)

Program Committee

Table of Contents

On the Influence of Variabilities on the Application-Engineering Process of a Product Family*

Lars Geyer and Martin Becker

System Software Research Group
p.o. box 3049
University of Kaiserslautern
D-67653 Kaiserslautern, Germany
{geyer, mbecker}@informatik.uni-kl.de

Abstract. Product Families typically comprise a set of software assets, which offer the possibility to configure the product family to the needs of a specific application. The configuration process is driven by the variabilities (i.e., the variable requirements that were implemented into the software assets in the form of variation points). During application engineering, a developer selects a consistent set of variabilities; this set is used to instantiate the family assets to the needed functionality. This paper describes the influence of this configuration step on the application-engineering process of a product family. In addition, it identifies the requirements imposed on a configuration technique by the described product family application-engineering process.

1 Introduction

In many application domains, software products are part of a product line (i.e., systems are used in similar environments to fulfill similar tasks). Experiences in recent years show that it is feasible to take advantage of this relationship by implementing a product line as a product family (i.e., by a common infrastructure), which builds the core of every product. With this basis it is only necessary to configure and adapt the infrastructure to the requirements of the specific application. If product family engineering is done right, this results in a considerable decrease in effort needed for the construction of a single system.

A key problem of the success of a product family is the handling of the differences between family members. The requirements relevant to the product family are typically separated into commonalities and variabilities. The commonalities are easy to handle. Since they are part of every system in the family, they can simply be integrated into the infrastructure and automatically reused during the development of the single applications.

Handling variabilities is more difficult. They are part of only some systems in the family, so, the infrastructure has to define the places in which a variability takes effect. These so-called variation points need to be identified, and there needs to be

---

* This research was supported by the Deutsche Forschungsgemeinschaft as part of Special Research Project 501.

G. Chastek (Ed.): SPLC2 2002, LNCS 2379, pp. 1–14, 2002.

trace information between the variation points and the corresponding variability. In [4], we proposed a variability model as a model, which captures the variability-related information of a product family, and which, therefore, documents the traceability information to the associated variation points in the assets of the product family.

In this paper, we first present a detailed definition to clarify the meaning of the concepts relevant to the handling of variability and their interconnections. Second, we discuss the handling of the offered variability during the application-engineering process (i.e., we describe how the configuration of the variability in the product family is embedded into the application-engineering process). Third, we analyze the resulting application-engineering process for requirements towards a configuration technique, which is suitable in the context of product families.

In the next section, we define key terms. In Section 3, we describe the embedding of the configuration into the application-engineering process. The subsequent section deals with some specific issues in the context of this embedding. Requirements for a configuration technique are summarized in Section 5. This paper concludes with some closing remarks and a look to the future in Section 6.

2   Concepts and Their Interconnections

2.1 Product Lines and Product Families

At first, we start with the definition of a software product line. A *software product line* or is a set of software-intensive systems sharing a common, managed set of features that satisfy the specific needs of a particular market segment or mission [1]. A *product family*, on the other hand, is a set of systems built from a common set of software assets [1] (i.e., the systems of a product family are based on the same reuse infrastructure). So, the main difference between these two terms is that they describe two different viewpoints. A product line describes a set of related systems from the viewpoint of common functionality, while the term product family describes a set of systems, which are build on common assets.

The definition of product family uses the term software asset. This term is defined as either a partial solution (e.g., a component or a design document) or knowledge (e.g., a requirements database or test procedures). Engineers use assets to build or modify software products [13]. The reuse infrastructure of a product family comprises a set of assets.

2.2 Commonality and Variability

A *commonality* is a quality or functionality that all the applications in a product family share. As a consequence, commonalities are the elements with the highest reuse potential because an implementation of a commonality is used in all family members. In contrast, a variability represents a capability to change or customize a system [12] (i.e., it abstracts from the varying but coherent qualities in regard to one facet between the members of the family [4]). Variabilities always represent a variable aspect from the viewpoint of the requirements (i.e., they abstract from a variable functionality or a variable quality of the system).

The range of a variability identifies the possible variants that represent the different incarnations of the variability found in the family members. The range may also represent a numerical variability, which offers the possibility to choose the value from a range of integer or real numbers. Other variabilities are simply open issues (i.e., for them, it did not make sense to specify a finite set of variants). Instead, an environment is defined in which a developer has to integrate a specific solution for the variability. In some cases, variants may already exist variants for an open variability, but this set is not finite (i.e., new variants may be integrated for a product family member).

The variability described above deals with qualitative aspects (i.e., different kinds of functionality are chosen from a set of variants). Another type of variability is concerned with quantitative aspects. In some domains, it is necessary to include related functionality with different characteristics more than once. For example, in the domain of building automation systems, a whole set of common and variable functionality describes how a system should control a room. Typically, there are several room types in a building, like offices, computer labs, or meeting rooms. For each room type, the control strategy is the same, but the strategy differs between different room types. This results in a separate specification of the variable functionality for each room type (i.e., a set of variable requirements needs to be instantiated several times during the configuration of the product family). This quantitative type of variability is an orthogonal type compared to the qualitative variabilities; the handling of it is different, as can be seen later in this paper.

2.3 Features

The requirements of a product family are typically abstracted to features. A *feature* is a logical unit of behavior that is specified by a set of functional and quality requirements [5]. They are structured in a feature model [11][8], which creates a hierarchical ordering of the features in a tree. The hierarchy expresses a refinement relationship between features. The high-level functionality groups are typically represented near the root of the tree. These groups are refined on the next step with more detailed features, which are further refined on the next step, and so on.

Features can be classified as mandatory (i.e., they are simply part of a system if its parent in the feature hierarchy is part of the system). Alternatively, features can be classified as optional (i.e., associated with the feature is the decision of whether the feature is part of a family member). In addition, features can be numerical (i.e., associated to the feature is a range of numbers). During the configuration, the value of the feature is chosen from this numeric range.

Related optional features may be arranged in groups that are associated with a multiplicity. In this way, they allow for the definition of dependencies between features, like the classic alternative features in the Feature-Oriented Domain Analysis (FODA) method [11]. Alternative features are represented as a group with an "exactly one"-semantic (i.e., exactly one of the optional features may be part of a system). The "exactly one"-semantic can be weakened to an "at most one"-semantic (i.e., it is permissible to choose none of the alternative features). Furthermore, groups can be used to express mandatory subsets (i.e., in a group of features with an "at least one"-semantic, at least one of the features has to be part of a system).

In addition to these simple dependencies between features, there are more complex relationships. Typically, *requires* and *excludes* relationships are found in the literature (e.g., in [8]). A requires dependency exists when the integration of a feature requires the integration of another feature. The excludes relationship, on the contrary, exists when two feature as incompatible (i.e., they are not allowed to be part of the same system). But dependencies can also combine more than two features. These relationships are typically formulated in Boolean expressions. Between features with a numeric range, relational or even functional dependencies can be defined. In some cases, it is necessary to hold an equation, which combines the values of numerical features; in this case, we have a relational dependency between the concerned features. In other cases, it is possible to compute the value of one feature out of the values of others, yielding a functional dependency.

A feature model can be used favorably for the description of the commonalities and variabilities of a product family. Typically, the commonalities build the core of the feature tree. Plugged into this core are the variabilities as branches of the feature tree; they are further refined by subordinate features, which can be classified as mandatory or optional. Qualitative variabilities are either represented by optional features or by feature groups. Optional features represent optional variabilities, while feature groups are used if a variability contains more than one variant. Numerical variabilities are expressed by numerical features, and open variabilities are expressed by abstract features (i.e., an abstract feature simply references an environment in which the open functionality has to be integrated). Quantitative variability is expressed by cardinalities associated to the link between a superior feature and a subordinate feature (i.e., a cardinality greater than one allows for a multiple instantiation of the subtree defined by the subordinate feature).

Feature models are a suitable basis for the configuration of the product family (i.e., they can be used as the basic structure of a decision model for the adaptation of the assets of a product family). The feature models can be described easily in a configuration technology, which is used during the configuration process to specify a consistent set of features. This feature set is mapped onto the reuse infrastructure, allowing a fast construction of the core functionality of an application. A detailed description of this process is given in the next section.

2.4 Variation Points

Jacobsen, et al. define a variation point as an identifier of one or more locations in a software asset at which the variation will occur [10]. We restrict this definition to one location, therefore allowing multiple variation points to identify locations where a specific variation will occur (i.e., a variation point always identifies one spot in an asset, but a variability may influence more than one variation point). Nonetheless, variation points reflect the variabilities' impacts in the assets. Typically, there is a set of solutions that can be integrated into one variation point. Each alternative of a variation point implements a solution for a specific variant of the variability.

The solutions, which resolve a variation point, are typically of three types [3]. The first type is a piece of the model in which the variation point is defined (e.g., it may be a piece of code or a part of an architecture). The piece is simply pasted into the model, thereby replacing the variation point. The new piece can contain additional variation points, so the resolution of variation points is a recursive process.

The second type is a variation point representing a parameter whose value is generated. This starts from a simple substitution of a symbol with a value. But it can also comprise the generation of a piece of the asset's model out of a high-level specification, which is completed by the selection of a variant for a variability. During the generation, new variation points can be inserted into the asset model, also resulting in a recursive resolution of variation points.

The third type simply defines an empty frame in which a solution must be created in a creative task by a developer. This type of variation point always comes into play if the range of the variability is open (i.e., not completely defined during the domain-engineering process). In some cases, a variation point is associated with an open set of alternatives. In order to resolve the variation point, it is possible to either choose one of the alternative solutions or integrate an application-specific solution that is developed in a creative task.

Associated with each variation point is a binding time, at which the resolution of the variation point takes place. Typical binding times are architecture configuration (component selection), component configuration (component parameterization), startup time, and runtime. The detailed dependencies between the resolution of variation points at the specified binding time and the application-engineering process are described in the next section.

The relationship between variabilities and variation points is *n to m* (i.e., one variability may affect several variation points and, conversely, a variation point may be influenced by several variabilities). One variability can have variants, which influence the system not only in different components but also at different binding times. Figure 1 shows the connection between assets, variation points, and variabilities.

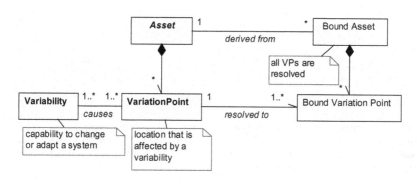

Fig. 1. The Connection Between Variabilities, Variation Points and Assets

3 The Application-Engineering Process

In this section, we will describe the embedding of variability handling into the application-engineering process of a product family. We describe the embedding in this section, and present some integration issues in the next section.

3.1 The Product Family Process

The product family process can be seen in Figure 2. In this figure, the well-known six-pack is presented (i.e., on the upper half of the picture, the domain-engineering process is shown, which comprises the domain analysis, the domain design, and the domain implementation tasks). Each of these steps has one equivalent in the application-engineering process, shown on the lower half of the figure. The counterpart of the domain analysis is the application requirements engineering, followed by the application design and the application implementation task.

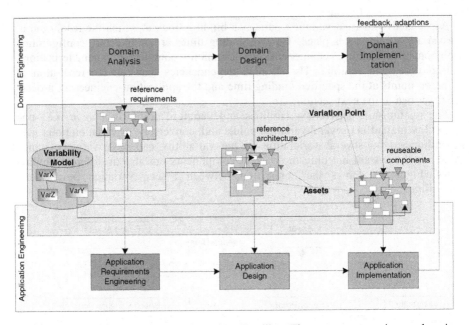

Fig. 2. The Development Process of Product Families: The process comprises a domain-engineering process, which implements the reuse infrastructure shown on asset base between the two subprocesses. The reuse infrastructure is used in the application-engineering process as the core for the development of family members.

In a product family approach, the domain-engineering process is responsible for the creation of reusable assets, which are shown in Figure 2 between the two processes in the middle. The domain-engineering process generates assets on each level (i.e., in the asset base are requirements templates, a generic software architecture, and reusable generic components). Each asset is associated to a specific process task, in which the contained variation points are bound to concrete solutions: the variation points with a binding-time architecture configuration are to be found in assets associated to the application design task. After this task is performed, all variation points with this binding time are bound to a solution. The variation points with a binding-time component configuration are to be found in assets associated to the application implementation task. After performing this task, all variation points with this binding time are bound to a solution.

After the component configuration, the assets of the product family contain only variation points with binding times of startup or runtime. These two binding times need to be handled in another way, which is described in the next section.

3.2 The Variability Model as Mediator Between Variabilities and Variation Points

An important question is how a solution is chosen for a specific variation point. As stated earlier, variation points are associated to variabilities (i.e., a variation point offers different solutions according to the possible variants specified for a specific variability). So basically, the selection of a solution for a variation point is done by choosing a variant of a variability. In order to map variants to associated solutions, we need a description of the connection between variabilities and variation points. This management functionality is the task of the variability model found on the left side of Figure 2.

The variability model is an orthogonal model, which affects all tasks of the application-engineering process. It contains information about all variabilities to be found in the product family. In addition, the model lists all traces between variabilities and variation points.

After the selection of variants for the variabilities, the variability model allows for the tracing of the chosen variants' impact on the associated variation points (i.e., with the information found in the variability model, it is possible to bind the variation points to solutions that match the set of variants selected for the specific application). It also prepares the assets for the integration of new solutions in the case of open variabilities (i.e., it helps the developer to identify places in the assets that need additional implementation effort).

3.3 The Influence of the Variability Model on the Application-Engineering Process

So basically, each task in the application-engineering process has a common structure. First, the unbound variabilities, which are associated with variation points of assets used in the task, are configured. In a possibly automated way, the assets are parameterized according to the chosen variants by following the trace information of the variability model. Open variabilities and additional requirements, which were not considered initially in the product family, are introduced into the application (i.e., open variation points are filled to meet the needs of the specific application). In addition, new requirements are integrated by adapting the assets of the reuse infrastructure. This last step is critical, since it is a creative step that integrates ideas into the product family for which it was not specialized (i.e., typically, this task is the most time consuming and comprises the highest risk of introducing errors).

Figure 3 shows the consequences of the application-engineering process. In the middle, the different process tasks are presented. Typically, we have two tasks, the application design and the application implementation. The requirements documents are completed step by step in each process task, by first selecting the matching variants for a variability and, second, by integrating new requirements into the documentation. In each task, assets are adapted to the requirements of the application. As stated earlier, this adaptation starts with a selection of variants for specific variabilities. But not all variabilities are relevant in this task. Only the variabilities, which have an impact on variation points found in assets used in the task, need to be considered in the configuration step. This is indicated in the figure on the left-hand side. The beams represent the set of variabilities of the product family. In each task, variants are selected for only a part of the variabilities. At the end of the application-engineering process, there may still be unresolved variabilities. The selection of variants for these variabilities takes place at startup or runtime, so the system contains some variation points and the necessary functionality for the selection of different variants, and the binding to the right solution for the associated variation point at the specified binding time.

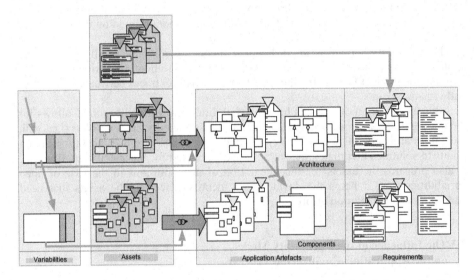

Fig. 3. The Application Design and Application Implementation Tasks of the Application-Engineering Process: In both tasks, the variation points of the associated assets are bound to solutions, which include functionality represented by variants of a variability.

As a consequence, the requirements elicitation is a continuous process within the application development (i.e., variabilities, which affect only late variation points, do not have to be selected early in the process). The selection of a variability may be postponed as long as there is an associated variation point integrated into the product family. This issue is analyzed in detail in the next section.

Because of this separation of the selection of variabilities into different process phases, the configuration step has to be supported by an adequate configuration technique. This technique has to offer the decisions for the tasks that influence variation points. We describe requirements for an adequate configuration technique in Section 5.

4 Additional Influences on the Application-Engineering Process

In this section, we describe some additional issues in the context of the application-engineering process. First, we describe in detail the connection between variabilities and variation points. Second, we take a look at the consequences of late bound variabilities (i.e., variabilities bound at startup or runtime). And last, we show the consequences on the requirements engineering.

4.1 Variabilities and Variation Points

An issue in this context is the connection between variabilities and variation points. Actually, there are two dimensions for the selection of a variability's variant. The first dimension is the variant, which is chosen for a specific application. This is the obvious dimension, which results in different functionality in the applications.

The second dimension is the time at which a decision is taken. It is possible to associate variation points with different binding times to one variability. For example, for one variability, there can be one variation point in the architecture, which allows the integration of highly optimized components during the application design task. If the selection of a variability is critical for the success of the application development, it may make sense to delay that decision to the application implementation task in order to minimize the risk. Therefore, an additional variation point is inserted into an asset associated to the application implementation task. This variation point allows the later integration of a solution for the variability, but at the potential cost of a less optimized solution.

As a consequence, the decision has to be considered in both tasks. During application design, the developer has the opportunity to select a variant out of the set of possible variants, or may postpone the decision. Postponing the decision also results in a binding of the variation points. In contrast to the highly optimized solutions, the binding results in the integration of a general component, which allows the integration of a solution in a later task. If the decision is postponed, the variability has to be considered once more during the application implementation task, in order to bind the variation points in the associated assets. If the variability is decided in the earlier task, the decision is carried along for the remainder of the development process. So, associated variation points in assets used in the later task can be bound automatically to the specified solution.

It is further possible to integrate variation points with even later binding times (i.e., the same variability which can be bound during application design or application implementation may also be bound as late as startup or runtime). Therefore, it is possible to once more postpone the decision during application implementation, resulting in the integration of solutions for all possible variants of the variability as well as a mechanism that allows the selection of a variant at the specified binding time.

The binding time, which offers the last possibility for a variability to be selected, is called the *latest binding time* of the variability. This does not have to be the last binding time for a variation point associated to the variability; the variation point may pinpoint a location in an asset that needs to be bound to a variant solution that must be selected at an earlier binding time. For example, a variation point may be needed in order to configure a component to the needs of a specific variant, which also requires the binding of a variation point to a specific solution in the earlier application design task. So, the variability needs to be decided in the design task and has additional impact on a variation point in the implementation task. The latest binding time in this case would be the application design task.

Naturally, the range of possible variants decreases with time, as more special variants of a variability need specific solutions that must be integrated early in the process. If the decision is postponed, the variation point is bound with a generic solution that does not allow the integration of the special variant any longer. For example, a specific variant of a variability may need the integration of a specific component during the application design task. If the decision is postponed, this variant is no longer selectable since the variation point in the asset of the design task is not bound to the required solution.

4.1.1 Example

In an operating system, there may be an optional feature *network support* (i.e., integrating network support into a runtime platform is optional). The runtime platform product family may now offer several variation points, which allow the integration of network support. On the architectural level, there may be some very specific components that implement efficient combinations of protocols and physical interfaces, such as a component that is specialized on TCP/IP over an ethernet or a component that runs AppleTalk over a token-ring network. If the decision is postponed in the architectural design task, the variation point for network support is resolved with a general component that offers the possibility to be parameterized to different network interfaces. This component may be parameterized to a specific network interface during the implementation phase, thereby inserting some overhead into the application, or the decision about the network interface may be further postponed to runtime (i.e., the general component needs to be parameterized to integrate network drivers for different network types at runtime). Consequently, a specific mechanism must be provided by the application that offers the possibility to select the network interface necessary at one point in time.

It is also possible that one variation point is influenced by more than one variability. An example for this case is a family that offers two functionalities. Both functionalities can be integrated into an application alone, but they need conflict management when integrated together. The conflict management component is integrated at a variation point that is influenced by the variabilities representing the two functionalities.

4.2 The Startup and Runtime Binding Times

A special treatment is necessary for the variation points with associated startup and runtime binding times. Typically, a variation point of these types is associated with other variation points that are bound to a solution during the application-engineering process (i.e., at an earlier binding time). The associated variation points are responsible for the insertion of different solutions for the still selectable variants into the application, as well as the integration of a specific mechanism that allows the binding of the variation points with these late binding times. For a variation point bound at startup time, there is a need for a mechanism that allows the binding of variation points at startup (e.g., a component), and that reads a configuration file and integrates the therein-specified solution into the application. For a runtime variation point, an additional mechanism like an option dialog box, which allows the user to select the required variant, is needed.

As can be seen, the handling of these two binding times always requires the integration of overhead into the application that is responsible for the resolution of the variation point at the specified binding time.

4.3 Consequences on Requirements Engineering

As described earlier, the application requirements engineering task is spread over the whole application-engineering process. Throughout the process, decisions have to be taken which affect the current engineering task. Requirements are pinpointed as late as possible to reduce the need to change already defined requirements. In Figure 3, this can be seen on the right-hand side. The requirements documents are carried along the different development tasks, and the variation points in these documents are bound to the selected solutions as a byproduct of the performed process task.

An important advantage of the described requirements engineering is the possibility to postpone critical feature decisions as long as possible within the product family. With the cost of a little overhead, it is possible to reduce the risk of a wrong decision to a minimum. The possibility of wrong decisions is further reduced by the fact that a customer is supported during the definition of the requirements, because he or she does not have to define the requirements from scratch. Instead, he or she is lead through the possible functionality offered by the product family and can select functionality out of the offered possibilities. Simultaneously, he or she takes advantage of the configuration technique, which prevents selection of an inconsistent feature set. The description of the dependencies combined with their evaluation using an inference machine takes care of that. This knowledge is furthermore communicated to the customer allowing him or her to understand the problems of the inconsistent feature combination.

Another advantage is the completeness of the requirements. Because the requirements model defines possible combinations of variants, it is easy to consider relevant requirements. As a result, the method prevents the customers from forgetting important requirements and, as a consequence, under specifying an application. On the other hand, the completeness allows the customer to grasp the possibilities of the product family, and supports the specification of only those additional requirements that are absolutely necessary. Since the integration of additional requirements is a time- and resource-consuming step, this reduction to the minimum helps in finding a satisfying solution for both the customer and the producer of the software.

5 Requirements for a Configuration Technique

In the last three sections, the basic principles of configuration in a product family were described. Configuration takes place during the whole application-engineering process. In all of the tasks, there is a configuration step based upon the variabilities of the product family. Variabilities are presented in all process tasks in which they have an influence on the associated assets' variation points. On the other hand, early decisions influence the binding of variation points in later process steps, so they have to be carried along the whole development process.

The configuration is based upon the variabilities in the variability model. Part of the variability model is a feature model described in Section 2. The feature model is used as the basis for the decision model of a product family. It abstracts the variabilities and structures them into a feature hierarchy (i.e., the core of the model is build upon the mandatory features that represent the common requirements of the family). Attached to this core are the variable requirements in the form of optional features. They can be grouped together in order to build alternative or subset feature groups. Additional dependencies have to be expressed to guarantee consistent feature selections, which result in well-configured product family assets. These dependencies have to be formulated within the feature model; an inference machine has to evaluate the dependencies during the application configuration.

As a consequence, a configuration technique has to allow the description of features as basic knowledge elements. These knowledge elements have to be integrable into a refinement hierarchy, which is basically an aggregation hierarchy. In addition, the links of the aggregation hierarchy define the status of the features (i.e., the links comprise cardinality information). This allows the definition of options [cardinality 0..1], mandatory features [cardinality 1..1], and quantitative variabilities [cardinality > 1]. It must be possible to define groups of knowledge containers for which a cardinality can be defined. With this mechanism, it is possible to define alternative or subset feature groups. The knowledge elements have to allow all types of possible ranges (i.e., besides enumerations and numerical ranges, the technique has to allow the representation of open variabilities).

The technique needs a constraint mechanism, which allows the definition of dependencies between features. The mechanism needs to be sufficient for the definition of all types of dependencies described in Section 2.

An important issue is the presentation of the model during modeling, as well as during configuration. In both cases, the aggregation hierarchy must be central to the presentation in order to make the understanding of the model and the navigation within the model as easy as possible. This seems to be obvious, but classical configuration techniques known from the knowledge-based system community concentrate on the inheritance structure, which is important to the understanding of configuration, but not necessary in the configuration process described above.

The technique needs a view mechanism, which allows the separation of the decision model into the parts needed in the different tasks (as described in Section 3). It must be possible to insert knowledge elements into more than one view to reflect the property and variation points in different process tasks may offer solutions for the implementation of a variability. Additionally, it is necessary to change the range of possible values in different views, since some alternatives may be not selectable in a specific process task. It must be possible to postpone decisions in one view, as well as to handle decisions already made in other views when presenting the relevant view in one process task.

Other requirements concern the support of the user during the configuration process. A strategy mechanism should help users to select the different features in an order that allows them to take advantage of the dependencies (i.e., that offers the opportunity to decide about as many features as possible automatically by the inference machine). Therefore the inference machine has to support the automatic selection of features; for example, in a requires dependency, if the condition is true, the required feature can be included into the feature selection automatically. On the other hand, in an exclude dependency, if one of the referenced features is chosen into the feature selection, the other feature can be excluded automatically.

These are basically the requirements for a configuration technique usable in a product family context.

6   Conclusion and Further Work

In this paper, we presented the consequences of variability on the structure of a product family as well as on the application-engineering process. We defined the basic terms typically used in the context of product families and described the dependencies between these terms. An important statement of the paper is the clear distinction of variabilities and variation points and the discussion of binding-time-related issues. In a recent paper [6] these two terms are used somewhat as synonyms.

Another statement is the distribution of the requirements-engineering task over the whole application-engineering process, allowing the customer to select requirements as late as possible. This is somewhat more general than a direct usage of features for the description of variabilities, as proposed in [7].

The technique proposed in this paper defines a set of requirements that have to be met by a configuration method. We summarized the induced requirements in a separate section of this paper. In the future we will define a configuration technique that meets the described requirements. This technique will be based on our earlier work about extended design spaces [2]. This technique will be further enhanced in order to meet the requirements. The concentration on this rather simple technique is necessary, since a survey on classical configuration techniques has shown that these techniques have a different understanding of configuration. This understanding renders them rather useless for the configuration problem described in this paper (see [9] for details).

References

1.   Bass, L.; Clements, P.; Donohoe, P.; McGregor, J.; Northrop, L.: Fourth Product Line Practice Workshop Report, http://www.sei.cmu.edu/publications/documents/00.reports/00tr002.html, November 1999
2.   Baum, L.; Geyer, L.; Molter, G.; Rothkugel, S.; Sturm, P.: Architecture-Centric Software Development Based on Extended Design Spaces, ARES 2nd Int'l Workshop on Development and Evolution of Software Architectures for Product Families, Feb. 1998
3.   Baum, L.; Becker, M.; Geyer, L.; Molter, G.: Mapping Requirements to Reusable Components using Design Spaces, Proc. of IEEE Int'l Conference on Requirements Engineering (ICRE 2000), Chicago, USA, 2000
4.   Becker, M.; Geyer, L.; Gilbert, A.; Becker, K.: Variability Modeling as a Catalyst for Efficient Variability Treatment, Proceedings of the 4th Workshop on Product Family Engineering (PFE-04), Bilbao, Spain, 2001

5. Bosch, J.: Design and Use of Software Architectures - Adopting and Evolving a Product Line Approach, Addison-Wesley, 2000
6. Bosch, J.: Variability Issues in Software Product Lines, Proceedings of the 4th Workshop on Product Family Engineering (PFE-04), Bilbao, Spain, 2001
7. Capilla R., Dueñas, J.C., Modeling Variability with Features in Distributed Architectures, Proceedings of the 4th Workshop on Product Family Engineering (PFE-04), Bilbao, Spain, 2001
8. Czarnecki, K; Eisenecker, U.W.: Generative Programming - Methods, Tools, and Applications, Addison-Wesley, 2000
9. Geyer, L.: Configuring Product Families Using Design Spaces, to be published in Proceedings of the Sixth World Conference on Integrated Design & Process Technology (IDPT2002), Pasadena, California, USA, 2002
10. Jacobson, I.; Griss, M.; Jonsson P.: Software Reuse - Architecture, Process and Organisation for Business Success, ACM Press / Addison-Wesley, 97
11. Kang, K.; Cohen, S.; Hess, J.; Nowak, W.; Peterson, S.: Feature-Oriented Domain Analysis (FODA) Feasibility Study, Technical Report, CMU/SEI-90-TR-21, Software Engineering Institute, Carnegie Mellon University, Pittsburgh, PA, USA, November 1990
12. Van Gurp, J.; Bosch, J.; Svahnberg, M.: On the Notion of Variability in Software Product Lines, Proc. of the Working IFIP Conference on Software Architecture (WICSA 2001), August 2001
13. Withey, J.: Investment Analysis of Software Assets for Product Lines, http://www.sei.cmu.edu/publications/documents/96.reports/96.tr.010.html, Software Engineering Institute, Carnegie Mellon University, Pittsburgh, PA, USA, 1996

Representing Variability in Software Product Lines: A Case Study

Michel Jaring and Jan Bosch

University of Groningen
Department of Mathematics and Computing Science
PO Box 800, 9700 AV Groningen
The Netherlands
{m.jaring, bosch}@cs.rug.nl
http://www.cs.rug.nl/Research/SE

Abstract. Variability is the ability to change or customize a software system (i.e., software architects anticipate change and design architectures that support those changes). If the architecture is used for different product versions (e.g., in a software product line context, it becomes important to understand where change has to be planned and the possible options in particular situations. Three variability issues have been identified in a case study involving a software company specializing in product and system development for a professional mobile communication infrastructure. These issues are discussed and analyzed and illustrate the need for handling variability in a more explicit manner. To address this need, this paper suggests a method to represent and normalize variability in industrial software systems. The method is exemplified by applying it to the software product line of the aforementioned company.

1 Introduction

The notion of constructing software systems by composing software components and a family of software products is not recent [23][25]. Combining both concepts has resulted in approaches towards software design that share the ability to delay design decisions to a later phase in the development process [19][20]. The recent emergence of software product lines provides an example of delayed design decisions. The core idea of software product line engineering is to develop a reuse infrastructure that supports the software development of a family of products. The differences between the products express variation or variability (i.e., it is a form of diversification).

The relationship between a family of products (e.g., a software product line) and variability has been identified in both research [1][10] and industry by, among others, the coauthor of this paper [7]. However, insight into this relationship is still limited, and the approach towards variability tends to differ in both areas of expertise. In general, the focus in research is to establish a commonly accepted concept of variability, whereas industry focuses on how to handle variability. Since architects have been able to handle variability in large-scale software systems in the past, it is likely that practice may lead theory at this point [15]. To establish a basis for

G. Chastek (Ed.): SPLC2 2002, LNC2379, p. 15–36, 2002.

understanding variability, it is necessary to investigate the current state of practice and the questions that arise in industry.

Several authors have reported on experiences with evolutionary software systems in an industrial context (e.g., [9][12][22]), but they do not explicitly address variability. In addition, most of this work reports primarily on large, American software companies that are often related to defense industry. Therefore, it is not necessarily representative for small and medium-sized enterprises.

This paper focuses on variability in industrial software product lines. The issues that were identified in a case study involving a Dutch-based company are discussed and analyzed and illustrate the need for handling variability in a more explicit manner. This company, Rohill Technologies BV, is a worldwide operating organization specialized in product and system development for professional mobile communication infrastructures, such as radio networks for police and fire departments. In our opinion, the organization is representative for small and medium-sized enterprises (SMEs) in software industry (i.e., a development department of approximately fifteen developers and products that are sold to industry and public organizations). The contribution of this paper is, we believe, threefold; it

- discusses an exemplar of an industrial software product line,
- presents variability related issues and
- suggests a method to represent and normalize variability.

The next section discusses variability with a focus on software product lines and provides terminology based on the work of others. Section 3 describes the case study and discusses the issues that have been identified. A method to represent and normalize variability is then suggested and exemplified by applying it to Rohill's software product line in Section 4. Section 5 surveys related work, and the paper is concluded in Section 6.

2 Variability in Industrial Software Systems

A common goal in software engineering is to prepare software for change, especially when an architecture for a family of products is designed [10]. A software architect will try to predict forthcoming changes (i.e., variations) and prepare the architecture accordingly. A boxes-and-lines diagram is sometimes used to document the architecture, where the implicit assumption is that the boxes are the points of variation [1]. However, a single variation is most often spread across multiple components due to interconnections, but a relation between two or more components is usually not documented with regard to variation. In other words, the relation between components is known, but the implications of variation through this relationship are not. In addition, it is likely that changes occur in the life cycle of an architecture that have not been anticipated in advance. If an architecture has to support unplanned changes, the dependencies among components will typically increase, which makes it harder to understand the impact of a change. Furthermore, the creators of an architecture are not necessarily the adaptors [11]. The architect generally has a concept for what to do when a change actually occurs and also understands the implications of the change. When this architect is involved in the analysis of a required variation, the result is probably sufficient [1]. However, in industrial software engineering, the adaptors of the architecture are most often not the creators. Consequently, adapting software architectures demands proper documentation, methods, techniques and guidelines for handling change (i.e., variability). Following this line, it also requires that all parties involved (customer, development, management, etc.) observe and identify variability from the same frame of reference.

The intention of identifying variability is to delay design decisions to a later phase in the software development process (i.e., to promote reuse). Recently, delaying design decisions towards later phases in the development process has received attention in both research and industry [18][21]. A software system that dynamically adapts its runtime behavior relevant to its environment by either selecting embedded alternatives or by binding modules is a typical example of a delayed design decision. The software architecture of such a product is said to be dynamic (i.e., it is static neither during development nor at runtime. Dynamic software architectures [24] are an extreme form of variability (i.e., it is not possible to delay design decisions any further). Even a conditional expression is sometimes considered as a form of variability (i.e., virtually all software architectures exhibit a certain dynamic behavior or flexibility).

Variability is generally expressed in terms of variation points. A variation point refers to the aforementioned delayed design decision (i.e., it indicates a specific point in the development or deployment phase of a software system). A typical example of variation points is the pre-processor directive shown in Figure 1.

```
#define EMBEDDED /* SIMULATION */

#ifdef SIMULATION
        #include <stdio.h>
#endif

#ifdef EMBEDDED
        #include <drivers.h>
#endif
```

Fig. 1. Selecting an embedded or simulation mode indicates a variation point (e.g., simulation mode does not require hardware drivers, but rather standard I/O instead).

A software system recognizes a number of development phases, and each phase relates to its own representation (e.g., requirement collection relates to requirement specification, whereas implementation relates to source code). As explained in [18], software development consists of transformations of these representations, and each phase can be regarded as a different abstraction level of the system. Design decisions are taken during each transformation, but some decisions are deliberately left open to support variability. These open design decisions are actually delayed design decisions (i.e., variation points). A variation point is introduced at a particular phase in the software development process and bound at either this phase, or at a phase further on in the software life cycle. Also see Figure 2.

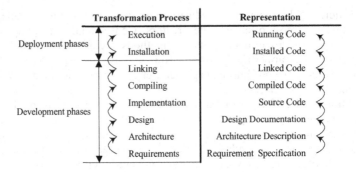

Fig. 2. Transformation and representation processes; the software life cycle is a combination of the development and deployment phases. The arrows are unidirectional, but traversing back and forth through the phases is possible (e.g., in the case of iterative software development).

In this paper, the life cycle of a software system consists of all transformation processes. The intention of designing a variation point into a system is to insert a variant (alternative) at a later phase in this life cycle. Each design decision constrains the number of possible systems that can be built [20] (i.e., during early development, there are many open design decisions). However, these decisions have not been deliberately left open and therefore do not refer to a particular point in the life cycle of a software system. From this perspective, a variation point is in one of the following three states [18]:

- Implicit: the design decision is not deliberately left open.
- Designed: the design decision is deliberately left open.
- Bound: a variant (drawn from a set of variants) related to the variation point is inserted into the system.

Each variation point relates to a set of variants that can be bound to it. With respect to this set, the following distinction between variation points is made [18]:

- Open variation points: the set of variants can be extended.
- Closed variation points: the set of variants cannot be extended.

For example, a range of wireless modems may support two profiles that aim for two groups of users: technical users, such as wireless-service-provider personnel who are interested in debugging problems using their wireless communications service; and non-technical users who do not require detailed information (they are only interested in general information about the current connection). The components that implement these profiles are the available variants to bind this designed variation point. For example, the variation is introduced at the design phase and bound at runtime. If the two profiles are the only variants possible, the variation point is closed.

2.1 Variability in Software Product Lines

A typical example of delayed design decisions is found in software product lines. The goal of the software product line approach is the systematic reuse of core assets for building related products (i.e., by developing a product line instead of single products, a more efficient development and maintainability process is anticipated [2][27]). Systematic methods with a focus on software product line engineering, such as the Family-Oriented Abstraction, Specification and Translation (FAST) process described in [31], emerged. In [6], the coauthor of this paper describes a software product line as follows: a software product line typically consists of a product line architecture, a set of components and a set of products. Each product derives its architecture from the product line architecture, instantiates and configures a subset of the product line components and usually contains some product-specific code. The IEEE Standard 1471 defines architecture as [13] "the fundamental organization of a system embodied in its components, their relationships to each other and to the environment and the principles guiding its design and evolution." In [3], the software architecture of a program or computing system is defined as "the structure or structures of the system, which comprise software components, the externally visible properties of those components, and the relationships among them."

In general, there are two relatively independent development cycles in organizations that use software product lines: product line development (domain engineering) and product instantiation (application engineering). Product instantiation is the process of creating a specific product that is based on a software product line. Domain engineering is responsible for the design, development and evolution of the reusable assets (e.g., the product line architecture and shared components). Application engineering, on the other hand, relates to adapting the product line architecture to fit the system architecture of the product in question. In other words, the product line domain is divided in reusable and non-reusable assets (i.e., domain and application engineering, respectively). This approach is also taken in [19], for example.

Variability in software product lines can be observed in two dimensions [8]: space (e.g., software artifacts appear in several products) and time (i.e., software artifacts change over time). Features are suggested as a useful abstraction to express variability [18] in both dimensions (i.e., to describe the differences between products). In [6], a feature is defined as a logical unit of behavior that is specified by a set of functional and quality requirements. The underlying idea is that a feature groups related requirements (i.e., they abstract from requirements). Features can be seen as incremental units of development [16], and dependencies make it possible to link them to a component or class. Features that are associated with (depend on) other features are so-called crosscutting features. Crosscutting features make it difficult to properly implement variability and generally demand a systematic and reproducible approach towards software system design.

3   Case Study: Rohill's TetraNode Software Product Line

This section details a case study conducted at Rohill Technologies BV and provides an example of an industrial software product line. The variability issues that have been identified in the study are discussed and analyzed. In the next section, this case study is used to exemplify a theory concerning variability representation.

3.1 Case Study Methodology

The case study methodology is, among others, based on [29] and [30]. The goal of this study is to exemplify relevant variability issues that may arise in SMEs (i.e., development departments of five to fifty developers) and products that are sold to industry and public organizations. The objectives deriving from this goal are

1. Analyze the variability in an industrial software product line.
2. Provide a context to verify and validate theories on variability.

Relevant to the organization in question, the research questions arising from the above objectives were as follows

- Where and in what form does variability occur in the software life cycle?
- What variability issues are applicable?

Several variability concerns are discussed in [8] by, among others, the coauthor of this paper. Based on previous studies that were not focused on variability (e.g., [4][7][9]), several of those concerns were expected to apply to the organization under consideration. However, suitable literature related to variability in SMEs is limited. In our opinion, the most appropriate method to answer the research questions was through interviews with key persons in the organization. The interviewed party, Rohill Technologies BV [26], develops hardware-dedicated software (object oriented, C++) for a range of products and employs approximately fifteen developers with an electrical engineering background. This organization is therefore, we believe, representative for a larger category of SMEs.

We conducted interviews with the chief architect and the main developer. The interviews were preceded by an introductory talk (at least a week prior to the interviews) to explain the reason of the interviews and to itemize the topics to be discussed. This allowed the interviewees to prepare themselves (e.g., to collect the architectural overviews to be shown during the interviews). A questionnaire was used during the interviews to guide the process, and the interviewee could elaborate, if necessary. Only individuals were interviewed to increase the possibility for having in-depth discussions and to ensure that the interviewee could speak freely. The results of the interviews were discussed with the interviewees who then provided feedback to prevent misunderstandings. Additional information has been collected from company documents and by having short talks with the developers in the company. The latter was particularly useful to verify the statements of the interviewees.

3.2 Rohill Technologies BV

3.2.1 Company Background
Rohill started in 1976 with the sales of conventional private mobile radio equipment to the domestic market. Nowadays, Rohill is a worldwide organization specialized in product and system development for professional mobile communication infrastructures such as radio networks for police and fire departments (exports account for 90 percent of its sales). Rohill's main activities include the development

and integration of trunked[1] mobile radio systems according to mandatory standards. In the early 1990s, the past had proven that professional communication users require specialized, tailor-made systems to maximize the result of their organization. The company therefore focused on research and development and contracted out most of the actual hardware production to so-called original equipment manufacturers. Their products are now tailored according to customer requirements by modifying a reusable software and hardware infrastructure.

3.2.2 TETRA versus GSM

Standard wireless communication solutions are based mainly on GSM (Global Standard for Mobile telecommunication) technology. However, the market not covered by GSM solutions requires customer-specific solutions (i.e., application-specific development is necessary). Most of the specialized products are related to trunked mobile radio systems that are compliant to several standards such as TETRA (Trans-European Trunked Radio). The TETRA standard is defined by the ETSI (European Telecommunications Standards Institute) that joins the interests of network operators, national administrations, equipment manufacturers and users. The ETSI publishes telecommunication standards that are mandatory for use in Europe, but also widely applicable outside Europe (this is the case with, among others, the GSM). The GSM is primarily a telephony standard for public cellular telephony, whereas TETRA is a professional mobile radio standard for demanding markets, such as railway and airline companies, and fire and police departments.

The TETRA and GSM standards overlap, but there are fundamental differences in their functional and quality requirements. The transmission architecture for the GSM is highly hierarchical and optimized for central delivery, and call validation is performed on each transaction. The consequences are long call-set-up times, high transmission costs and limited inherent resilience (i.e., a single system failure can cause major disruption in services). TETRA, on the other hand, relies on an intelligent, distributed network architecture optimized for local delivery and call validation performed per session. Such an architecture results in low transmission costs, fast call-set-up times, and inherent system resilience, and is scalable (with regard to the GSM transmission architecture).

3.2.3 TetraNode Software Design Model

The trunked mobile radio product range developed by Rohill is referred to as TetraNode. It is an implementation of the TETRA standard and the focus of the case study. The general architecture of TetraNode does not use the hierarchical model of the traditional (mobile) telephone network. Instead, it uses a model similar to the Internet. A central switch is therefore not necessary, and reliability is increased due to redundant pathways and distributed functionality. The protocol for data transport is based on the TCP/IP standard, which allows adding new nodes to the network to extend its coverage. Figure 3 depicts the overall decomposition of the software design model of TetraNode in terms of components and subsystems.

---

[1] Trunking is the automatic and dynamic allocation of a small number of radio repeaters among many users.

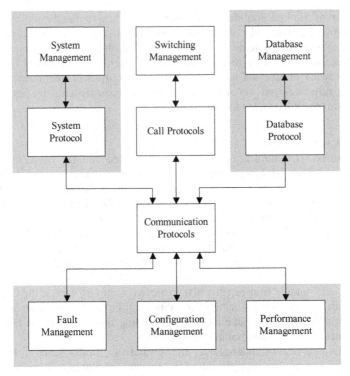

Fig. 3. Software Design Model of the Trunked Mobile Radio System (TetraNode): The shaded boxes indicate related subsystems of functional modules.

3.2.4 Quality Issues
The high level of quality demanded by the professional telecommunications market and regulatory bodies requires a quality system that relates to the organization, products and services. For the development and implementation of the adopted quality system, the company refers to the ISO 9004-1 guidelines. The actual production is contracted out to ISO 9002 certified subcontractors. The specifications and procedures for quality assurance in final inspection and testing have been documented (i.e., each product has to meet the relevant requirements with respect to safety, durability, liability, type approvals and ETSI regulations). Over the last few years, several large companies such as Dutch PTT, AEG Germany and GEC Marconi England have successfully audited Rohill according to the ISO 9000 model.

3.3 Rohill's Software Product Line

3.3.1 Software Architecture
As illustrated in Figure 4, Rohill applies a layered software architecture that allows building applications according to the software product line approach. Three TetraNode products are the professional, medium and minimal solution. This range of products is characterized by differences in both software and hardware that are anticipated prior to implementation. Specific customer requirements are met by

adapting one of these three products after product instantiation. For example, a Dutch electricity supply company requested a trunked radio network that would allow radio communication in case of power supply, radio channel, site, or switch failure. An appropriate product was selected from the product line and adapted by adding additional components that implement the required functionality.

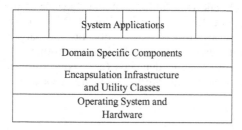

	System Applications	
Domain Specific Components		
Encapsulation Infrastructure and Utility Classes		
Operating System and Hardware		

Fig. 4. The Layered Software Architecture of TetraNode

The general architecture of TetraNode is designed and maintained by the architect. In addition, the architect also controls the header files and reviews the source code directly related to the quality requirements of the system. Documentation, such as the architecture design document and quality assurance documents is available.

3.3.2 TetraNode Software Product Line
The TetraNode product line is based on single software architecture that is reduced to yield one out of the three products (i.e., it is a software product line according to the so-called maximalist approach). In other words, the product line architecture supports all (hardware-related) features, and disabling specific features creates the professional, medium or minimal solution. As illustrated in Figure 5, a product is selected from the product line and, if necessary, adapted to meet additional requirements.

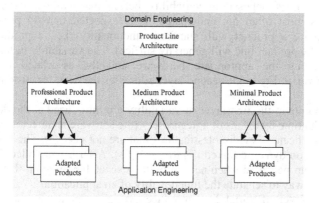

Fig. 5. The TetraNode Product Line Architecture, Product Architectures and Derived Products

The product line and product-specific life cycle refer to domain and application engineering, respectively. In other words, change occurs before and after product instantiation. Change before product instantiation relies on the reuse infrastructure, whereas change after instantiation relies on non-reusable code.

An object-oriented approach is used, mainly to facilitate program modifiability (C++). The subsystems and functional modules in Figure 3 are ultimately decomposed into classes and class utilities. A developer is assigned to one or more classes and is responsible for the functionality of these classes. Classes that are (partially) implemented are tested extensively on the target hardware and, if necessary, adapted in an iterative manner. Tests are performed by Rohill, but also by regulatory bodies to meet specific demands (e.g., concerning reliability and radio transmitter power). In general, an internal software release is available for testing every few months.

3.3.3 System Size

As opposed to their hardware platform, Rohill's software is proprietary and based on the TetraNode Foundation Classes (TFC). These classes are developed internally and provide a library for protocols, routing, security, and so forth. The TetraNode system has been under development for four years, and the TFC has recently been finished. The remainder of the system is still under development, and the total size of the system is expected to be 100 KLOC (thousand lines of code). Interestingly, the TFC implements almost all functionality, but is only about 30 KLOC. This implies that the code currently being developed is focused on selecting the appropriate features from the TFC to create the product line. In other words, the dependencies among features require more programming than programming the features themselves. This is probably due to the dependencies of crosscutting features.

3.4 Variability in the TetraNode Software Product Line

As illustrated in Figure 6, variability is identified before and after product instantiation, and, as opposed to variability before instantiation, variability after instantiation is most often not anticipated. It is expected that 80 percent of the customers require a product with standard functionality (i.e., a product selected directly from the product line will generally suffice). The variability in the first layer is about targeting the appropriate hardware and the associated functionality. Unanticipated variability in the second layer addresses the need for customer-specific solutions.

Variation points in the first layer of variability are introduced at the design phase and bound at runtime by means of a license key (the software architecture supports all features and the license key disables features that are not needed). The license key is based primarily on dynamic linked libraries (DLLs). A DLL is a collection of small programs that can be called when needed by the executable program that is running. DLLs provide a way to separate the functionality of an application.

The second layer of variability introduces variation points at the requirement specification phase and binds them at the implementation or link phase. This layer refers to customer-specific requirements and is based primarily on makefiles and product-specific code. A makefile defines those files that are needed to compile a program and how those programs are to be compiled. Product-specific code is source code that appears only in a single product (i.e., it is not to be reused).

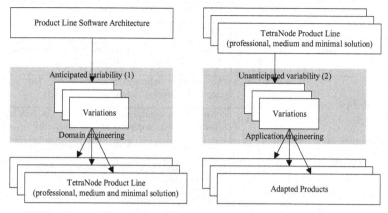

Fig. 6. Variability is identified before (1) and after product instantiation (2).

3.5 Variability Concerns in Rohill

The case study underpins several variability concerns as discussed in 7. The following concerns were identified as relevant with respect to the organizational and technical aspects of Rohill:

- Mechanism: a means to describe differences between products (e.g., pre-processor directives and makefiles)
- Phase: particular phases in the life cycle introduce and bind variation points (e.g., a variation point is introduced during design and bound during implementation)
- Representation: a notation format to describe variability
- Dependencies: the relationships between variability and features
- Tool support: the means to maintain variability information (i.e., the number of variation points, associated variants and dependencies)

Table 1 lists how these concerns are handled in Rohill from the domain (DE) and application engineering (AE) perspectives.

3.6 Variability Issues in Rohill

Three issues regarding variability have been pinpointed in Rohill: variability identification, variability dependencies and tool support. Each issue is a combination of variability concerns and is discussed together with an example taken from Rohill.

3.6.1 Variability Identification
Mechanism. Typically, variability is mapped to a single mechanism, which particularly simplifies the design phase with a risk of obstructing future maintenance. The process of selecting a variability mechanism is often based on earlier experience,

Table 1. Variability Concerns in Rohill

Mechanism	DE	DLLs
	AE	Makefiles and product-specific code
Phase (with respect to the majority of variation points)	DE	Introduced at design phase and bound at runtime
	AE	Introduced at the requirement specification phase and bound at the implementation or link phase
Representation	DE	No explicit representation available. The architect implicitly discerns variability
	AE	No explicit representation available, the architect and the developers implicitly discern variability.
Dependencies	DE	The architect implicitly discerns dependencies.
	AE	The architect and the developers implicitly discern dependencies.
Tool support	DE	No tool support available
	AE	No tool support available

but the associated costs and impact are not always understood. If a variation point has to be bound at another moment in the life cycle, a redesign to replace the current variability mechanism is necessary. The consequences of a particular variability mechanism on resource usage are generally not clear until runtime, and changing the mechanism at this phase, if possible, is probably costly.

Example. Three variability mechanisms are used in Rohill: DLLs, makefiles and product-specific code. The first applies to instantiating the product line, whereas the latter two apply to adapting the products that are selected from the product line to meet customer-specific requirements. The mechanisms selected by Rohill are in accordance with the skill level of the organization. For example, pre-processor directives were also used in the past, but after slightly reorganizing the development process (i.e., increasing the number of code reviews), this particular mechanism was replaced by makefiles. In other words, the software system was made more flexible as soon as the organization was able to do so. The architect considers the consequences of selecting a particular mechanism with respect to resource usage and underlying dependencies in an implicit manner. The architect determines how variability is handled to support the required functionality and future maintenance based on his experience and insight into the system.

Phase. Variation points are introduced and bound at particular phases in the life cycle, and selecting the optimal phase for each of these activities has a considerable impact on the flexibility of the system, as well as on the development and maintenance costs. If a variation point is bound too early, flexibility of the product line artifacts is less than required. Binding it later than necessary typically results in a more costly solution. Identifying variability is often based on analyzing commonalities and differences between products, but actually specifying the optimal phases is difficult due to lacking methods, techniques and guidelines.

Example. Methods, techniques and guidelines for optimal phase selection are not used in Rohill. Phase selection is based primarily on the experience of the architect who takes product and organizational characteristics, such as technical aspects, competence and business considerations, into account. This may explain why variability tends to accumulate at certain phases in the life cycle (i.e., phase selection is probably related to the cultural facets of the organization). To meet customer-specific requirements after product instantiation, different phases are selected at the beginning of the life cycle to introduce and bind variation points. In other words, customer-specific design decisions appear earlier in the life cycle than design decisions related to the reuse infrastructure.

3.6.2 Variability Dependencies

Representation. A notation format to describe variability is not available, so, insight into variability is difficult to obtain. In addition, the perception of variability often depends on the organization in question and the area of expertise of the people involved. There is a need for a common frame of reference (i.e., a system-independent notation to describe variability).

Example. In Rohill, variability is observed as the ability to deliberately form different products in a repeatable manner. As a result of developing products according to standards like TETRA, the differences between products are well documented, especially from a hardware perspective. Since most variability is related to the target hardware, variability and dependencies are observed mainly from a hardware perspective. The architect manages and implicitly represents variability from this perspective, which implies that (in-depth) knowledge on the product line technology is necessary to discuss variability in Rohill. In other words, Rohill's frame of reference concerning variability is technology based.

Dependencies. In general, the dependencies between variability and features are not made explicit, that is, they are (indirectly) implied, undocumented and sometimes even unintended. As a result, it is not always clear what assets should be selected to compose a product with the required functionality. This problem is strongly related to the problem of variability representation (i.e., to describe the dependencies it is, in the first instance, necessary to describe variability).

Example. Rohill develops a software architecture that supports all features of the product line. This architecture is then reduced to yield one out of three product architectures (the maximalist approach). Removing functionality from an architecture results in fewer dependencies (i.e., the complexity decreases). Despite the fact that the architect manages all dependencies, this approach works well in Rohill. However, the management of all dependencies by just one person is more than likely to become difficult, if not impossible, if the size of the system increases.

3.6.3 Tool Support

The number of variation points, associated variants, and dependencies tend to increase rapidly. Consequently, tool support for maintaining variability information is necessary, especially in the case of large-scale software systems. However, current software configuration and management tools have not been developed from a life cycle perspective and lack many required characteristics (i.e., most tools refer to a particular development phase and not to interacting transformation processes).

Example. The architect manages most of the variability in Rohill, and, strictly speaking, tool support to maintain variability information is not mandatory at the moment. However, when the size of the system increases, proper tool support is probably beneficial, if not necessary (especially in the case of the maximalist approach). In addition, it may make Rohill less dependent on key persons, since it would add explicit variability knowledge to the organization.

3.7 A Common Understanding of Variability

The three issues that have been identified in the study are (indirectly) related to each other (i.e., tool support implies insight into variability dependencies, which in turn relies on variability identification). In addition, these issues are characterized by a lacking frame of reference; how variability is observed often depends on the organization in question and the issue at hand. To handle variability, a common understanding of variability is necessary, which may support methods, techniques, tools and guidelines that are needed by software architects and developers. Several research communities study this problem from their own perspective (e.g., object-oriented frameworks, maintainability and configuration management). However, the common denominator is, in our opinion, variability representation, which implies an integrated approach towards finding a common frame of reference.

It would be beneficial if different areas of expertise, such as engineering and management, could refer to the same representation of variability. However, this requires a frame of reference that does not assume in-depth knowledge of the software system in question, but, at the same time, it should provide a proper level of information. A common understanding of variability may pave the way for identifying the variability rate of (parts of) a software system, which would make it possible to decide on variability in a more explicit manner. The next section suggests a representation and normalization of variability (i.e., a frame of reference).

4 Variability: A Frame of Reference

This section suggests a representation and normalization of variability (i.e., a first step to address the need for a system-independent frame of reference). The theory is exemplified by applying it to Rohill's software product line.

4.1 Representing Variability

There are many ways to support variability, ranging from conditional statements, pre-processor directives and inheritance to the runtime selection of the appropriate components. Such variability-realization techniques are diverse, but characterized by their introduction and binding phase in the software life cycle. To represent variability, we classify variability-realization techniques according to these phases by introducing variability sets. A variability set relates to a particular combination of an introduction and binding phase, and each variability realization technique with an introduction and binding phase that concurs with this combination is a member of this set. In other words, a variability realization technique is a member of exactly one variability set, and a variability set may consist of zero or more variability realization techniques. Grouping variability-realization techniques according to their introduction and binding phase forms a two-dimensional, triangular space (see Figure 7).

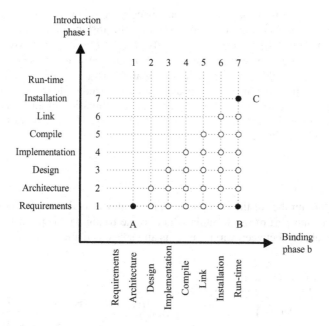

Fig. 7. A variability set is represented by a single, discrete point in a fixed-size space. The combination of the introduction and binding phase of the variability-realization techniques included in a variability set specifies the coordinates of this set.

In the context of this paper, the variability space comprises 28 variability sets. Set A indicates minimum variability, whereas set C indicates maximum variability. Sets B and C share the same binding phase, but they have different introduction phases. We have taken the line that set C indicates maximum variability (e.g., set C is more variable than set B). As said, a design decision, whether it is delayed or not, constrains the number of possible systems that can be built. When a variation point is introduced, the possible options are limited for all subsequent phases, regardless of whether the variation point is bound. For example, in Rohill, the differences between the professional, medium and minimal solutions are introduced at the design phase, but product instantiation is at runtime. The phases in between have to take these differences into account, which limits the number of options (i.e., it is less variable).

4.2 Normalizing Variability

To suggest a normalization of variability independent from the system under consideration, we assume the following with respect to Figure 7:

• A variability set relates to a certain rate of variability.

- The variability-realization techniques associated with a particular variability set relate to the same rate of variability.
- Set A indicates minimum variability, whereas set C indicates maximum variability.

The area covered by a two-dimensional space is commonly used in various fields to express a normalized measure. For example, the instantaneous power (work per unit time) consumed by a resistor is simply $P = V \cdot I$. For V in volts and I in amperes, P comes out in watts. Both V and I can be mapped on a relative scale ranging from (e.g., 0 through 1 to yield a normalized value for the consumed power). Considering that the axes in Figure 7 provide a normalized scale from 0 through 7, the area of variability space covered by a particular combination of an introduction and binding phase provides a relative measure for variability. The area of variability space covered by a variability set is

$$A(i,b) = i \cdot b - \frac{i^2}{2} \ ,$$

where i is the number of the introduction phase, and b is the number of the binding phase (the second part of the formula is due to the triangular shape of the variability space). The relation between variability sets and space is depicted in Figure 8.

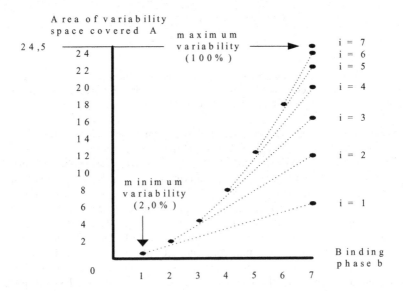

Fig. 8. Accumulation of variability space covered per introduction phase i. For clarity, only the extreme values for each introduction phase are depicted.

4.3 Case Study: Representing Variability in Rohill's Software Product Line

In Rohill, products that are instantiated directly from the product line account for approximately 80 percent of the products shipped. Instantiation is based on a license key (DLLs). The remaining products are customer specific (i.e., these products are adapted after instantiation). In general, makefiles account for approximately 5 percent and product specific code accounts for 15 percent of the variability supported in customer-specific products. Also see Table 2.

Table 2. Variability-realization techniques in Rohill's TetraNode product range.

Variability-Realization Technique	Introduction Phase	Binding Phase
A: DLLs (80%)	Design	Runtime
B: Makefiles (5%)	Requirement specification	Link
C: Product specific code (15%)	Requirement specification	Implementation

Figure 9 exemplifies the theory of representing variability graphically. Point A represents DLLs (product instantiation, 80%); point B represents makefiles (customer specific, 5%); and point C represents product specific code (customer specific, 15%). The ratio between the different variability realization techniques corresponds with the diameter of the solid points in the figure.

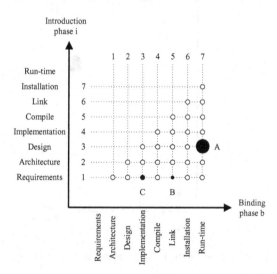

Fig. 9. Graphical representation of variability in Rohill's TetraNode product range. A: DLLs (product instantiation, 80%). B: makefiles (customer-specific, 5%). C: product specific code (customer specific, 15%)

As shown in Table 3, calculating the area covered according to equation 1 for A, B and C, respectively, yields normalized variability values. The maximum, normalized value for variability is 24,5 when $i = 7$ and $b = 7$ (the total area of variability space).

Table 3. Normalized values for the variability supported in Rohill's TetraNode product range. These values indicate the variability of each realization technique (i.e., 0 per cent implies no variability, whereas 100 percent implies maximum variability).

Varibility-Realization Technique	Normalized: absolute	Normalized: relative (%)
A: DLLs ($i=3$, $b=7$)	16,5	67
B: makefiles ($i=1$, $b=5$)	4,5	18
C: product-specific code ($i=1$, $b=3$)	2,5	10

The normalized values are plotted in Figure 10, with points A, B, and C defined as they were in Figure 9. The position of the solid points indicates the rate of variability, whereas its size indicates the rate of use.

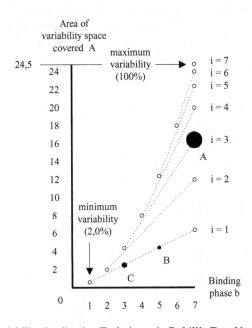

Fig. 10. The Variability-Realization Techniques in Rohill's TetraNode Product Range

Moving from one line to another (in this case, from the line associated with $i=1$ to the line associated with $i=3$) implies a nonlinear increase of variability.

Taking into account that the entire product range (including customer-specific products) is based on point A, the total rate of variability for Rohill's software system is [2]

$$((100 \cdot 16,5)+(5 \cdot 4,5)+(15 \cdot 2,5))/120 = 14,3$$

This yields a relative, normalized variability of

$$(14,3/24,5) \cdot 100\% \approx 58\% .$$

---

[2] All products (100 percent) use the license key for initial instantiation.

This measure provides an insight into the variability supported by Rohill's software. For example, makefiles have replaced the pre-processor directives in the past; the relative, normalized variability used to be

$$((100 \cdot 16,5) + (5 \cdot 3,5) + (15 \cdot 2,5)) / 120 = 14,2 \cong 58\% \,.$$

In other words, replacing pre-processor directives by makefiles has hardly affected the variability in Rohill's product range. Suppose that the variation points related to product instantiation are introduced at the implementation instead of the design phase (point A is then positioned at the end of the line $i = 4$ in Figure 10). The absolute area of variability space covered for point A then equals 20, and the normalized value becomes

$$((100 \cdot 20) + (5 \cdot 4,5) + (15 \cdot 2,5)) / 120 = 17,2 \cong 70\% \,.$$

In other words, delaying the introduction of the professional, medium and minimal solutions' characteristics would substantially increase the variability supported by Rohill's product line architecture.

5 Related Work

The notion of variation points was introduced in [19]. This book discusses topics related to software reuse, including variability. In [20], several variability mechanisms are discussed, and it sets forth how design decisions remove variability from an architecture (i.e., how variability is constrained). Using patterns to model variability in software product families is explained in [21] with a focus on the design phase. Design patterns are discussed in detail in [14] (a pattern is an element of reusable software). A domain-independent model of software system design and construction is presented in [5]. The model is based upon interchangeable software components (variants) and large-scale reuse. A categorization of features (variants) is suggested in [17], which is slightly related to the types of variation listed in [1]. The issues that have been identified in the case study relate to earlier work presented in [8] by, among others, the coauthor of this paper. A framework of terminology and concepts regarding variability is discussed in [18] that presents three recurring patterns of variability and suggests a method for managing variability in software product lines. Case studies and experience reports from our research group (e.g., [7] [28]) indicate that evolution in a family of software products is more effortful than in stand-alone products due to dependencies between products and conflicting features.

6 Conclusions

Software architects and developers have been able to handle variability in software systems in the past in an implicit manner. However, present-day software systems (e.g., software product lines) require a more explicit approach. It becomes important to represent variability in advance to understand where change has to be planned and the possible options in particular situations.

This paper focuses on variability in industrial software product lines. The variability issues listed in Table 4 have been identified in a case study involving a Dutch software company. In our opinion, this company, Rohill Technologies BV, is representative for small and medium-sized enterprises in software industry and provides a suitable context to verify and validate theories on variability. The issues identified in the study have been discussed and analyzed and illustrate the need for handling variability in a more explicit manner.

Table 4. Variability issues that have been identified in Rohill

Issue	Analysis
Variability Identification	• Limited insight into the consequences of selecting a particular variability mechanism • Methods, techniques and guidelines to select the optimal mechanism are not available.
Variability Dependencies	• A notation format to describe variability is not available. • Dependencies between variability and features are not made explicit.
Tool support	• Tools to maintain variability information are not available.

These issues are (indirectly) related to each other and characterized by a common denominator, variability representation. This implies an integrated approach towards finding a common frame of reference for variability, which may contribute to making variability more explicit.

A system-independent method to represent and normalize variability is suggested in this paper. This method consists of a graphical representation and normalization of the variability supported in a software system and is based on classifying variability-realization techniques according to their introduction and binding times in the software life cycle. The method is exemplified by applying it to Rohill's software product line. For example, the case study shows that replacing pre-processor directives by makefiles has hardly affected the variability supported in Rohill's software. On the other hand, the variability related to product instantiation has a substantial impact on the software system as a whole. In general, the method can be used to illustrate the variability of a software system without focusing on specific engineering aspects.

Acknowledgements

We would like to thank Rohill Technologies BV for participating in the case study.

References

1. F. Bachmann, L. Bass. Managing Variability in Software Architectures. Proceedings of the 2001 Symposium on Software Reusability, May 2001, 126-132.
2. J. Bayer, O. Flege, P. Knauber, R. Laqua, D. Muthig, K. Schmid, T. Widen, J.-M. DeBaud. PuLSE: A Methodology to Develop Software Product Lines. Proceedings of the Fifth Symposium on Software Reusability, May 1999, 122-131.
3. L. Bass, P. Clements, R. Kazman. Software Architecture in Practice. Addison-Wesley, 1998.

4. L. Bass, P. Clements, S. Cohen, L. Northrop, J. Withey. Product Line Practice Workshop Report. Technical Report CMU/SEI-97-TR-003, Software Engineering Institute, 1997. http://www.sei.cmu.edu/publications/publications.html

5. D. Batory, S. O'Malley. The Design and Implementation of Hierarchical Software Systems with Reusable Components. ACM Transactions on Software Engineering and Methodology, Vol. 1, No. 4, October 1992, 355-398.

6. J. Bosch. Design & Use of Software Architectures - Adopting and Evolving a Product-Line Approach. Addison-Wesley, 2000.

7. J. Bosch. Evolution and Composition of Reusable Assets in Product-Line Architectures: A Case Study. Proceedings of the First Working IFIP Conference on Software Architecture, October 1999, 92-97.

8. J. Bosch, G Florijn, D. Greefhorst, J. Kuusela, H. Obbink, K. Pohl. Variability Issues in Software Product Lines. Proceedings of the Fourth Workshop on Product Family Engineering, October 2001, to be published at Springer LNCS.

9. L. Bronsword, P. Clements. A Case Study in Successful Product Line Development. Software Engineering Institute, CMU/SEI-96-TR-016, 1996. http://www.sei.cmu.edu/publications/publications.html

10. J. Coplien, D. Hoffman, D. Weiss. Commonality and Variability in Software Engineering. IEEE Software, Vol. 15, No. 6, November/December 1998, 37-45.

11. P. Clements, L. Northrop. A Framework for Software Product Line Practice - Version 3. Software Engineering Institute, 2001. http://www.sei.cmu.edu/plp/framework.html

12. D. Dikel, D. Kane, S.Ornburn, W.Loftus, J.Wilson. Applying Software Product Line Architecture. IEEE Computer, August 1997, 49-55.

13. D. Emery, R. Hilliard, M. W. Maier. Software Architecture: Introducing IEEE Standard 1471, IEEE, Vol. 34, No. 4, April 2001, 107-109.

14. E. Gamma, R. Helm, R. Johnson, J. Vlissides. Design Patterns: Elements of Reusable Object-Oriented Software. Addison-Wesley, 1995.

15. R. L. Glass. The Relationship Between Theory and Practice in Software Engineering. Communications of the ACM, Vol. 39, No. 11, November 1996, 11-13.

16. J. P. Gibson. Feature Requirements Model: Understanding Interactions. Feature Interactions in Telecommunications IV, IOS Press, June 1997.

17. M. L. Griss, J. Favaro, M. D'Alessandro. Integrating Feature Modelling with the RSEB. Proceedings of ICSR98, IEEE, June1998, 36-44.

18. J. van Gurp, J. Bosch, M. Svahnberg. On the Notion of Variability in Software Product Lines. Proceedings of the Working IEEE/IFIP Conference on Software Architecture, August 2001.

19. I. Jacobson, M. Griss, P. Jonsson. Software Reuse - Architecture, Process and Organization for Business Success. Addison-Wesley, 1997.

20. M. Jazayeri, A. Ran, P. van der Linden. Software Architecture For Product Families: Putting Research into Practice. Addison-Wesley, May 2000.

21. B. Keepence, M. Mannion. Using Patterns to Model Variability in Product Families. IEEE Software, July/August 1999, 102-108.

22. R. R. Macala, L. D. Stucky, D.C. Gross. Managing Domain-Specific Product-Line Development. IEEE Software, 1996, 57-67.

23. M. D. McIlroy. Mass Produced Software Components. Report on a conference of the NATO Science Committee, 1968, 138-150.

24. P. Oreizy, M. M. Gorlick, R. N. Taylor, D. Heimbigner, G. Johnson, N. Medvidovic, A. Quilici, D. S. Rosenblum, A.L. Wolf. Self-Adaptive Software: An Architecture Based Approach. IEEE Intelligent Systems, 1999.

25. D. Parnas. On the Design and Development of Product Families. IEEE Transactions on Software Engineering, Vol. 2, No. 1, 1976.

26. Rohill Technologies BV. http://www.rohill.com

27. K. Schmid. Scoping Software Product Lines - An Analysis of an Emerging Technology, in Software Product Lines: Experience and Research Directions. Proceedings of the First Software Product Line Conference, Kluwer Academic Publishers, August 2000, 513-532.
28. M. Svahnberg, J. Bosch. Evolution in Software Product Lines: Two Cases. Journal of Software Maintenance - Research and Practice, Vol. 11, No. 6, 1999, 391-422.
29. W. Tellis. Introduction to Case Study. The Qualitative Report, Vol. 3, No. 2, July 1997. http://www.nova.edu/ssss/QR/QR3-2/tellis1.html
30. W. Tellis. Application of a Case Study Methodology. The Qualitative Report, Vol. 3, No. 3, September 1997. http://www.nova.edu/ssss/QR/QR3-3/tellis2.html
31. D. M. Weiss, C. T. R. Lai. Software Product-Line Engineering: A Family-Based Software Development Process. Addison-Wesley, 1999.

Variation Management for Software Production Lines

Charles W. Krueger

BigLever Software, Inc.
10500 Laurel Hill Cove
Austin TX 78730 USA
ckrueger@biglever.com

Abstract. Variation management in a software product line is a multi-dimensional configuration management problem. In addition to the conventional configuration management problem of managing variation over time, software product lines also have the problem of managing variation among the individual products in the domain space. In this paper, we illustrate how to "divide and conquer" the variation management problem into a collection of nine smaller problems and solutions. We also show how to address the nine problems with lightweight solutions that can reduce the risks, costs, and time for establishing and maintaining a software product line.

1   Introduction

Variation management is the key discriminator between conventional software engineering and software product line engineering. In conventional software engineering, variation management deals with software variation over time and is commonly known as *configuration management*. In software product line engineering, variation management is multidimensional. It deals with variation in both time and space. In this context, managing *variation in time* refers to the configuration management of the product line software as it varies over time, while managing *variation in space* refers to managing differences among the individual products in the domain space of a product line at any fixed point in time [1][2][3][4][5][6]

In the same way that configuration management is an essential part of conventional software engineering, variation management is at the core of software product line engineering. However, the potentially complex interactions between variation in time and variation in space can make the design, implementation, and deployment of a variation management solution a daunting task. Practitioners have historically relied on intuition, ad hoc approaches, and a pioneering spirit to establish variation management strategies and techniques for their product lines. As a result, the associated risks, costs, and time of establishing and maintaining a software product line approach can be high [6][7][8].

This paper illustrates how to "divide and conquer" the variation management problem into a collection of nine small, manageable, and interrelated problems. We also show how to address these nine problems with lightweight solutions that can significantly reduce the risks, costs, and time for establishing and maintaining a software product line.

G. Chastek (Ed.): SPLC2 2002, LNCS 2379, p. 37–48, 2002.

Even more interesting is that a complete and consistent variation management solution as defined herein can be used as the fundamental basis for software product line engineering. Elevating variation management to a central role in software product line engineering offers several advantages:

- Return to single-system engineering. Collectively, the common, variant, and infrastructure artifacts in a software product line can be treated as a single software production line that evolves over time.
- Lower adoption barrier. Incremental adoption strategies, the reuse of existing technology and assets, and lightweight extensions to one-of-a-kind techniques reduce the time, cost, and effort required to adopt a product line approach [11].
- Flexible product line methodology. Different methods for different business conditions include the reuse of legacy assets versus reengineering, proactive versus reactive variation engineering, and the refactoring of variation/commonality [12].
- Formality options. Engineers can choose appropriate levels of formality, including no formal domain analysis, no formal architecture, and no componentization.

2   Divide and Conquer Variation Management

The issues of variation management in software product lines can be viewed as an extension to the issues of configuration management in one-of-a-kind systems. This view of variation management is useful, because we can reuse the proven technologies and techniques of configuration management, and then incrementally extend them as needed with technologies and techniques to cover the remaining issues of variation management.

2.1   Two Dimensions of Variation Management

Variation management can be "divided" into nine smaller issues and then "conquered" by addressing each of these subproblems. Because we have defined variation management as an extension to configuration management, some of the subproblems will be addressed by conventional configuration management technology and techniques. The division of variation management issues is represented in two dimensions by the nine-cell grid in Table 1.

Table 1. Two-Dimensional View of Variation Management

	Sequential Time	**Parallel Time**	**Domain Space**
Files	–	–	–
Components	–	–	–
Products	–	–	–

The columns in this table represent the dimension of *variation types*, while the rows represent the dimension of *granularity of software artifacts*. Each cell in the table represents a variation management issue for a given type of variation (sequential, parallel, or spatial) and for a given granularity of artifact (file, component, or product).

The first two columns in Table 1, *Sequential Time* and *Parallel Time*, are the types of time-based variation supported by conventional configuration management systems. Sequential time variation is the evolution of an artifact along a single development branch. Parallel time variation is parallel evolution along multiple development branches, which is typically associated with parallel maintenance branches. The third column, *Domain Space*, represents the type of variations that arise to support multiple products in the domain space of a software product line. Combined, these three columns represent the complete set of variation that exists in a software product line.

The rows in Table 1 are the different granularity of artifacts that are supported by convention configuration management and, likewise, must be supported by variation management in software product lines. Variations of *files* are composed to create variations of *components*, and variations of *components* are composed to create variations of *products*.

Modeling variation at the granularity of files may seem counterintuitive at first. However, by using files, components, and products for the artifact granularity in variation management, we have preserved an important property of conventional configuration management – neutrality to architecture, design, and language. That is, neither configuration management nor variation management are concerned with the content of files or the semantics of the file collections used to create a component or product.

2.2   Solution Clusters in the Variation Management Grid

Solutions to the nine subproblems in the variation management grid come from three different technology areas. These three solution technologies and the subproblems that they address are shown as three clusters in Table 2: *Basic Configuration Management, Component Composition, and Software Mass Customization.*

Table 2. Variation Management Clusters

	Sequential Time	**Parallel Time**	**Domain Space**
Files	Basic Configuration Management		Software Mass Customization
Components			
Products	Component Composition		

Basic Configuration Management technology, available in commercial configuration management systems, addresses four of the time-based variation management cells. *Component Composition* technology, either homegrown or commercially available in a few configuration management systems, addresses the other two time-based variation issues. *Software Mass Customization* technology, either homegrown or commercially available, addresses the three issues of variation in the domain space column.

2.3   Nine Subproblems of Variation Management

Table 3 illustrates the nine subproblems of variation management. The clusters from Table 2 are also drawn in the table and are used to organize the following descriptions of the subproblems. Details on these problems and their solutions are provided in later sections.

2.3.1   Basic Configuration Management

- Version management. Versions of files as they change over time.
- Branch management. Independent branches of file evolution.
- Baseline management. Snapshots of consistent collections of file versions.
- Branched baseline management. Independent branches of baseline evolution.

Table 3. Nine Subproblems of Variation Management

	Sequential Time	**Parallel Time**	**Domain Space**
Files	Version management	Branch management	Variation point management
Components	Baseline management	Branched baseline management	Customization management
Products	Composition management	Branched composition management	Customization composition management

2.3.2   Component Composition

- Composition management. Snapshots of consistent compositions of component versions.
- Branched composition management. Independent branches of component compositions.

2.3.3   Software Mass Customization

- Variation point management. Variants of files in the domain space.
- Customization management. Consistent compositions of common and variant files.
- Customization composition management. Compositions of customized components.

3   Production Line Versus Product Line

The effectiveness of variation management in a software product line depends on the way that software artifacts are structured in the engineering process. We offer the following rule of thumb:

"Variation manages the *production line* rather than the *product line*."

That is, the artifacts under variation management should include all of the common artifacts, variant artifacts, and the product instantiation infrastructure (collectively the production line), but not the individual products that are instantiated (collectively the product line). The individual products should be treated as transient outputs of the production line that can be discarded and re-instantiated as needed.

Figure 1 and Figure 2 illustrate why we emphasize this distinction between product line and production line. Figure 1 illustrates a general approach to variation management, such as the one described in [6], that allows each product to be refined and independently configuration managed, after it is instantiated from the core assets. Although some organizational and business constraints demand this generality (for example, see [9]), there are some undesirable implications of structuring variation management around a product line that should be avoided if possible.

The bold box in Figure 1 encloses all of the artifacts under variation management, including the common and variant artifacts created during domain engineering (i.e., the core assets), the instantiation infrastructure used to assemble common and variant artifacts into a product instance, and all of the product instances that can be further refined after instantiation via independent product development.

From a variation management perspective, the structure and process in Figure 1 has several negative properties.

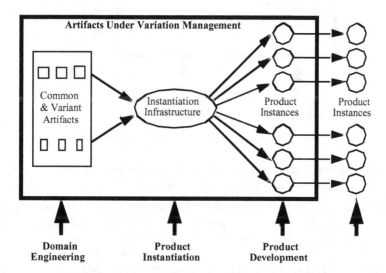

Fig. 1. Variation Management of a Product Line

- Each product instance becomes a clone that takes on a life of its own after instantiation as it undergoes further refinement via product development. For example, if there are 100 product instances, then there are 100 independent, divergent product evolutions in variation management.
- Modifications made to a product instance during product development are not reflected back into the common and variant artifacts (core assets), nor are they reflected in other product instances. A separate engineering activity is required to refactor changes made to a product instance back into the core assets and other products.
- Enhancements and fixes applied to the common and variant artifacts cannot be applied directly to the product instances, since product development may have introduced incompatible changes to some of the product instances.

In contrast, Figure 2 shows variation management structured around a production line. In this case, only the common and variant artifacts and the instantiation infrastructure are variation managed. The product instances are outside of variation management and are used directly without any further modification via application engineering.

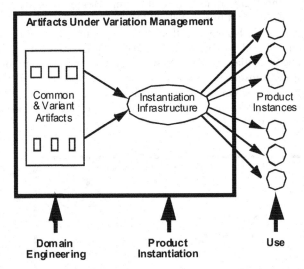

Fig. 2. Variation Management of Production Line

From a variation management perspective, the structure and process in Figure 2 offers several distinct advantages over that of Figure 1:

- There is only a single "product" under variation management – the production line. This eliminates the potential for large numbers of independent product-evolution branches that have to be maintained under variation management.
- All modifications are made directly to the common and variant artifacts. This eliminates the need to make duplicate changes to product instances and core assets.
- Enhancements and fixes applied to the common and variant artifacts are immediately and directly available to all product instances.

Automotive production lines offer an insightful analogy to the production line approach to software variation management. The mass customization of automobiles – that is, individualized automobiles produced with the efficiency of mass production – is made possible by focusing all of the engineering efforts on the common and variant components plus the automotive "instantiation infrastructure," not on engineering the individual automobile instances. Similarly, we can achieve true efficiencies in software mass customization by taking an analogous production line approach to variation management.

In order to take advantage of the variation management benefits of the production line approach illustrated in Figure 2, some of the generality implied in the product line approach of Figure 1 must be sacrificed. Most importantly, the production line approach in Figure 2 implies a single, tightly coordinated engineering effort in order to engineer the common and variant artifacts and the instantiation infrastructure. This does not support the possibility of one organization developing the core assets and a separate organization developing the products based on core assets, as described in [6]. Nor does it support advanced recursive product line approaches such as those described in [9], where multiple product lines can be derived from a single platform of core assets. In these cases, the automobile production analogy resembles going to an automotive parts supplier to get all of the parts for a particular automobile and then performing "product development" to complete the construction.

4   Technology Layers for Variation Management

Section 2.2 described three different solution technologies used for variation management: basic configuration management, component composition, and software mass customization. Figure 3 illustrates how these technologies relate to each other and to other software engineering technology. In the diagram, when two layers are directly adjacent to each other, the layer above is dependent on the services of the layer below.

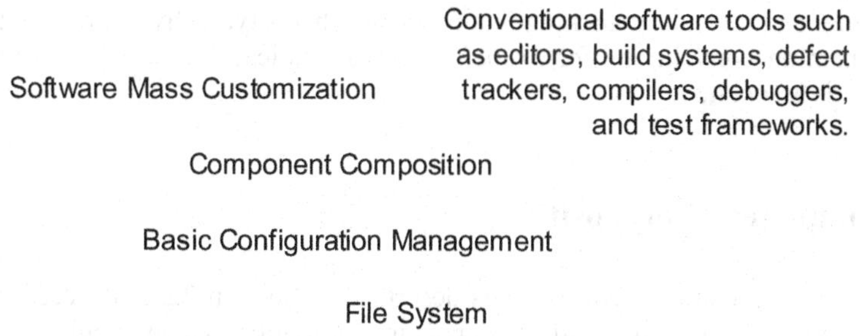

Conventional software tools such as editors, build systems, defect trackers, compilers, debuggers, and test frameworks.

Software Mass Customization

Component Composition

Basic Configuration Management

File System

Fig. 3. Technology Layers for Variation Management

Basic configuration management technology relies on the underlying operating system's file system. Keeping the entire production line under variation management means that the component composition and software mass customization layers always depend on basic configuration management to supply versioned artifacts for a complete and consistent collection of versions at a fixed point in time. Software mass customization operates on variations at the file and component level to produce customized products.

5 Basic Configuration Management

As illustrated in Section 2.2 and Section 2.3, publicly or commercially available configuration management technology is suitable for solving four of the nine subproblems in variation management. These four subproblems are associated with managing sequential and parallel time variation for files and components.

In Section 3 we demonstrated that all artifacts in the production line should be under variation management. This is essential for *reproducibility*, where any product in the product line can be reproduced, exactly as it was at some point in the past, using only artifacts under variation management. At the basic configuration management level, that means that all common files, variant files, and instantiation infrastructure files must be placed under basic configuration management.

Following are descriptions of the four subproblems and how they can be solved by basic configuration management technology.

1. Version management. Sequential versions of files must be managed over time. *Solution: Check-out* and *check-in* operations create sequential file versions on the main trunk.
2. Branch management. Independent branches of file evolution must be supported. *Solution:* Parallel *file branches* created off of the main trunk or other file branches.
3. Baseline management. It must be possible to create a baseline of file versions for all files in a component. This provides a reproducible snapshot of the state of a component at a given point in time. *Solution: Labels* create a persistent named "slice" of file versions.
4. Branched baseline management. Independent branches of component baselines must be supported. *Solution:* Naming conventions for *labels* used to create baselines can indicate branching in a baseline. This is typically done in conjunction with naming conventions for *branch* names to indicate the label with which the branch is associated.

6 Component Composition

Component composition technology as described in Section 2.2 and Section 2.3 will address two of the nine subproblems in variation management. These two subproblems are associated with managing sequential and parallel time variation for the composition of components into products. Some commercial configuration management systems provide this capability, though straightforward homegrown approaches can be implemented easily.

Component composition issues arise when products in a product line are assembled out of independent components and when the components can be evolve independently of each other. That is, if components evolve together as part of a product baseline rather than separately with independent component baselines, then component composition support is not necessary. Components in the latter case are simply modular partitions, or subsystems, within a whole software product.

There are two general approaches to assembling component versions for the construction of a product. The first approach, termed "the shelf," maintains all the versions of all the components on a reusable parts "shelf." To construct a product, you go to the shelf and select one version of each component. With this approach, guidance is needed in determining consistent compositions of component versions, since many of the version combinations will be incompatible.

The second approach, termed "the context," maintains an evolving "context" of component versions. In contrast to the "shelf" approach where all component versions are maintained as peers on the shelf, a "context" represents only one possible composition of component versions. A context typically evolves incrementally as new component versions are developed and integrated into the context.

Following are descriptions of the two subproblems and how they can be solved by "shelf" or "context" component composition technology.

1. Composition management. The sequential versioning of the valid component compositions, from component versions into a product version, must be managed as the valid compositions change over time. **Solution:** The combinatorics of component composition can be a challenge. In a product with 10 components, where each component has 4 baselines, there are over one million possible component compositions, most of which may be invalid combinations. The "shelf" approach may require an expert system, with significant overhead associated with maintaining the composition rules. To support the sequential versioning of composition, the composition engine and rules should be maintained in configuration management.

   The "context" approach is much simpler and should be used when possible. The "context" can be implemented as a simple list in a single file that tracks the "latest and greatest" composition of components for a product. This list can evolve as a new sequential file version each time a new component baseline is released, validated, and entered into the context list for the product.

2. Branched composition management. Independent branches of component compositions must be supported. **Solution:** With the "shelf" approach, the composition engine and rules can be branched using the underlying configuration management branching mechanism. Similarly, with the "context" approach, the context file can be branched using configuration management branches.

7   Software Mass Customization

The remaining three variation management subproblems described in Section 2.2 and Section 2.3 deal with variations that come from the domain space of the product line. These are variations of files, components, and products that exist at a fixed point in time rather than over time. They are addressed by *software mass customization* technology and techniques. One commercial system (from Big Lever Software) provides this capability, and homegrown approaches are also possible [10].

Software mass customization introduces some new abstractions to variation management [12][13][14]. First is a means of expressing the dimensions of variation that exist in the domain. Second is the ability to identify points of variation in the software artifacts for the production line and how these points depend on the dimensions of variation. Third is a mechanism to assemble common and variant artifacts into customized components based on the dimensions of variation and the variation points within the components. Fourth is a mechanism to compose customized components into customized products.

All of the software mass customization infrastructure should be maintained under configuration management, along with the common and variant artifacts used to compose components and products. This assures reproducibility of the customized components and customized products in the domain space, from any baseline in time.

Following are descriptions of the three subproblems and how they can be solved by software mass customization technology. "Standard" software mass customization conventions do not exist in the same way that configuration management or component composition conventions do. Therefore we describe solutions based on the conventions we have adopted as a result of our research on software mass customization.

1. Variation point management. Points of variation in the software artifacts of the production line must be managed, including the different ways that they can be instantiated and how the instantiation depends on the dimensions of variation in the domain space. **Solution:** Variation points are implemented to include a collection of file variants and logic for selecting among the variants, based on the dimensions of variation in the domain space. Given a point in the domain space, a file variant can be identified for each variation point.

2. Customization management. A customized component is created by assembling the component's common and variant artifacts and then instantiating any variation points. Reproducible assembly and instantiation component customizations must be supported by software mass customization. **Solution:** Logical names, corresponding to a point in the domain space, can be assigned to a component customization, similar to a label in configuration management. The logical name can then be used to identify the associated point in the domain space in order to instantiate each variation point in the component, thereby instantiating the customized component.

3. Customization composition management. Customized products are composed out of customized and common components. Reproducible product composition from customized components must be supported. **Solution:** A customized product is a composition of customized components. Associating a logical name for a customized product with a list of customized components is sufficient to look up or instantiate the customized components for a product.

8   Putting It All Together

We have shown that variation management in software product lines is a multidimensional configuration management problem, where variation in time and space must be effectively managed. In order to "conquer" the variation management problem, we "divided" it into nine smaller subproblems with simpler solutions. We covered this solution space with three technology clusters, each of which provides the solutions to several of the nine subproblems.

To illustrate how all of these solutions work in concert to provide variation management for a software product line, we conclude with a simple scenario for instantiating a custom product instance.

1. Get a baseline for the production line from which to build a product instance. The baseline might be from the latest development activity on the main trunk, from a baseline on a release branch for a production line released two months ago, or from a branch being used to do quality assurance testing prior to the next release. Items of interest in the production line baseline are the component composition "context" (see Section 6) and the customization composition lists for the product instances (see Section 7).

2. Use the component context from step 1 to get the baseline version of each component (see Section 6). The baselines that can be customized will include all of their common artifacts and variant artifacts in the uninstantiated form.

3. Using the logical name for the product instance to be built, get the customization composition list from step 1. This list provides the logical name for each customized component instance needed for the product (see Section 7).

4. For each component, use the logical name from step 3 to identify the desired point in domain space in order to instantiate all of the variation points in the component (see Section 7). The source for each component is fully instantiated after this step.

5. Apply conventional build tools as needed to the component source in step 4 to create an installable and executable product instance.

6. A custom test suite matching the custom product instance should be a part of what is produced in steps 1-5. Use this test suite to test the product instance.

9   Conclusions

An interesting observation that we made while "dividing and conquering" the variation management problem is that it can serve as a complete and consistent basis for creating a product line. For example, we have taken a one-of-a-kind software system built out of components, added software mass customization capability as described in Section 7, and created a software product line without doing any domain reengineering, re-architecting, redesign, and so forth. We have even seen this approach applied to a legacy software with no formal or documented domain analysis, architecture, or design.

This observation is not a recommendation to omit analysis, architecture, and design. Rather, it demonstrates that software product line approaches can be adopted very quickly and incrementally, starting with whatever legacy artifacts might serve as a suitable starting point and then adding formality as needed during the evolution of the product line. In contrast to some of the more heavyweight methodologies that require significant up-front investments to adopt a product line approach, an incremental approach based on variation management may offer a more palatable adoption strategy to "in production" software projects.

References

1. Software Engineering Institute. The Product Line Practice (PLP) Initiative, Carnegie Mellon University, www.sei.cmu.edu/activities/plp/plp_init.html
2. Weiss, D., Lai, R. 1999. Software Product-line Engineering. Addison-Wesley, Reading, MA.
3. Bass, L., Clements, P., and Kazman, R. 1998. Software Architecture in Practice. Addison-Wesley, Reading, MA.
4. Jacobson, I., Gris, M., Jonsson, P. 1997. Software Reuse: Architecture, Process and Organization for Business Success, ACM Press / Addison-Wesley, New York, NY.
5. Software Product Lines. Experience and Research Directions. Proceeding of the First Software Product Lines Conference (SPLC1). August 2000. Denver, Colorado. Kluwer Academic Publishers, Boston, MA.
6. Clements, P., Northrop, L. 2001. Software Product Lines: Practice and Patterns, Addison-Wesley, Reading, MA.
7. Dagstuhl Seminar No. 01161: Product Family Development. April 2001. Wadern, Germany.
8. Postema, H., Obbink, J.H. Platform Based Product Development. Proceedings of the 4th International Workshop on Product Family Engineering. October 2001. Bilbao, Spain. Springer-Verlag, New York, NY.
9. van der Linden, F., Wijnstra, J.G. Platform Engineering for the Medical Domain. Proceedings of the 4th International Workshop on Product Family Engineering. October 2001. Bilbao, Spain. Springer-Verlag, New York, NY.
10. BigLever Software, Inc. Austin, TX. www.biglever.com
11. Krueger, C. Using Separation of Concerns to Simplify Software Product Family Engineering. Proceedings of the Dagstuhl Seminar No. 01161: Product Family Development. April 2001. Wadern, Germany.
12. Krueger, C. Easing the Transition to Software Mass Customization. Proceedings of the 4th International Workshop on Product Family Engineering. October 2001. Bilbao, Spain. Springer-Verlag, New York, NY.
13. Krueger, C. Software Reuse. 1992. ACM Computing Surveys. 24, 2 (June), 131-183.
14. Krueger, C. 1997. Modeling and Simulating a Software Architecture Design Space. Ph.D. thesis. CMU-CS-97-158, Carnegie Mellon University, Pittsburgh, PA.

Adopting and Institutionalizing a Product Line Culture

Günter Böckle[1], Jesús Bermejo Muñoz[2], Peter Knauber[3], Charles W. Krueger[4],
Julio Cesar Sampaio do Prado Leite[5], Frank van der Linden[6], Linda Northrop[7],
Michael Stark[8], and David M.Weiss[9]

[1] Siemens AG, Otto Hahn Ring 6, D-81730 Munich, Germany
Guenter.W.Boeckle@mchp.siemens.de
[2] Telvent, C/ Tamarguillo 29, 41006 Sevilla, Spain
jesus.bermejo@sainco.abengoa.com
[3] Fraunhofer IESE, Sauerwiesen 6, D-67661 Kaiserslautern, Germany
knauber@iese.fhg.de
[4] BigLever Software, Inc, 10500 Laurel Hill Cove, Austin, TX 78730, USA
ckrueger@biglever.com
[5] Departamento de Informática, PUC-Rio,
R. Marquês de São Vicente, 225, Rio de Janeiro, Brasil 22453-900
julio@obatala.inf.puc-rio.br
[6] Philips Medical Systems, Veenpluis 4-6, 5684 PC Best, The Netherlands
Frank.van.der.Linden@philips.com
[7] Software Engineering Institute, Carnegie Mellon University,
Pittsburgh, PA 15213-3890, USA
lmn@sei.cmu.edu
[8] University of Maryland, College Park, MD 20742, USA
mstark@cs.umd.edu
[9] Avaya Labs, USA
weiss@avaya.com

Abstract. The strengths of product line engineering have been described before. But how can an organization make the move from developing one-of products to product line engineering without major interruptions in the day-to-day work? This paper describes how to perform the transition to product line engineering and lists the various strategies for such a transition. It also describes how to create an adoption plan and how to institutionalize product line engineering in an organization.

1 Introduction

There are several approaches to successfully bringing products to the market. For software-intensive systems, the product-family approach promises significant improvement in time to market and various other success parameters. The basic idea behind the product line approach is planned reusability. Once a software organization deploys such an approach, producing a new product that belongs to a family can be done at a fraction of the cost and time of a usual production process.

This document describes how an organization can perform the transition from a standard product development of one-of products to product line engineering. It is primarily the result of a working group at the Dagstuhl symposium on Product Family Development, April 16 - 20, 2001.

G. Chastek (Ed.): SPLC2 2002, LNCS 2379, pp. 49–59, 2002.
© Springer-Verlag Berlin Heidelberg 2002

2   The Task

Transforming an organization to create products as members of a product family requires the directing of the business towards product-family development by installing corresponding processes, organization structures, and methods. Central to the introduction of the product line culture lies the challenge of convincing the different organization-decision levels about the appropriateness of investing in this technology. For mechanical and electronic systems, product line engineering is current practice. However, for software and for software-intensive systems, particular topics have to be considered.

This paper aims at describing a general process strategy for the adoption and institutionalization of a product line culture for software-intensive systems. Business cases have to be developed to justify adopting a product line approach and to define the actions required to accomplish that. A business case depends on which decision level in the organization we are trying to convince. Different roles have different interests and have to be addressed in different ways by such a business case to achieve the implementation of a product line culture.

3   The Big Picture

Figure 1 depicts the overall context of directing a business towards a software product line. It shows the major phases of the transition process.

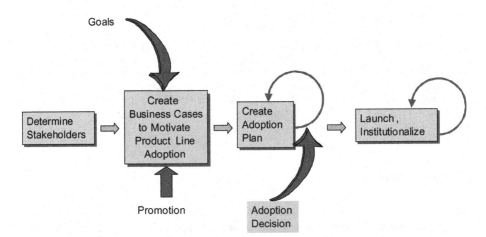

Fig. 1. The Big Picture - the Major Phases for Transition to Product Line Development

First of all, we have to consider the goals of a product line approach; these goals will vary according to the stakeholders we are addressing and their decision level in the organization. These goals will then be elaborated in business cases that promote the product line idea. The business cases and a first draft of the adoption plan will be the base for the decision to adopt a product line culture. After a positive decision, the adoption plan will be elaborated in more detail and refined iteratively. After launch, the major concern is in institutionalizing the product line culture by integrating it in the organization culture. Launch and institutionalization are themselves iterative process phases, too.

4   The Stakeholders

The first step in the transition process is to determine the stakeholders. The different decision stakeholders (roles) are interested in different aspects of the product line concept. As a consequence, the business cases are role dependent and the plans will have to be adjusted accordingly.

There are often organization-specific roles that have to be considered. However, there are some general roles that will occur in most organizations:

- Product managers: Their interest is in marketing and customer analysis; their goals are revenue based. Time to market is important to them and their interest is in market breadth; often they are the ones who are involved in the assignment of budgets and strategy definition.
- Managers: They are interested in technical feasibility, but also in project planning, measuring progress, risk analysis, and getting presentable results early.
- Project managers: They are interested in technical feasibility, but also in project planning, measuring progress, risk analysis, and getting presentable results early.
- Engineers: They must be convinced that the approach is technologically sound and can help them in engineering; managers may ask their opinions about the approach.
- Quality assurance: They must be convinced that the approach increases quality. Managers may ask their opinions about the approach.

5   Business Cases

For each of these roles, a business case has to be developed that defines how product-family engineering helps them to achieve each of their specific goals. These business cases are used to convince the corresponding people of the advantages of the product-family approach.

Persons representing these roles will be involved in directing a business towards product-family engineering. They have to be motivated with the business cases and their tasks and responsibilities have to be defined.

The direction of the business case will first start with an adoption plan. It has to show certain measures that are relevant for the roles addressed in the business case. These are for instance revenues and profits, costs and return on investment (ROI), comparing one-of products to a family of products that is targeted to specific markets. More about business cases is described in [1] and [5].

6   The Adoption Plan

The persons doing adoption planning represent any one of the roles described in Section 4. In any case, the person(s) should have the responsibility to carry it out, trace it, and evolve it. The structure of the adoption plan has three major parts:

1. Characterization of current state: The state of the organization is characterized by its process, the staff and their expertise, the organizational structure, the project management methods, the engineering methods, and many other business parameters.
2. Characterization of desired state
3. Strategies, objectives, and activities to get from the current to the desired state

6.1   Characterization of the Current State

For characterizing the current state, the maturity of the organization has to be analyzed and described. The adoption of a product-family engineering approach starts with the assessment of the current state. Such an assessment may be similar to a Capability Maturity Model® (CMM) assessment; however, its purpose is not to obtain a number to compare the organization to other organizations. This assessment shall determine the strengths and weaknesses of the organization for product-family engineering and the points where special care (and thus measurement) has to be taken for the adoption. The following topics have to be assessed:

- Market characterization
- Competition in the market
- Degree of globalization
- Management commitment
- Organizational maturity
- Organizational stability
- Staff turnover
- Process maturity
- Project management maturity
- Expertise in product-family engineering (warm start vs. cold start)
- Domain expertise
- Other staff competence
- Contractors' expertise and reliability
- Communication with third parties
- Existing assets
- Software infrastructure

® CMM is registered in the U.S. Patent and Trademark Office.

6.2   Characterization of the Desired State

After having characterized the current state by a CMM-like assessment, the desired state is described in the same structure so that an easy comparison of current and future states is possible. Thus, the topics to be considered are

- The markets that shall be addressed by the product family
- The competition in these markets
- The degree of globalization that is necessary for these markets
- The management commitment necessary for moving to product line engineering
- The organization structures proposed for product-family engineering and the requirements for the organizational stability
- The staff stability required to prevent know-how from getting lost
- The processes proposed for product-family engineering and methods to ensure that the processes are really enacted
- The required project management skills and methods
- The expertise of the staff that is necessary for product-family engineering
- The domain expertise required for the targeted markets and products
- Other competencies of the staff required for product-family engineering
- The expertise that has to be delivered from contractors because it cannot or need not be built up in the organization; the reliability and kinds of contracts required
- The communication with third parties (e.g., communication infrastructure to contractors, communication rules, milestones)
- List of other assets needed for product line engineering
- The software infrastructure needed for product line engineering (e.g., tools for product planning, scoping, requirements engineering, architecture modeling, design, design management, asset management)

6.3   How to Get from the Current to the Desired State

There are several strategies for getting from the current state to the desired state. The adoption plan has to characterize and prioritize them and suggest the best-suited strategy for transition. Figure 2 lists the major strategies for this transition.

```
Incremental introduction
        -    Expanding scope
    •   Incremental investment
        -   Tactical
    •   Pilot first
        -   New product
        -   Toy product
        -   Prototype
    •   Big bang
```

Fig. 2. Product Line Adoption Strategies

6.3.1   Incremental Introduction

The expanding scope strategy may start with a single department doing product line engineering and when they are successful, other departments are added incrementally. Mostly, there will be several departments developing products. One department for developing core assets may be installed and their results used by the other departments, as they get ready. The other departments may then be reorganized accordingly.

6.3.2   Incremental Investment

At the beginning a certain, limited investment is assigned to product line engineering while the major part remains in conventional product engineering. It has to be planned carefully which activities will be funded to start the product line; typically this is in writing reusable components or making existing components reusable. However, the product line scoping and planning stage has to be introduced as early as possible to ensure the significance of the efforts and to make them measurable and predictable. The budgeting plan for incrementally introducing product line engineering may be informal or more or less rigorous but planning and measuring is central!

The tactical strategy is driven by problems with the conventional approach, e.g., with configuration management for multiple related one-of products. Reusing core assets will reduce the complexity of configuration management. This approach may start informally. However, the scoping of and the planning for the further development and application of cores assets has to be performed early so that the results can be made measurable and predictable.

6.3.3   Pilot First

The New Product strategy is started as the first member of a new product line, or an existing series of related products, is extended by a new product for which certain activities of product line engineering are applied. For this approach, particular methods are important, like architecture recovery.

The Toy Product strategy recognizes that the risk of creating a new product with a new approach may be assessed as being too high in certain environments. In this case, a toy product may be created that is sufficiently close to the organizations' products, so that some of the results can be reused if product line engineering is introduced later for the "real" products.

The Prototype strategy recognizes that a prototype may be the first product in a new product family or a new product in a series of existing related products. In either case, the product line engineering that will be applied during the pilot project has to be planned beforehand, and the process has to be determined accordingly.

6.3.4   Big Bang

In cases where the management of an organization is convinced of the advantages of a product line engineering approach and where it is essential for the business to achieve the business results of this approach as early as possible, a big-bang approach may be the best one. In this strategy, the product-family engineering approach is adopted for the new products of the organization immediately.

Whatever the strategy for product line adoption may be, it is always necessary to introduce review points in the transition process where the current state of the adoption is evaluated and the results of the new engineering approach are compared to the conventional approach. This requires the introduction of measurements during the transition process that can be used for these evaluations. These reviews have to adjust the transition process, and may even lead to a change in the adoption strategy.

The objectives and activities for transition depend on the strategy chosen. They include ways of integrating the transition process into the everyday work so that the process of developing products for the customer is not disturbed. Also included are activities from the business cases, including the necessary training for the staff and management. These activities for transition shall include estimations of effort and cost so that a decision about adoption can be supported. These estimations can be derived from the business cases.

7   Launching

The initial version of the adoption plan is used to decide about the product line adoption. If the adoption is chosen, the product line is launched.

The following are common parts of the launch for the activities described above:

- Recognition of stakeholders, their interests, needs, biases and culture.
- Determination of roles and responsibilities in the current and future state, together with a corresponding migration path.
- Definition of a product-family engineering process for the organization, considering the products, skills, environment, and so forth.
- Definition of the production process.
- Motivation of all affected stakeholders, using the business cases (see Section 5).
- Cultivation of champions and angels for all-important activities.
- Introduction of data collection, metrics, and tracking.
- Plans for funding.
- Plans for staffing, including consultants and providers.

Champions are staff members who are convinced of a new idea (e.g., product line engineering) and try to convince other staff members, too. They support others in applying the approach; they present practical tips and support the proliferation of the idea. Angels are members of management or senior engineers who have influence due to their role in the hierarchy or due to their experience and expertise. They give the necessary weight to the launch of an approach like product line engineering.

8   Institutionalization

Just launching the product line is not sufficient. It has to be institutionalized so that the involved managers and staff will consider it as part of their working culture.

Permanent organizational fixtures are then installed that support and enforce product-family engineering.

Institutions are considered stable structures [3]. "Organizations become institutions as they become valued in and of themselves: their disappearance would create drastic problems for various members and groups in the environment" [4].

Software product line institutionalization occurs when the product line processes are perceived as stable and indispensable to a given software organization. Iacono and Kling [2] believe that large scope computer-based information systems should be viewed as social institutions. As such, those systems are a complex web of interactions among actors, equipment, roles, procedures, rules, and activities. However, such systems can only be viewed as an institution when they are stable and indispensable to the organization.

This said, we do not contradict the fact that those systems, to fight entropy, need to be in constant evolution. Once a product line approach is institutionalized, it continues to evolve, but does so in a stable position and with a high demand from the organization that will see it as an indispensable part of its way of doing business. Although institutions strive for immortality [6], of course they are not immune to changes.

The institutionalization has to consider the organizational structures and ensure that product-family engineering is engrained in the organization's processes. Incentives have to be defined and installed; funding has to be put into place by proven funding sources; and measures that reflect product-family engineering have to be installed and used as bases for reviews. There are two aspects to understanding institutionalization: what determines the extent to which an action or structure is institutionalized and the consequences of actions or structures being institutionalized. Iacono and Kling [2] list several determinants and consequences of institutionalized computer-based information systems. Using their list as a basis, we point out the main determinants and consequences of institutionalized software product line below.

8.1   Determinants

- Social arrangements such as policies, procedures, conventions, and the distribution of resources are developed and utilized by the main actors (audience).
- There are key stakeholders in the environment who wish to maintain or increase their control, despite the fact that no actor or coalition has complete control.
- There are negotiations, commitments, and future obligations among the main actors (audience) that are not easy to reverse.

The successful launch of a product line, for a given family of products, will bring new social arrangements to the organization. These will be seen as new policies, procedures, conventions, and distributions of resources in software production, but as well on the cooperation with customers and quality assurance. When these ensembles of resources and people are in place, we have a strong determinant towards making a product line an institution.

The champions of the idea as well as their angels will drive to maintain or increase control over the organization as a natural consequence of product line success. This is a main driving force towards institutionalization. Champions and angels will strive to use marketing strategies to ensure that the whole organization perceives the advantage of product lines over traditional methods.

Of course in the process of marketing the product line, several commitments and future obligations will have to be established by the key stakeholders who have other interests in the organization. These commitments and obligations will persist since they represent a huge investment of the organizations.

8.2   Consequences

• Social arrangements between the main actors persist over time, making it difficult for small coalitions to change the status quo.
• People believe that the social arrangements will persist.
• Stable arrangements ease cooperation along routine behaviors and constrain substantially different behaviors.
• Change is localized.

Once a product line is institutionalized, change is localized, usually by add-on technologies, and people believe that the product line will persist. The product line framework will guide the cooperation among software personnel, customers, and quality assurance personnel in such a way that changing procedures or conventions will be difficult.

On the other hand, once a product line is institutionalized, the organization will benefit from better efficiency overall. With social arrangements working properly and the technology infrastructure in place, the organization will be producing software products faster, better, and cheaper.

9   A Bottom-Up Approach

A common challenge that organizations face with all of the adoption strategies is the "adoption barrier" – the overhead associated with starting the software product line. Typically resources have to be shifted from existing projects, and rarely do existing projects have resources to spare.

BigLever Software [7] promotes a *bottom-up* approach to address this problem. BigLever Software GEARS is a technology that allows organizations to gradually convert existing one-of-a-kind software and processes into product line software and processes [9]. The premise of GEARS is that any existing software product is a valid software product line with only one member and that new members can be added incrementally using the GEARS *infrastructure* to manage variation among the product members.

For example, during two weeks in August 2001, two engineers at Salion [8] allocated approximately 25% of their time using GEARS to convert their one-of-a-kind enterprise software product into a software product line with three members. Although the three initial members varied in simple ways, Salion had truly adopted a product line approach that could incrementally grow more sophisticated over time.

The key to this low adoption barrier is GEARS' *separation of concerns*. GEARS is an extension to the current arsenal of software engineering languages, tools, and techniques. It provides a *software product line infrastructure* that can be inserted into any collection of source files and directories in order to introduce parameterized variation. The GEARS infrastructure is comprised of four basic constructs:

- Feature declarations – parameters of variation for the software product line.
- Product definitions – assignment of values to feature-declaration parameters for each product member.
- Automata – the encapsulated mapping from parameter values to source-code variants among the product members.
- Actuator – the mechanism for instantiating product members from the product source code and the GEARS infrastructure.

When using the GEARS technology during software product line adoption, BigLever distinguishes between three different adoption strategies that can be used independently or in combination:

- Extractive – a "bottom-up" approach where one or more existing legacy systems are reused as the basis for the product line.
- Reactive – an "incremental" approach where product line members are built on demand as new product requirements are identified.
- Proactive – a "big-bang" approach where a significant number of the product line members are identified and built upfront.

10   Summary

This paper demonstrates the importance of the following steps for a successful transition from producing one-of products to product line engineering:

- Prepare business cases that determine the activities, efforts and costs from the perspectives of the major stakeholders, as a basis for deciding about the transition.
- Make an adoption plan with the activities needed for the transition so that staff and management will support the transition.
- Institutionalize product line engineering in the organization so that it becomes part of the company culture.

References

1.   The Business Case Web Site, http://www.solutionmatrix.com/
2.   Iacono, S. and Kling, R.: Computer Systems as Institutions: Social Dimensions of Computing in Organizations, in *Proceedings of the Ninth International Conference on Information Systems*, 1988, pp.101-110.
3.   Meyer, J.W. and Rowan, B.: Institutionalized Organizations: Formal Structure as Myth and Ceremony, American Journal of Sociology, vol. 83(2), 1977.
4.   Perrow, C.: Complex Organizations, A Critical Essay, Soctt Foresman and Company, 1979.
5.   A Framework for Software Product Line Practice - Version 3.0, http://www.sei.cmu.edu /plp/framework.html

6. Selznick, P. Leadership in Administration: A Sociology Interpretation, New York –
    Harper and Row, 1957.
7. BigLever Software, Inc.: *www.biglever.com*, Austin, TX. 2001.
8. Salion, Inc.: *www.salion.com*, Austin, TX. 2001.
9. Krueger, C.: Using Separation of Concerns to Simplify Software Product Family
    Engineering. April 2001. Proceedings of the Dagstuhl Seminar No. 01161: Product Family
    Development. Wadern, Germany.

Establishing a Software Product Line
in an Immature Domain

Stefan Voget[1] and Martin Becker[2]

[1]Robert Bosch GmbH, Corporate Research and Development, Software Technology, P.O.
Box 94 03 50, D-60461 Frankfurt, Germany
stefan.voget@de.bosch.com
[2]System Software Research Group, University of Kaiserslautern, P.O. Box 3049 D-67653
Kaiserslautern, Germany
mbecker@informatik.uni-kl.de

Abstract. Often product lines are applied to "stable domains" (i.e., a set of common features is identifiable in advance and the evolution of the domain is manageable during the lifetime of the product line). These prerequisites are not always given. But there may be market pressure that requires developing products with systematic and preplanned reuse in a domain that is difficult to grasp. In such a case the product line approach also offers a set of methods that helps to overcome the risks of an immature domain.

In this paper we discuss some risks in context of immature domains. For some challenges we present approaches to manage them. The considerations are substantiated by experiences in the domain of entertainment and infotainment systems in an automotive context. The development is deeply influenced by technological changes (e.g., Internet, MP3-player, UMTS) that challenge the successful deployment of product line technology.

1 Introduction

Approaches like product line engineering or product population engineering use systematic reuse in families of related systems, in contrast to single system engineering. Planned and systematic reuse, however, implies that the common software artefacts are especially developed for reuse. The engineering of such reusable artefacts is usually called domain engineering.

To succeed with a pre-planned strategy, the engineers must obviously be able to plan the reuse. The success is tightly related to the nature of the domain itself (its properties). Therefore, domain-engineering approaches typically require that the respective domain is well understood, mature, and stable (i.e., the set of common features is identifiable in advance, and the evolution of the domain is manageable during the lifetime of the product line). There are considerable risks if these conditions are not fulfilled. The literature offers some adaptations of the product line approach, which help to manage the risks of an immature domain.

In this paper we present our experiences with these approaches during the establishment of a product line in the domain of entertainment and infotainment systems (EIS) in an automotive context. EIS is considered to be an immature domain.

G. Chastek (Ed.): SPLC2 2002, LNCS 2379, p. 60–67, 2002.

The market for EIS is divided into two segments. In the first segment, the customers are vehicle manufacturers that include the EIS directly into the vehicle production line. This market is an oligopolistic market controlled by a few worldwide operating manufacturers. The second segment is the after-sales market. EIS has neglected this segment and will continue to in the near future. We will focus our considerations on the first segment.

The remainder of the paper is structured as follows: Section 2 defines the underlying notions of this paper in order to define what we want to understand by an immature domain. The domain of entertainment and infotainment systems and the drivers for a product line approach in this domain are presented in Section 3. Section 4 discusses the respective risks. A set of approaches to manage the aforementioned risks is pointed out in Section 5. The paper ends with a conclusion and some words on further work.

2   Domains, Product Lines, and Scope

In the literature a lot of different definitions for the term "domain" can be found – all of them emphasize different aspects [2], [4], [9]. The main difference is that some of them concentrate on knowledge and others focus more on applications. Bass [2] defines a domain in a general way as "an area of knowledge or activity characterized by a set of concepts and terminology understood by practitioners in that area."

With a more application oriented view, [4] gives two characterizations for a domain: "a domain is a collection of current and future (software) applications that share a set of common characteristics and a well-defined set of characteristics that accurately, narrowly, and completely describe a family of problems for which computer applications solutions are being and will be sought." In this document we will follow the application-oriented definition of domain given by [4].

The activity in a product line development process, that lays down what is "in" and what is "out" of the scope of a product line is called scoping. Thorough scoping is essential for the success of a product line. A detailed discussion of scoping can be found in [7]. Normally three different kinds of scoping are distinguished which address three different levels of abstraction [9]:

- *Product portfolio definition* – identifies the products and the coarse requirements the products shall fulfil
- *Domain-centric scoping* – bounds the domain that should be in the focus of the product line development
- *Asset-centric scoping* – identifies the specific assets that should be developed as part of the reuse infrastructure

Scoping decisions on these levels are not always obvious and above all not easy to make [11]. Various factors have to be considered during the decision making in the context of a product line approach, for example the:

- Extent and kind of functional requirements and quality attributes
- Market circumstances (e.g., regional differences [USA, Europe] or kind of market [1st tier supplier, after sales])
- Costs (from low-end to high-end devices) and many more

The risks considered in this document can only treat a subset of the characteristics. Only risks correlated to the evolution of technology and the market will be considered.

As product lines typically require up-front investments for the companies and promise long-term benefits, it is a commonly accepted requirement of product line approaches that the respective domains are at least well understood, mature, and stable. This ideally means that the scope characteristics listed above are assessable and remain more or less the same for most of the product line's lifecycle. Thus, the common set of features among the envisioned products can be identified in advance, and the evolution of the domain is manageable during lifetime. In contrast to such stable domains, we want to denote domains as immature if most of the scope characteristics cannot be assessed in advance or change considerably over time.

3   The EIS Domain

Vehicles improve by adding comfort and safety functionality. As these technologies progress, drivers have to interoperate with more non-uniform user interfaces of single box devices.

The vision of an EIS is that one harmonized human-machine interface allows interaction to all kinds of

- Comfort services (seat adjustment, adjustable mirrors, air-conditioning)
- Vehicle information (oil temperature, average petrol consumption)
- Entertainment (Radio, CD, MD, CC, DVD, TV, games)
- cell phone
- Navigation
- Telematics (internet, WAP, traffic information, remote control)
- Mobile office services (text system, dictating machine, e-mail)

The evolution of this domain is driven mainly by the technology changes (e.g., only two years ago, no one considered the integration of MP3-players in an EIS. Only one year later, the integration of a MP3-player has become standard). As a consequence of the technological evolution, a new market grew up. For the manufacturers of EIS this means that they have to move to protect their market share.

Considering this environment, the main drivers for developments in the EIS domain are:

- *Get and protect market share* – an EIS introduces and integrates new kinds of functionality in the vehicles. It is a new market, which arises in the environment of the automotive industry.
- *Variability* – all vehicle manufacturers emphasize their individual corporate identity. At least the user interface has to be customer specific. In most cases this is true for the telematic services, too.
- *Reuse potential changes* – the market itself is not clear and changes in time. A decision what has to be developed for reuse, and what has to be developed with reuse may become quickly outdated.

- *Time to market* – the supplier that is first in the market makes the most profit. The prices for such systems decrease extremely in time.

But there are some market characteristics that are fixed and therefore certain:

- *Start of production* of a vehicle is always defined very early, usually 6-7 years in advance. This date only changes in very exceptional cases. It is accompanied by a loss of image. The start of production of a vehicle often coincides with the delivery of the EIS from the supplier to the vehicle manufacturer. Therefore, the external time schedule is given early and precisely.
- *From high end to low end* – the introduction of new services usually starts in the high-end vehicles. Products in the middle class come later. The high-end products do not provide a large return of investment because of the low production figures. Therefore, the products in the middle class – offering the main profits – have to be part of the product line and the product line planning from the beginning.

These drivers do not necessarily force the decision to develop an EIS using a product line engineering process. But the product line engineering technology delivers many methods to exploit the reuse potential and reduce the risks associated with the mentioned drivers.

4   Risks for a Product Line in an Immature Domain

4.1   Scope-Related Risks

Two major risks concerning the scope have been identified: the scope can be vague, and can be subject to change, especially by extensions and reductions.

The *vagueness* of the scope impedes the analysis of what is "in" and what is "out". The phenomenon of vagueness has been experienced on all three scoping levels mentioned above (e.g., the separation between the EIS and mobile computers becomes increasingly blurred). As a consequence it is hard to decide on domain level, and therefore, on which products are really in the scope. This considerably impedes the assessment of the product line's potential: it complicates the identification of the commonalities and the decision about which core assets to provide and when to provide them during the product line's lifecycle.

Extensions of the scope are critical if the joined elements are outside the previously considered product portfolio. The joined elements can cause additional development and integration efforts, and extensions can interfere with elements that are inside the portfolio. Extensions are very common for the EIS domain.

Reductions are critical if elements of the product line scope disappear before the pre-planned benefit has been realized. An example is the radio with cassette player, which will most likely disappear in the near future.

4.2   Product and Market-Related Risks

Although the automotive industry is a so-called "old economy", the EIS is a product that has to be assigned to the "new economy". The amount of software included is much higher than in formerly developed devices. With the introduction of an EIS in vehicles, the two economies collide. As a consequence the borders between different market segments become blurred. EIS are developed more and more by suppliers, who increasingly come from non-automotive branches.

As mentioned before, new services are introduced in the high-end vehicles first. This rule influences the development of the product line. Instead of a thorough domain analysis of the mass market and the engineering of corresponding core assets, the establishment of the product line is driven considerably by the development of a few full-fledged, prestigious high-quality products. Those products have to be developed first to protect the market share. The mass-market products are derived afterwards from the high-end products. As a consequence, special attention has to be paid to retain the features in the high-end products: they must be designed to be removable and scalable.

4.3   Knowledge-Related Risks

In an EIS, the software as well as the hardware is based on new and previously unused technologies. As a consequence, there is little experience with the specific needs of the customers, their requirements and the respective solutions. This raises the probability of misunderstandings between the customer and the EIS supplier.

In particular, new standards and technologies that influence the EIS are often unknown, not fully specified, or not completely established. The use of such a technology and its associated first-time development is always risky.

5   Approaches to Manage the Risks

The previously mentioned risks for an immature domain like the EIS domain mainly emanate from

- An unknown and changing market
- Uncertain technological evolutions

The approaches presented in the subsequent section only focus on the technological evolution and do not address the first group of risks.

5.1   Light-Weight Domain Engineering

Instead of an extensive, and therefore heavyweight, domain analysis before application engineering, domain engineering can be done on-the-fly concurrently with application engineering. During the development of applications, the work products are assessed for their reuse potential with respect to the envisioned products [1], [8]. Special emphasis is placed on the documentation of the potential commonalities in the work products. Core assets, in the sense of the product line approach, are built from the respective work products when the first reuse occurs. Obviously, the success of such an approach depends substantially on the knowledge, the skills, and the intuition of the application engineers.

Lightweight domain engineering can be considered in some sense as implicit domain engineering that is done in the heads of the application engineers during the application engineering. This approach deals mainly with the scope-related risks, the vagueness of scope, and the changes in the scope.

Our experiences from the EIS domain show that it is good practice to start with an emphasis on application engineering. But a continuous and conscientious analysis assessing the artefacts' reuse potential has to take place from the beginning. In this phase, as many domain engineering activities as possible should be done. A specific domain engineering team should be set up later. This team should start with a small set of reusable artefacts and take more analysis results into account over time.

5.2   Stable Subdomains Start-Up

Although a domain as a whole may be immature, the situation for the subdomains can vary. As a consequence, product line endeavour can focus on those subdomains. This typically results in a hierarchical domain engineering, and consequently in a hierarchy of product lines. A product line defined on a higher level in the hierarchy can be seen as a framework for product lines defined on a lower level in the hierarchy. On a larger scale, such hierarchies are often called "product populations".

This approach also addresses scope-related risks. In contrast to light-weight domain engineering, this approach isolates the stable areas from unstable ones. This reduces the risk of the scoping of the whole system changing significantly due to the changes in unstable areas. The stable subdomains can serve as starting points for the incremental construction of the product line.

This principle is used intensively for our developments in the EIS domain. Some of the subdomains, like the CD or the address book, form stable subdomains. Others, like navigation or user management, are very unstable. The reasons for the variabilities may vary for different subdomains. On the other hand this approach contradicts the vision of a totally integrated EIS without borders between the formerly-known devices. A balance between the isolation of subdomains and the integration aspects has to be found and steadily taken into account.

5.3   Commonality-Oriented Assets

The reuse potential of the variabilities is typically less than that of the commonalities. In contrast, the effort required to make a variability reusable is typically higher than that required to make a commonality reusable. In this approach only sparse effort is spent on the variabilities during the construction of the core assets. The minimal support that should be provided for variabilities, to this end, is the identification of the appropriate variation points [10].

This approach is comparable to the previous one in the sense that in both approaches the development focuses on one special aspect (stability in contrast to commonality) and isolates the parts of the products which are stable with respect to the specific aspect in mind.

In a simplified manner an EIS can be seen as a collection of different applications (radio, CD, DVD, navigation) and some central components (profile, access control, system management). Normally the central components are typical candidates for the commonality-oriented assets. But sometimes they include variabilities. These often cannot be handled by mechanisms that cause only local effects. The situation is quite different in the applications. Here the variabilities typically can be solved locally with appropriate mechanisms. Moreover, in most of the cases the major part of the applications are revealed to be free of variablity. Therefore, it depends on both the kind and the number of variabilities to determine if a component can be taken as a commonality-oriented asset or not.

5.4   Sound Variability Treatment Support

The sound treatment of variabilities, a necessity if commonality is supposed to be exploited beyond the initial construction of the products, can be supported by methodologies that are particularly aware of the variabilities [3]. This includes:

- A thorough support for an efficient change impact analysis [5]
- Adaptable core assets [1]
- (semi-)automatic evolution of core assets and the corresponding applications
- Integration of legacy code with integrated refactorisation support [6]

These approaches have not been tried in the EIS domain up to now. They are mentioned here, since they concentrate more on the treatment of variability than the commonality-oriented assets approaches presented above. Especially in an immature domain, it is always a difficult question of what is more important to manage: the variabilities or the commonalities.

6   Conclusion and Further Work

We presented some risks that may arise while establishing a software product line in an immature domain. The literature contains these and other approaches for handling risks. None of the approaches consider all the risks. Some risks, especially the market related risks, are not addressed by any of the presented approaches. The handling of these remaining risks is actually an open question.

For the EIS domain the market will actually grow and consolidate. On the other hand, it is assumed that the technology-related risks will be of interest in coming years, and it is expected that new ones will come up (e.g., the current architectures for the whole electronic system of the vehicle is not suitable for future services). This will influence the EIS and will bring other technologies (e.g. related to real-time aspects) into that domain.

References

1. Bassett, P.G.: Framing Software Reuse - Lessons From the Real World, Yourdon Press Computing Series, 1997
2. Bass, L.; Clements, P.; Donohoe, P.; McGregor, J.; Northrop, L.: Fourth Product Line Practice Workshop Report, Software Engineering Institute, USA, November 1999
3. Becker, M.; Geyer, L.; Gilbert, A.; Becker, K.: Comprehensive Variability Modelling to Facilitate Efficient Variability Treatment, Fourth International Workshop on Product Family Engineering (PFE-4), Bilbao, Spain, October 2001
4. Berard, E.: Essays in Object-Oriented Software Engineering. Prentice Hall, 1992
5. Bosch, J.; Högström, M.: Product Instantiation in Software Product Lines: A Case Study, 2nd International Symposium on Generative and Component-Based Software Engineering (GCSE'00), 2000
6. Butler, G.; Xu, L.: Cascaded Refactoring for Framework Evolution, Proc. of 2001 Symposium on Software Reusability, Toronto, Ontario, Canada, May 2001
7. Clements, P.C.: On the Importance of Product Line Scope, IV'th International Workshop on Product Family Engineering, Bilbao, 2001
8. Krueger, C.W.: Easing the Transition to Software Mass Customization, Fourth International Workshop on Product Family Engineering (PFE-4), Bilbao, Spain, October 2001
9. Schmid, K.: Scoping Software Product Lines, Software Product Lines – Experience and Research Directions; Donohoe, P. (Editor); Kluwer Academic Publishers, 2000
10. Voget, S.; Angilletta, I.; Herbst, I.; Lutz, P.: Behandlung von Variabilitäten in Produktlinien mit Schwerpunkt Architektur, Proceedings of 1. Deutscher Software-Produktlinien Workshop (DSPL-1), Kaiserslautern, Germany, November 2000
11. Withey, J.: Investment Analysis of Software Assets for Product Lines, http://www.sei.cmu.edu/publications/documents/96.reports/96.tr.010.html, Software Engineering Institute, Carnegie Mellon University, Pittsburgh, PA, USA, 1996

Critical Factors for a Successful Platform-Based Product Family Approach[1]

Jan Gerben Wijnstra

Philips Research Laboratories
Prof. Holstlaan 4, 5656 AA Eindhoven, The Netherlands
JanGerben.Wijnstra@philips.com

Abstract. The notion of software product families is becoming more and more popular, both in research and in industry. In presentations of ideal applications, the benefits of product families are stressed and very little attention is paid to possible problems. However, in practice, it is important to know what such problems could be and how they could be dealt with. In this paper we want to identify some of the most critical issues, and explain how they can be handled or even avoided. This will be done on the basis of experiences gained with three industrial product families for professional markets. The focus will be on product families that use platforms with reusable assets for the development of the family members.

Keywords: Product Family, Platform, Business, Architecture, Process, Organization

1   Introduction

Products in the various embedded system markets are becoming more complex and more diverse, and must be easily extendible with new features. Important factors are a short time to market, low development costs and high demands on the quality of the software. One way of meeting such requirements for a range of products is by defining a product family with a shared architecture and reusable assets organized in a platform.

In practice it is relatively difficult to introduce a product family approach. Many initiatives do not achieve their goals or even fail because their impact and potential problems were not properly identified. Introducing a product family approach is not a matter of simply using a new technique (i.e., a platform with reusable components). A product family approach involves more than architectural issues alone; it also affects a company's business, processes and organization. For example, the product-management, marketing and project management departments must be familiar with the approach, and requirements management must take account of it. If no due allowance is made for all these aspects, then the chances of the introduction of such an approach proving a success will be small.

---

[1] This work was performed in the context of the Eureka Σ! 2023 Programme, ITEA project ip00004, CAFÉ.

G. Chastek (Ed.): SPLC2 2002, LNCS 2379, p. 68–89, 2002.

In this paper we discuss some of the issues that are of importance in the context of product families on the basis of three industrial cases. To structure our discussion, we will use two dimensions, as shown in Figure 1.

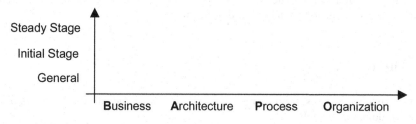

Fig. 1. Two Dimensions

The first dimension comprises Business, Architecture, Process, and Organization (BAPO), which is a reasoning framework introduced in [1] and [9]. It places architecture in the context of business, process and organization; see Figure 2. It also defines logical relations between them (the arrows in Figure 2). For example, processes are ideally defined in such a way that they optimally support the realization of the architecture. The architecture is further refined into five views (see [9]):

- Customer (the customer's world)
- Application (applications important to the customer)
- Functional (requirements for a system used in a customer application)
- Conceptual (architectural concepts of the system)
- Realization (realization technologies for building the system)

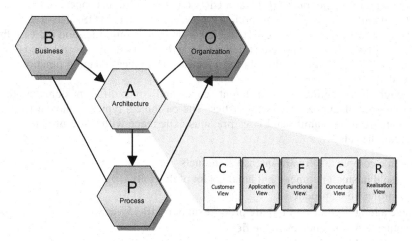

Fig. 2. BAPO/CAFCR Framework

The second dimension comprises issues that apply to a product family approach in general, issues in the initial stage (when a product family approach is introduced) and issues in the steady stage (when it has already been applied for several years).

The paper is organized as follows. In Section 2, the three industrial cases will be briefly introduced. Sections 3 through 6 will cover the BAPO issues. Each of these sections will discuss general product family issues and will conclude with a subsection on initial stage issues (in this paper, no special attention will be paid to the steady stage). Conclusions can be found in Section 7.

2   Three Cases

In this paper we will use experiences gained with three industrial product families from two domains, namely:

- Telecommunication switching systems (TSS)
- Medical modality systems (MMS)
- Medical imaging systems (MIS)

The TSS product family covers telecommunication infrastructure systems. This family has been designed for niche markets with a high variety of features. A key requirement was to achieve a reasonable price even with a low sales volume. Products of this family include public telephony exchanges, GSM radio base stations, technical operator service stations, operator-assisted directory services and combinations of the aforementioned.

The other two product families come from the medical domain. Philips Medical Systems builds products that are used to make images of the internal parts of the human body for medical diagnostic purposes. The different types of equipment used for acquiring images are called 'modalities', for example Magnetic Resonance (MR), X-ray, Computed Tomography (CT), and Ultrasound (US). In this paper we shall take a product family for one such a modality as a case, called MMS. There are also similarities across these modalities. To benefit from these similarities and increase the synergy, a platform is being constructed that will be used by several modalities (including the MMS family). This platform focuses on medical imaging functionality, and is called MIS.

Although these families have different scopes and cover different domains, they share a number of important characteristics. The customers typically have a number of products from one family and have previous experience with those products. The product families also

- Include complex, software-intensive products
- Are sold in small numbers, but having a lot of diversity
- Are professional products
- Have a long lifetime and require product support (10-15 years)
- Require software updates in the field
- Are extensible with new features
- Have standards for interconnection
- Have relatively mature and stable domains

It must be noted that the three cases described here are product families intended for professional markets. These markets and the products for these markets are somewhat different than, for example, a high-volume market with customer appliances. Even so, we are of the opinion that the BAPO issues discussed in the next sections are also relevant for product family approaches in other domains.

3   Business Aspects

Business is concerned with a company's mission and market. A strategy must be defined that supports the mission. Several elements make up a company's strategy. In this paper we focus on a product family platform as such a strategic means. A product family platform should thus be seen as a means and not as a goal.

3.1.   Why Platform-Based Development?

According to the BAPO framework, the rationale for a platform architecture and platform-based development can be found in the business. So, what are the business drivers for applying such an approach? These drivers can be external (i.e., matching a customer's need), or internal (i.e., supporting the development of the products internal to the company). The main reasons mentioned in the context of the three cases are:

- *Variation on a shared basis*: The systems are being made in small numbers. The customers on the other hand have their own specific demands. This leads to a range of similar, yet different systems.
- *Feature propagation:* A single customer will usually own not one, but several telecommunication switching or medical systems. As a result, a customer may request that a feature present in one system also be provided in the other systems.
- *Timely availability:* In order to be competitive, new features must be introduced into the market in a timely manner. Deadlines agreed upon with the customer must be met.
- *No unnecessary diversity:* Unnecessary diversity must not be exposed to the systems' users, who will usually have to deal with several similar systems. For example, a physician may have to be able to operate different types of X-ray systems. And a field-service engineer will have to know how to service various systems in the hospital. If the systems are similar, less training and fewer manuals will be needed to use or service the systems, which will lead to greater efficiency.
- *Limited development costs, shortage of skilled labor:* In the current economic situation, it is important to be able to limit development costs so that products can be offered at reasonable prices. There may also be a shortage of skilled staff needed to develop the systems.
- *Software complexity* (>100 man years, $>10^6$ lines of code): The systems we are talking about are complex and contain over 1 million lines of code. Such systems cannot be developed from scratch each time.
- *Higher quality:* The functionality within the platform will be reused in difference places, which will increase confidence in it. In addition, the testability of the functionality will increase with regression tests, etc. This however holds only for unmodified reuse; if components need to be altered, this will apply to a much lesser extent.

- *Interoperability:* The individual systems within a family must be able to interoperate with each other because a single customer will usually use several family members. This can be ensured by including interoperability functionality in the platform itself.
- *Evolvability:* Because of the large investments, the same basis must be used for building the products over relatively long periods of time. Because of new requirements and new technologies, this basis must evolve over time. If this basis consists of a component-based platform, the individual components will be able to evolve gracefully, assuming an appropriate separation of functionality is chosen.

3.2. Product Lines and Product Families

In this paper we use the term product family as a set of related products that are realized on the basis of a shared architecture, using assets from a platform. This focuses on the internal part of the business. For the external view, we will use the term product line, which represents a set of related products for the customers of a business. It is often assumed that a product line is related to a product family on a one-to-one basis. For example, the definition of product line in [3] mentions both a market segment and a common set of core assets (platform). There are, however, more possible relations between product line and product family, as illustrated below.

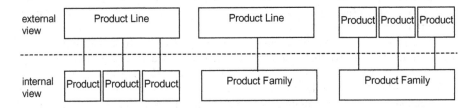

Fig. 3. Product Line and Product Family

The middle picture represents the 'common' situation. Another possibility is that a set of products is commercially marketed as a product line, while the individual products are developed independently (left picture). Alternatively, a set of products may be developed as part of a product family, while the products are marketed individually (right picture). We will return to this later.

3.3. Value and Levels of Reuse

In [6], four levels of reuse are described; see Figure 4. These levels range from ad-hoc reuse, which means that a developer reuses code when (s)he sees suitable code, to strategy-driven reuse, with which the reuse is aimed directly at supporting the company's strategy. This means that business people will also be involved when making the decision to pursue strategy-driven reuse. Strategy-driven reuse means, for example, that by having a reusable platform, it will be easier to enter new adjacent markets.

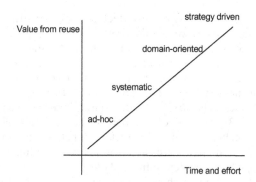

Fig. 4. Levels of Reuse

As graphically shown in Figure 4, the time and effort needed to achieve strategy-driven reuse are greatest because of the large scope and impact of this form of reuse. The option of applying such reuse must therefore be carefully considered. If, say, you have not yet worked out your strategy in full detail, it would be dangerous to try out such a new way of working, not knowing whether it will prove to be effective.

The three cases considered in this paper all have a flavor of strategy-driven reuse. The MIS platform, for example, has to support important business goals; it must allow for an integrated product portfolio and a common look-and-feel across products. The TSS platform was developed to be able to quickly enter new niche markets with low-priced products.

When starting to apply a product family platform, it is important to also embed it in the company in order to obtain optimum results. The real value of applying a platform approach in a certain context is hard to predict. There are still no clear rules to exactly predict the value of this kind of reuse. In [12], some information is given on the costs and benefits of a platform approach. Since a product family's scope must be known to determine the value of the approach, we will now discuss scoping.

3.4.   Scoping of Product Families and Platforms

In this paper we make a distinction between family architecture and platform architecture. By platform architecture we mean the architecture that is used to build the reusable assets within a platform. By family architecture we mean the shared architecture with which the family members must comply. The rules of the family architecture must enable reuse of platform components, but may also contribute, for example, to more commonality in the family so that it will be possible to merge individual systems in the future. The family architecture focuses on the shared architectural issues of the family members; the platform architecture focuses on the platform's internal structure.

The product line scope must be based on the external market. The family and platform scopes depend on external and internal issues. Some of the reasons mentioned for a product family approach (e.g., the feature propagation, an external driver), can be serviced well if there is a one-to-one relation between product line and product family. However, if the focus is more on cost reduction, an internal driver, and the family platform focuses on reuse in technical or infrastructure subdomains[2] and not on application subdomains, this product family may show no external similarities, and thus not be considered a product line as illustrated in the right picture in Figure 3. So, internal business considerations can also lead to a product family approach. All these consideration must be taken into account when roadmapping a platform within a business strategy. The TSS and MMS product families are also marketed as product lines. The MIS case lies somewhere between the middle and right pictures of Figure 3; the products are part of the same portfolio, but the reuse currently focuses on technical and infrastructure functionality. In the future, the platform focus will evolve more towards application (external) functionality.

When a family scope has been determined, platform support for that scope must be investigated iteratively. The main shared functional parts must be identified on the basis of the family scope. The main architectural rules and concepts supporting the qualities of the products within the family must also be considered. The platform's scope must be such that the architecture-shaping qualities are shared for this scope. If the platform scope includes too diverse systems, a platform approach may become counter productive. An initial architecture can be generated on the basis of the architecture-shaping qualities and be used for a first cost-benefit analysis. These considerations will lead to the definition of a platform scope within the product family's scope.

Another more technical choice is the asset content of the platform; have all assets been included (including product-specific ones), or only the assets that are used within several family members? Figure 5 graphically represents the various platform and product scopes. The family functionality is represented as white rectangles divided into a number of subdomains, and the platform functionality is represented as gray rectangles.

- The TSS platform contains all the components of all the systems in the family; the family architecture is the same as the platform architecture. The right components must be selected for a specific product.
- The MMS platform contains components relevant to two or more systems in the family; only family-member-specific functionality has to be provided for each family member. The family architecture is more or less the same as the platform architecture.
- The MIS platform contains components for the imaging subdomain that are relevant to two or more systems in the family; each family member still has to add product-specific functionality for this subdomain and all functionality for the other subdomains. The family scope is broader than the platform scope.

---

[2] By 'subdomain' we mean a sub-area within a system which requires some specific knowledge, for example the image processing subdomain, or the image acquisition subdomain. These subdomains may relate to the application knowledge of the user, to technical knowledge relating to the peripheral hardware or to computing infrastructure knowledge.

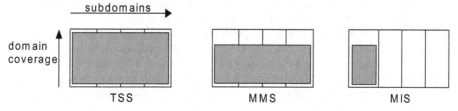

Fig. 5. Platform Coverage of Product Functionality

On the basis of the two dimensions used in Figure 5, the three cases can also be classified in a table, as shown in Table 1. The columns indicate whether the platform covers all the subdomains of the products in the family or only a subset. The rows indicate whether the platform contains all the functionality of the products, or only the generic functionality (i.e., whether it applies to at least several family members).

Table 1. Platform Types

	subset of domain	**complete domain**
generic functionality	MIS platform	MMS platform
all functionality		TSS platform

So far, we have assumed that a product family is based on one platform. But in view of the large scopes of product families with diverse family members, it is also possible to build a product based on several platforms, as shown in Figure 6. On the left-hand side, a platform is used to make another platform, which is again used to make the final products. This situation holds for the combination of MIS and MMS; the MMS platform is built using components from the MIS platform. The users of the MMS platform use it as a single platform and do not see the MIS platform as a separate one. The right-hand side of the figure illustrates a situation in which products are built on the basis of two platforms. Such platforms will usually focus on different subdomains of the family.

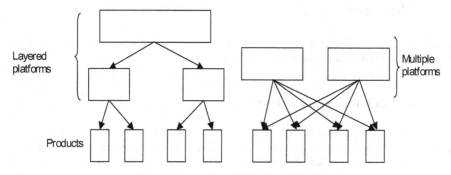

Fig. 6. Layered and Multiple Platforms

Depending on an organization's size and market scope, one or more platforms can be applied to support its mission. When only one platform is used for a large part of the business, there will be a risk of the platform capabilities being overstretched. We experienced this in some respect in the case of the MMS platform, which covers high- to low-end products, leading to a broad range of architectural requirements. This is hard to realize within a single platform. When several platforms are used, it must be made clear how the scopes of the various platforms complement each other.

3.5.   How Stable Is a Platform?

It is important to note that a platform should not be regarded as a stable unchangeable base. Changes will usually have to be made in a platform to meet the requirements of a new product. There should be no risk of missing market opportunities for the reason that 'they could not be incorporated in the platform'.

3.6.   Initial Stage

Some business-related issues that will have to be considered in the initial stage are:

- *Maturity and stability of the market:* It is important to note that all three cases are based on existing systems intended for relatively mature and relatively stable markets. So the important domain concepts are known and are not likely to change very fast. This is very important when a platform approach is introduced, since such an approach forms a (reusable) consolidation of these concepts, and should not innovate too much. However, a platform should enable the business to enter adjacent markets if necessary.
- *Vision of the future:* A business roadmap is needed to describe what is expected from the platform in the years to come and how it will fit in the plan for the release of products. The future expectations for the platform should help to identify evolution requirements required staffing, how it should be introduced, etc.

4   Architecture Aspects

In this section we will discuss the diversity mechanisms used for the families and how the platform architectures cover the five CAFCR views.

4.1.   Platform Integration and Diversity

The main concept guiding the platform's use depends on the requirements specified for the platform and its architecture. If only a single system is needed, the architecture can describe a number of fixed functional blocks. If greater variations of a system are needed, this can be solved by, for example, introducing component frameworks (right picture in Figure 7). In the case of even greater diversity and flexibility a set of components can be used (component kit), from which the relevant components can be selected (left picture in Figure 7). A platform's integration level may lie between that of a complete system and those of individual components as illustrated in Figure 7.

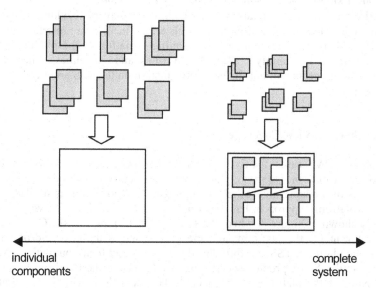

individual
components

complete
system

Fig. 7. Platform Integration and Diversity

Below, the software architecture of the three cases will be described, focusing on the support of diversity.

- The TSS architecture defines four horizontal layers. The layers contain components (called building blocks), based on a proprietary component model. A collection of component frameworks and plug-ins is used as the diversity mechanism. These component frameworks together constitute the system's architectural skeleton (right side in Figure 7). More information on this architecture can be found in [7].

- Since this platform is already highly integrated, the platform architecture also constitutes the product architecture. As a consequence, a lot of documentation can be made in the context of the platform, which can be reused for the specific products. For example, a product is described as a list of features. These features are described as part of the platform documentation.

- The MMS architecture is somewhat similar to the TSS architecture. The system is also divided into a number of layers. Each layer contains a number of units, which can be regarded as kinds of subdomains (e.g., image processing and the administration of patient data). Each unit contains one or more components, realized with the aid of COM. Component frameworks and plug-ins are used as a diversity mechanism. More information on the architecture and variation mechanism for MMS can be found in [10] and [13].

- As in the case of TSS, this platform architecture also constitutes the product architecture. Product requirements documentation is handled as an extended subset of the set of requirements documentation provided by the platform.

- In the development of the MMS platform, it was not always easy to take all different architectural requirements into account. For some parts of the system, a component kit approach would have offered better flexibility.
- The MIS family architecture also defines a number of layers. In addition, a number of generic interfaces and information models are defined. These interfaces must be implemented by specific components, forming a platform. The platform's users must adhere to the family's architectural rules and guidelines, otherwise the platform components will not fit. More information on the MIS architecture can be found in [8].

4.2.   Architecture View Coverage

In the TSS and MMS cases, the five CAFCR views have been reasonably covered by the platform from the start (e.g., analysis of customer needs, requirement specifications of products, and realized components). Although this is similar for both cases, the platform approach has been introduced in a different way. This is graphically shown in Figure 8, where the five rectangles represent the CAFCR views that are relevant for the platform, and the gray shape is the coverage of the first version of the platform. TSS was introduced with a product focus, but with a vision of a product family. Some product-specific parts fell outside the platform, and not all relevant parts of the platform were covered. This was dealt with in later releases (indicated by the arrows). MMS was introduced with a platform focus and with known platform boundaries, although not all platform functionality was integrated from the beginning.

For MIS, the introduction had a platform orientation. Furthermore, the initial focus was on the realized components (Realization view) and not as much on the earlier views of CAFCR. The idea is that this will grow over time (indicated by the two arrows in the right picture of Figure 8).

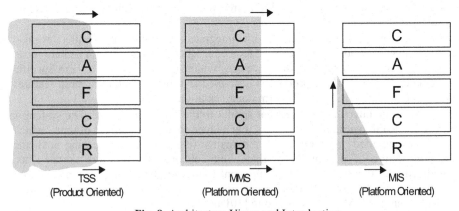

Fig. 8. Architecture Views and Introduction

4.3. Initial Stage

Some issues relating to the architecture that must be taken into account in the initial stage are:

- *Domain concept selection:* In the initial stage, the main concepts in the domain must be identified (e.g., subscriber and trunk lines or images and patient records). The stable and well-known concepts can already be introduced in the platform, so that they can be used for the development of generic interfaces or components. However, since the development of a platform has only just started, it will not be possible to define all relevant concepts. That is why the first step should not go all the way; evolution of the platform will always be necessary.
- *Guard conceptual integrity:* Important in the initial stage is to define the right architectural rules, guidelines, qualities, aspects, etc. Changing these architectural decisions afterwards will be hard and have a negative impact on conceptual integrity. Fortunately, these architectural decisions are usually stable and are not impacted too much by changes in domain concepts.

5   Process Aspects

In this section we will discuss some process structure and planning issues.

5.1. Process Structures

The three cases described here have different process structures. To enable comparison of these structures, we have mapped them onto the three activities described in [4]. These activities are:

- Application Family Engineering (AFE), which is responsible for the family architecture and ensuring reuse
- Component System Engineering (CSE), which focuses on the development, maintenance and administration of reusable assets within the platform
- Application System Engineering (ASE), which focuses on the development of products

The processes of TSS can be mapped to these activities as shown in Figure 9. The architecting is a continuous process and is not related to a single project. Most projects are defined to create one or more products. Sometimes a project is defined for an architectural redesign only. Several projects can run parallel to one another. A project to create a product deals not only with the product, but usually also contains some platform work (e.g., creating or modifying component frameworks).

The MMS and MIS cases also involve an architecting process. But unlike TSS, there are separate projects for working on the platform and on the products; see Figure 10. There will be only one project working on the platform at a time.

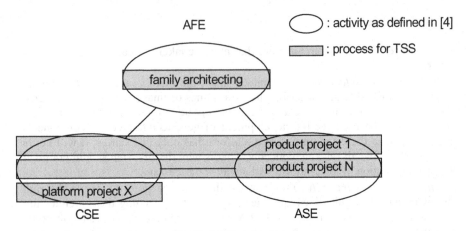

Fig. 9. TSS Process Structure

Each platform project of MMS focuses on a particular subset of platform users. The purpose is to extend the platform towards these users. Each MIS platform project focuses on adding new functionality to the platform. All interested groups in the MIS family may use this new functionality. This difference in focus is related to the type of platform architecture that is applied. The MMS platform is based on architectural frameworks for the entire family, forming one skeleton. The possibilities of this skeleton must sometimes be fine-tuned with respect to the users. The MIS platform, on the other hand, is a component kit, to which new components can easily be added.

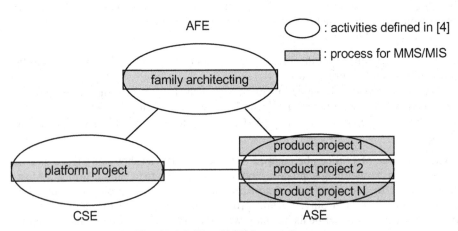

Fig. 10. MMS and MIS Process Structure

Below, some additional issues relating to the process structure will be discussed.

- *Family and platform architecting:* In the MIS case, the family architecture is broader than the platform architecture, as already discussed in the section on scoping. For MIS there are thus two architecting activity areas: the internal platform architecture, and the architecture with which the family members must comply. For the TSS and MMS cases, these two architectures are largely the same.

- *Relation between CSE and ASE activities:* The TSS case differs from the other two cases in that there is a one-to-one relation between CSE and ASE activities. This gives a clear product focus within TSS. For the MMS case, this relation is one-to-few (i.e., the subset of products (about 3) on which the platform project focuses). For MIS this relation is one-to-many. The platform activity is further removed from the actual products. The difference in focus on platform or product work is shown in Figure 11 (derived from the HP Owen approach [11]). The MMS and MIS cases have a much more pronounced platform focus than the TSS case. This involves the risks of the architecture activity becoming too platform-focused and the product focus decreasing. If there is no clear product focus, the development goal may not be clear and this may lead to 'floating' (i.e., the development becomes too generic and deadlines are missed). This can be tackled by increasing the cooperation between the CSE and ASE activities, as will be discussed in the section on organization. A risk involved in product orientation is pollution of the platform by 'fast hacks' that are not cleaned up afterwards.

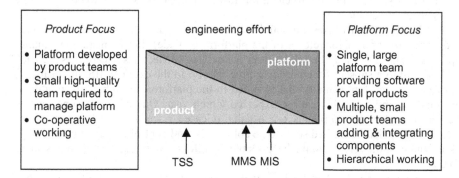

Fig. 11. Product vs. Platform Focus

- *Type of communication:* Of the three cases, TSS involves the smallest number of developers (taking into account both the platform and the product development). Furthermore, there is no clear separation between platform and product development; one developer can work on both a component framework and its specific plug-ins. The consequences of this are that the communication may be relatively informal and the amount of documentation required to transfer knowledge may be limited. The two other cases are more complex, and moreover entail clear separation between platform and product development. This requires more formal communication and elaborated documentation on how the platform can be used to build products. Extra attention must be paid to specifying clear interfaces. This has led to problems in the past: the documentation became too bulky or the product developers could not find the right information.

- *'Openness' of development:* Because of the nature of development at TSS, it is a kind of open-source development; a developer can modify both the sources of the component frameworks and the plug-ins in the platform. Such an open-source activity at a company is sometimes called inner source. This is a consequence of the combination of the CSE and ASE activities. The CSE activities of the MMS and MIS cases deliver black-box components; they should in principle not be modified by the product projects. Although MIS is currently in a closed-source mode, there are ideas to go in the direction of open-source that would encourage contributions from the product builders to the platform.

5.2. Planning

At TSS, most projects are defined on the basis of products that have to be made. In these projects, the platform is also modified if necessary. For planning purposes, a similar 'component topology' diagram as described for HP Owen [11], is used in which it is indicated which platform components have to be updated or added to realize the new product. Several projects are performed per year, according to the customers' demands for specific products. Each project generates a set of compatible components from which one or more products can be assembled. A set of compatible components is called a construction set. To limit the number of different construction sets existing side by side and to clean up 'fast hacks', projects are defined to remove unnecessary diversity.

The MMS and MIS cases are both based on a heartbeat (release cycle) of one year (i.e., once a year a major release of the platform is made). In the meantime, smaller updates or bug fixes may be released. In the case of MMS, these heartbeats are each year related to a subset of the product in the family. In the case of MIS, the heartbeat is related to new functionality that is added to the platform. In both cases, roadmaps are made to indicate what can be expected which year. One of the reasons for this heartbeat is that new products are usually released once a year. The number of releases must also be limited so as to be able to test and control the set of components as a whole, although it would be possible to release individual components more frequently.

We have found that feedback is very important. This is especially true when platform development takes place separately from product development. At TSS, where platform and product development are merged, deadlines were not missed very often. Sometimes a 'fast hack' was introduced to meet a deadline, but it was usually corrected afterwards. In the case of MMS and MIS, platform development has no real feedback from the market. A problem that occurred with MIS was that a lot of time was spent on defining generic interfaces, but they were not immediately realized in components. As a consequence, feedback from the implementation was missed. The interface specification could have been made much faster if feedback had been frequently provided. Feedback from the market is thus available for TSS more often (several releases per year) than for MMS and MIS (one release per year).

5.3. Initial Stage

Two issues relating to processes that must be taken into account in the initial stage are the weight of the introduction and tool support.

5.3.1. 'Weight' of Introduction

During one of the sessions of the 4th Product Family Engineering workshop in Bilbao (October 2001), attention was paid to lightweight introduction of a product family approach. For example, Krueger [5] describes a family approach on code level that can be introduced without too much impact. Since several product family initiatives did not succeed, lightweight introduction is now receiving more and more attention. Although the introduction itself is lightweight, it should be based from the very outset on a clear view of the underlying architecture; otherwise there will be no sound basis.

The ideal approach (see Figure 12), in which large investments are made initially (revolution) and recovered later. This is, however, a risky undertaking since this approach may fail because it costs too much and/or takes too long. The more realistic scenario that is sketched assumes partial, stepwise introduction without too much impact. This will lower the risk and result in benefits at an earlier stage. Feedback is obtained at an earlier stage this way, and acceptance can be built up gradually. However, the benefits may not increase as fast as in the ideal situation, because the approach will have to be improved gradually over time.

The TSS platform was introduced gradually. The focus was on products. The various component frameworks were introduced (and redesigned) one by one. The MMS system, which involves an architectural approach similar to that followed with the TSS system, was introduced as a revolution. The MMS family, which had the high ambition of having a clean platform architecture from the start, had a longer introduction time than expected. Furthermore, with MMS we noticed that it is very hard to have the right requirements at the beginning and to identify all important concepts. The MIS system, based on a component-kit architectural approach, is being introduced step-by-step. Each release contains more functionality. This is made easy by the architectural approach of individual components. The focus is initially on realized components, similar to Krueger [5]. Later, other views will also be taken into account; see the right picture in Figure 8.

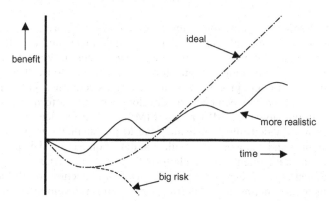

Fig. 12. Ideal vs. Realistic Introduction

5.3.2. Tool Support

Tools are needed to support the various processes. Tools are particularly important in the context of products based on a platform, because the platform will be used many times, allowing for automation of certain activities. For example, code for interfaces that are required to interact with the platform functionality can be generated. Another example consists of test specifications for generic interfaces that can be reused for specific components. The provision of such support must be planned at an early stage.

6   Organization Aspects

In this section we will discuss the organization structures and their mapping onto the process structures.

6.1.   Organizational Structures

The organizational structure of TSS is depicted in Figure 13. There is one system team. This team is responsible for defining the requirements and the architecture. The architecture is designed and implemented by a number of development teams, one for each layer. All the teams work at the same site, and there is no separation between platform development and platform usage.

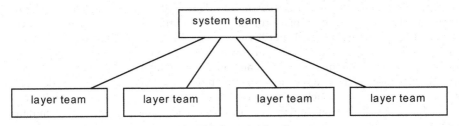

Fig. 13. TSS Organization Structure

In the case of MMS the situation is more complex (see Figure 14). There is one platform team that is responsible for the platform requirements and architecture. The platform is designed and implemented by several teams, each of which is responsible for one or a few units. Some units are outsourced to a software house. The platform is used by a number of product groups, working in various countries. The management has to enable cooperation between platform development and platform usage.

Something similar holds for MIS as for MMS. One difference is that platform development is not divided into unit teams, due to the smaller size of the platform team. Outsourcing and cooperation with another company take place in the development of the components of the platform, too. Another difference is that there is an additional team that is responsible for the shared architecture for all members of the family. This team contains members from both platform-development and product groups.

A comparison of Figures 13 and 14 reveals a difference in the main decomposition of the organization. In the case of TSS, the main decomposition is along the layers (subdomains) of the architecture of the product family. Within such a layer team, work can be performed on several products in parallel. In the case of MMS and MIS, the main decomposition is into platform and product development. In [2] Bosch describes a number of organizational structures for product family development. The

TSS case can be compared with the development department model. The difference is however that in the case of TSS the department is split into a number of teams, each dealing with their own subdomain, making this approach more scalable. The MMS and MIS cases can be compared with the domain engineering unit model. When the MIS and MMS cases are combined, this can be compared with the hierarchical domain engineering unit model.

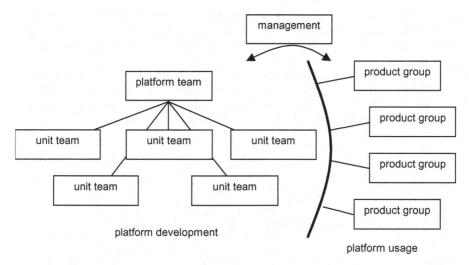

Fig. 14. MMS Organizational Structure

In [11] it is assumed that when there is a separation into platform and product groups, the platform group is large and makes all the components, and the product groups are small and simply have to assemble the components into products (right-hand side of Figure 11). However, this does not apply to the MMS and the MIS cases. The reason is that these platforms contain only the shared components; specific functionality still has to be provided by the product groups. Furthermore, the MIS platform covers only one subdomain. This means that the product groups using MIS must be larger than the platform group.

6.2.   Process to Organization Mapping

After the discussion of the processes in Section 5, it is interesting to see how the processes map onto the organization. The easiest mapping would theoretically be one-to-one, but that is not always the case in practice. In the case of TSS, the system team is responsible for the architecting. The product projects run across the layer teams.

Unlike TSS, MMS and MIS introduce a separation between platform development and platform usage. This separation introduces a 'communication barrier' that has to be taken care of. For the MMS and MIS projects, the following solutions are applied:

- At MMS, members of the product groups (temporarily) participate in the platform development. This way, expertise from the product groups is used in the platform development and the members of the product group acquire knowledge of the platform. The architects and requirement engineers from the product groups are also involved in defining the platform's requirements and architecture.

- At MIS, there is a special team that is responsible for the shared architecture in which platform and product architects participate. Furthermore, when new functionality is added to the platform, this is usually done via a pilot project in which one or more product groups also participate.

Although the platform's components are currently made by the platform group, the product groups should in the future also be able to insert their components that can be reused by other groups into the platform. This comes close to the business unit model described in [2].

So, to improve communication between platform and product development, processes are needed that cross this organizational boundary. In Figure 15 this is graphically shown for the MIS case. In this figure the product groups also participate in the definition of the shared architecture and in writing components for the platform.

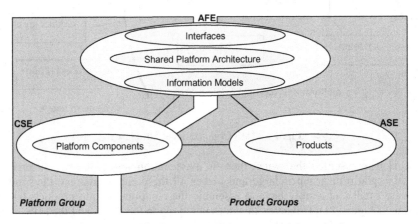

Fig. 15. Relation between MIS Processes and Organization

6.3.   Initial Stage

Some issues relating to the organization that must be taken into account in the initial stage are:

- *Platform acceptance:*

  It is important to promote broad acceptance within the organization for a product family approach. It is especially important to create support within the product groups. These groups may see the introduction of a platform as a threat to their own freedom; they now have to adhere to the shared architecture. Since there are no separate product groups for TSS, this problem does not play a role in that context.

  In the case of MMS this is more of a problem. Here, the product groups defined their own architecture and made their own decisions. This has changed, since the family prescribes an architecture that more or less corresponds to the product architecture. For the MIS platform this is less of a problem, since the MIS platform is only intended for a subdomain of the products, and a more flexible mechanism is used (i.e., the product groups are free to select the components they need). As a consequence, resistance will be much less than in the case of MMS; MIS is seen as something that can be beneficial to use, MMS is seen as something that must be used.

- *Distributed groups*
  Both the MMS and the MIS cases have distributed development groups and apply outsourcing. This adds to the complexity involved in the development of a product family. As switching to a product family approach is already a very big step that involves a lot of changes, any additional complexity should be minimized where possible in the initial stage. Feedback cycles must be short because a lot of decisions must be made; outsourcing in this stage could imply less frequent feedback. Furthermore, if the groups are working in different countries, differences in culture could complicate introduction.

- *Growth*
  During the development of a new system (initial system stage) it is preferable for an organization to be small. The reason for this is that a number of issues have to be investigated and discussed before the system can be introduced, and this can be done more effectively in a small group. Later, when the requirements of the system, the software architecture, design concepts and principles are known and have been formulated, the number of people may increase (steady system stage). Only in this way can conceptual integrity be safeguarded from the outset.

7   Conclusions

In this paper we have discussed three product family approaches, and each of their strengths and weaknesses. Product family approaches discussed in the literature usually focus on architectural issues. However, architectural issues are but a few of the many issues that have to be considered, as has been pointed out in this paper. To bring structure into these issues, we applied the BAPO reasoning framework. This helped us in comparing business, architectural, process and organizational aspects of the approaches. In Table 2 we have listed the most important issues in the form of questions that need to be answered when defining a product family approach.

This is only a subset of the issues that need to be defined for a product family approach. In this paper we have discussed some ways of dealing with these issues. For example, the problem of the 'communication barrier' introduced by the separation of platform and product groups can be dealt with by temporarily moving people between organizational units, or by involving members of different groups in pilot projects.

Special attention has been paid to the initial stage in which a product family approach is introduced in a company. This involves a considerable change effort, which must be well prepared. Some of the main problems that may be encountered are: underestimation of the change effort needed, wrong/incomplete requirements for the platform, wrong platform architecture, resistance within the company, restriction of freedom, no tool support.

Table 2. BAPO ASPECTS FOR Product Families

Business	***product line - product family relation;*** What is the mapping between the product line (external) and the product family (internal) like? ***business integration;*** To what extent is the platform taken into account in the business planning? ***platform coverage;*** To what extent is the platform covered in the family? To a too great extent?
Architecture	***platform integration and diversity;*** What is the level of platform integration? Which architectural diversity mechanism is most suitable? ***Architecture views coverage;*** Where lies the focus of the architecting (e.g., realized components and family/product requirements)?
Process	***family and platform architecting;*** Is the platform architecture the same as the family architecture? ***product or platform focus;*** What is the relation between the CSE and ASE activities; how is it organized? ***type of communication;*** How must the communication be organized (e.g., via documentation, exchange of persons, and shared pilot projects)? ***heartbeat and feedback;*** How often is the platform released; frequency of feedback?
Organization	***separation of platform and product groups;*** Must platform and product groups be separated (in relation to the size of the organization)? ***acceptance;*** How is the platform approach accepted in the various groups; how could this be improved?
Overall	***matching of BAPO aspects;*** Do the various business, architectural, process and organizational choices agree with one another (e.g., does the platform architecture conform to the business requirements)? Are the process and organizational structure in agreement with the platform architecture?

Acknowledgements

We would like to thank Lothar Baumbauer, Frank van der Linden, Ben Pronk and Tobias Rötschke for their comments on earlier versions of this paper.

References

1.   Pierre America, Henk Obbink, Rob van Ommering, Frank van der Linden, CoPAM: A Component-Oriented Platform Architecting Method Family for Product Family Engineering, Proceedings of the SPLC1, Denver, August 2000.

2. Jan Bosch, *Design & Use of Software Architectures – Adopting and Evolving a Product line Approach*, Addison-Wesley, 2000.
3. Paul Clements, Linda Northrop, *Software Product Lines – Practices and Patterns*, Addison-Wesley, 2001.
4. Ivar Jacobson, Martin Griss, Patrik Jonsson, *Software Reuse - Architecture, Process and Organization for Business Success*, Addison-Wesley, 1997.
5. Charles W. Krueger, *Easing the Transition to Software Mass Customization*, Proceedings of PFE-4, Bilbao, Spain, October 2001.
6. Wayne C. Lim, *Managing Software Reuse: A Comprehensive Guide to Strategically Reengineering the Organization for Reusable Components*, Prentice Hall, 1998.
7. Frank J. van der Linden, Jürgen K. Müller, *Creating Architectures with Building Blocks*, IEEE Software, November 1995.
8. Frank van der Linden, Jan Gerben Wijnstra, *Platform Engineering for the Medical Domain*, Proceedings of the PFE-4, Bilbao, Spain, October 2001.
9. Henk Obbink, Jürgen Müller, Pierre America, Rob van Ommering, Gerrit Muller, William van der Sterren, Jan Gerben Wijnstra, *COPA: A Component-Oriented Platform Architecting Method for Families of Software-Intensive Electronic Products*, Tutorial at the SPLC1, August 2000.
    (http://www.extra.research.philips.com/SAE/COPA/COPA_Tutorial.pdf)
10. Ben J. Pronk, *An Interface-Based Platform Approach*, Proceedings of the SPLC1, Denver, August 2000.
11. Peter Toft, Derek Coleman, Joni Ohta, A *Cooperative Model for Cross-Divisional Product Development for a Software Product Line*, Proceedings of the SPLC1, Denver, August 2000.
12. David M. Weiss, Chi Tau Robert Lai, *Software Product line Engineering - A Family-Based Software Development Process*, Addison-Wesley, 1999.
13. Jan Gerben Wijnstra, Supporting Diversity with Component Frameworks as Architectural Elements, Proceedings of the ICSE 2000, June 2000.

Product Line Architecture
and the Separation of Concerns

Jay van Zyl

Rubico (Pty) Ltd, Postnet Suite 22, Private Bag X87, Bryanston, 2021 Johannesburg,
South Africa
http://www.jayvanzyl.com/, jay@rubico.com

Abstract. Software product lines present many benefits over the traditional
methods of building systems. With the diverse implementation of product lines,
organizations are faced with complex design constraints. Layered architectures
assist with breaking down complexity through separating architectural elements
based on their use and applicability. It is difficult to achieve high levels of reuse
and productivity by focusing on one architectural style. This paper discusses
three primary concepts, namely, the product line architecture, the separation
continuum and application assembly. It starts by presenting a product line
architectural view that shows how various concepts are separated based on
abstraction. The separation continuum shows how vertical and horizontal
layering can assist with separating user interface from business logic and data at
an implementation level, and the separation of customer facing processes from
infrastructure facing processes at a business or abstract level. An application
assembly approach is discussed whereby a product line architecture is tied to
the separation continuum, showing how high levels of productivity can be
achieved when realizing product lines. The approach presented in this paper is
still under development with implementation on a limited number of product
lines only. It is intended that the content will provoke and stimulate the thinking
and experimentation needed to deal with application assembly by means of
having a product line architecture overlaid onto a separation continuum.
Keywords: product line, architecture, separation of concerns, separation
continuum, patterns, software assembly.

1 Introduction

Reusability is a topic that is constantly under discussion. The reality is that there are
no "silver bullets", no easy process, no easy software solution and no bullet-proof
architecture to assist with building and using reusable software assets. In this era of
objects, components and service based architectures, how do architects and software
practitioners implement large-scale usable, reusable software products that are fit for
the purpose? How are the benefits of product lines fully realized once implemented?
These kinds of questions are answered in this paper.

This paper ties together three essential concepts, namely, the separation continuum,
product line practices, and a product line architecture. The three concepts "morph"
into one, yielding benefits that all revolve around the ability to: "assemble" software
systems safely, quickly, and easily into product lines. The complex nature of large-

G. Chastek (Ed.): SPLC2 2002, LNCS 2379, pp. 90–109, 2002.

scale software systems requires a clear separation of the concerns represented by a *separation continuum*. *Product line practices* are a frequently adopted and well understood means of facilitating the processes needed in the production, maintenance and management of product lines. A *product line architecture* is needed in order to realize the various concerns in a software product by using product line practices.

Emerging approaches, such as the Model Driven Architecture (MDA) [12] and the Reusable Asset Specification (RAS) [14], show that the need to have a common method for understanding how requirements are realized, independently of the implementation, is receiving a fair deal of attention. The MDA framework is based on modelling different levels and abstractions of systems, and exploiting the relationships among these models. The RAS provides guidelines for description, development and application of different kinds of reusable software assets. Neither of these initiatives focuses on producing product lines.

The Product Line Management v2.0 [16], page 3, presents the following definition: "A software product line is a set of software-intensive systems sharing a common, managed set of features that satisfy the specific needs of a particular market segment or mission". Common software assets are invented, designed and built in such a way that they can be used in a multitude of product lines. The ability to build and evolve these separately has major benefits because architectural, resource and other dependencies can be balanced. Independent synchronized product delivery, where assets are constructed in parallel, is now possible as products are assembled depending on the customer's needs.

In order to have a clearly separated technology and platform architecture [9] suggests that certain elements of flow control must be removed from the underlying architectures. Components might be independently defined and built, but the flow of processes and data presents many platform-specific challenges. The core software assets must include tools to perform these tasks without having a specific platform feature implemented.

This paper contributes to the research already underway in the field of assembling systems from previously constructed software assets.

Section 2 introduces the separation continuum and the way in which the various dimensions are identified.

Section 3 discusses the platform implementation layering of the separation continuum model. It also shows that the separation of concerns must be taken into account in product line architectures.

Section 4 introduces the concept of assembling new product lines from pre-defined software assets. It also shows how product lines are realized.

Section 5 closes with some specific comments on the implementation of the principles described in this paper.

2   Separation Continuum

The principle of "the separation of concerns" has been used by various architectural styles. Essentially, it is used to deal with the complexities that exist in the definition and use of software systems. Principally, if the inherently static rules that require high speeds of execution are placed in an environment where they are best suited, and are separated from the dynamics of user interface metaphors, the risk of having an imbalance between performance and dynamic capability is reduced radically.

The continuum described here attempts to extend the thinking already prevalent in layered architectures. Architectures always describe a system that is made up of smaller parts [2]. Complexity is managed by understanding the continuums that exist when describing, defining and assembling product lines using these parts.

2.1.   Separation of Concerns

The Separation Continuum can be defined as: "a systemic view of a system to understand its parts and their relationship, through understanding vertical and horizontal continuums needed where abstraction and implementation are on the vertical continuum, and human and machine facing aspects to have attributes of adaptability, context and relevance are on the horizontal continuum."

Model Driven Architecture [10] has a vision that overlaps with the separation continuum: "An integrated enterprise is one whose business areas, strategies, architectures, organizational units, processes, machines, technology platforms, data and information – and the organization's understanding of these – form a consistent, cohesive, and adaptive whole".

It is reasoned that the separation continuum will assist in the implementation of product line practices. The ability to understand interrelated layers of a system and the levels of reusability required in producing software intensive product lines has many benefits, including:

- Agility – the ability of the business to respond to market demand by having highly adaptive software systems.
- Time to market – the ability to assemble new software products by using software assets in a highly productive and easy to use manner.
- Operational optimization – the ability to have focused teams produce relevant assets based on functional and non-functional requirements.
- Innovation ability – new products can be produced as prototypes by using different combinations of assets.

When architectures are designed for new product lines, there needs to be one main objective [13], namely, "avoiding a monolithic design by extreme de-coupling of components and localization of functionality so that every component can be replaced or upgraded in isolation". The separation continuum takes this concept one step further in that other dimensions in systems delivery need to be considered.

"Horizontal separation" is concerned with how the user interface is independent of the connectivity and, in turn, separate from the business logic and data access. "Vertical separation" is the layering needed to implement platform elements separately from the higher levels of abstraction needed at application levels typically represented in business requirements.

Architectures from many platform vendors are available that specialise in different kinds of separation. Both J2EE and Microsoft .NET platforms are focused strongly on the notion of separating out the various dimensions of a system on both the vertical and horizontal axis. The continuum assists with the thinking required to bring vertical and horizontal layering into one construct.

2.2. Horizontal Continuum

The horizontal continuum can be seen as having two areas, namely, "client facing aspects" and "infrastructure facing aspects". The horizontal continuum at a *platform implementation* continuum level is typically made up of the following elements:

- User interface: the interface seen by the system user that might include a multitude of devices (e.g., web browsers and personal devices).
- User interface controller: this controller is needed to manage the behaviour of the interfaces (for example, web pages) that connect to the business logic layer.
- Services and business logic layer: the ability to have a cluster of business and/or technical services exposed to the user interface.
- Connection or middleware layer: the ability of the user interface to connect to a server that directs the way in which the interface is used.
- Data provision layer: the ability to store in a reliable fashion that which may be used by the services layer to deal with transactional, system and meta-data data definitions.

Architectural patterns can assist in determining the optimal groupings of architectural elements on the horizontal continuum. [5] describes in "Pattern-Oriented Software Architecture" many architectural constructs that can be used.

The *layering abstract* continuum relates to the platform implementation in the following way. Customer facing processes in organizations can be implemented by using various technologies. Human-only processes do not require any physical implementation but still need to be defined and understood in order to provide the optimal human-technology interaction. An example could be a system that can be accessed via the web to perform certain transactions. When something out of the ordinary happens, the user can telephone a call centre, where a human can assist with queries. In this example there is an overlap between what the technology needs to provide and what humans need to provide.

By taking an internal customer-facing perspective, the separation continuum can be implemented in its entirety as the realization of an infrastructure process. The call centre example above is seen by the external customer as an infrastructure-facing process. The call centre operator, using visual tools, sees a customer facing view of the system used to deal with the inquiry.

2.3. Vertical Continuum

The separation of dimensions, based on context and relevance, is fundamentally important when defining a product line architecture [9]. Aspect-Oriented Frameworks [8] can assist with the challenge that is faced by so many designers and architects. "Aspects" refer to the properties of the system that do not align directly with a system's functional requirements, but instead cut across functional components and increase their interdependencies. The "vertical continuum" essentially deals with the aspects needed to produce product lines. In order to understand this continuum, two concepts need to be defined briefly; namely, models and architecture.

"Models" can be defined as a simplified description of a complex problem that is represented by designs of a projected implementation. The separation continuum uses models to analyse and communicate abstract business related requirements.

"Software Architecture" as defined by [3] is the structure (or structures) of a system which comprises software components, the externally visible properties of those components, and the relationships between them. "Architecture" in the context of the separation continuum, as adapted from [3], is defined as the high level design that can be realized by the overall structure of the system that includes all the interrelationships of elements in whatever style was used.

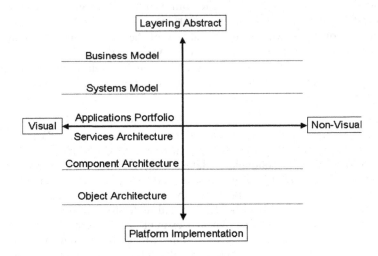

Fig. 1. The Separation Continuum

Vertical separation of contexts in the organization or system considers the following levels, moving from abstract layering to platform implementation:

- Business Model – This layer represents the basic concept of "doing business".
- Systems Model – The systems model deals with the systems required to satisfy a specific business model.
- Applications Portfolio – Systems are required to automate required systems by means of producing software assets, product lines and product families.
- Services Architecture – This architecture is concerned with the breadth of functionality needed to implement the business systems via the applications portfolio. A generic term that could be used here is "web service" or "service based architecture".
- Component Architecture - The component architecture view presents a complete view of the business components that can be exposed as services. Components are typically coarse-grained software elements that satisfy a particular requirement.
- Object Architecture – Components are created from object or other technologies and exposed as business components. Objects are the finest granularity of functionality in a typical system.

This continuum also assists with application context realization [1] and refers to this as "zoom-in" and "zoom-out". These "zooming" concepts can be used in order to move up or down the vertical continuum, for example, a particular business model is realized by a number of systems models. It also means that there is traceability between the various layers. This ability allows for the direct mapping onto the Model Driven Architecture through platform independent and platform dependent models [12].

The next two sections will explore the vertical continuum. Firstly the *layering abstract* is discussed where it is shown how business requirements are used to derive an applications portfolio that is used to assemble a product line. Secondly, the *platform implementation* is discussed and it is shown how software architectures are used to realize software assets. These assets are used to realize the product line through an assembly process.

2.3.1. Layering Abstract

This continuum is concerned with the relationships that are required to ensure that the *platform implementation* is relevant to the *layering abstract* it will implement. The layers defined in the *layering abstract* can overlap, and probably will, with existing business design and modeling methods. Most organizations today have business plans, strategies, processes and other artefacts that describe the way in which the business operates. These can be used to determine the required models.

Benefits of continuity and common understanding can be realized when an organization, or a unit in an organization, understands business requirements in terms of the horizontal continuum. The systems model layer and the layers below can form a critical map for the chief information officer or technology executive in that, once continuity is achieved, all dependencies are understood and new development and packaged product purchases can be seen in the context of the overall organization.

2.3.2. Applications Portfolio

Well thought out business systems are required in order to automate these systems. The software required to undertake customer management, for example, might be the same for both business models and their related systems. Differences will be prevalent when the various audiences use the software interfaces, for example, the "electronic banking" user will have a specific means to maintain information, whereas the "personal banking" agent might have access to more confidential information relating to the client, such as internal banking ratings.

A typical applications portfolio might involve software applications that might be classified as legacy. This means that this portfolio is the implementation view of the systems model without the manual operations. It does, however, show the relationship between human and machine, resulting in flow-of-activity definitions that are specific to the way in which a certain role would utilize the software product.

The applications portfolio lives on the abstract continuum and forms the bridge between the *layering abstract* and *platform implementation* continuums. Application engineering [1], as a concept of producing applications, uses all the concepts as articulated at the various levels in the continuum. Even though the applications portfolio might seem more "platform implementation" specific, it is not. Overlaps into the "layering abstract" become more apparent when systems can be constructed quickly, and the stakeholders decide to accept changes in this level rather than in the technology [19]. This means that deployable software will include the definitions of the application portfolio in some platform independent fashion such as an Extensible Markup Language (XML) definition.

This was a high level introduction into the layering abstract. It is provided in order to show the platform implementation for what it is: a realization of business requirements.

3   Platform Implementation

Product lines that cover a wide spectrum of functionality can only be produced if the underlying architecture is independent of the business functionality required by the ultimate user. A number of architectures cover the ability of software developed objects and components to be transformed from one type of implementation to another. This still proves problematic because the skills shortage and the level of understanding of the architecture are critical elements in transforming strategic features into products.

This part of the continuum is affected by the implementation and usage of international standards. Standards help to integrate diverse software assets, and assure the purchaser that lock-in is minimized. But, there are standards ... and there are standards. The selection process of implementing standards is as important as selecting an entire architecture in some cases, as these are closely interrelated. Standards also assist with basic requirements that need to be included to make architectures more competitive.

The three layers in the platform implementation can be grouped into two main areas, namely, services and components. Typical component implementations will not expose the objects used as these are typically part of the underlying frameworks used.

3.1.   Services Architecture

This architecture is concerned with the breadth of functionality needed to implement the business systems via the applications portfolio. A generic term that could be used here is "web service" or "service based architecture". It means that the application portfolio is constructed from independently usable software components that are exposed as services. A typical service might be "DoCustomerManagement" that entails all the basic elements of maintaining information about a customer. Another related service could be "ObtainCustomerPortfolio", that is, the portfolio of the account that the customer has with a particular institution.

Services need to be defined in such a way that they can be used in a loosely coupled way. This means that an assembly process is applied to tie together the different functionality areas at the run-time of the software system's execution. People performing the role of assemblers need not have the technical skill of a component builder or developer. Safety is a major factor when non-technical people assemble systems. A concept such as design-by-contract can be used to ensure that services have the correct inputs, produce the appropriate outputs, and are controlled by means of pre- and post-conditional checks.

3.2. Component Architecture

The component architecture presents a complete view of the business components (components constructed for more general business use) that can be exposed as services. Components are typically coarse-grained software elements that satisfy a particular requirement and are constructed using an object oriented or other technology. The customer management service requires a number of components in order to realize functionality (for example, there might be different components to read customer information and to create new customer accounts). More generic components might be grouped together in order to realize more business-related functionality (for example, when a generic storage management or security component is used). More generic components might have associated configuration environments to direct the behavioural and data usage principles applied.

Components that live in the same technical component architecture can be tightly coupled to ensure good performance. "Tightly coupled" means that there is specific work involved in getting components wired together, where they share and have optimal ways to execute using high performance implementation techniques. "Loosely coupled" differs from tightly coupled by the dynamic ability to wire components together either on one platform or across platforms. Loosely coupled components are typically done via services, as described in the previous section.

3.3. Object Architecture

Components are created from object or other technologies and exposed as business components. Objects are the finest granularity of functionality in a typical system. The term is used in this context more generically than in object orientation. Data objects for example might be realized in a particular database technology, where connectivity might be realized using a particular transport mechanism. Functionality provided by objects is grouped and used as components.

Object usage would normally involve the use of an underlying technical architecture. It involves a programming model that has specific semantics, characteristics, and usage criteria. When used in programming, objects are applied in a tightly coupled fashion, meaning that programming would be required to change the way in which an execution sequence is implemented, for example.

The platform implementation continuum is realized using one or more technical architectures. Specific styles can be applied depending on the characteristics of how the final systems need to function.

3.4. Software Architecture

The software architecture can be implemented by using object, component, and service-based architectures. The software architecture needs to be designed in such a way that applications can be created dynamically. There will be tradeoffs when applying the various architectural styles during the design process.

A number of basic architectural patterns has stayed the same over the history of computer systems. These basic patterns are applied repeatedly in the design and development of systems. To be "design centric" means to be focused on the timeless concepts needed to construct systems. Patterns have been used to fill this gap to a certain extent. Programming languages have come and gone, but the basic design of language, semantics and usage has remained the same or similar in nature.

Design needs to take into account both functional and non-functional requirements when designing architectures. Design processes, such as those by [4], can be applied to all architectures on the *platform implementation* continuum.

4   Assembly Using a Product Line Approach

The previous three sections discussed the separation continuum. There was an emphasis on the *platform implementation* continuum because this section will describe how a product line architecture can be used to implement the continuum.

4.1.   Introduction

Product lines are defined in order to realize a specific customer requirement, market need or market niche. Product line features, or requirements, are determined from the *systems models* that require software *applications* to function. "Assembly" is the process of exploring and reusing existing software assets. In the case where a requirement cannot be satisfied, a development life cycle will be initiated to construct the relevant asset.

Principles of altering behaviour and information requirements of more dynamic assets can be applied in assembly processes. In "Software Product Lines", Clements and Northrop [7] state that: "In a product line, the generic form of the component is evolved and maintained in the asset base. In component-based development, if any variation is involved, it is usually accomplished by writing code, and the variations are most likely maintained separately". The next section will describe one such implementation, where executable patterns can be seen as software assets, and the variations on the patterns as asset parameters.

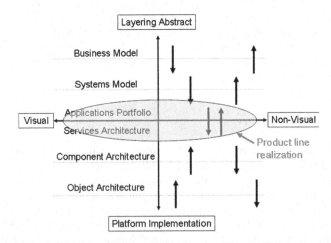

Fig. 2. Separation Continuum and Product Line Realization

During system assembly the focus should be on the tying together of a predefined set of assets that comes in the form of web services, components or objects. It must be considered that these assets could have been acquired from different sources.

Assembly using software as assets is needed to realize the benefits of agility, time-to-market, operational optimization and increased innovation ability.

Component and object architectures form the nucleus of software execution. Product lines are realized where the abstract layers join the implementation layers. The diagram above shows that there are two ways to realize product lines:

- Top down: The business model drives strategic initiatives from the top down to the implementation. All the interpretations of how the business systems must function are realized in the application portfolio specification. The platform implementation continuum needs to be flexible enough to respond to changes with quick turn-around times. *Business consultants* or *systems analysts* typically function in this domain.
- Bottom up: The architectures already implemented either present enablers or inhibitors to the business model. Web services are a good example of how business is affected and how a new means of realizing functionality quickly can facilitate new business products to be taken to market. *Developer, architect* and *assembler* are roles typically seen in this domain.

4.2. Product Line Architecture

The separation continuum is realized by having a high-level product line architecture mapped onto it. The product line architecture needs to separate out the essential elements needed to produce product lines productively – software assets can be used in many different product families and product lines.

Figure 3 shows three distinct groupings of concepts used to realize a software system using the separation continuum. Technology and platform architectures form the basis on which software assets are built – these can include platforms provided by, for example, IBM, BEA or Microsoft. This paper is focused on commercially related software - hence the use of widely used commercial platforms.

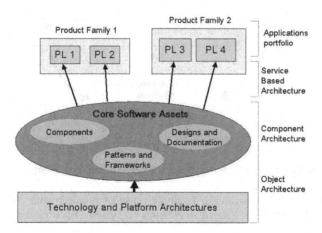

Fig. 3. Assembly, the Product Line Architecture, and the Separation Continuum

Core software assets are the different elements that make up a complete software product. All assets need to be stored in a repository for ease of search and use. Software components, designs and documentation are built using patterns and frameworks, and are all included as assets. Product families are made up of product lines that are, in turn, assembled from core software assets.

Product lines are produced from software assets to satisfy a specific product space. This production exercise should be executed with rigour, based on processes that reflect mature capabilities. Scoping of product lines has posed challenges to the production of product lines [15]. Producing the product, by using the independent synchronized product delivery [20] concept, poses risks to the team if the scope of the asset and overall product line is not clearly defined and communicated.

Part of the message here is that the separation continuum is used to layer elements of a software system – *layering abstract* into *platform implementation,* and that assembly by means of using software assets forms the basis of productivity and time-to-market gains.

4.3.   Separation Continuum Implementation

The approach described next relies on the understanding that systems have elements that are stable and others that are volatile in the context of ongoing systemic evolution. Basically, one needs to understand the things that will stay the same versus the things that might or will change over a particular time period. The things that stay the same are developed in the underlying software technology platform and represent stability. The things that change are used to tell the software how to behave and represent volatility. This is done by means of using patterns when assembling systems.

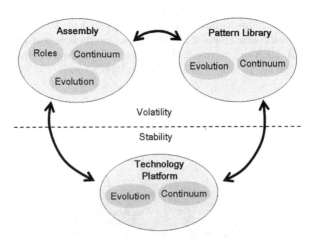

Fig. 4. Software Asset Creation Using a Pattern-Technology-Assembly Method

Patterns are used as a means to facilitate reuse of requirements, software assets, designs, and other artefacts needed to construct a system. Each pattern describes the solution to a known problem and is stored in the library. It also describes the structural and behavioural solutions.

Patterns are classified as per the separation continuum. It means that business model patterns have certain system model patterns linked to them. Certain system model patterns have application portfolio elements linked to them, and so on.

Analysed business needs can be mapped to business patterns relevant to a particular domain. If new patterns are identified, a process is initiated to create them. These patterns form the basis on which the final software system will be constructed. The availability of patterns that show how specific problems have been solved presents many opportunities for business analysts to apply defined knowledge. When used in productivity tools, patterns realized previously give the development teams comfort as reuse is implemented by means of pattern recognition and application.

Looking at the separation continuum, it was seen that the abstract layers describe only the patterns and requirements needed by a business audience. The *platform implementation* revealed software assets that are used to construct the various product lines using services and components. Once services are put to use, the resultant product line reveals a "look and feel" that are specific to the intended user. The user interface and other user-facing aspects are typically part of the things that change between two product line implementations.

Figure 5 shows a "tree-view" on the left most panel that is constructed based on the user logon credentials, role definition and process definition. The panels in the work areas are also created using a role-based definition to ensure that attribute usage on

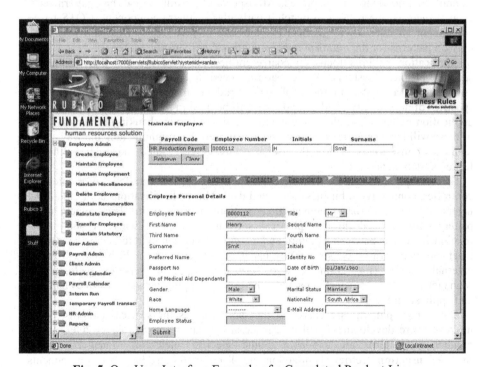

Fig. 5. One User Interface Example of a Completed Product Line

forms is appropriate for the intended application. Many other non-visual software assets make up the completed product line. The non-visual software assets, for example, web services used to obtain the data that are filled in on the form, can be used by a number of different visual devices.

The next section will explore how assets are built and acquired through using the pattern technology assembly method.

4.4.   The Product Space

The previous section provided an introduction to the concepts separating volatility from stability for software product lines. This section will show how a final product is constructed using the *pattern library, assembly* and *technology platform* areas.

4.4.1.   Pattern Library

The pattern library provides descriptions of the potential solutions that a client might require in a specific domain. The separation continuum is used to ensure the structure of the library is such that new patterns can be added over time. The horizontal continuum ensures the completeness and effective separation of the various architectural elements by having considering the correct user interface, user interface controller, connectivity, business logic, and data.

The pattern library is the central location and method where process and technology knowledge are captured. All aspects of a solution can be "patternized", even if there is one pattern to match a particular software component, COTS based component, or even a web service. For the sake of focus, this discussion will focus only on patterns for the *platform implementation* continuum.

Application patterns focus on coarse-grained software systems that implement specific business systems. These patterns need to cover all the aspects of an application that make up the deployable product line. They typically cover the specifics of how services and components will be used in a final application. Example application patterns are: electronic banking and self-service banking terminals. Each of these will have specific characteristics when used that might include the way a user identifies himself/herself, how the user interface is represented and used, and how a legacy system is accessed.

Services patterns can be classified in the areas of user interface, user interface controller, connectivity, business logic and data. These classifications apply to all the layers on the *platform* implementation continuum. This is the layer where these patterns are realized through physical software – a point where a one-on-one relationship exists between a pattern and its implementation by referencing a software asset. Services can be constructed by using components, or might be used from an external source (for example, web services). Example services patterns are ManageCustomer, TransferFunds, etc. There is a mapping between services patterns and application patterns.

Component patterns are classified the same way as the services patterns. Since most software development will take place at this layer and the object layer, a vast number of patterns are available. Some specific ones are: ManageHierarchy, **StoreTransaction**, RetrieveTransaction, etc. There could also have been components called ManageCustomer and TransferFunds – the services layer becomes the "externalization" of these components.

Each pattern should have behavioural and structural definitions. Pattern behaviour is the common set of stimuli, actions and responses that the pattern implements. The pattern structure is the more static definitions that the pattern needs, for example, data. Each of these definitions can be made up of other related behavioural and structural definitions.

The tool shows available patterns, documentation of the patterns and possible properties of a pattern. The two primary areas in the tool are used as follows:

- The tree view on the left indicates the patterns as classified in the library that is being browsed.
- The documentation for the selected pattern is shown in the window on the right. Each pattern has abstract, behaviour and structure definitions as per the Y-Model [21].

The population of the pattern library should be done only once a clear understanding is formed of how a product can be realized in the context of an application. Analysis techniques are needed to ensure adherence to the appropriate levels of abstraction. The population and usage of patterns involve various roles throughout the life cycle.

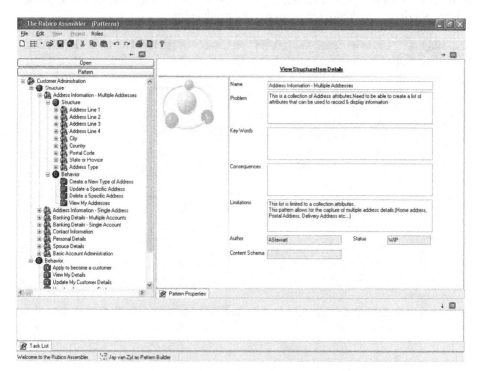

Fig. 6. An Example of Patterns in the Rubico Assembler Tool

4.4.2. Assembly

The assembly of software assets takes place in the context of available patterns. Patterns are "instantiated" by assigning values to a set of properties, making them ready for a technology platform. Specific roles throughout the process of constructing software assets need to apply pattern usage characteristics to ensure secure implementations.

The process of assembling systems starts with a product definition or business need and follows through to the final deployment of the executable software. Roles in the assembly process might change depending on the organizational requirements. Roles like *business analysts, component builder* and *assembler* need productive tools that assist with reusing pre-built assets. The business analyst defines the requirement; the component builder develops components, and the assembler ties the various components together.

When using patterns at the application layer, the assembler role focuses on producing a product line that can be deployed with all its related assets. The application will contain all the services, components and objects needed to execute on a selected technology platform. The result is a definition of an application package that can be deployed.

Constructing or using services can be done via using the patterns at the services layer. When a product line is realized, new services are constructed or existing ones used. The assembly process facilitates this process of creating new services, using existing services, and deploying services for a product line.

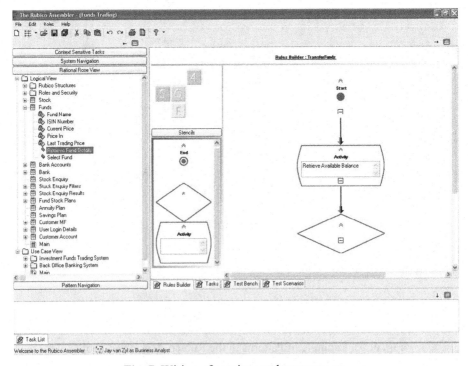

Fig. 7. Wiring of services and components.

When software assets are created in the assembler from a pattern library, they can be referred to as "top-down development". If existing assets are explored (for example, legacy system components, custom developed components and COTS based systems) and are registered in the assembly environment, they can be referred to as "bottom-up development". The process of "wiring" components and services together to form a product line is largely simplified due to the ability of separating out the various continuums.

4.4.3.   Technology Platform

The technology platform is used to realize the pattern and its associated assembly attributes. Together these three areas make up the finally deployable component and/or service as part of a software product. Patterns implemented in particular technology platforms (for example, Java versus C++ based), might require specific environmental implementation variations where security, data access and component invocation might be different.

There always needs to be a set of core software assets in order to execute on a particular platform. Components need to be abstracted [9] in order to allow for changes in COTS-based systems over time. This requires a number of non-functional requirements to take preference over others (for example, interoperability becomes very important in cross-technology deployment).

Certain patterns are used as software requirements to develop software assets. It must be taken into account that the assembly process will define the ways in which the pattern, once turned into a software asset, can be executed. Behavioural and structural requirements are specified by the assembler and should not be developed in the underlying software code. This means that the developer of a core software asset, using the pattern as the specification, needs to design and develop code that is flexible enough to execute within the constraints of the pattern's specification. The combination of pattern, assembly properties and technical platform code form a deployable component.

COTS-based components can be registered in the technology platform and used in the assembly process. It must be considered that certification of COTS-based systems needs to be taken into account when assembling product lines [24]. Functional attributes include the functionality inherent in the COTS component and quality of service criteria (like reliability ratings and security criteria). Structural attributes include understandability and adaptablility. Operational attributes relate to the execution environment and rate efficiency of implementation and user interface characteristics.

Once a product line is deployed onto a particular platform, it must be possible to view the installed software assets. The example in Figure 8 shows a list of software assets, as services, that are exposed on a particular application server in the list view on the left-most panel. These services represent implementations of components from a multitude of unrelated platforms. They also provide the entry point into registry standards like Universal Description, Discovery and Integration (UDDI) [17]. The interface specification (that is, the contract) does not reveal the "real" implementation but is a façade to the component that contains the functionality. The window on the right is where the contract is shown – the interface to the service and component. All the inputs, outputs and related information, which make up the contract, are revealed to the inquirer. Based on this example, it can be seen that the software assets available on a particular platform can be exposed by means of using an XML contract [23]. This XML contract can be exposed as a Web Services Description Language (WSDL) [22] to describe it as a web service.

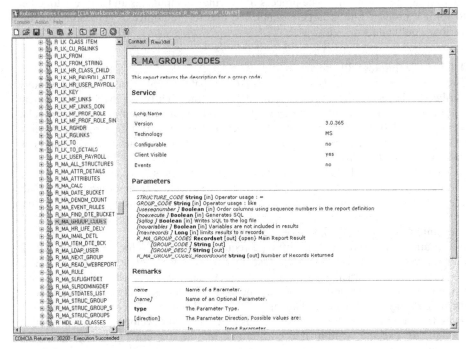

Fig. 8. An example of how a tool can be used to query services that are exposed on a particular application server.

4.5.   Producing Product Lines

The separation continuum presented a means by which many different techniques can produce product lines. Domain analysis or domain engineering techniques are used to extract features systematically from existing stakeholders of a product line [11]. This process is cumbersome and can take a long time. Griss [11] proposes that "aspect-oriented" methods can be used to simplify the process of delivering product line features. Each feature that is obtained must be realized in a fragment or code or component implementation. Only the features and aspects of the components should be managed while the components are being built.

Product lines require an understanding of the continuums in the final product. An architecture is required for a systemic view and to effectively implement system.

5   Discussion

Software product lines have emerged as a very important paradigm in delivering systems. Major benefits are derived from the practice of using common assets to build systems. Remarkable increases in time to market, product quality, and customer satisfaction are realised through this framework. With the "component" paradigm maturing and the emergence of "web services", companies can construct systems from commonly available software assets, through a process of application assembly. The technological aspects are not without their problems, but the process of product line practices presents more benefits than existed previously.

One major challenge of this kind of implementation – that of assembling solutions – is that design architects try to deal with as many eventualities as possible (even for the unforeseen) when designing and building the underlying software infrastructure. Projects like "San Francisco" (now called IBM Business Components), found similar issues [6] as developers try to build "tanks", that is, "bullet-proof" software. It took a long time and was very expensive, and by the end industry had moved on. The separation continuum must be seen as a means by which developers, architects, design specialists, and business analysts can participate when creating large and complex systems in harmony. The continuum facilitates the use of architectural principles that need to be applied when using Web services. It also assists to provide a means to reuse code written by others, elsewhere, using their own set of tools.

The separation of business and technology has never been more relevant than now. Assembling systems from software assets (including web services) has been implemented in a variety of languages and architectures and provides the vision for the provision of application software. It opens an entirely new thread of discussion as to what software is available on an organization's infrastructure versus that of its software-as-service supplier.

The separation continuum and product line architecture described in this paper formed the basis of work performed between 2000 and 2002. Examples included were taken from actual software products, either available or currently under development. Strategic product development [18] and product line practices provided the process and product line thinking required in order to produce these products.

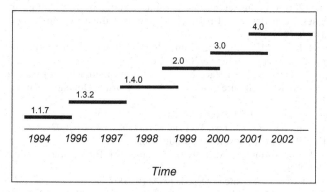

Fig. 9. Rubico Technology Product Family Lifeline (Version ff Product Family Over Time)

The major releases of Rubico Technology products are reflected in Figure 9 and were used in a paper presented at the first Software Product Line Conference (SPLC1) called "Strategic Product Development" [18]. Even though no quantitative results are presented here, the benefits were realized over the time frame while developing versions 2 and 3 and the architectural definition of version 4. Version 4 is currently under development and is benefiting from the product line practices implemented in the past.

References

1. Atkinson C., Bayer J. and Muthig D. (2000). Component-based product line development. Software product lines: Experience and research directions. Edited by Patrick Donohoe. Kluwer Press. ISBN 0-7923-7940-3.
2. Bachman F., Bass L., Carriere J. and Clements P. (2000). Software architecture documentation in practice: Documenting architectural layers. CMU/SEI Special Report CMU/SEI-2000-SR-004.
3. Bass L., Clements P. and Kazman R. (1998). Software architecture in practice. Addison Wesley Press. ISBN 0-201-19930-0.
4. Bosch J. (2000). Design and use of software architectures: Adopting and evolving a product-line approach. Addison Wesley Press. ISBN 0-201-67494-7.
5. Buschmann F., Meunier R., Rohnert H., Sommerlad P. and Stal M. (2000). Pattern-oriented software architecture: A system of patterns. John Wiley & Sons. ISBN 0-471-95869-7.
6. Carey J.E. and Carlson B. A. (1998). Deferring design decisions in an application framework. IBM Corporation. ACM Computing Surveys.
7. Clements P. and Northrop L. (2001). Software product lines, practices and patterns. Addison Wesley Press. ISBN 0-201-70332-7.
8. Constantinides C.A., Bader A., Elrad T.H., Fayed M.E. and Netinand P. (2000). Designing an aspect-oriented framework in an object oriented environment. ACM Computing Surveys. March.
9. Doerr B.S. and Sharp D.C. (2000). Freeing product line architectures from execution dependencies. Software product lines: Experience and research directions. Edited by Patrick Donohoe. Kluwer Press. ISBN 0-7923-7940-3.
10. Dsouza D. (2001). Model-driven architecture opportunities and challenges. Kinetium. http://www.kinetium.com/. Website accessed: 15 April 2002
11. Griss M.L. (2000). Implementing product-line features by composing aspects. Software product lines: experience and research directions. Edited by Patrick Donohoe. Kluwer Press. ISBN 0-7923-7940-3.
12. Architecture board MDA drafting team. (2001). Model driven architecture: A technical perspective. Document Number ab/2001-02-01.
13. Pronk B.J. (2000). An interface-based platform approach. Software product lines: Experience and research directions. Edited by Patrick Donohoe. Kluwer Press. ISBN 0-7923-7940-3.
14. Rational Corporation. (2001). Reusable asset specification. http://www.rational.com/eda/ras/. Website accessed: 15 April 2002
15. Schmid K. (2000). Scoping software product lines.
16. Clements P. and Northrop L.M. (1999). A framework for software product line practice. Version 2.0, SEI.
17. http://www.uddi.org/ Website accessed: 15 April 2002
18. van Zyl J.A. (1999). Strategic product development. SPLC1. Denver, USA, 28-31 August 2000

19. van Zyl J.A. (2001). Class of solution dilemma. IEEE Engineering Management Conference proceedings. IEEE Electronic Library.
20. van Zyl J.A. (2001). Product line balancing. IEEE Engineering Management Conference proceedings. IEEE Electronic Library.
21. van Zyl J.A. (2001). A model that deals with system complexity. Unpublished PhD thesis, University of the Witwatersrand, Johannesburg, South Africa.
22. http://www.wsdl.org/ Website accessed: 15 April 2002
23. http://www.xml.org/ Website accessed: 15 April 2002
24. Yacoub S., Kaveri C. and Dehlin M. (2000). A hierarchy of COTS certification criteria. Software product lines: Experience and research directions. Edited by Patrick Donohoe. Kluwer Press. ISBN 0-7923-7940-3.

Model-Driven Product Line Architectures

Dirk Muthig and Colin Atkinson

Fraunhofer Institute Experimental Software Engineering (IESE)
Sauerwiesen 6, D-67661 Kaiserslautern, Germany
{muthig, atkinson}@iese.fhg.de

Abstract. It has long been recognized that successful product line engineering revolves around the creation of a coherent and flexible product line architecture that consolidates the common parts of a product family for reuse and captures the variant parts for simple adaptation. However, it has been less clear what form such architectures should take and how they should be represented. One promising approach is offered by the new Model-Driven Architecture (MDA) paradigm of the Object Management Group (OMG). This paradigm holds that an organization's key architectural assets should be represented in an abstract "platform-independent" way, in terms of Unified Modeling Language (UML) models, and thereby be shielded from the idiosyncrasies and volatility of specific implementation technologies. In this paper, we discuss the opportunities and challenges involved in using the MDA paradigm for product line engineering and explain how model-driven, product line architectures can be developed, maintained and applied. After first outlining the core concepts of product line engineering and the ad hoc strategies currently used to support it, the paper provides a detailed metamodel of the information that needs to be stored within a product line architecture.

1 Introduction

Of all the software reuse approaches currently under investigation, product line engineering offers potentially the highest return on software development effort. By consolidating all the common features of a family of software products within a high-quality, reusable core, and packaging the variant parts for simple customization, product line engineering maximizes the size of the reusable assets in a particular development domain. In contrast, other reuse approaches typically encapsulate smaller grained units of reusability.

Although the general principles of product line engineering have been understood for some time, practical examples of product line engineering in industrial development settings are few and far between. One of the main reasons for this slow industrial uptake is the high-level nature and early life-cycle focus of most published product line engineering approaches. These approaches typically deal with high-level, up-front issues such as domain analysis, product line scoping and infrastructure definition, but pay little if any attention to the impact of product line engineering on the "lower-level" development activities that come later in the life cycle, such as design and programming. This often leads to the perception among developers that product line engineering has little do with everyday development activities, or that it

G. Chastek (Ed.): SPLC2 2002, LNCS 2379, pp. 110–129, 2002.

is incompatible with the single-system-implementation vehicles in which they have invested many years of effort.

To overcome this problem and make the benefits of product line engineering more practically accessible in mainstream development situations, it is necessary to

1. Provide a more concrete link between abstract product line concepts and detailed software development activities such as design and programming
2. Make the techniques of product line engineering systematically usable with widely applied, mainstream software development technologies

Only then will the lingering suspicions about product line techniques be overcome, and product line engineering will be applied more widely in industry.

A development paradigm, which offers a highly practical strategy for addressing this problem, is the new Model-Driven Architecture (MDA) paradigm of the OMG. The goal of the MDA approach is to provide a concrete mapping between high-level, platform-independent representations of a system and the platform-specific artifacts resulting from detailed design and programming, and in addition to make the platform-independent representations readily compatible with as many lower-level implementation technologies as possible. The MDA, therefore, directly addresses the two issues listed above, but not specifically in connection with product line engineering. Applying the principle of MDA to product lines, therefore, promises to make product line engineering more applicable in industrial development situations and to extend the benefits of the MDA approach beyond those initially envisaged by the OMG.

The foundation of a successful product line engineering program is the creation, application and maintenance of a comprehensive product line architecture, which explicitly captures the commonalities and variabilities that define the domain and distinguish the family members. In the context of an MDA, such a product line architecture would be represented in a platform-independent way in the form of inter-related UML models. Enhancing the MDA paradigm to support product line engineering therefore involves the extensions of the UML to capture key product family information such as commonalities and variabilities. It also involves the definition of systematic techniques for resolving variabilities and mapping the result to suitable product-specific and platform-specific representations.

In this paper, we explore the issues involved in integrating the MDA and product line engineering approaches. Section 2 introduces the core ideas of product line engineering and identifies the essential information that needs to be captured within a product line architecture. It also identifies some of the existing ad hoc ways in which the UML has been used in a product line context. Section 3 continues with an abstract metamodel of the key product line concepts, and the most general ways in which product line information needs to be captured within product line architectures. Finally, Section 4 provides some concluding remarks.

2   Product Line Engineering

The goal of product line engineering is to support the systematic development of a set of similar software systems by understanding and controlling their common and distinguishing characteristics. It is thus an approach for software reuse driven by the concepts from the real-world domain of the software products, which are used to tackle the main reuse challenges. These challenges are depicted in Figure 1 in relation to the overall life cycle of a product line. The concepts, entities, and relationships in the application domain are analyzed and used to build a product line infrastructure, which includes reference architecture for the systems in the domain. Concrete applications can then be constructed largely by instantiating and reusing this product line infrastructure.

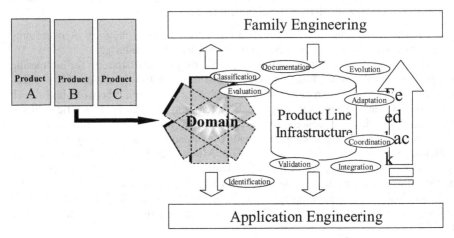

Fig. 1. Product Line Life Cycle

2.1   Documenting Product Line Architectures

Product line engineering is distinguished from single-system engineering by its focus on the systematic analysis and management of the common and varying characteristics of a set of software systems, and their ultimate integration into a common product line or reference model. For these purposes, commonalities and variabilities are equally important. At the architecture level, commonalities define the architectural skeleton; variabilities bound the space of required and anticipated variations of the common skeleton. Both must be documented in a suitable way.

2.1.1   Commonality

Product line engineering is only useful when an organization develops several systems in a single application domain. By definition, this implies that these systems have at least some characteristics in common; otherwise it would be difficult to view them as occupying the same domain. In a sense, therefore, the common features of a family of products serve to characterize the domain. Typically, organizations limit themselves to the domain or domains in which they have expertise.

Commonalities are important for establishing a common understanding within an enterprise of the kinds of applications that it provides. The determination of whether a characteristic is a commonality or variability is often a strategic decision rather than an inherent property of the product family. For example, the execution platform can be a commonality when an organization decides to provide a solution for only one particular platform.

2.1.2   Variability

Variabilities are characteristics that may vary from application to application. In general, all variabilities can be described in terms of alternatives. At a coarse-grained level, one artifact can be seen as an alternative to another. Then during application engineering, the artifact that best matches the context of the system under development is selected. Although simple in theory, providing an effective representation of the variabilities in a product family is an important factor in successfully managing a product line infrastructure.

Simply identifying and modeling alternatives among the products in a product line does not define what features are associated with what products, as well as what dependencies and interrelationships exist among variabilities. This information must also be captured, which is often the role of a decision model. Essentially, a decision model consists of decisions that relate user-visible options to specific system features and finally to variation points within generic assets. The goal is to support the evolution of the product line infrastructure and to guide application engineers in using the infrastructure while building new applications.

2.2   Documenting Variabilities and Commonalities

For an effective approach to product line engineering, the commonality and variability information that characterizes the members of a product family must somehow be integrated into a single coherent description of the product line. One way of achieving this is to describe and contrast a set of systems within a single document but to keep each system individually visible. Such a separation of system information is typically required at two places in the product line life cycle (see Figure 2): first, in the initial "scoping" phase where each system is characterized and compared to all other systems to be considered as part of the product line, and second, during application engineering where each customer is only interested in his/her system.

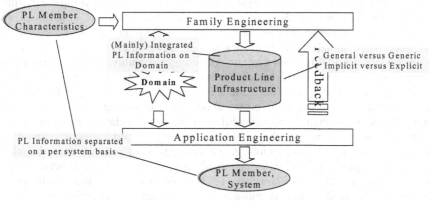

Fig. 2. Product line (PL) assets in the product line life cycle

However, in the remaining parts of the product line life cycle (which includes the creation and documentation of the product line architecture) the characteristics of systems should be handled and captured in an integrated way. That is, the product line architecture represents an integrated platform satisfying commonalities and variabilities in an application domain, rather than a comparison of architectures of similar systems.

When product line information is integrated, commonalities and variabilities are part of one asset. This is nothing unusual in the context of software: by their very nature, software systems are inherently full of variabilities because their execution paths are driven largely by runtime input. When looking at a set of systems, however, variability typically exists that is not runtime variability within a single system but rather variability across systems. In other words, the key difference between a single system's runtime variability and the variability in an application domain is that the former is an inherent part of a delivered software system, while the latter must be explicitly controlled to effectively and successfully manage a product line and use it to create systems. Consequently, all activities in the product line life cycle require information on what varies from one system to another, what motivates these variations, and where these variations impact software solutions and related assets.

Even if there is agreement on the importance of variability information and the need to handle it differently from usual runtime variability, the right level of detail and presentation style of (development-time) variabilities must still be determined based on the circumstances of particular organizations.

2.3   Modeling Product Line Architectures with the UML

The Unified Modeling Language (UML) is a "graphical language for visualizing, specifying, constructing, and documenting the artifacts of a software-intensive system [1]. Thus, if it is to effectively support the development of families of software products (which is the need faced by the majority of software development organizations today) the UML must support the explicit modeling of product line information as explained above. Various UML variants and modeling techniques have consequently been proposed and applied for using the UML (or one of its predecessors) for this purpose [3-10].

In principle, product line architectures can be modeled by simply using the existing generalization concepts of the UML That is, development-time variabilities are handled in the same fashion as runtime variabilities, so that information is generalized to the point where it makes statements that accommodate all members of the family.

Figure 3 depicts a UML class diagram containing variability. Libraries loan books to their users, and allow some users also to reserve books. At a given point in time, a physical book can be loaned to only one user, but can be reserved by multiple users. A user can both borrow and reserve several books at the same time. This situation is captured by the multiplicity constraints between the relevant classes. In a product line context, it may be desirable to have a library with no support for book reservation. This would mean that reservation is an optional feature (and thus the class *Reservation* is optional). The UML diagram already accommodates the fact that users can have zero reservations; however, so that the variability that distinguishes members of the product line is subsumed by the runtime variability of a single member of the product line.

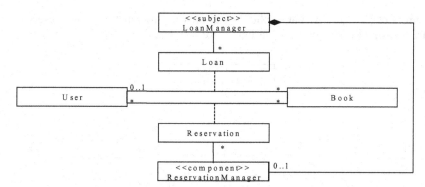

Fig. 3. UML generalization mechanism used to model variability

The example shows that, when generalization is used to model product lines, variabilities that distinguish family members in a product line are mixed up with the runtime variabilities that are "common" to all members of the product line. In short, it suppresses the very information that is essential for effectively understanding and using a product line. Even when the generalized models are supported by constraints describing how the general information changes among family members, this drawback is not completely solved because the information about variabilities is actually captured in separate constraints rather than integrated with the artifacts to which it relates. This still defeats the whole object of easily accessing and understanding variability information, because information must always be intellectually related to the attached constraints. Hence, a better way is needed that allows variabilities to be modeled explicitly.

Most of the published ways of using the UML for modeling product lines either use the Object Constraint Language (OCL) to capture product line information separately from the graphical models [11], exploit the extension mechanisms offered by the UML itself, define variability patterns analogously to the famous design patterns [12], or combine some of these possibilities. Most of them, however, do not provide a sound definition of the used concepts. Instead, they seem to be more pragmatic solutions resulting from practical modeling experiences in a particular domain or environment. Additionally, they are often constrained or impacted by the used UML modeling tools, so that tool support can be provided without major effort. In other words, most existing approaches are pragmatic initiatives that use an ad hoc application of the UML's existing concept. We look more closely now at one of these pragmatic methods and discuss the associated strengths and weaknesses of such approaches.

The KobrA method, a concrete instance of PuLSE™ (Product Line Software Engineering)[1], is a systematic method that integrates component-based development with product line engineering [14, 15, 16]. In the first step, to enable the method to be usable with existing UML tools, KobrA makes use of the extension mechanisms of the UML just like most other approaches. Figure 4 shows the simplified realization class diagram of the *LoanManager* component, which is responsible for managing loans and reservations. The diagram covers the same runtime variability as the

---

[1] PuLSE [13] is a registered trademark of Fraunhofer IESE (www.iese.fhg.de/PuLSE).

diagram above (Figure 3) but explicitly captures the optionality of the reservation feature by using the stereotype <<variant>> for the class *Reservation*.

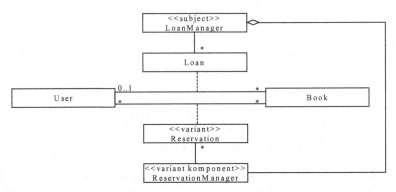

Fig. 4. Generic KobrA class diagram

Although this approach allows variability to be modeled explicitly, it has two major drawbacks. First, the use of stereotypes for capturing variability information conflicts with the original usage of stereotypes in a single-system context. For example, *ReservationManager* is, on the one hand, a subcomponent of *LoanManager* and thus, in KobrA, must be a class of the stereotype <<komponent>>. On the other hand, *ReservationManager* is optional and must, therefore, be of the stereotype <<variant>>. The pragmatic solution chosen by KobrA is to define a new stereotype that mixes the two facets of *ReservationManager*. The mixed stereotype, however, is not a clean solution of the underlying conceptual conflict.

Second, the stereotype concept is typically used for modeling variability, because it is the standard extension mechanism offered by the UML, and thus allows variability information to be made graphically and explicitly visible in diagrams. However, the meaning of variability-related stereotypes is usually not well defined, and even if it is defined, the definition must be interpreted by the modelers and is not semantically integrated with the other UML concepts.

To provide a clean and systematic solution to these problems, in the next section we introduce a general metamodel for product line assets. This provides more concise and user-accessible descriptions of the key concepts involved in the model-driven description of product lines. A clean, consistent metamodel is also the prerequisite for flexible tool support.

3   A Metamodel for Product Line Assets

A metamodel can be viewed as "an information model for the information that can be expressed during modeling" [http://www.metamodel.com]. The metamodel for the product line assets described in this section is thus an information model for the assets capturing the explicit and integrated product line information as defined above. The purpose of the metamodel is to

- Help understand, in general, the concepts needed by product line engineering methods
- Help understand the relationships between general product line concepts and how they are realized in different methods
- Provide the conceptual schemas required for realizing product line tools

The description of the metamodel given in this section defines product line concepts and their interrelationships in a general way with a view to their eventual integration into the UML metamodel. In the same way that the UML metamodel [1] is used to model itself, therefore, we use the UML notation to describe our metamodel.

The metamodel for product line assets consists of three packages. These packages and their dependency relationships are shown in Figure 5. The *Asset* package contains the metamodel for general assets including assets used in single-system development. This is described in Section 3.1

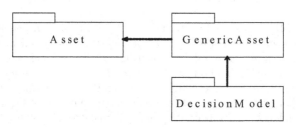

Fig. 5. Package structure of the metamodel for product line assets

The *GenericAsset* package depends on the *Asset* package and defines genericity as an add-on characteristic for any asset. The main concepts in the *GenericAsset* package are variant asset elements, which are variation points concerned with variant information at local points within an asset. The GenericAsset package is described in Section 3.2.

The *DecisionModel* package builds on generic assets and extends the variation-point concept to decisions. Decisions are variation points that typically constrain other variation points and provide a question that must be answered during application engineering. These questions and the constraints among them support application engineering by guiding the instantiation of generic assets. The constraint network of decisions is the decision model. Its structure is defined in the *DecisionModel* package, which is described in Section 3.3.

3.1   Asset

The *Asset* package, shown in Figure 6, contains the metamodel for general assets including assets used in single-system development. From an abstract point of view, an *Asset* consists of a finite set of interrelated elements, *AssetElements*. Each conceptual element has one or more *PresentationElements* that represent the *AssetElement* in views on an *Asset*.

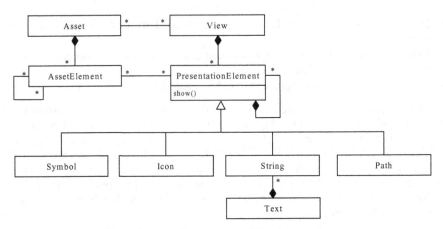

Fig. 6. Information structure of the *Asset* package

As in the UML, there are four basic types of *PresentationElement*s that can be composed of several other *PresentationElements. Icon* is a graphical figure of fixed size and shape. *Symbol* is a two-dimensional figure with variable height and width so that it can be expanded to hold other *PresentationElements. Path* is a sequence of line segments whose end points are attached to other *PresentationElements. String* is a sequence of characters. *Text* has been included to show how the presentation of formatted, textual assets have been fitted into the metamodel, and to give an example of constructs composed of multiple *PresentationElements. Text* is composed of *Strings*. The composition is defined in the *show()* operation of *PresentationElement*, which is responsible for drawing the element.

Figure 7 shows an asset capturing a business process in which a library loans some books to a user. First, the user is identified, then the books are loaned, and finally the loan information is printed and handed to the user. Figure 8 shows the metamodel for the asset, capturing simple business processes that we will use throughout this section to illustrate the described metamodel by a concrete examplary instance. The asset has two specialized *AssetElements: Activity* and *ControlFlow. Activities* can be connected using *ControlFlow* elements with multiple, subsequent activities. The presentation elements are a rectangle for *Activity* (including the name of the activity), and an arrow for *ControlFlow*. The *show()* operation of *ActivityBox* defines where the name is placed with respect to the *Rectangle* representing the *Activity*.

Fig. 7. Loan books: an example business process in the library domain

In the model of Figure 8, the UML pattern construct is used (as it is several times in the paper) to show which classes play which roles. The ellipse represents the pattern (with the pattern name inside), and each role name is shown beside the connecting relationship. As a consequence, each class logically inherits from the class in the pattern definition that represents the role it is assigned in the pattern instance. In our example, the used pattern *AssetElement* is defined in the metamodel (see Figure

6). The role names correspond to the class names. That is, *ActivityBox* is a *PresentationElement* and thus inherits the *show()* operation, *Activity* is an *AssetElement,* and therefore it is part of an *Asset* and related to other *AssetElements.*

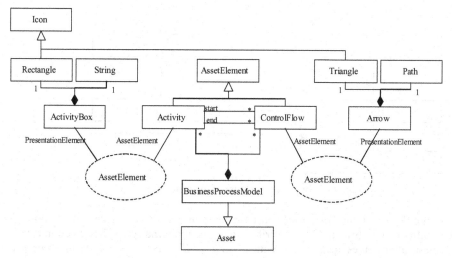

Fig. 8. Metamodel of a basic asset, capturing business processes

3.2   GenericAsset

The *GenericAsset* package depends on the *Asset* package and contains the concepts that make an asset generic when they are added to the structure described above. That is, it enables assets to capture product line information. Figure 9 shows that the existence of variation points, which represent *Variability*, makes an asset a generic asset. *VariationPoint* is a new concept, defined more fully in Section 3.2.1. Additionally, a specialized but still abstract *AssetElement, VariantAssetElement,* is introduced. It represents variation points within a generic asset. This dualism of *AssetElement* and *VariationPoint* is captured using multiple inheritance. *VariantAssetElement* is explained in Section 3.2.2, as well as possibilities for presenting a variant asset element and the relationship between its presentation and that of its super *AssetElement.*

3.2.1   Variation Point

Jacobson, Griss, and Jonsson define variation point in their book on software reuse as follows: "a variation point identifies one or more locations at which the variation will occur" [4]. In general, we will stick with this definition, but to simplify the introduction of the approach, we first limit the definition in this subsection to the following subset: a variation point identifies exactly <u>one</u> location at which the variation will occur. We remove this limitation later and return to the original definition in Section 3.3. Here, a *VariationPoint*, which represents a *Variability*, is related only to a single asset element. The location of this asset element in the asset is the one location where the variation occurs.

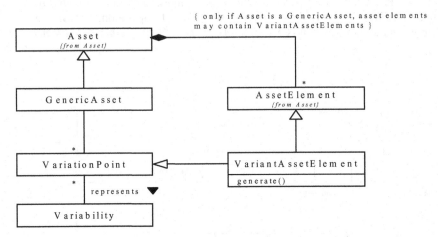

Fig. 9. Information structure of the *GenericAsset* package

More details about *VariationPoint* are shown in Figure 10. As described above, a variability can, in principle, be described in terms of alternatives. The selection of one of these alternatives means resolving the *Variability* and also its *VariationPoints*. From the *VariationPoint*'s point of view, each alternative corresponds to a *Resolution*. That is, while resolving a *VariationPoint*, one must choose one of these *Resolutions*, which are captured in the *VariationPoint*'s attribute choices.

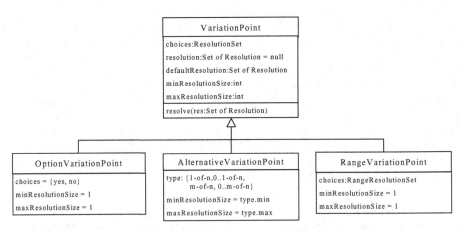

Fig. 10. *VariationPoint* and specialized types

In general, more than one alternative, or *Resolution*, can be selected to resolve a variation point correctly. The minimal and maximum numbers of *Resolutions* to be selected is specified by the attributes *minResolutionSize* and *maxResolutionSize*. A default *Resolution* may specify the choice typically chosen for a product line member. The resolution activity itself, the *resolve()* operation of *VariationPoint*, is specified in Table 1 in a form originally defined by the Fusion method [17] and enhanced by the

KobrA method [14]. The nature of the variation depends on the semantic meaning of the *VariantAssetElement*. Hence, the resolution's effect on an asset is described in the section on *VariantAssetElement* below. Note that the chosen resolution of a variation point is important information for sharing the maintenance and evolution effort spent on product line assets. Therefore, this information is stored for each system derived from the product line infrastructure. The collection of all pairs consisting of variation points and the chosen resolution is a system's resolution model.

Table 1. Specification of the operation *resolve()* of *VariationPoint*

Name	VariationPoint.resolve()
Informal description	A VariationPoint vp is resolved by selecting a subset of its choices offered.
Receives	res:Set of Resolution
Assumes	res subset of choices r1,r2 in res: r1 != r2 0<=minResolutionSize<=#res<=maxResolutionSize<=#choices
Changes	vp.resolution
Result	vp.resolution has been set to res

With the general *VariationPoint* concept, any kind of variability can be captured. However, there is a set of *VariationPoints* specialized for particular types of variation: *OptionVariationPoint*, *AlternativeVariationPoint*, and *RangeVariationPoint* (see Figure 9). This set covers all the *VariationPoints* supported by existing product line methods [18]. Hence, this set seems to cover the kinds of variation that typically occur among members of a product line. An *OptionVariationPoint* references information that is either relevant for a product line member or is not. That is, there are only two choices, and exactly one must be chosen to resolve an *OptionVariationPoint*. An *AlternativeVariationPoint* is not very different from the general *VariationPoint*, but it provides four types that control the minimal and maximal sizes of a valid *ResolutionSet*. The types and corresponding valid sizes of *ResolutionSet* are listed in Table 2.

Table 2. Parameter combinations for standard alternative types

Alternative type	1-of-n	0..1-of-n	m-of-n (m>0)	0..m-of-n
Minimal resolution	1	0	k (k>0)	k (k>=0)
Maximal resolution	1	1	l (k<=l<=n)	l (k<=l<=n; l>0)

The choices offered by a *RangeVariationPoint* correspond to a possibly infinite range of values of a continuous data type, such as numbers or characters. For the realization of a *RangeVariationPoint*, a special *ResolutionSet* is required that simulates the behavior of a finite set of concrete choices for a continuous range. The data structure *ResolutionSet* is shown in Figure 11.

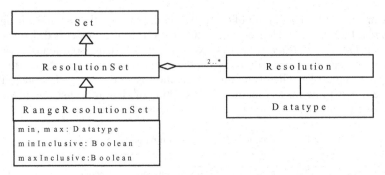

Fig. 11. Data structure for resolution sets of variation points

3.2.2   VariantAssetElement

VariantAssetElement represents a variation point within a generic asset. Consequently, it is both a *VariationPoint* representing a *Variability* and an *AssetElement* that is a naturally integrated part of a *GenericAsset*. This dualism of *AssetElement* and *VariationPoint* is captured using multiple inheritance (see Figure 9). The dualism causes a new behavior that is specific to *VariantAssetElement*. This behavior is specified by the *generate()* operation (see Table 3). *Generate()* modifies the *PresentationElement* of its *AssetElement* facet dependent on the actual resolution of its *VariationPoint* facet. The modification depends on the semantic meaning of the *AssetElement* and thus can only be further refined for concrete cases.

Table 3. Specification of the operation *generate()* of *VariantAssetElement*

Name	VariantAssetElement.generate()
Informal description	Views that present the variant asset element are adapted according to its resolution.
Assumes	VariationPoint.resolve() has terminated successfully.
Changes	VariantAssetElement->Asset->Views
Result	The views on VariantAssetElement.Asset have been adapted according to the Resolution of the related VariationPoint.

A concrete *VariantAssetElement* is defined by applying the *VariantAssetElement* pattern. That is, a specialized *VariantAssetElement* is derived from a specialized pair of *AssetElement* and *VariationPoint*, and its *PresentationElement* is defined. Figure 12 gives an example of the *BusinessProcessModel* introduced above, and a *VariantAssetElement*, *OptionalActivity*, is defined. *OptionalActivity* integrates *Activity* with the *OptionVariationPoint*. As motivated in Section 2, an integrated and explicit representation of variant information is required. To keep the changes to an asset natural and minimal, the *PresentationElement* of a *VariantAssetElement* should be a specialization of the *PresentationElement* of the *AssetElement* from which the *VariantAssetElement* is derived. In the example, the *PresentationElement* of *OptionalAlternative* is derived from *AlternativeBox*, the *PresentationElement* of *AssetElement Activity*. The specialized *PresentationElement*, *OptionalActivityBox*, only changes the fill color of *ActivityBox* to gray. To keep an asset simple and consistent, this change to a *PresentationElement* should be similar for all *VariantAssetElement* in a *GenericAsset*.

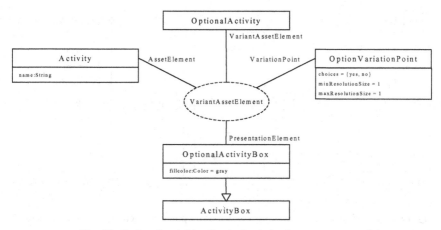

Fig. 12. Optional activities for the basic business process model

A generic business process, a user reserving a library book, is shown in Figure 13. First, the user is identified, then the book is reserved to the user's account, and finally (but not in every library) a reservation fee is collected.

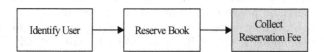

Fig. 13. Reserve book: A generic business process

For a new *VariantAssetElement*, the *generate()* operation must be specialized. The *generate()* operation for *OptionalActivity* is specified in Table 4.

Table 4. Specification of the operation *generate()* of *OptionalActivity*

Name	OptionalActivity.generate()
...	...
Result	**If** resolution=="yes" the background of the *PresentationElement* representing the *OptionalActivity* has been set to white, **else** if resolution=="no" the *PresentationElement* has been hidden, as well as all *PresentationElements* of related *ControlFlows*. **else** /* not resolved */ the background of the PresentationElement has been set to gray.

Its effects for both possible resolutions are illustrated in Figure 14, for the generic business process "return books." When a user returns books to the library, that user is identified. Then the book is returned, and finally (but not in every library) a loan fee is collected. The *VariationPoint* in this process can be resolved with "yes" or "no." Depending on the particular resolution, the optional collection of a loan fee is shown as a non-variant activity in the process, or it is completely removed together with its incoming control flow.

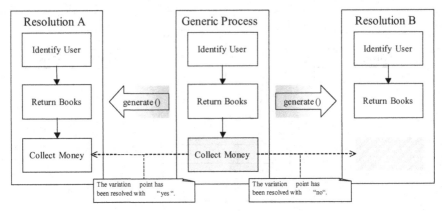

Fig. 14. Effect of generate() on a resolved variation point in a generic business process

3.3   DecisionModel

The *DecisionModel* package builds on the *GenericAsset* package and extends the variation point concept to decisions. Its information structure is shown in Figure 15. Decisions are variation points that constrain other variation points and that can be related explicitly to a domain concept. Hence, *Decisions* are meant to structure and document *VariationPoints*, especially their inter-relationships and dependencies. *Decisions* are the subject of Section 3.3.1. The different types of *ResolutionConstraints* are described in Section 3.3.2. The constraint network spread by the interrelated *Decisions* is analyzed in Section 3.3.3.

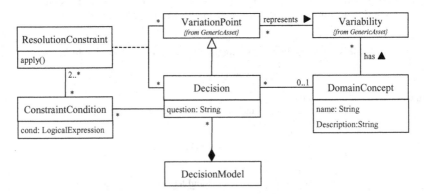

Fig. 15. Information structure of the *Decision* package

3.3.1   Decision

Decisions are variation points that typically constrain the resolution of other variation points. A *Decision* is related to a variability that is caused by a varying domain concept. Each *Decision* defines a question that captures the essence of the related variability in the sense that answering this question corresponds to resolving the

Decision, which is a *VariationPoint*. Realizing that a *Decision* is, like *VariantAssetElement*, also a *VariationPoint*, explains why *VariationPoint* is a separate concept. A *Decision* is not an *AssetElement*, and thus it is only intended to structure *VariationPoints* that include *VariantAssetElements*. A *Decision* that is directly related to a *VariantAssetElement* and that does not constrain further *VariationPoints* is called a *simple decision*.

An example for a *simple decision* is a one that is directly related to the optional activity in the return books business process (see Figure 14). Its question may read as follows: is a loan fee collected after returning books to the library? The *simple decision* for the optional activity in the reserve book business process (see Figure 13) is defined analogously.

Decisions may constrain several *VariationPoints*. According to the limited definition of variation point given above, each of these constrained variation points identifies exactly one location at which variation may occur. Consequently, a *Decision* referencing multiple variation points identifies more than one location at which variation may occur. Understanding *Decisions* as *VariationPoints* allows us to remove the limitation of the variation point definition and return to the original definition given in [4] (see Section 3.2.1). Now, *VariantAssetElements* and *simple decisions* are *VariationPoints* identifying one location. *Decisions* constraining several variation points are *VariationPoints* identifying multiple locations.

Like *VariationPoint* types, *Decision* types can be defined. Again, because *Decisions* are *VariationPoints*, the same types are typically needed: options, alternatives, and ranges. These *Decision* types can be derived directly from the *VariationPoint* types. For instance, *OptionDecision* is derived from *OptionVariationPoint*, and so forth.

For the example, we define two non-simple *decisions* in addition to the *simple decisions* given above. First, an *OptionDecision* related to the domain concept "library fees" is defined. Its question is whether a library user must pay fees for any of the library's services. The *decision* constrains both *simple decisions*. Second, another *OptionDecision*, which is related to the domain concept "reservation," is defined. Its question is whether a library allows its users to reserve books. This *decision* directly constrains only one *simple decision*: the decision related to the collection of a reservation fee. *Decisions'* constraints are described in the following section.

3.3.2   ResolutionConstraints

A *ResolutionConstraint* captures a dependency between the *Resolution* of a *Decision* and of another *VariationPoint*. There are three types of potential dependencies: resolution, partial resolution, and exclusion.

The resolution dependency means that resolving a decision also resolves the depending variation point. That is, the decision fully subsumes the dependent variation point. The partial-resolution dependency means that resolving a *decision* also partially resolves the depending variation point. That is, the resolution of the constraining *decision* disables some of the choices offered by the dependent variation point so that they are no longer valid choices for a later resolution of the constrained variation point. The exclusion dependency means that resolving a *decision* excludes the depending variation point. That is, the *decision* excludes a larger optional part containing the dependent variation point whose resolution is thus not relevant anymore.

Except for the exclusion dependency, dependencies have similar meanings when a dependent variation point is resolved before the constraining *decision*. In the case of a resolution dependency, the resolution of the dependent variation point may also completely or only partially resolve the constraining *decision*. In the case of a partial resolution, resolving a dependent variation point means partially resolving the constraining *decision*.

As an example, we analyze the constraints between the two non-simple *decisions* defined above. The fee-related *decision* constraining both *simple decisions* and both dependencies is a partial-resolution dependency in both cases. If the constraining decision is resolved by "no," both *simple decisions* are also resolved with "no." If the constraining decision is resolved by "yes," one of the *simple decision*s must be resolved by "yes," too, but which one cannot be determined before one of them is resolved. In the other direction, the constraints have the following meaning: if one of the *simple decisions* is resolved with "yes," the constraining *OptionDecision* is also resolved with "yes." If both *simple decisions* are resolved with "no," the *OptionDecision* is also resolved with "no." Note that an *AlternativeDecision* could be used instead of an *OptionDecision*. Then, the dependency would be of resolution dependency.

The other reservation-related *decision* directly constrains only one *simple decision*, the *decision* related to the collection of a reservation fee. It excludes the *simple decision* in the case when no reservation service is offered in a library, because the whole business process becomes obsolete. Note also, that an indirect relationship to all other introduced *decisions* exists that via the *simple decision*. Therefore, one must be careful while constructing a *decision* model. A *decision* model is only valid when it allows all *VariationPoints* to be resolved that are not excluded. Figure 16 shows the object diagram of the example *decision* model.

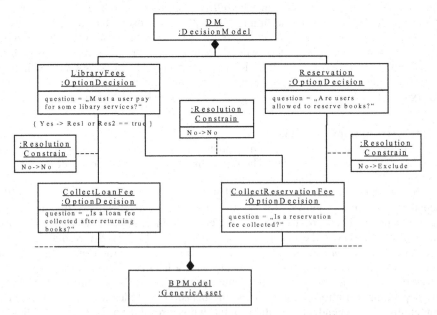

Fig. 16. Object diagram of an example *decision* model

The OCL comment represents the instance of *ConstraintCondition* related to the LibraryFee *decision's* constraints. A more practicable representation of a *decision* model is shown in Table 5. There, the attributes of the *decisions*, as well as of the related constraints, are mapped into a tabular form.

Table 5. Tabular notation of the decision model of Figure 16

Asset	ID	Name or Question	Type	AssetElement	Constraints
Business Processes	1	Must a user <u>pay</u> for some library services?	Option Decision	-	No: resolve 3, 4 Yes: resolve 3 or 4
Business Processes	2	Are users allowed to reserve books?	Option Decision	-	No: exclude 3
Business Process "Return Books"	3	Is a reservation fee collected?	Optional Activity	"Collect Reservation Fee"	-
Business Process "Reserve Book"	4	Is a loan fee collected after returning books?	Optional Activity	"Collect Money"	-
...	...	...	...	...	...

3.3.3   Decision Hierarchy

Up to this point, *VariationPoints* have been considered as part of the same generic asset. The decision model is then also related to a single asset, and thus it is called the asset's decision model. If patterns of identical relationships among *VariationPoints* in a single asset are identified, the modeling of this pattern can be simplified by realizing the pattern by a special *Decision* or *VariantAssetElement*. In the latter case, relationships among variant asset elements are visible in views on an asset. An example is the pattern of alternative classes described in [6].

However, the three library processes could also be regarded as three separate assets, each describing a single business process. Then, a decision model is constructed that covers multiple assets. Consequently, a decision model can be constructed that integrates and relates all variation points of all assets capturing information on the same product line. These assets may cover all life-cycle stages ranging from the scope definition to implementation assets to user manuals and tutorial material. In an ideal case, a feature in a product line's scope definition is related to a decision that constrains all variation points somehow related to the reservation feature. Exclusion of the feature means an automatic exclusion of all feature-specific information. For instance, excluding the reservation feature excludes a component in the architecture responsible for managing reservations, and the user manual says nothing about reservation functionality.

4   Conclusions

Combining the concepts of product line and model-driven architectures promises to address some of the key shortcomings of the former and to make the benefits of the latter available in the context of a family of products. As well as making product line engineering more attractive for industrial projects, therefore, it also provides a systematic way of leveraging the benefits of a product line viewpoint in tandem with the component and middleware technologies commonly associated with the MDA, such as CORBA, EJB, XML, SOAP, and .NET.

The development of a model-driven, product line architecture depends on the adaptation/application of the UML to capture key product-engineering concepts such as the commonalities that define the domain, and the variabilities that distinguish the family members. As explained in this paper, numerous ad hoc adaptations of the UML for this purpose have been defined in the literature. Most, however, manipulate only the syntactic aspects and do not cleanly integrate product line concepts with the UML metamodel. The result is that the product line aspects of a model have to be handled manually, and cannot be subject to automated consistency checking or generation. Nevertheless, we believe that the ideas presented in this paper capture the essential concepts needed for providing product line support within model-driven architectures, and thus point the way towards enhanced product line engineering capabilities in future versions of the UML.

References

1. OMG Unified Modeling Language Specification, www.omg.org, Version 1.3, First Edition, March 2000
2. P. Donohoe. Software Product Lines - Experience and Research Directions, Kluwer Academic Publishers, Proceedings of the 1st Software Product Line Conference, 2000
3. H. Gomaa, L. Kerschberg, V. Sugumaran, C. Bosch, I. Tavakoli, and L. O'Hara. A Knowledge-Based Software Engineering Environment for Reusable Software Requirements and Architectures, in Automated Software Engineering, vol. 3, Aug. 1996
4. I. Jacobson, M. Griss, and P. Jonsson. Software Reuse - Architecture, Process, and Organization for Business Success, Addison-Wesley, 1997
5. D. D'Souza and A. Wills. Objects, Components, and Frameworks with UML - The Catalysis Approach, Addison-Wesely, Object Technology Series, 1999
6. B. Keepence and M. Mannion. Using Patterns to Model Variability in Product Families, IEEE Software, Jul./Aug. 1999
7. G. Larsen. Designing Component-Based Frameworks using Patterns in the UML, in Communications of the ACM, Vol. 42, No. 10, October 1999
8. M. Coriat, J. Jourdan, and F. Boisbourdin. The SPLIT Method - Building Product Lines for Software-Intensive Systems in [2]
9. O. Flege. Using a Decision Model to Support Product Line Architecture Modeling, Evaluation, and Instantiation, in Proceedings of the Product Line Architecture Workshop with SPL-C, 2000
10. S. Thiel and F. Peruzzi. Starting a Product Line for an Envisioned Market – Research and Experience in an Industrial Environment, in [2]
11. J. Warmer and A. Kleppe. The Object Constraint Language - Precise Modeling with UML, Addison-Wesley, 1999
12. E. Gamma, R. Helm, R. Johnson, and J. Vlissides. Design Patterns: Elements of Reusable Object-Oriented Software, Addison-Wesley, Reading, 1995
13. J. Bayer, O. Flege, P. Knauber, R. Laqua, D. Muthig, K. Schmid, T. Widen, and J.-M. Debaud. *PuLSE: A Methodology to Develop Software Product Lines*, in the Proceedings of the Symposium on Software Reuse (SSR'99), May 1999
14. C. Atkinson, J. Bayer, C. Bunse, O. Laitenberger, R. Laqua, E. Kamsties, D. Muthig, B. Paech, J. Wüst, and J. Zettel. Component-based Product Line Engineering with UML, Component Series, Addison-Wesley, 2001
15. C. Atkinson, J. Bayer, and D. Muthig. Component-Based Product Line Development: The KobrA Approach, in [2]

16. C. Atkinson and D. Muthig. A Concrete Method for Developing and Applying Product Line Architectures, submitted to the Third Working IEEE/IFIP Conference on Software Architecture (WICSA-3), Montreal, August 2002
17. D. Coleman, P. Arnold, S. Bodoff, C. Dollin, H. Gilchrist. F. Hayes, P. Jeremaes. Object-Oriented Development: The Fusion Method, Prentice-Hall International, 1994
18. D. Muthig. A Light-weight Approach Facilitating an Evolutionary Transition towards Software Product Lines, Ph. D. Thesis, University of Kaiserslautern, Germany, 2002

Systematic Integration of Variability into Product Line Architecture Design

Steffen Thiel and Andreas Hein

Robert Bosch Corporation
Corporate Research and Development, Software Technology
P.O. Box 94 03 50
D-60461 Frankfurt, Germany
{steffen.thiel | andreas.hein1}@de.bosch.com

Abstract. Product lines consider related products, their commonalities and their differences. The differences between the single products are also referred to as variability. Consequently, variability is inherent in every product line and makes a key difference as compared to single systems. While, on the requirements level, the methods for analyzing product line variability are understood today, their transition to architecture remains vague. Bringing variability to architecture as an "add-on" is just a provisional solution and forebodes the risk of violating other intentions. This paper presents a systematic approach to integrate variability with product line architecture design. In particular, it promotes variability as an architectural driver, embeds variability requirements in the architecture design framework "Quality-Driven Software Architecting" (QUASAR), and gives guidelines and examples for documenting variability in architectural views.

1 Introduction

Architectural considerations play a key role in the success of any software-based development project. An architecture is "the structure or structures of the system, which comprise software and hardware components, the externally visible properties of those components, and the relationships among them" [2]. It is the first design artifact that places requirements in a solution space. Quality attributes such as performance, modifiability, and reliability are largely promoted or hindered by an architecture. An architecture determines the structure and management of the development project as well as the resulting system, since teams are formed and resources allocated around architectural components. For anyone seeking to learn how a system works, the architecture is the place where understanding begins. Getting the architecture right is a prerequisite for the success of a development project. Getting it wrong may be disastrous for a company's business.

In the context of a product line approach, additional demands on an architecture arise. A product line simultaneously considers several related products that may vary from each other in terms of their functionality, quality attributes, network,

G. Chastek (Ed.): SPLC2 2002, LNCS 2379, pp. 130–153, 2002.

middleware, or by other factors. The variability of a product line is usually captured in a feature model during analysis [8] [17] and must consequently be reflected and supported by its architecture. In other words, a product line architecture must allow all product variants that can be defined through the feature model. In addition, it must contain knowledge about how single variation points are to be used in order make a desired product variant. As a result, the explicit representation of variation becomes an integral part of a product line architecture description, including the mechanisms for a systematic resolution of the variation points during product creation.

When talking about variability with respect to product line architectures one must distinguish between variability at derivation time, and variability at runtime. The topic of interest concerning the design of product line architectures (and this paper) clearly is the derivation time variability. Variability that is bound after that point will be encapsulated from a product line point of view and does not come into play before a product has been instantiated from the common architecture.

Although the presence of derivation-time variability in product line architectures provides the fundamental difference – and benefits – compared to a single-system architectures, it is often dismissed as a secondary subject during architecture design. However, correcting this failure is not for free. Integrating the variability afterwards is likely to cause costly architecture transformations, as with any other quality that is not considered in time [2] [6] [26] [33]. Therefore, variability should be planned and systematically handled from the very beginning of architecture design.

In this paper we will present essential issues related to variability modeling in software product line architectures. In Section 2 we explain in more detail why it is important to plan for variability, and how variability can systematically be integrated into software architecture design using the QUASAR framework. Section 3 introduces consistent enhancements to the IEEE P1471 Recommended Practice for Architectural Documentation with respect to product lines in general, and architectural variability in particular. Section 4 illustrates the proposed variability documentation practices based on examples of a software architecture for an automotive product line. In particular, the practices are applied to the architecture's logical, process, physical, and deployment view. In Section 5 we discuss the tradeoffs that must be made due to feasibility in industrial settings. Section 6 refers to related work. Finally, Section 7 summarizes and gives a brief outlook on further research activities.

2   Understanding Variability
as a Quality of Product Line Architectures

Generally, an architecture lays down the fundamental structures of a system. For example, an architecture may comprise logical and deployment structures. If an architecture is intended for different related products (a product line), fixed structures are no longer sufficient. Rather, the points where the products differ must be explicitly represented as well as the common parts. These variation points allow adaptation of the architecture according to the variable requirements within the product line. This means that the essential (and differentiating) characteristic of product line architectures is their integrated variability. The number of variation points in the architecture will most probably differ from the number of options among the requirements. For example, a single requirement may correspond to multiple architectural solutions, or an architecture may contain "hidden variability" that is not propagated to the customer of the system. At the end, a product line architecture must allow all products and product variants that are foreseen at the requirements level.

2.1 Modifiability vs. Configurability

Modifiability and configurability both address the flexibility of product line architectures and therefore are prerequisites for reuse. Nevertheless, these attributes have a different focus. As illustrated in Figure 1, modifiability is concerned with *evolution* (i.e., it addresses the variation over time). In contrast, configurability concentrates on the *variability* in the product space. It therefore addresses the differences between related products at a given point in time. In the product line context, configurability can be defined as the ability to build consistent product line members from a common architecture through selecting, parameterizing, and synthesizing provided design elements.

Nevertheless, incorporating new variation that is not explicitly prepared in the architecture, but comes with evolution, is a matter of modifiability. As product lines are made for long-term use, modifiability clearly is one of several vital requirements that has to be carefully considered during product line architecture design. But even though modifiability is concerned with change, variability in a product line is not automatically addressed by modifiability mechanisms. Rather, a product line's variability and the way it allows the derivation of new product variants at a given point in time need to be regarded as additional qualities that must be explicitly handled through configurability mechanisms. In the following, we will concentrate on product line variability and the required design tradeoffs.

2.2 Design Tradeoffs

As explained above, variability is an inherent quality of product lines. The success of a product line initiative strongly depends on the ability to exploit the variability effectively. Therefore, considerations with respect to configurability play a key role in product line architecture design. Although dealing with configurability at the architecture level is challenging, many modeling strategies that are used for developing individual systems can be adopted (e.g., attribute-driven design) [1] [33]. Including configurability as a quality attribute in early design considerations guarantees that the desired product variants can finally be built efficiently.

Configurability addresses the features that are captured in the feature model and the variations that they allow. Feature models describe variability through optional, alternative, optional alternative, and 'or' features [10]. Including and excluding such variable features must be supported by a product line architecture.

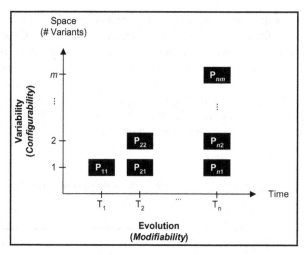

Fig. 1. Variability (addressed by Configurability) and Evolution (addressed by Modifiability)

But even though configurability is a driver for product line architecture design, it is definitely not the only quality requirement that shapes the architecture. In the domain of embedded automotive systems, for example, performance, safety, and reliability also play an important role. The different architectural drivers conflict by nature (i.e., they normally cannot be realized all at once to their full extent). Compromises must be found based on a tradeoff analysis and may lead to architecture transformations. Consequently, an architecture's configurability may be affected by concessions that must be made to other quality attributes. Indirections that have been introduced into a product line architecture through inheritance or patterns (like Adapter [12]) to represent different variants and that remain in the architecture after derivation may conflict with product performance requirements. Depending on its realization, configurability interferes more or less strongly with other qualities. Therefore, finding effective mechanisms for configurability and evaluating them with respect to other architecturally significant requirements is essential.

2.3   The QUASAR Framework

QUASAR is a process framework developed by the authors that supports the systematic Quality-Driven Software Architecting of complex systems and product lines. It gives guidance on bridging the gap between high-level requirements and detailed design through providing essential documentation, design, and assessment practices for the critical phases of architecting. QUASAR allows for iterative and incremental development and is organized in three interrelated workflows (see Figure 2): Preparation, Modeling, and Evaluation. Each workflow describes a meaningful sequence of activities that produce some valuable result for architecture design. The *Preparation* workflow comprises activities that support early architectural considerations. The activities of the *Modeling* workflow are concerned with modeling architectural views and the variability within each view. The *Evaluation* workflow includes activities for analyzing the achievement of architectural qualities. Each activity of a workflow has associated input and output artifacts. An artifact is a piece of information that is produced, modified, or used by a process and may take various shapes (e.g., models, model elements, documents).

In the remainder of this section we will give a brief outline of the modeling workflow since the concepts presented in the next sections will provide refinements of this workflow. A more comprehensive description of QUASAR can be found in [33].

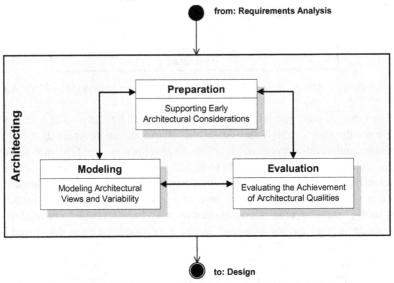

Fig. 2. The QUASAR Framework for Product Line Architecting

The purpose of the Modeling workflow is to provide techniques and guidelines for modeling architectural views and the variability within those views. For modeling architectural views, one has to instantiate the key mechanisms identified for the architecturally significant requirements during the Preparation workflow. Architectural drivers are a combination of quality attributes (e.g., performance), critical functionality, and business considerations (e.g., build-or-buy decisions). In the case of a product line, configurability adds to this list, as different products must be supported based on one common architecture. Mechanisms are design primitives such as architectural styles [29] or patterns [7] that contribute to the achievement of such requirements.

Applying mechanisms causes architectural transformations where new design elements with new responsibilities are added and existing design elements are modified. Usually, the application of a mechanism has an impact on more than one view. For example, realizing robustness in the presence of failures will affect the logical view (replication of logical components), the process view (a new process must be introduced in order to allow switching to the replicated component when the process running the other one crashes), and the deployment view (the replicated component may reside on an extra processor node for increased robustness). Repeated application of mechanisms evolves the design and makes it more stable and robust with respect to the qualities.

As mentioned before, configurability is an inherent driver for a product line design. Consequently, the variability identified in the requirements must be represented in the architecture. In the next section we will present some fundamental concepts for modeling architectural variability.

3 Architectural Variability Metamodel

To cope with the specific needs of documenting architectures for product lines we introduce a proposal to extend and refine the IEEE P1471 recommended practice for architectural description [19].

The P1471 was developed by the IEEE Architecture Working Group (AWG) and defines conventions for architectural descriptions. It standardizes documents and other artifacts which define or describe an architecture. In particular, the framework gives specific meaning to stakeholder concerns, views, and viewpoints, and defines minimal documentation criteria for those aspects. However, the P1471 is focused on single products and does not cover specific documentation needs for product lines.

In order to cope with the specific challenges of modeling product line architectures, we propose to evolve different aspects of the P1471, as represented by the metamodel in Figure 3. The purpose of this metamodel is to lay down an overall scheme for representing product line architectures. We propose four basic extensions to the P1471:

1. *Product line extension* – captures the basic relationships between a product line, product, and product line architecture
2. *Feature variability extension* –represents variability on the requirements level
3. *Architecture variability extension* – covers the explicit representation and specification of variability in architectures
4. *Design element extension* – provides the component and connection types that are used to describe an architecture and shows how they integrate with the representation of architectural variability

In the remainder of this section we will concentrate on the explanation of the last three extensions. A detailed description of the IEEE P1471 can be found in [19]. In the next section we will show how the concepts recorded in the metamodel were applied during architecture design of a product line of car periphery supervision systems. Note that the description of the metamodel is based on the UML notation [28]. The extension of the metamodel is a work in progress.

3.1 Feature Variability Extension

In the context of product lines, a feature is understood as "a product characteristic that users and customers view as important in describing and distinguishing members of the product line"[14]. Features represent requirements and thus describe the problem space for a product line development effort. A feature can be either common or variable. In the first case, the feature is included in all product members of the product line. In the latter case, the feature is implemented in a single member or a set of members, but not by all.

Features can be organized in a feature model. A feature model usually captures additional details about features and their relationships. Note that these details are beyond the scope of this paper. For a more comprehensive overview we refer to [8] [10] [23]. Feature models may be used to create feature configurations [17]. A feature configuration represents the set of features selected by the customer to be included in a specific product. The configuration thus can be understood as an initial requirements specification for that product. The architectural decisions that must be made to realize a feature are not covered in such a specification, but must be captured in the product line architecture description.

3.2 Architectural Variability Extension

As defined by the IEEE P1471, the description of an architecture should be organized into multiple views. Each view addresses one or more stakeholder concerns. In the context of product lines, each architectural view contains architectural variability to cope with the variety of characteristics that must be implemented for the different product line members. Architectural variability reflects the existence of alternative design options that could not be bound during architectural modeling. Architectural variability is usually expressed by a set of architectural variation points, as shown at the bottom right in Figure 3. A variation point shows part of the architectural solution of the feature variability. The resolution of variability may be postponed up to runtime, in principle. In this paper we will concentrate on derivation-time variability since it is essential to make this type explicit in the documentation of a product line architecture.

Similar to features, architectural variability can be summarized in an architectural variability model that can be used to create architecture configurations. An architecture configuration describes which design elements and responsibilities are included in a product architecture, and how they work together. To define an architecture configuration, the set of architectural variation points needs to be consistently resolved and bound to concrete design options. Particularly, the feature configuration can be used as an input to define the correlated architecture configuration.

In order to enable an unambiguous derivation of product architectures based on a feature/architecture matching, the variation points need to be specified in more detail. Typically, a variation point specification must include information about binding times, resolution rules, and dependencies to other variation points, as shown in Figure 3.

The binding time represents the point in time when a variation point has to be resolved – that is, when the design decision has to be made. Resolution rules capture the strategies to be applied when a variation needs to be resolved. In its simplest case, the resolution rule may describe alternative design element selections. A more common and realistic case is the instantiation of multiple elements with different options. Dependencies must be recorded since architectural variation points usually are not independent of each other. Those relationships may exist within one architectural view, but may also be distributed over more than one view, since the design elements in the different views are usually correlated.

3.3 Design Element Extension

As mentioned above, an architectural variation point affects one or more design elements. Design elements make the content of architectural views. As shown at the bottom left in Figure 3, each design element conforms to one design element type – (i.e., a component or a connection type). The types are the vocabulary to describe a view. The vocabulary specified to be used for a view depends on the viewpoint that is addressed by that view. For example, a viewpoint may be the physical interconnection of design elements. Then the "viewpoint language" may contain design element types such as a processor node, a point-to-point link, and a shared bus.

Note that three basic types of variability may be distinguished at the architecture level: a variation point may have an impact on (1) exactly one design element in one view, (2) multiple design elements in one view, or (3) multiple design elements in multiple views. Particularly, the latter two types of variability require special attention during architecture design since they may strongly influence structural properties of the architecture.

4 Modeling Architectural Variability: Examples from a Case Study

In this section we will show examples derived from applying the architectural variability modeling concepts introduced in the previous sections to a product line of *Car Periphery Supervision* (CPS) systems. CPS systems can be characterized as a family of automotive products that are based on sensors installed around the vehicle to monitor its local environment, as illustrated in Figure 4. Different sensor measurement methods and evaluation mechanisms enable the realization of various kinds of higher level applications which guarantee more safety and comfort for car drivers and passengers. Examples of such applications are parking assistance, automatic detection of objects in vehicles' blind spots, the adaptive operation of airbags and seatbelt tensioners, and automatic cruise control.

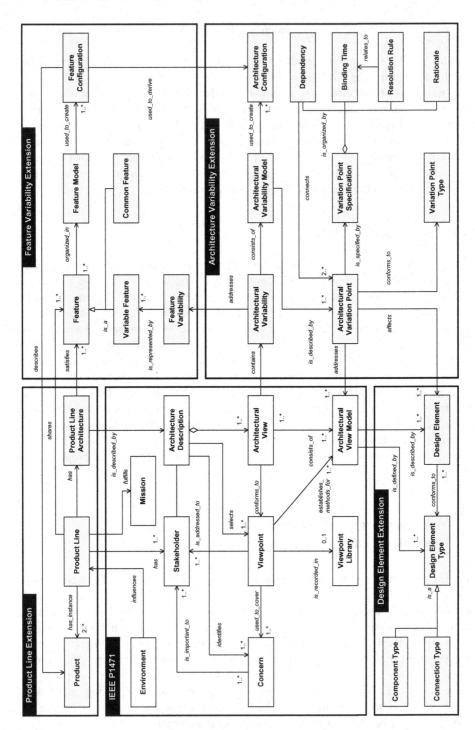

Fig. 3. Proposed Variability Extensions of the IEEE P1471

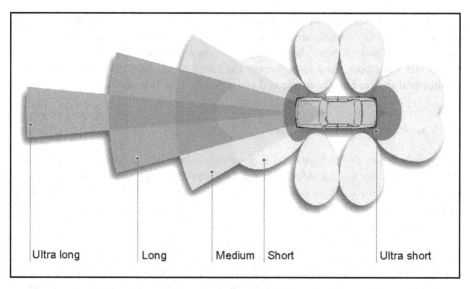

Fig. 4. Car Periphery Supervision

In order to create the architecture of CPS we went through several iterations of analysis and feature modeling [8] [16] [32] based on a defined business case. During the preparation phase of the QUASAR framework we determined architecturally significant requirements and key mechanisms to satisfy those requirements. When starting architectural modeling, one of our concerns was to document the points of variation that came into play as we introduced the mechanisms for satisfying driving configurability requirements (e.g., easy functional adaptation). In order to cope with the huge number of variations, we used the existing business case description to generate a starting set of the most important product feature configurations in the CPS scope.

Figure 5 shows a simplified feature configuration example for three candidate CPS product variants: a reverse parking aid (RPA), a parking assistant system (PAS), and a parking aid system with pre-crash detection capability (PAP).

Features	Feature Configuration		
	V1: Reverse Parking Aid (RPA)	V2: Parking Assistant System (PAS)	V3: Parking Aid w/ Pre-Crash (PAP)
Parking Support			
F1: Service Activation	YES	YES	YES
F2: Indicate Distance	B	F, B	F, B
F3: Detect Parking Space	--	YES	YES
F4: Assist Steering	--	YES	--
Pre-Crash Detection			
F5: Range	--	--	F

Legend: F = Front, B = Back

Fig. 5. Three Sample Feature Configurations

In the next subsections we will describe how we recorded the necessary variation points in essential architectural views for the three given product variants. In particular, we outline how the concepts of variability modeling defined in our metamodel have been used to document the variation in the CPS product line. The architectural figures have been adapted and simplified for that purpose.

4.1 Variability in the Logical View

In Figure 6, a part of the high-level *logical* view of the product line architecture for CPS is shown. In the QUASAR preparation phase, UML subsystems and usage dependencies were used as design element types of this view. A subsystem is a package of elements with a specified behavior that is treated as a coherent unit. A usage dependency connects a client element (tail of the arrow) to a supplier element (arrowhead), the change of which usually requires a change to the client element.

The subsystems of the CPS product line form a layered structure with defined responsibilities. The lowest layer is defined by Environment Description and Sensor Control. They provide basic services for obtaining and abstracting the sensor data. The middleware layer consists of subsystems for evaluating the environment model (Situation Evaluation) and for mediating the appropriate measurement data to upper layers (Measurement Coordination). The application layer provides high-level functionality that is specific to the different applications. In our example, the application layer consists of these subsystems: Distance Indication, Steering Assistance, and Pre-Crash Detection.

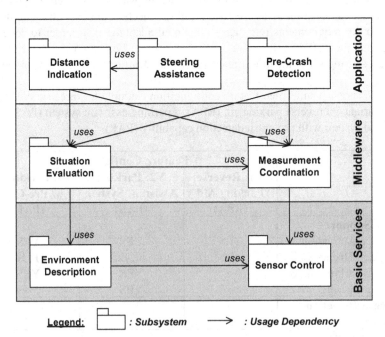

Fig. 6. Logical View of the CPS Architecture

Variability mechanisms were introduced into the logical view to configure the product variants defined in Figure 5.

Figure 7 shows a simplified variability model of the logical view containing four variation points. The first variation point (VP1) has a direct impact on Steering Assistance as well as on two component groups (Pre-Crash Detection & Situation Evaluation and Distance Indication & Situation Evaluation), as indicated by the arrows. The other variation points (VP2, VP3, VP4) affect only single logical components (Distance Indication, Sensor Control, and Measurement Coordination, respectively). In addition, there exist inter-variation-point-dependencies between VP1 and VP3, VP4, as well as VP2 and VP5. The latter case represents a global variation point dependency (i.e., it interrelates with a variation point in another architectural view (the physical view), as we will see later).

As mentioned before, the variability model in Figure 7 also shows that a variation point may affect single design elements or groupings of design elements. Groupings reduce the complexity of the model, as they allow the identification of strongly coupled configuration entities that are the basis for feature-oriented configurations.

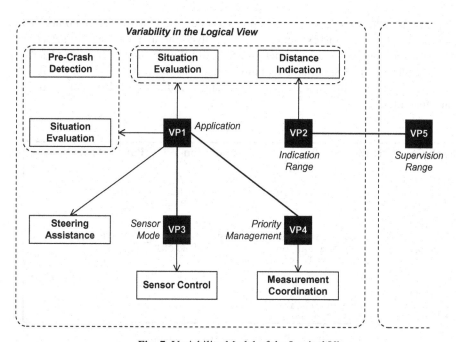

Fig. 7. Variability Model of the Logical View

As discussed in the previous section, variation points must be introduced at the architecture level in order to satisfy feature variability. According to our metamodel, each variation point is characterized by a variation point specification. The table of Figure 8 summarizes the rationales for the variability model of Figure 7. It also shows which features are affected by the particular architectural variation points.

VP	Name	Rationale	Feature#
1	Application	Different application subsystems are required to realize the high-level functionality and to present the results to the user.	F1, F2, F3, F4, F5
2	Indication Range	Detection of objects is constrained by environmental monitoring.	F2
3	Sensor Mode	Different applications require different types of sensor data. The type of data provided by a sensor during operation is defined by the sensor mode.	F2, F3, F4, F5
4	Priority Management	The number of concurrent applications affects the priorities for delivering the appropriate measurement data in the required time frame.	F1, F5

Fig. 8. Rationales for the Variation Points

Figure 9 sketches resolution rules (in pseudo code) of the two variation points VP1 and VP2 obtained from the example. VP1 is resolved through a subsystem selection mechanism in order to reduce the memory footprint. For example, VP1 includes the Distance Indication and Situation Evaluation subsystems for product variant 1 (RPA).

VP2 then adapts the range of the Distance Indication subsystem through parameterization.

```
Resolution VP1: (Selection)          Resolution VP2: (Parameterization)

CASE VP1(V1):                        CASE VP2(V1):
  #INCLUDE Distance_Indication;        #SET Distance_Indication :=
  #INCLUDE Situation_Evaluation;          { BACK };

CASE VP1(V2):                        CASE VP2(V2), VP2(V3):
  #INCLUDE Steering_Assistance;        #SET Distance_Indication :=
  #INCLUDE Distance_Indication;           { FRONT, BACK };
  #INCLUDE Situation_Evaluation;

CASE VP1(V3):
  #INCLUDE Pre-Crash_Detection;
  #INCLUDE Distance_Indication;
  #INCLUDE Situation_Evaluation;
```

Fig. 9. Resolutions for Variation Points

Figure 10 shows the logical architecture of the RPA product variant after instantiation of the four variation points presented in Figure 8. The selected design options chosen during instantiation for binding the variation points are illustrated in brackets. Note that this view does not contain derivation-time variability anymore.

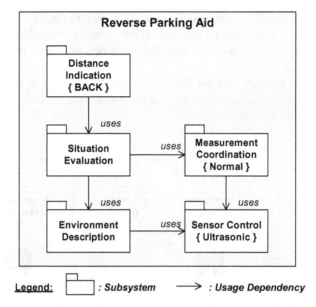

Fig. 10. Logical View of the Reverse Parking Aid (RPA)

4.2 Variability in the Physical View

Another important aspect of architectural modeling, especially for embedded systems, is the representation of physical elements. The physical organization of processors, devices, and communication lines is usually described by a dedicated *physical* view. Figure 11 illustrates an example of the CPS high-level physical structure. It shows two electronic control units (ECU1 and ECU2) and several smart sensor units for mid-front, left-rear, and right-rear surveillance. The sensors communicate with the electronic control units via a shared bus connection.

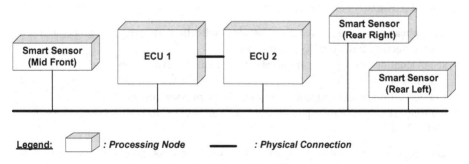

Fig. 11. Physical View of the CPS Architecture

As mentioned in the previous subsection, VP2 represents a variation point that affects variations in other views. Whereas VP2 parameterizes the software for the indication range, VP5 (supervision range) and VP6 (sensor type) are responsible for configuring elements of the physical platform, as shown in Figure 12. Consequently, VP5 and VP6 are part of the CPS physical architecture. The variation points describe which sensor equipment must be installed in order to allow for the specified functionality.

Note that the number and quality of the sensors is not only driven by the functionality to be provided but also by non-functional aspects, such as the market or price segment to be addressed.

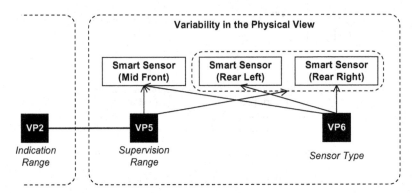

Fig. 12. Variability Model for the Physical View

4.3   Variability in the Process View

Variability does not only affect structural concerns of an architecture, as described in the logical and physical view. It also has a strong impact on dynamic and distribution aspects. We will concentrate on the dynamic impact in this section.

Figure 13 shows a simplified *process* view of the CPS product line architecture. A process view is dedicated to record dynamic concerns of an architecture, such as processes, tasks, and inter-process communication (IPC). As we can see, CPS is organized into several main processes:

- an application process, executing distance indication, steering assistance, and pre-crash detection functionality at run-time
- an evaluation process, responsible for situation evaluation, and environment description
- a coordination process, running the measurement coordination
- multiple sensor control processes, each managing the low-level access to a particular sensor

Each process can communicate with every other process, except for the application and sensor control processes, which do not communicate with each other directly.

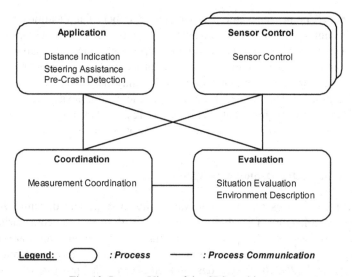

Legend: ⬭ : Process   ──── : Process Communication

Fig. 13. Process View of the CPS Architecture

During architectural modeling, the general process organization shown in Figure 13 has evolved as a reasonable solution to cope with driving safety and reliability requirements. However, performance with respect to the communication between data evaluation and delivering that data to the applications is critical when multiple applications are active and request sensor data concurrently. Particularly, the time needed for context switching between the processes may prevent the correct delivery of data in the specified time frame for product variants with a large number of different applications on a single ECU. In order to cope with this problem, a variation point VP7 (IPC Reduction) was introduced at the architecture level, as shown in Figure 14.

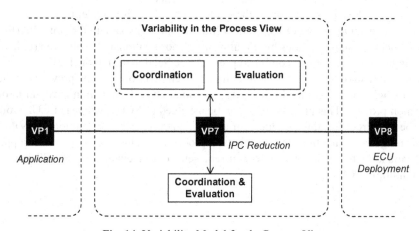

Fig. 14. Variability Model for the Process View

This variation point comes into play when the number of applications for a product variant – configured through VP1, see Section 4.1 – exceeds a certain upper limit on a single ECU solution (which is known at derivation time). It enables it to run evaluation and coordination in a combined process. This decision reduces time-consuming inter-process communication significantly. However, running evaluation and coordination in a combined process adds more complexity for achieving the safety and reliability requirements. This is one reason why this combination is not chosen in general. Next we will see how VP7 is related with VP8.

4.4 Variability in the Deployment View

In the previous sections we explained variability in static and dynamic views of a product line architecture. Distribution aspects are of special concern during design when the process and the physical structure of an architecture are complex. Distribution aspects are usually covered in a separate view, often referred to as the *deployment* view [26]. It relates design elements of the process view to design elements of the physical view. Since it does not introduce additional components, the deployment view can be understood as a "combined view."

In the product line context, the deployment view is special because it refers to two external potential sources of variation: the variation in the process view and the variation in the physical view. When the variation in the process and physical views are fixed according to a certain configuration, the deployment view shows the reasonable allocations between the components of those views. Whether a deployment configuration is reasonable or not depends on the driving architectural requirements. A fixed process and physical structure may lead to multiple deployment alternatives – one for the best performance and another one for easy scalability, for example. In summary, the deployment view adds information to the product line architectural documentation by showing the mapping and the variation of the mapping between process and physical view elements.

Figure 15 shows an example of the deployment variability model that was created during architecture design of the product line. It represents variation point VP8 (ECU deployment) which is responsible for allocating coordination and evaluation (either as two single processes or one combined process, see Section 4.3) to the ECUs.

One alternative to resolve VP8 has already been mentioned in the previous section (i.e., a single-ECU variant). In this case, coordination and evaluation may run in one common process. This process may then be assigned to ECU1, whereas ECU2 would not be required for this product variant. Another possible resolution of VP8 is replicating the evaluation process on two processors. This decision would support performance since it allows for concurrent sensor data evaluation in CPS variants with multiple ECUs.

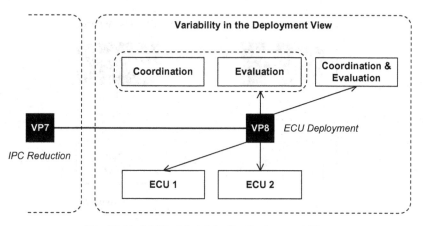

Fig. 15. Variability Model for the Deployment View

5 Discussion

In the previous section we presented variability modeling examples pertaining to a product line of car periphery supervision systems. The concepts we used to introduce and represent the variations rely on our metamodel described in Section 3. As has been mentioned several times, each architectural view of a product line may contain variability which is expressed by a set of architectural variation points. In the case study, we gave variability modeling examples for representative architectural views. In particular, we described variation points within static (logical and physical view), dynamic (process view), and distribution (deployment view) structures, respectively. The views presented address software, physical, and system aspects, as illustrated in Figure 16.

Moreover, it has been shown that architectural views are not independent of each other. Figure 16 illustrates relationships between the views that were used in the example of the previous section. A relationship between two views denotes that the design elements of the one view are semantically connected to those of the other view. For example, the design elements of the process view (e.g., processes) are related to the design elements of the logical view (e.g., subsystems). The elements of the deployment view are related to elements of the physical and elements of the process view.

The interdependencies between architectural views include the variation points that may also relate to each other across view boundaries (see Figure 3). So to integrate variability in product line architectures and in order to support the instantiation of product architecture variants, adequate descriptions of the relevant architectural views, the variation points within these views, and the resolution of the variations are needed.

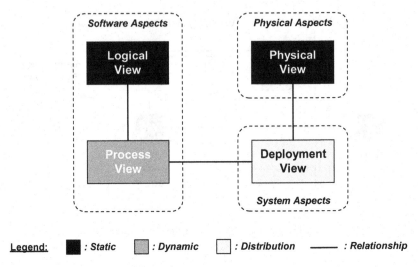

Fig. 16. Variability and View Interdependencies

In order to drive the configuration, the feature model and the product line architecture have to be associated so that a feature selection binds the corresponding variation in the architecture. Therefore, the variability concepts defined in the metamodel must be integrated into the QUASAR framework to support and improve the systematic development of product line architectures as well as their usage for product derivation. In the following, some basic issues with respect to employing the represented variability and the tradeoffs that must be made are discussed.

5.1 Traceability from Analysis to Design

A feature model that is intended to be the starting point for configuration encapsulates product characteristics and their variations from an user's or customer's point of view, rather than with respect to design paradigms like object orientation. A feature variation point may affect only single architecture design elements or responsibilities in an isolated case, but functionality typically involves several design elements or – even worse – aspects that crosscut the design are the units of variation. Therefore, groupings have been introduced as a means for encapsulating these variable units so that they can be explicitly addressed in the architecture.

Anyway, there is an actual association between the variability on the requirements level captured in the feature model and the variation points in the product line architecture that finally realize the single feature variants. At the one extreme, the complete mapping may be made explicit. At the other extreme, the mapping may be left unspecified.

In the first case, a lot of modeling effort may be needed, resulting in a presumably complicated assignment. Nevertheless, it would be possible to understand every single trace from the features to the architecture so that it would be clear why a particular variation point has been introduced into the architecture and which feature variant it supports, respectively. In addition, the associations could be used for product derivation.

In the second case, the mapping would have to be redone every time one tries to understand the architecture in the context of the feature model, principally for every single product derivation. Every mapping would then be inevitably subjective. Leaving the association between features and architecture open brings the risk of errors and misinterpretations, which conflict with the goal of a systematic product derivation.

Therefore, a tradeoff must be made depending on the number of expected product developments that make use of the mapping. On the one hand, a minimum traceability and a systematic production of variants should be guaranteed, while on the other hand the initial effort for representing the mapping must be reasonable with respect to the expected benefit.

5.2 Representing Variability in Architectures

The same argumentation holds for representing variation points and their interdependencies. For example, there is a tradeoff between making all dependencies explicit, which would ensure that instantiations of the product line architecture are valid, and leaving dependencies open, thereby exposing them to interpretation. Not all combinations of components are possible in general, either because they are not compatible or not in scope. Even if one tries to modularize the variability and to keep the units of variation independent of each other, dependencies cannot be totally avoided. This holds for feature interdependencies as well as for variation point interdependencies in the architecture. Another open issue is where to model (i.e., in the feature model, architecture, or code) which kind of configuration information (i.e., resolution rules, dependencies). This may vary with the application context and must be shown by experience.

5.3 Supporting the Configuration Process

Finally, our goal is to create feature models that allow configuration of product architectures through domain abstractions. Therefore, the variability in a product line must generally be made explicit and specified in detail. Furthermore, the individual representations must be formalized. In particular, adequate notations for feature models as well as for architectures are needed. Again, the question is to which extent a formalization will pay off. In this case, a tradeoff must be made between formal representations enabling advanced tool support for feature, architecture, and code configuration on the one hand, and a presumably higher modeling and maintenance effort on the other hand. An obvious migration path is to start with formalizing parts of the derivation process (e.g., those parts that are most error-prone or easiest to automate).

6 Related Work

Our work is concerned with the systematic integration and management of variability within product line architecture design. There are a couple of research areas that are related to our work. These areas are briefly sketched next.

Traditionally, variability modeling is part of feature analysis. Feature modeling approaches such as [23] [24] [34] [13] [9] [16] deal with the identification and representation of similarities and differences among requirements. Fundamentally, feature analysis aims at defining the problem space of a product line but does not consider technical solutions.

An architecture defines the solution space of a system or product line. Architectural design methods such as [5] [27] [21] which focus on functionality or [26] [2] [18] which emphasize the importance of quality attributes provide useful design guidelines, but are mainly restricted to single systems. Other approaches, notably [6] [22] [35], address product line architectures but do not cover variability modeling in detail. In [25] an approach for expressing feature variability on the architecture level using simple inheritance and aggregation patterns is described. As such, this approach deals with structural aspects of architectural variability, but does not treat dependencies to dynamic and distribution concerns.

Variability is bound to specific instances based on design decisions. This process is also referred to as configuration. Approaches to configuration are discussed in [15] [4]. System composition using domain-specific languages and code generators are described, for example, in [3] [10]. However, these approaches do not address the different shapes of variability at the architecture level.

Note that some basic concepts of this work for product line configuration can be found in [17]. The QUASAR framework is described in [33].

7 Summary and Future Directions

In this paper we have presented steps towards a systematic integration of variability into product line architecture design. We started with highlighting the pivotal and often neglected role of variability modeling during architecture design of product lines. In this context we pointed out that variability and configurability, respectively, must be regarded as additional quality attributes in concert with other attributes such as performance, safety, and reliability. Variability adds complexity to product line design. Therefore, we presented a metamodel that lays down a comprehensive conceptual scheme for representing variability in product line architectures. Particularly, the metamodel refines the IEEE P1471 recommended practice and describes how architectural variation points can be specified, how they are related to architectural views, and how they connect to feature variability. Next, we presented examples of applying these variability concepts to car periphery supervision systems by performing iterations of QUASAR. The examples demonstrate that variation points may be found in multiple architectural views and that they usually depend on each other. We then discussed important traceability, representation, and formalization issues that must be considered for a systematic development of product line architectures as well as for an efficient product derivation. Finally, we gave a short overview of related work.

Our future research activities include the refinement of QUASAR, especially with respect to variability management. In particular, activities and artifacts of the modeling workflow need to be extended for this purpose. Furthermore, the specification and representation of variation points and variation point dependencies must be improved in order to gain a better understanding of the consequences of variability at the architecture level. This would contribute to a more efficient derivation of product variants.

References

1. F. Bachmann, L. Bass, G. Chastek, P. Donohoe, F. Peruzzi: The Architecture Based Design Method; Technical Report CMU/SEI-2000-TR-001, Software Engineering Institute, Carnegie Mellon University, January 2000.L. Bass, P. Clements, R. Kazman: Software Architecture in Practice; Addison-Wesley, 1998.
2. D. Batory, S. O'Malley: The Design and Implementation of Hierarchical Software Systems with Reusable Components; ACM Transactions on Software Engineering and Methodology, October 1992.
3. L. Baum, M. Becker, L. Geyer, G. Molter: Mapping Requirements to Reusable Components using Design Spaces; Proceedings of the IEEE International Conference on Requirements Engineering (ICRE2000), Schaumburg, Illinois, USA, June 19-23, 2000.
4. G. Booch: Object-Oriented Analysis and Design with Applications (Second Edition); Benjamin/Cummings Publishing Company, 1994.
5. J. Bosch: Design and Use of Software Architectures - Adopting and Evolving a Product-Line Approach; Addison-Wesley, 2000.
6. F. Buschmann, R. Meunier, H. Rohnert, P. Sommerlad, M. Stal: Pattern-Oriented Software Architecture: A System of Patterns; Wiley, 1996.
7. G. Chastek, P. Donohoe, K. C. Kang, S. Thiel: Product Line Analysis: A Practical Introduction; Technical Report CMU/SEI-2001-TR-001, Software Engineering Institute, Carnegie Mellon University, June 2001.
8. J Coplien, D. Hoffmann, D. Weiss: Commonality and Variability in Software Engineering; IEEE Software, pp. 37-45, November-December 1998.
9. K. Czarnecki, U. W. Eisenecker: Generative Programming. Methods, Tools, and Applications. Addison-Wesley, 2000.
10. P. Donohoe (ed.): Software Product Lines - Experience and Research Directions; Kluwer Academic Publishers, 2000.
11. E. Gamma, R. Helm, R. Johnson, J. Vlissides: Design patterns. Elements of reusable object-oriented software. Addison-Wesley, 1995.
12. M. L. Griss, J. Favaro, M. d'Alessandro: Integrating feature modeling with the RSEB. Proceedings of the 5th International Conference on Software Reuse (ICSR'98). IEEE Computer Society Press. Victoria BC, Canada, June 2-5, 1998.

13. M. L. Griss: Implementing Product-Line Features by Composing Aspects; P. Donohoe (ed.): Software Product Lines - Experience and Research Directions; Kluwer Academic Publishers, pp. 271-288, 2000.

14. A. Günter, C. Kühn: Knowledge-Based Configuration – Survey and Future Directions. XPS-99, Knowledge-Based Systems, Würzburg, Germany.

15. A. Hein, M. Schlick, R. Vinga-Martins: Applying Feature Models in Industrial Settings; P. Donohoe (ed.): Software Product Lines - Experience and Research Directions; Kluwer Academic Publishers, pp. 47-70, 2000.

16. A. Hein, J. MacGregor, S. Thiel: Configuring Software Product Line Features; Proceedings of the Workshop on Feature Interaction in Composed Systems, 15th European Conference on Object-Oriented Programming (ECOOP 2001), Budapest, Hungary, June 18-22, 2001.

17. C. Hofmeister, R. Nord, D. Soni: Applied Software Architecture; Addison-Wesley, 1999.

18. IEEE Recommended Practice for Architectural Description of Software-Intensive Systems (IEEE Standard P1471); IEEE Architecture Working Group (AWG); 2000.

19. I. Jacobson, G. Booch, J. Rumbaugh: The Unified Software Development Process; Addison-Wesley, 1999.

20. I. Jacobson, M. Christerson, P. Jonsson, G. Övergaard: Object-Oriented Software Engineering - A Use Case Approach; Addison-Wesley, 1992.

21. I. Jacobson, M. Griss, P. Jonsson: Software Reuse - Architecture, Process and Organization for Business Success; Addison-Wesley, 1997.

22. K. C. Kang, S. G. Cohen, J. A. Hess, W. E. Novak, A. S. Peterson: Feature-Oriented Domain Analysis (FODA). Feasibility Study. Technical Report CMU/SEI-90-TR-21, Carnegie Mellon University, Software Engineering Institute, 1990.

23. K. C. Kang, S. Kim, J. Lee, K. Kim: FORM: A Feature-Oriented Reuse Method with Domain-Specific Reference Architectures. Annals of Software Engineering, Vol. 5, pp. 143-168, 1998.

24. B. Keepence, M. Mannion: Using patterns to model variability in product families. In : IEEE Software, July/August 1999, pp. 102-108.

25. P. Kruchten: The Rational Unified Process - An Introduction (Second Edition); Addison-Wesley, 2000.

26. J. Rumbaugh, M. Blaha, W. Premerlani, F. Eddy, W. Lorensen: Object-oriented modeling and design; Prentice Hall, 1991.

27. J. Rumbaugh, I. Jacobson, G. Booch: The Unified Modeling Language Reference Manual; Addison-Wesley, 1999.

28. M. Shaw, D. Garlan: Software Architecture: Perspectives on an Emerging Discipline; Prentice Hall, 1996.

29. M. Svahnberg, J. van Gurp, J. Bosch: On the Notion of Variability in Software Product Lines; Department of Software Engineering and Computer Science, University of Karlskrona, Ronneby, 1999.

30. S. Thiel, F. Peruzzi: Starting a Product Line Approach for an Envisioned Market: Research and Experience in an Industrial Environment; P. Donohoe (ed.): Software Product Lines - Experience and Research Directions; Kluwer Academic Publishers, pp. 495-512, 2000.

31. S. Thiel, S. Ferber, A. Hein, T. Fischer, M. Schlick: A Case Study in Applying a Product Line Approach for Car Periphery Supervision Systems; Proceedings of In-Vehicle Software 2001 (SP-1587), pp. 43-55, SAE 2001 World Congress, Detroit, Michigan, USA, March 5-8, 2001.

32. S. Thiel: On the Definition of a Framework for an Architecting Process Supporting Product Family Development; Proceedings of 4th International Workshop on Product Family Engineering (PFE-4), pp. 123-139, Bilbao, Spain, October 3-5, 2001.
33. A. D. Vici, N. Argentieri, A. Mansour, M. d'Alessandro, J. Favaro: FODAcom: An Experience with Domain Analysis in the Italian Telecom Industry. Proceedings of the 5th International Conference on Requirements Engineering (ICRE'98). IEEE Computer Society Press. Victoria BC, Canada, June 2-5, 1998.
34. D. M. Weiss, C. T. R. Lai: Software Product-Line Engineering - A Family-Based Software Development Process; Addison-Wesley, 1999.

Adaptable Components
for Software Product Line Engineering

T. John Brown, Ivor Spence, Peter Kilpatrick, and Danny Crookes

School of Computer Science, The Queen's University of Belfast,
Belfast BT7 1NN
{tj.brown, i.spence, p.kilpatrick, d.crookes}@qub.ac.uk

Abstract. This paper explores techniques for implementing adaptable software components. Such techniques can greatly facilitate the implementation of software product lines. The techniques we present allow the construction of large transparently adaptable components via composition and parameterization. Functional and structural adaptation, to any level of nesting, is achieved at the point of instantiation via recursive argument lists whose structure mirrors that of the component. The techniques are currently based on the C++ language, although work is under way to extend them to other languages (particularly Java™).

1 Introduction

One of the major emerging strategies for maximizing software reuse in specific circumstances is referred to as *Product Line* software engineering [1]. This is an approach that is particularly relevant when a *family* of related software systems are to be fielded. Typically, the systems to be produced will differ in many ways, but will also have many points of similarity. This kind of situation is found in many industries.

We are currently exploring the development of software engineering methods for the application of product line methods to the production of software for telecommunications products, as part of a cooperative research initiative with Nortel Networks. Products in this domain often exhibit a significant level of underlying commonality, and product line methods are clearly relevant.

The traditional approach to building software systems in this, as in other fields, has been what may be termed the *one-system-at-a-time* approach. Individual systems are built by individual teams. In this situation, the reuse of software can and often does occur. However, the reuse achieved is essentially opportunistic and depends on informal cooperation between engineering teams. Individual teams remain primarily responsible for their current projects. The software they produce is targeted at the requirements of those projects in the first instance. Any future reuse in other projects is an added bonus, but software is not necessarily designed from the outset to be used across multiple products. An organization can achieve only a certain level of reuse in this way.

™ Java and all Java-based marks are trademarks of Sun Microsystems, Inc. in the U.S. and other
countries.

G. Chastek (Ed.): SPLC2 2002, LNCS 2379, pp. 154–175, 2002.
© Springer-Verlag Berlin Heidelberg 2002

By contrast, a *Product line* approach attempts to put in place a systematic engineering process that supports the construction of *software families* rather than individual systems. To make such an approach work, new skills and techniques must be mastered. For example, at the requirements engineering stage, it is no longer enough to analyse the requirements for one system, often a difficult task in its own right. Instead, analysis must focus on the requirements for a complete family of systems. The aim must be to recognise and abstract out the common features across the product family, and also the features and characteristics that differ from product to product. The term *commonality-variability* analysis has emerged to describe this form of analysis process. The variable features relate to the distinctions and differences between individual members of the family. The common features reveal the potential for reuse. When the engineering process moves forward beyond the requirements stage, the results of commonality-variability analysis must somehow be used to design software that both embeds the commonality revealed by the earlier analysis and provides mechanisms to accommodate the variability. The ability to accommodate variability is the key to realising in practice the level of reuse that is potentially possible.

To this end, the ability to design and build *adaptable* software components is therefore a valuable enabling technological skill for the successful practice of product line engineering methods. The development of design and implementation techniques for adaptable software components is therefore an important research theme. This paper is focused specifically on implementation techniques for adaptable components. However the research which has led to these techniques is much wider in scope. It encompasses domain analysis and architecture design and description methods using an architecture-description language. Taken together, the analysis, design and implementation techniques are ultimately intended to form an integrated methodology for engineering software families, including families of embedded systems.

It is difficult of course to discuss software implementation methods in a wholly abstract way, without relating the discussion to some practical implementation framework. In this case, the implementation approach is based on the use of the C++ language. Currently, this remains a widely used language for large-scale software engineering projects, despite the steadily advancing popularity of Java. The underlying concepts behind this approach should be transferable to other implementation-language frameworks, though perhaps with some loss of elegance.

It should be noted that not all available C++ compilers fully support the most recent language standard. This is particularly true in the case of templates. Clearly this is a situation which might be expected to improve over time. Some of the coding techniques we have developed make use of modern features of the language, and may not be compatible with all current compilers. In our work, we use the GNU compiler version 2.95.1.

The remainder of this paper first explores the granularity range of the components, which may need to be made *adaptable*. The paper then introduces the notion of *skeleton objects* as a basis for functionally adaptable components and shows how they can be composed progressively to form large components, which remain *transparently* adaptable. Finally, the issue of structural (or architectural) adaptability is considered. Here the issue is how to design components that can vary their internal architecture at the point of instantiation. The key concepts needed to design and implement components with this capability are then presented.

An important point to note is that the underlying programming concepts on which this approach is based will already be familiar to most software engineers with a

C/C++ background: only the context in which they are used may be unfamiliar. These implementation techniques therefore entail only a short learning curve, while at the same time providing the means to construct highly adaptable software components at any level of granularity.

2   Component Granularity and the Concept of *Transparent Adaptability*

How big should an adaptable software component be? There is probably no definitive answer to this question. Clearly a small adaptable component is likely to be easier to design and implement than a large one. On the other hand, the real aim is to maximize software reuse. Reusing a large component is clearly potentially more beneficial than reusing a small one, although there are likely to be more circumstances where a small component may be reused. There is a conflict therefore between what is economically desirable and what is easily manageable.

An obvious way to escape from this dilemma is to begin by building small adaptable components, whose design and implementation can readily be managed, and then to compose them to form larger adaptable components. Those components can be composed again to form even larger adaptable components, and so forth. However, there is a critically important requirement which must be fulfilled if this kind of strategy is to be practised. It concerns the time at which adaptable components are bound to their final form. Most software engineers will be familiar with the concept of *binding time* and will be aware of the general benefits of late binding. It is conventional to think in terms of compile-time binding, or runtime binding. In the context of product line software engineering, the terms *platform time* and *product time* are perhaps more appropriate. Platform time refers to the time when effort is focused on the design of a common architecture and the construction of components or other artifacts that are to be used across the whole family of products. Product time refers to the time when actual products with particular features and characteristics are under construction. At product time, stored components will be retrieved and bound to parameters that customize them to match the requirements of the actual product being constructed.

When the components being used are large components and are formed as compositions of smaller ones, the component-adaptation mechanism must be one which provides the ability to compose small adaptable components to form larger ones, without being forced to bind the variability of the small components. In other words, the large components must exhibit *transparent adaptability*. If, on the other hand, the component-adaptation mechanism does not allow this, it may be necessary to sacrifice at platform time some of the flexibility and adaptability that ideally should be retained to product time. One of the key considerations therefore in designing adaptable components is to have a uniform mechanism for component adaptation that is transparent in the context of composition.

The following sections introduce simple, but powerful techniques that support the requirement for transparent adaptability through composition without difficulty.

3 Higher Order Functions and the Template Pattern

The prevalence of object-oriented programming in industrial software production makes it easy to forget that there are other programming paradigms with equal (or even greater) expressive power. One such paradigm is *functional* programming. It has never been very widely used within the software industry, and few functional programming languages are comparable in efficiency to modern procedural or object-based languages. One of the significant features of the functional programming paradigm is that it treats functions as first-class objects, in the same way as data objects. Modern functional languages typically support a variety of capabilities including the ability to pass functions as arguments to other functions. A function which accepts function parameters is a *higher order* function, and it has long been recognized that higher order functions can provide a powerful mechanism for software reuse [4].

Consider a higher order function defined in a pseudo language as follows:

```
returnType higher(aFunctionParam, aDataParam)
```

Function *higher* accepts two parameters of which the first is a function parameter and the second a data item. It performs some computation in the course of which it invokes and uses its function parameter. In this situation, the functionality actually executed derives from two sources. The first is the fixed functionality that is defined within the main higher order function called *higher*. The second is the functionality passed in as the function parameter. This can clearly vary from one invocation to another. In essence, we have a mechanism for packaging common functionality in such a way that it can easily be combined with functionality that varies from one situation to another. The function parameter lets us adapt the functionality, which actually gets to be executed. The body of *higher* contains the common functionality, which is reused each time higher is called.

Higher order functions are sometimes called *skeletons* (or more precisely higher order functions provide an implementation mechanism for skeletons). Moreover, in the arena of parallel programming research, the use of skeletons has been a major subject of investigation for some time [8]. In this case, the interest is in viewing them as a vehicle for reuse.

The next step is to return from the functional programming arena back to the object-oriented arena and look at a very well-known design pattern, namely the *template* pattern [5]. The template pattern may be illustrated by first considering the C++ abstract class definition below.

Note that the method *performSomeAction* is not a virtual function and cannot be overridden within any class derived from this one. However, it can be seen that *detailFunction1* and *detailFunction2* are called within the body of *performSomeAction*, and that they are pure virtual functions that have no definition within this class. Thus the precise action performed by *performSomeAction* is not fully defined until we derive a concrete class and provide concrete definitions for *detailFunction1* and *detailFunction2*.

```
class anAbstractClass
{
 public :
   anAbstractClass( params)   ;     // constructor
   double performSomeAction(int x, float y, double z)
      {
       float f1 ;
       int i1,i2   ;
       i1 = detailFunction2(z) ;
           f1 = detailFunction1(x, y) ;
           i2 = i1 * i1 ;
           return (double)(i2 + f1) ;
      } ;
 private :
   virtual float detailFunction1(int a, float b) = 0 ;
   virtual int detailFunction2(double d) = 0 ;
} ;
```

The key idea behind the template pattern is that any number of concrete classes can be derived from the abstract class *anAbstractClass*, and each concrete class can define different functionality for *detailFunction1* and *detailFunction2*. In this way, a degree of adaptability can be achieved. This can be depicted diagrammatically in Figure 1.

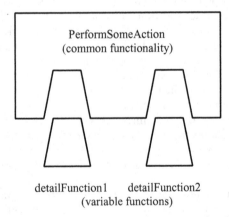

PerformSomeAction
(common functionality)

detailFunction1   detailFunction2
(variable functions)

Fig. 1. Providing Common and Variant Functionality

In essence, the template pattern provides a way to combine functionality that is fixed with functionality that can vary from one instance to another.

But the earlier discussion demonstrated that a higher order function can do a very similar thing. The main difference is that one concept has emerged from the object-oriented programming paradigm, where inheritance and class derivation are fundamental mechanisms, whereas the other has emerged from the functional programming paradigm, where treating functions as first-class objects and passing them as parameters is common practice.

There are however some differences between the two situations. An important benefit of the object-oriented approach is that a class usually has a local state that persists beyond the occurrence of calls to its member functions. It binds state and functionality in a way that is not true of the functional approach. The big disadvantage of the template method as an approach to securing adaptability comes when we try to use composition and nesting. A higher order function can have a function parameter which is itself a higher order function. Furthermore, within the definition of a higher order function, it is possible to call any number of existing higher order functions. Thus it is possible to retain the adaptability, which higher order functions provide, through composition and nesting. It is often harder to compose and nest instances of the template pattern without creating a large proliferation of derived classes.

4   Combining Aspects of the Above Approaches with Skeleton Objects

This section introduces the concept of a *skeleton object*. The term skeleton has been used earlier to describe a higher order function. A skeleton object is simply an object whose constructor is a skeleton (i.e., a higher order function). Its function parameters, provided at the point of construction, supply the functionality missing from the skeleton object as it is defined initially. To illustrate the concept, consider the C++ definition below:

```
class aSkeletonObject
{
 public :
   aSkeletonObject(float (*detailFunc1)(int,float),
                   int (*detailFunc2)(double)) :

detail1(detailFunc1),detail2(detailFunc2) {} ;
   double performSomeAction(int x, float y, double z)
     {
       float f1 ;
       int i1,i2   ;
       i1 = detail2(z) ;
       f1 = detail1(x, y) ;
         i2 = i1 * i1 ;
         return (double)(i2 + f1) ;
     } ;

 private :
     float (*detail1)(int a, float b)   ;
     int (*detail2)(double d)   ;
} ;
```

This class has a constructor that accepts two function pointers. In addition, it has two private attributes that are also function pointers with corresponding type signatures. These are instantiated by the constructor and then used within the definition of the member function *performSomeAction*. It is important to understand that this is not an abstract class, and we do not need to derive any other class from it before we can declare an instance of the class. On the other hand, the functionality of the member function *performSomeAction* is only partially defined, in the same way as was the case with the similarly named function within the abstract class illustrated earlier. Because it uses the functions pointed to by *detail1* and *detail2*, the constructor must execute before the class is unified to its final functionality. The example below illustrates how this may be done.

```
float function1(int a, float b)
        {return (b * (float)(a * a)) ; } ;
int function2(double d)
        {return (int)(d  /  25.0) ; } ;

aSkeletonObject Sk(&function1, &function2) ;
```

Function1 and *Function2* are two (relatively trivial) function definitions, and *Sk* is an instance of the class *aSkeletonObject* whose functionality is now completely defined. Its member function *performSomeAction* may now be invoked in the normal way. If, on some later occasion, there is a requirement for another instance of the object whose functionality differs, this can be supported by defining two more functions (with the same two signatures) and using them to create a new instance of the object with modified functionality. There is no need to use inheritance, as is the case when the template pattern is used as the basis for providing adaptability. Parameterisation with functions at the point of declaration provides an equivalent capability. There is a minor disadvantage, which can readily be overcome, as will be seen later. There is also a major advantage, which will become clear when consideration is given to the way skeleton objects can be composed to build large adaptable components.

5   Using Skeleton Objects in Product Line Software Engineering

In the earlier discussion of product line software engineering, a distinction was made between platform time and product time. During platform time (often called the domain-engineering phase) the first task is to analyse and understand the requirements across the family of products in terms of commonality and variability. The second task is to map the results of commonality and variability analysis into a common architecture and component library for the product family. The components collectively need to capture the common features and capabilities of the product family and to support sufficient *adaptability* to accommodate the expected variability. It is not difficult to see how skeleton objects can be used as an implementation framework for adaptable components within this context. Functionality that is fixed can be captured within the object's methods, which can be designed as illustrated above, to invoke function parameters that are only passed to the constructor at the point of declaration. Then, at product time (often called the application-engineering phase), when an instance of the object is declared within the software for a specific product, it can be provided with function parameters written to provide the detailed functionality required specifically for that product.

The problem with this is that individual skeleton objects are likely to provide components that are too small, and the ability to vary the functionality of individual methods within an object, provides only fine-grained adaptability. What are really needed are medium- to large-scale components, because reuse in the latter is what delivers serious changes to software production costs. This can be achieved by composing skeleton objects to form larger components. A critical requirement is that the larger objects should be *transparently adaptable*. In other words, when an instance of the larger object is declared, not only should it be possible to adapt the methods of the outer object, but it should also be possible to adapt the functionality of its nested components at the same time. The skeleton object concept makes this a relatively easy thing to achieve.

Consider a situation where there is a need to define a component that contains a nested component, and both the inner and outer components are required to be adaptable. For the inner component a suitable definition as a skeleton object might be:

```
class inner
{
 public :
    inner( innerFuncType1 in1, innerFuncType2 in2) :
          inFuncPtr1(in1), inFuncPtr2(in2)
               {.. other code .. } ;
    anyType innerMethod(  … params … )  ;

 private :
    innerFuncType1 *inFuncPtr1 ;
    innerFuncType2 *inFuncPtr2 ;
};
```

where *innerFuncType1* and *innerFuncType2* are function types (these can be pre-declared as typedefs at some earlier point), and *innerMethod* is a callable method whose definition invokes the functions pointed to by *inFuncPtr1* and *inFuncPtr2*, in the manner illustrated earlier.

An instance of *inner* can be included readily within a larger component in the following way:

```
class outer
  { public :
    outer(innerFuncType1 in1,innerFuncType2 in2,
          outerFuncType out1):
      outerFuncPtr(out1)
      {
        ………… ;
        myInnerComponent = new inner(in1, in2) ;
        ………… ;
      } ;
        anyType outerMethod(  … params … )
      {
           ………… ;
           outerFuncPtr( …… ) ;
           ………… ;
           MyInnerComponent -> innerMethod(……) ;
           }
    private :
      outerFuncType    *outerFuncPtr ;
      inner * myInnerComponent ;
};
```

It can be seen that *outer* contains a pointer to an instance of *inner*, as well as a function pointer *outerFuncPtr*. Its constructor takes three function pointers, two of which are destined to be used to initialise the inner component pointed to by *myInnerComponent* and one of which is used to initialise *outer's* own function parameter. The outer component's constructor creates and configures the inner component simply by calling its constructor and passing it the appropriate function pointer parameters. In this way, the inner component is created and configured only when the outer component is declared. Figure 2 illustrates the calling pattern and allocation of parameters implicit in this example.

Any method defined within the outer component can freely use the functionality provided by the inner component by invoking its methods. It can also, of course, freely use the function pointed to by *outerFuncPtr*. If, on some other occasion, another instance of *outer* (say outer1) is declared with a different set of function pointer parameters, this will create a new version whose inner component is configured differently. It is this capability to delay the configuration of inner components until the point of declaration of the outer component that is referred to as *transparent adaptability*. Of course there can be as many inner components as required. Moreover, there is no reason why a compound component such as *outer* cannot become a nested component within an even larger adaptable component.

This means that it is possible to design and build large adaptable components at platform time, using the nesting and composition of smaller adaptable components, without in any way binding the variability provided by the nested components. At product time, when an instance of the large component is declared, its constructor is supplied with a set of function parameters that support configuration of the outer component and all the nested components to whatever depth of nesting is used. There is no need to produce large numbers of derived classes or to bind the inner components in any way when we compose them into larger components.

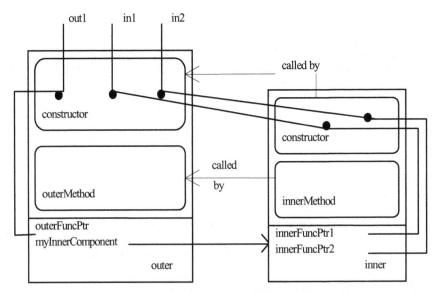

Fig. 2. A skeleton object containing a single nested skeleton object with calling patterns and parameter assignments.

Clearly the management of possible large lists of parameters is one issue that arises with this scheme. Techniques for the management of large parameter lists will be considered later in this paper. There is one other issue to note. The functions that are actually passed to the constructor of a skeleton object (via their pointers) are not member functions of the object. They cannot directly access attributes of the object that receives them. If they need to use attribute values, then these must be made available as parameters to the function. This is a minor inconvenience, albeit one that can readily be circumvented.

6   Optional and Alternative Subcomponents

The skeleton object concept provides the ability to define components whose detailed functionality is configurable at the point of declaration and which supports transparent adaptability through composition and nesting. This makes it possible to construct components with the kind of structure illustrated below in Figure 3. In this case, there are three nested subcomponents, each of which comes into existence when the outer component comes into existence and which will be destroyed when the outer component is destroyed. These inner components each have a set of interfaces (represented by the arrows) that are not callable from outside the outer component. They may be called within the definitions of the outer component's methods. It could be the case that each of the outer component's methods are implemented as direct calls to one inner component method. In this case, the outer component would act as a *façade* (a well-known design pattern [5]). The façade pattern can serve as a convenient framework for grouping a number of components to form a single larger component [5][7]. More generally, however, the outer component would be expected to contribute some additional functionality.

It is of course possible to consider a situation where an inner component, such as *inner3*, was only required to be present within some members of the product family, but not others. In other words, *inner3* and the capabilities that it provides are *optional* within the family. This is a much more radical form of adaptability. It might be described as *structural* or *architectural* adaptability. Moreover, optional subcomponents are not the only form of structural adaptability. There can be alternative subcomponents. For example, there might be three alternative subcomponents that could take the place of *inner2* (inner2a, inner2b, and inner2c) with only one of the three being present at any time.

To cope with components that have optional and (or) alternative subcomponents, it is no longer enough for the constructor of the outer component to construct and configure the functionality of the inner components as well as the outer component itself. It must now have the ability to decide on whether or not to include optional subcomponents, and it must have the ability to choose among alternative subcomponents. Of course, if the optional subcomponent (*inner3* in this case) is present, its functionality will still have to be configured, as will that of whichever alternative subcomponent is to be included. Moreover, the outer component itself may be included as a member of an even larger component. The large component must remain transparently adaptable, irrespective of the final subcomponent structure.

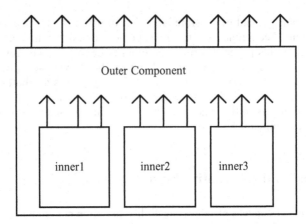

Fig. 3. A Component with 3 Inner Components: Inner component interfaces are not accessible from outside the outer component.

How this can be achieved is the next issue to consider. It turns out to be much easier than expected, but it requires the introduction of some further new component design concepts.

7   Indirect Function Arguments

Indirection is well recognised as a very powerful tool in computer science. Many design patterns succeed because they introduce an element of indirection that decouples the aspects of a design problem that need to be separated. It turns out that in order to design constructors that can choose among alternative subcomponents and decide whether or not optional subcomponents should be present, the key ability needed is the decoupling of a function from its arguments.

Consider first the case of a component with an optional subcomponent. When the optional subcomponent is required to be present, the constructor arguments must include those arguments needed to configure it. When it is not required to be present, these arguments can be omitted. In fact an easy way for the constructor to decide whether or not to build the optional subcomponent is by inspecting the arguments it has been given. If the arguments needed by an optional subcomponent are present, this can be used to indicate that it should be included.

To use this approach effectively, it is necessary to be able to vary the set of arguments presented to the constructor, and the constructor will in turn need to analyze its arguments and make decisions on the basis of what it finds to be present. However, in contemporary languages like C, C++ or Java, a function is normally defined syntactically with its arguments directly specified, as for example:

```
float aFunction(int x, float y, double z)
```

At the point of call, a function such as this must always be supplied with the arguments it expects; otherwise a compilation error will arise. The strategy proposed above requires more flexibility than this. Specifically, it must be possible to leave constructor arguments out at will, and the constructor needs to be able to detect the fact that some arguments are missing. Almost certainly, there is more than one way to achieve this required flexibility. However, the approach outlined below provides both the required flexibility and the means to easily marshal constructor arguments for large components with complex internal architectures.

The key facility needed is a device that might be called an *envelope*. An envelope is simply a container that can provide type-safe storage for a value of any type. This paper will not elaborate on how such a device may be implemented. However, a very concise and elegant implementation is described in detail elsewhere [6]. This implementation makes use of a small number of advanced features of the C++ language, and the term *variant_t* (short for variant type) is used to describe objects of this type. It is conceptually easier, however, to think of these objects as envelopes that can contain a value of any type. A user of the concept does not need to have any knowledge of the way envelopes are implemented in order to use them. It is enough to understand their key properties and the relatively small number of operations that may be performed with them. The first issue to consider is the way that containers of this kind provide an effective device for decoupling a function from its arguments.

An envelope is just a container that can be used to store a value of any type. It is implemented as a C++ class (not a template) so that an envelope holding a value of one type is no different from one holding a value of another type. Thus a function declared as

```
float aFunction(envelope e)
```

is effectively a function whose actual argument (which is the contents of the envelope) may be of any type. It is easy to create an envelope and place a value inside it as follows:

```
float f = 6.45 ;
envelope e(f) ;   // e now contains the value 6.45
```

Testing the type of an envelope's contents may be achieved by invoking a member template of the envelope class, which has the form

```
e.is_type<float>()
```

which will return *true* in this case.

The value from inside an envelope may be recovered using a generic operation, which returns a copy of the value contained. In this case, we can write

```
float value = float(e) ;
```

It should be noted that it is impossible to recover a value whose type differs from the type originally placed in the envelope. Attempting to do so will not be detected by the compiler, but will generate an exception at runtime. In this sense therefore, envelopes provide type-safe storage. For a fuller description of the mechanism by which this is achieved, we refer the reader to [6].

With the facilities that envelopes provide, it is possible to write code of the following form:

```
float aFunction(envelope e)
  {
```

```
    float result ;
    if (e.is_type<float>()) //if the contents of e is of
type float
        {
float f_contents = float(e);
            // retrieve the float value and
result = f_contents * f_contents ;
            // square it to get the result
        }
    else if (e.is_type<int>())
            // if the contents of e is of type int
        {
int i_contents = int(e) ;
            // retrieve the int value and cube it
result = (float)(i_contents*i_contents) * i_contents ;
        } ;
    return result ;
    };
```

This function is written with an envelope as its argument, but in reality it is designed to process two different *types* of value which may be contained within the envelope argument. Furthermore, the processing performed does not depend on the *value* of the envelope's contents; rather it depends on the *type* (in effect, type is being used as if it were a value). Having an envelope as a function parameter doesn't only mean that we can pass arguments of any type to the function. It also means that we can write the function so that it first determines what type of argument it has been given, and then uses this knowledge to choose among different processing operations with different types of argument. It is reasonable to describe this kind of function as a *smart function*.

However, many functions take more than one parameter, so a mechanism is needed for packaging multiple parameters, which can be of any type, into a single object. The kind of object needed to achieve this can be constructed easily as either a fixed- or variable-length list of envelopes. For a variable-length list, we could consider constructing a class using a vector (from the Standard Template Library) of envelopes (as described in [6]). In many cases however, a fixed-length list will be adequate, and some of the important implementation code for such a device is shown below:

```
template <int N>
  struct argList
  {
  ............ ;
  template <typename T>
  T operator [] (int n) {return T((*this)[n]) ; } ;

  envelope args[N] ;
  } ;
```

Note that the *argList* is a structure template rather than a class template, and that it has no constructor or destructor, these being generated by the compiler. By default, everything within a C++ struct is public, so an errant programmer could in theory directly access the single attribute *args*. The benefit of providing the object in this way is that it can be initialised by enumeration in the same way as a *C* array. So, for example, it is possible to write

```
float f = 8.9 ;
double d = 19.3345 ;
int produceValue( ) { return random(100) ; } ;

argList<3> threeArgs =

{envelope(f),envelope(d),envelope(produceValue) } ;
```

Here, the three arguments are placed inside envelopes, and the envelopes are placed into the *argList*, all in one operation. Directly retrieving a value from inside an argList object may be performed easily by making use of the generic indexing operator, as in

```
double d1 = double(threeArgs[1]) ;
```

which directly retrieves the value of type *double* from the middle component of *threeArgs*.

Recall that an envelope can contain a value of any type. This means that it is perfectly feasible for an envelope to contain an argList! But since an argList is composed of envelopes, this implies, in turn, that the individual values within an argList may themselves be argLists. An argList whose values include argLists is a *recursive data structure*, and the facilities provided by the envelope and argList classes are sufficient to enable the assembly and disassembly of these structures. In the remainder of this paper, we use the term *recursive argument list* to describe this kind of structure, and we will see that recursive argument lists are precisely what is needed to manage the parameterisation of recursively nested, transparently adaptable components.

8   Using Recursive Argument Lists with Adaptable Components

Now consider the adaptable component illustrated in Figure 3. It has one outer component and three inner components, and the inner components are individually adaptable (i.e. their constructors require function arguments). Suppose that *inner1* requires one function parameter, *inner2* requires two function parameters, and *inner3* requires three. Assume, for simplicity, that the outer component itself requires no further parameters. A recursive argument list that will act as a parameter to the outer component's constructor may then be built in the following way:

```
argList<1> inner1Args = {envelope(innerfunc1) } ;
argList<2> inner2Args =
{envelope(innerfunc2),envelope(innerfunc3)} ;
argList<3> inner3Args =

{envelope(innerfunc4),envelope(innerfunc5),envelope(inn
erfunc6)} ;
argList<3>outerArgs =
```

```
{envelope(inner1Args),envelope(inner2Args),envelope(inn
er3Args)} ;
```

The assumption is made in the above code fragment, that *innerfunc1, innerfunc2*, and so on refer to function pointers of anappropriate type. Then *outerArgs* is a single object that packages all the parameters that need to be passed to the constructor for the outer component. The constructor for the outer component may be written as a function that takes a single parameter of type *argList<3>*. Inside the constructor, the *argList* argument is disassembled into its components. These become arguments to the individual constructors for the inner components. The C++ code fragment below gives an indication of the way this can be done.

```
class outer
{
 public :
   Outer(argList<3> outerArgs)     // constructor for outer
     {
       argList<1> inn1Args = argList<1>(outerArgs[0]) ;
       inner1Ptr = new inner1(inn1Args) ;
           // construct inner1 component
       argList<2> inn2Args = argList<2>(outerArgs[1]) ;
       inner2Ptr = new inner2(inn2Args) ;
           // construct inner2 component
             etc. ;
     } ;

 private :
   inner1 *inner1Ptr ;
   inner2 *inner2Ptr ;
   inner3 *inner2Ptr ;
} ;
```

The constructors for the inner components are, in turn, each written to take a single argList as a parameter. Inside these constructors, their argList parameters will again be disassembled to yield the function pointers which can be assigned directly to their private function-pointer attributes, in the manner that has been demonstrated earlier in Sections 5 and 6.

9   Managing Optional Subcomponents with *Smart Constructors*

In Section 8, it was assumed that all three inner components were present all the time. Now consider the situation discussed earlier where it is assumed that *inner3* is in fact an optional subcomponent. Sometimes the constructor for the outer component will have to include *inner3* in the constructed component, and sometimes *inner3* will need to be excluded. Of course, if *inner3* is not present, any interface methods of the outer component that make use of *inner3* cannot be called safely. The constructor must take action that causes these to be disabled.

It turns out that these requirements can be achieved relatively easily. The key concept needed is the concept of a *missing* argument. What is required is a convenient way to symbolise and test for a missing argument within any argList. The following code fragment illustrates how this may be achieved.

```cpp
#define MISSING   -9999 // some convenient
representation

bool argumentIsMissing(envelope e)
          // a function which tests for an
  {       //   argument which is MISSING
  if (e.is_type<int>() )
    {
    int val = int(e) ;
    if (val == MISSING)
    return true ;
    else return false ;
    }
  else return false ;
  };

class outer
{
  public:
    outer(argList<3> outerArgs)           // constructor
for outer
      {
      argList<1> inn1Args = argList<1>(outerArgs[0]) ;
      inner1Ptr = new inner1(inn1Args) ;
       // construct inner1
      argList<2> inn2Args = argList<2>(outerArgs[1]) ;
      inner2Ptr = new inner2(inn2Args) ;
       // construct inner2
      if (argumentIsMissing(outerArgs[2]))
                  // inner3's arguments
        {         // are missing so
         inner3Ptr = NULL ; // don't construct it
         inner3Present = false ;
        }
      else          // inner3's arguments
        {           // are available
        argList<3> inn3Args = argList<3>(outerArgs[2])
;
        inner3Ptr = new inner3(inn3Args) ;
         // construct inner3
      inner3Present = true ;
        }
      } ;

      anyType outerMethod ( ...... Params ......)
                  // a method which makes use of
      {           // Inner3.
      if (! Inner3Present)     // the method has been
        {                      // called erroneously
          error_action
```

```
                    ("invalid call to interface method") ;
               return someDefaultValue ;
          }
        else      // normal implementation code goes here
        { … code to implement this method … } ;
      } ;

   private :
     inner1 *inner1Ptr ;
     inner2 *inner2Ptr ;
     inner3 *inner3Ptr ;
     bool inner3Present ;        // indicates
   presence/absence of inner3
   } ;
```

The first step is to define the constant MISSING to be -9999 and provide a simple function that will test any envelope to see if its argument is MISSING. Within the constructor, this function is used to see if the third element within the outer argList is MISSING. If it is, the subcomponent *inner3* is not constructed. Moreover, the private boolean attribute *inner3Present* is set to false, so that interface methods of the outer component that make use of the functionality of *inner3* (e.g. *outerMethod*) can be written to take the appropriate error action if they are called inadvertently. A missing subcomponent does not take up memory beyond that required for the pointer, which will be NULL, and the Boolean flag, which will be false. However, code may still be generated for an outer component method that is not needed, leading to some redundant consumption of memory. Some modern compilers are able to detect this situation and avoid code generation, which is a welcome trend.

It is easy to design the constructor so that it can readily determine whether or not to build optional subcomponents simply from the contents of the argument list. This provides a simple way to achieve the structural or architectural adaptability of components and maintain transparent adaptability at the same time.

10   Managing Alternative Subcomponents with *Smart Constructors*

The final issue to be addressed is the management of alternative subcomponents. Here there are in reality two situations to deal with, although the techniques required are closely similar. Suppose that there are two alternative subcomponents, and only one may be present within a larger component. The first situation is one in which the two alternative subcomponents have identical interface specifications. In such a situation, one can be swapped for the other without having to make any other changes and without any effect on the availability of interfaces at the outer component level. On the other hand, if the two components do not provide identical interface methods, it would be expected that the availability of the outer component's interface methods would depend on which of the two inner components was present. In this case, it will be necessary to manage the availability of the outer component's interface using similar techniques to those illustrated earlier (Section 9).

For simplicity, this minor complication can be ignored and the assumption made that the two alternatives have identical interfaces. Note that this does not necessarily imply that the constructors need to have identical signatures, merely that all other methods should. To select between them in this situation, it is necessary to build an argument list that contains a *key* of some kind, as well as the appropriate parameters for the component. An integer-valued key is perfectly appropriate.

Referring back to the component illustrated in Figure 3, assume that *inner2* may be one of two alternative inner components, either *inner2a* or *inner2b*. Assume also that the first is parameterised by, say two function parameters and the second by three. Then, to build an argument list for the outer component, which would cause the second of the two alternatives (inner2b) to be included, the code needed would be as follows:

```
argList<1> inner1Args = {envelope(innerfunc1)} ;
argList<3> inner2bArgs =
    {envelope(innerfunc2),
envelope(innerfunc3),envelope(innerfunc4} ;
argList<2> inner2Args = {envelope((int)2),
envelope(inner2bArgs)} ;
argList<3> inner3Args =

{envelope(innerfunc5),envelope(innerfunc6),envelope(inn
erfunc7)} ;
argList<3>outerArgs =

{envelope(inner1Args),envelope(inner2Args),envelope(inn
er3Args)} ;
```

The first action is to construct the appropriate argument list for the required component, and then to embed that as the second of two arguments within a further argument list. The first argument in this argList is just an integer-valued key that indicates that it is the second of the two alternative subcomponents that should be chosen.

This time, the constructor for the outer component is written as follows:

```
class outer
{
 public :
  outer(argList<3> outerArgs)
    {
      argList<1> inn1Args = argList<1>(outerArgs[0]) ;
      inner1Ptr = new inner1(inn1Args) ;
      argList<2> inn2Args = argList<2>(outerArgs[1]) ;
      int key = int(inn2Args[0]) ;
      if (key == 1) // indicates that inner2a is required
        {
          argList<2> inn2aArgs = argList<2>(inn2Args[1]) ;
          inner2Ptr = new inner2a(inn2aArgs) ;
        }
      else if (key == 2)// indicates that inner2b is required
          {
              argList<3> inn2bArgs =
argList<3>(inn2Args[1]) ;
```

```
inner2Ptr = new inner2b(inn2bArgs) ;
} ;
etc. ;
```

An important point is that only one of the alternative subcomponents will actually be created. The constructor uses the *key* to determine which component is needed and then constructs that component. Hence there is no undue waste of memory with this approach. Note that when dealing with a situation of alternative subcomponents, the argList that is required in the first instance will always be of length 2, and its first component will need to be extracted into an integer variable. The value of this variable identifies the alternative subcomponent to choose. In this case, if the key has a value of 1, the constructor *knows* that the alternative inner component required is *inner2a*, so it creates an argList of length 2 (recall that component *inner2a* takes two function parameters), into which the actual arguments for *inner2a* are extracted. The constructor for *inner2a* is then called to build the subcomponent. Alternatively, if the key value is 2, the constructor *knows* that component *inner2b* is required, so it extracts an argList of length 3 and subsequently calls the constructor for *inner2b*.

It is worth noting that this strategy does require an additional level of nesting within the recursive argument list, but otherwise presents no real difficulty. At platform time, the component's constructor is written to expect an argList of length 2 in the first instance. The first element is the integer key, and its value tells the constructor which of the component alternatives it must construct. The second element is the actual argument list for that component alternative. When dealing with subcomponent alternatives at product time, the first step is to build the recursive argument list that the desired subcomponent requires. This is then embedded, as the second element within an argList of two elements. The first element is simply an integer key to indicate which component alternative is required.

11   Some Practical Considerations

These techniques have been used successfully on small-scale evaluations, but not on any industrial-strength projects. Despite this limited experience, a number of practical considerations have been recognized and the following observations can be made.

First, a user of this form of adaptable component requires a detailed knowledge of the parameters that must be supplied. This includes knowledge of the role performed by function parameters, so that the appropriate code can be written, or an appropriate choice can be made from candidate functions already available. A user must also be aware of the inner components and the parameters required to construct them, again including knowledge of the requirements of any function parameters that the nested subcomponents require. In any library of such components for use within multiple products, it will be necessary to store this form of information with the component. However, a user will not necessarily need a full knowledge of all aspects of an inner component's interface, beyond the knowledge of constructor parameters and the role and requirements for function parameters in particular. Thus one disadvantage is that components of this form cannot be considered as *black-box* components for use by those with no knowledge of their internal make up.

A second consideration is that the outer component must *know* what internal components are included. It is therefore necessary to store this information in some form, for example, using Boolean flags to indicate the presence or absence of optional subcomponents. This does add some additional complexity that designers of this form of component must attend to and that inevitably has some memory overhead.

There are some further considerations that arise in the case of memory-constrained software, such as embedded systems. In striving for memory efficiency, it can be helpful for the outer component's constructor to keep a track of memory usage as subcomponents are constructed. A number of techniques may be useful for this purpose. The starting address at which the component is being constructed may be accessed via the *this* pointer. The *sizeof* operator may be used to identify the memory requirements for nested components. C++ also provides an alternative form of the operator *new* with placement syntax, and this may be used to map nested components into successive areas of memory. The judicious use of these techniques can improve memory efficiency, although they undoubtedly add further complexity to the construction process.

A further very general issue is the use of a language like C++ for this form of system, as opposed to the C language, which is, in general terms, more memory efficient. However, in this paper, the pros and cons of using C++ for embedded systems will not be debated. C++ is generally recognised to be more demanding in its use of memory than C, and the adaptable component-implementation methods do have some memory overheads.

These are the disadvantageous factors, but they must be weighed against the high degree of adaptability conveyed. The benefits of these techniques may be enumerated as follows:

1. The ability to adapt the functionality of individual methods within the outer component or any of its nested subcomponents to any level of nesting, at the point of declaration of the outer component
2. The ability to regulate the inclusion/exclusion of optional subcomponents within the outer component, and to similarly regulate the internal architecture of nested subcomponents to any depth of nesting. Regulation is again via parameters supplied at the point of declaration of the outer component. Note that, as discussed above, the outer component must be aware of its internal component composition.
3. The ability to regulate the choice of subcomponent alternatives, again at any level of nesting, and at the point of declaration of the outer component. The subcomponent alternatives from which the choice is made do not need to have the same constructor signature. The outer component will need to know which subcomponent alternative has been installed, if the interfaces differ.

Collective, these capabilities provide the means to build large adaptable components, as compositions of smaller adaptable components, following a bottom-up construction approach.

12 Discussion

This paper has introduced a number of ideas which, when taken together, enable the construction of very adaptable software components. The paper has been written to introduce these ideas gradually. It argues first that the template pattern, which is a key design pattern for achieving the functional adaptability of components, is in reality linked closely to the concept of higher order functions, (skeleton functions). Then it introduces the initial concept of a skeleton object as a class whose constructor is a higher order (skeleton) function and demonstrates that such objects give us essentially the same capability for the design of functionally adaptable software, as does the template pattern. The big advantage comes when we want to compose small adaptable components to form larger ones. Since the mechanism of adaptation does not rely on inheritance, it is easy to include skeleton objects within larger components to create components that retain transparent adaptability. This allows the construction of large components having nested subcomponents while retaining the ability to modify, via parameterisation, the detailed functionality of either the outer component's methods or the methods of any nested components, to any level of nesting. There is however the potential disadvantage of large lists of function parameters.

The next concept introduced is that of recursive argument lists, built from envelopes that are designed as containers for values of any type. The paper then demonstrates how these may then be used both to organise and manage lists of constructor arguments and to support the structural adaptability of large components. Such components may be designed so that their constructors can determine the inclusion or otherwise of optional subcomponents and can distinguish also among alternative subcomponents, solely on the basis of the recursive argument list given at the point of construction. These techniques give us a very powerful and also simple framework for building large adaptable components designed for use in multiple products. To use such components, we need only assemble the recursive argument lists they need in the correct way for each individual product. The fully configured components (given correct initial design) are then ready for incorporation into the final products.

An important point is that the underlying concepts are not difficult to grasp. Passing pointers as arguments is a familiar concept, though passing function pointers to class constructors and then invoking the functions pointed to within the class's methods may seem more unusual. Likewise, recursive data structures are well known, although the specific combination of techniques for building and using recursive argument lists may not be. Nevertheless, the learning curve associated with the introduction of this approach within an industrial software engineering environment should be short. The benefit, in terms of the adaptability that may be built into components, is considerable.

It is worth noting that there are other ways to implement recursive argument lists that do not require the use of envelopes. In particular, techniques have been reported using template meta-programming methods [11] to implement recursive argument lists that are similarly capable of storing values of any type. We have also employed these approaches successfully within our adaptable component framework. The differences in terms of coding complexity, performance and code size do not seem to be significant.

It is worth mentioning *mixin programming*, which is another emerging implementation strategy for product line engineering [9] [10]. The most recent developments in this area exploit the facilities for the parameterised inheritance provided by C++ templates. We regard our techniques as being broadly complementary to mixin programming methods. We are currently exploring ways to combine these methods and expect to report on this work in the near future.

Finally, it should be mentioned that recent work has focused on transferring these implementation concepts to Java. Despite superficial syntactic similarities, Java and C++ are very different languages. Java does not provide pointers to functions or (currently) templates, and it enforces a strictly object-oriented approach. With Java, it is therefore impossible to pass pointers to functions. Our approach uses lightweight *specialiser* objects which in effect act as wrappers for individual customizing functions. A full description is beyond the scope of this paper, but by the judicious use of Java's features one can construct components with a similar level of adaptability.

In the case of the C language, these techniques can not really be fully employed with the more restricted facilities available.

Acknowledgements

This research has been financed under the framework of the Jigsaw Project, which is a multidisciplinary research programme supported by Nortel Networks and the I.R.T.U. The authors wish to express their gratitude to both sponsors for the financial support, which has made this work possible.

References

1. "A Framework for Software Product Line Practice – version 2", Software Engineering Institute, Carnegie Mellon University.
2. "Adaptation of Software Components", George T. Heineman, Technical Report TR-99-04 Worcester Polytechnic Institute, 1999.
3. "Composing Software Systems from Adaptable Software Components", George T. Heineman, Technical Report TR-97-9, Worcester Polytechnic Institute, 1997.
4. "Higher Order + Polymorphic = Reusable", Simon Thompson, unpublished manuscript available from the Computing Laboratory, University of Kent. (http://www.cs.ukc.ac.uk/pubs/1997).
5. "Design Patterns : Elements of Reusable Object Oriented Software", by Erich Gamma, Richard Helm, Ralph Johnson and John Vlissades, Addison - Wesley Publishing Co.1995.
6. "An improved variant type based on member Templates", Fernando Cacciola, C/C++ Users Journal October 2000.
7. "Component-based Product development of Avionics Software", David C. Sharp, The Boeing Company, published in Software Product Lines: Experience and Research Directions ed. Patrick Donohoe pp 353 - 369 Kluwer Academic Publishers, August 2000.
8. "Skeletal Parallelism HomePage", at http://www.dcs.ed.ac.uk/home/mic/skeletons.html, maintained by Murray Cole.
9. "Mixin-Based Programming in C++", Y. Smaragdakis and D. Batory, Second International Symposium on Generative and Component-Based Software Engineering (GCSE 2000), Erfurt, Germany, October 9-12, 2000.
10. 10."Implementing Layered designs with Mixin layers", Y. Smaragdakis and D. Batory, ECOOP1998.
11. 11."Tuples and Multiple Return Values in C++", J. Jarvi, Technical Report TR No 249. Turku Centre for Computer Science, Finland.

Using First-Order Logic
for Product Line Model Validation

Mike Mannion

School of Computing and Mathematical Sciences, Glasgow Caledonian University
70 Cowcaddens Road, Glasgow, G4 0BA, Scotland, UK
Tel: +44 (0)141-331-3285
M.A.G.Mannion@gcal.ac.uk

Abstract. Product line models are used to drive the generation of requirements for single systems in the product line. They are difficult to validate because they are large and complex. By modelling variability and dependency between requirements using propositional connectives, a logical expression can be developed for the model. Validation of the selection of requirements from the model can be achieved by satisfying the logical expression. This approach can be used to validate the model as a whole. A detailed worked example is presented, and the computational aspects of the approach are discussed.

1   Introduction

A product line is a group of similar applications within a market segment, for example, mobile phones, pensions, or spacecraft-control operating systems. To achieve large-scale software reuse within a product line, many product line methods [1-4] advocate deriving implemented reusable components from early life-cycle work products including requirements. *Single systems* are then built from a selection of reusable components. In building single systems, the first task is to select desired requirements from the set of product line requirements. Many existing methods do not provide process details for this task.

A product line model consists of a pool of numbered, atomic, and natural-language requirements, a domain dictionary and a set of discriminants. It contains all the requirements in all the existing systems in the product line, can be constructed as a lattice of parent-child relationships and is typically large. The requirements in the model are all related to each other in parent-child relationships or through their relationships with the discriminants. A discriminant is the root of a tree in the lattice. The nodes below the root are the variants. Requirements belonging to each variant appear in the tree beneath the variant.

A discriminant is any requirement that differentiates one system from another. Feature-oriented domain analysis (FODA) [2] and FeatuRSEB [5] take a similar approach to modelling, but use features not requirements. Although defining commonality and variability is a step in most product line methods, details on it are

G. Chastek (Ed.): SPLC2 2002, LNCS 2379, p. 176–187, 2002.

sparse. The Scope, Commonality and Variability (SCV) analysis approach [6] addresses this gap. The identification of requirements and discriminants is a technique that can be used within the SCV approach.

In previous work [7][8], we assumed that the product line model had been constructed and validated. We identified 2 methods of requirements selection. *Free selection* allows a requirements engineer to browse a product line model and simply copy and paste a single requirement from anywhere in the model to the new instance. It does not use the constraints built into the lattice structure to guide model traversal and can lead to selection combinations being made that are invalid but that initiate the product line model being redesigned. Flexibility is a characteristic many engineers are reluctant to give up.

However, under this approach there can be an untenable number of choices, and random choices can mean illegal choices (e.g., 2 mutually exclusive requirements can be selected or requirements that must be included can be omitted). As a result, single system specifications can be time consuming to generate and contain errors.

Discriminant-based selection is grounded in using the lattice structure to drive selection and permits choices to be made only at discriminant points. This ensures that the choices produce a valid set of single-system requirements and reduces the time spent on specification. However, it reduces the flexibility for the single system requirements engineer.

Regardless of the selection method used, the construction and validation of a product line model remains difficult because of its size and linkage complexity. By validation we mean that prior to the model being used, we can be confident that there is at least one set of single-system requirements that can be generated from the product line model and that satisfy the constraints of the model.

To address these issues, we describe how a product line model can be represented using propositional logic. By considering each requirement as an atom and each relationship between requirements as a logical expression, a logical expression for the product line model can be developed. A selected combination of requirements drawn from the product line model can then be tested using this expression. This validation approach is independent of the selection method.

This paper is organised as follows. First we describe a detailed worked example of a mobile-phone product line model. Then we discuss some of the issues that concern product line model validation. Next we show how a product line model can be represented using propositional connectives and how selections from the model can be validated using propositional calculus. Finally we discuss some computational and other issues.

2   Product Line Models

In a product line model, the links between requirements are parent-child links so that requirements can be modelled hierarchically in a lattice. This is a reasonable assumption and a reflection of common-requirements document structures. A requirement can have zero to many children. A requirement can have zero to many parents.

Product line requirements can be categorised as directly reusable requirements and variable requirements. Directly reusable requirements are common to each product in a product line. R1 - R1.3 illustrates some directly reusable requirements for a mobile phone.

<DR> R1 There shall be an address book facility.

> R1.1   There shall be the facility to add an address.
> R1.2   There shall be the facility to search for an address.
> R1.3   There shall be the facility to delete an address.

A variable requirement is a *discriminant* (i.e., a requirement that differentiates between systems). Discriminants can take three forms:

- mutual exclusion (*single adaptor*): a set of mutually exclusive requirements from which only one can be chosen in any system in the application family. R2 - R2.2 show that a mobile phone user can switch from carrier A to carrier B without having to buy a new phone (i.e., the phone can deal with either, but it is possible to use the services of only one of these carriers).

    <SA> R2 The mobile phone requires the network services of one telecommunications carrier at a time.

    R2.1   The telecommunications carrier shall be A.
    R2.2   The telecommunications carrier shall be B.

- a list of alternatives (*multiple adaptor*), which are not mutually exclusive, but from which at least one must be chosen. R3 - R3.4 show there can be several ways of making a mobile phone call, but there must be at least one.

    <MA> R3 There shall be the facility to make a telephone call.

    R3.1   A telephone call shall be made by pressing the numeric digits.
    R3.2   A telephone call shall be made by storing the number in memory and then pressing a memory recall button.
    R3.3   A telephone call shall be made by pressing a ringback facility to dial the number of the last incoming call.
    R3.4   A telephone call shall be made by using speech recognition technology to say the numbers aloud.

- option: a single optional requirement that may or may not be chosen. R4 shows a mobile phone that may or may not have an Internet connection.

    <O> R4 The mobile phone shall support e-mail.

Dependencies between discriminants can be represented in the hierarchy. R5 - R5.3 shows that while e-mail maybe an option, the list of e-mail protocols it supports will be a list of alternatives from which at least one will be chosen.

<O> R5 The mobile phone shall support e-mail.

> R5.1   There shall be the facility to use the Post Office Protocol.

R5.2   There shall be the facility to use the Internet Message Access Protocol.
R5.3   There shall be the facility to use the Simple Mail Transfer Protocol.

Figure 1 shows a lattice structure for R1 - R5.3.

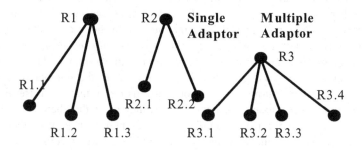

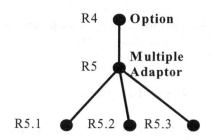

Fig. 1. Example of Lattice Structure

3   Product Line Model Validation

The value of a product line model lies in the cleanness and efficiency with which it can be used to generate a valid set of single-system requirements. The success of this task depends on the validity of the product line model. Ensuring that models are valid is difficult because they are larger and more complex than single-system requirement models. Techniques designed to support product line model validation should address the following questions.

- Question 1: *Does any single system exist that satisfies the relationships in the product line model?* A valid product line model is one in which it is possible to select at least one set of single requirements from the model that satisfy the relationships between the requirements in the model. An invalid product line model is one from which it is not possible to make such a selection.
- Question 2: *Given a subset of product line requirements, how can we know if it forms a valid single system?* The motivation for building a product line model is often to seek efficiency gains in the specification, design and production of a set of

products that already exist and/or a set of products that are visualised for the future. Typically validation activities will focus specifically on ensuring that these product sets can be specified from the model.

- Question 3: *What requirements do the valid single systems contain?* As a product line model becomes larger, it becomes difficult to see by inspection all the possible products that can be built from the product line model. New product ideas may be spawned from valid requirement selection combinations not previously considered.
- Question 4: *How many valid single systems can be built using this product line model?* Product line models contain many points of variation. The number of single systems that can be generated is proportional to the number of variation points. The number returned as a response to this query may be a useful design guide for product line models. A small number may mean that there is insufficient flexibility in the system for future markets. A large number may mean that there is unnecessary flexibility and that the model should be further constrained. Such interpretations will depend on the product type, the organisation's market share and its marketing strategy.

The more selection decisions there are to be made at each variation point, the longer it will take to construct a single-system specification.

4   Product Line Models as a Logical Expression

We can express the relationships between requirements in a product line model using propositional connectives and propositional calculus.

4.1.   Subgraphs

The logical expression of a product line lattice is the conjunction of the logical expressions for each of the subgraphs and is achieved using logical AND. If G_i and G_j are the logical expressions for 2 different subgraphs of a lattice, then the logical expression for the lattice is

$$G_i \wedge G_j$$

4.2.   Dependency Relations

The logical expression for a single adaptor discriminant is logical AND. If a_i is a parent requirement and a_j is a child requirement such that the selection of a_j is dependent on a_i, then

$$a_i \wedge a_j$$

If a_i also has other children $a_k \dots a_z$, then

$$a_i \wedge (a_k \wedge \dots \wedge a_z)$$

4.3. Single Adaptor Discriminant

The logical expression for a single adaptor discriminant is exclusive OR. If a_i and a_j are requirements such that a_i is mutually exclusive to a_j, then

$$a_i \oplus a_j$$

4.4. Multiple Adaptor Discriminant

The logical expression for a multiple adaptor discriminant is logical OR. If a_i and a_j are requirements such that at least one requirement must be chosen, then

$$a_i \vee a_j$$

4.5. Option Discriminant

The logical expression for an option discriminant is a bi-conditional[1]. If a_i is the parent of another requirement a_j, then the relationship between the 2 requirements is

$$a_i \bullet a_j$$

Table 1 summarizes the relationships and logical definitions of the model. The general expression for a product line model is

$$G_1 \wedge G_2 \wedge \ldots \wedge G_n$$

where G_i is $a_i \bullet a_j \bullet a_k \bullet \ldots \bullet a_n$ and $\bullet$ is one of $\wedge$, $\vee$, $\oplus$, or $\bullet$.

The logical expression for the mobile phone product requirements shown in Figure 1 is

$$((R1 \wedge (R1.1 \wedge R1.2 \wedge R1.3)) \wedge \ldots\ldots\ldots\ldots(G_1)$$
$$(R2 \wedge (R2.1 \oplus R2.2)) \wedge \ldots\ldots\ldots\ldots\ldots(G_2)$$
$$(R3 \wedge (R3.1 \vee R3.2 \vee R3.3 \vee R3.4)) \wedge \ldots(G_3)$$
$$(R4 \bullet (R5 \wedge (R5.1 \vee R5.2 \vee R5.3))).\ldots\ldots(G_4)$$

Table 1. Product Line Model Relations and Formal Definitions

Product Line Relation	Formal Definition
Subgraph	$G_i \wedge G_j$
Dependency	$a_i \wedge a_j$
Single Adaptor Discriminant	$a_i \oplus a_j$
Multiple Adaptor Discriminant	$a_i \vee a_j$
Option Discriminant	$a_i \bullet a_j$

---

[1] $a_i \bullet a_j$ is TRUE when a_i and a_j have the same values.

5   Worked Example of Product Line Model Validation

The logical expression of a product line model can be used to assist with its validation. During the construction of a single system, TRUE is assigned to those requirements that are selected, and FALSE is assigned to those not selected. These selection values are substituted into the product line logical expression. A valid single system is one for which the product line logical expression evaluates to TRUE. An invalid model is one in which every selected combination of requirements causes the model to evaluate to FALSE. For example, the product line model expression in Figure 2 is

$$(A \land ((X \land K \land Y) \oplus (Y \land X)))\ldots\ldots\ldots\ldots\ldots(G_1)$$

(G_1) will always evaluate to FALSE regardless of the combination of X, K, and Y selected. The model in Figure 1 however is a valid model.

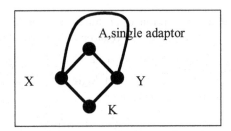

Fig. 2. Invalid Product Line Model

There are a number of different methods for traversing the lattice structure of the product line model and making selections from it. Regardless of the selection method, the same set of selected requirements should generate the same result (i.e., a valid or invalid set). We will consider 2 methods: free selection and discriminant-based selection.

5.1.   Free Selection

If free selection is used, then the dependency and other relationships between requirements in the lattice structure are not used to guide selection.

5.1.1.   Example 1
Suppose that the selected requirements are

(R1, R1.1, R1.2, R1.3, R2, R2.1, R3, R3.1, R3.2, R4, R5, R5.1)

The product line logical expression becomes

$$(T \land (T \land T \land T)) \land \ldots\ldots\ldots\ldots\ldots\ldots(G_1)$$
$$(T \land (T \oplus F)) \land \ldots\ldots\ldots\ldots\ldots\ldots(G_2)$$

$$(T \wedge (T \vee T \vee F \vee F)) \wedge..................(G_3)$$
$$(T \bullet ((T \wedge (T \vee F \vee F)))..................(G_4)$$

(G_1), (G_2), (G_3) and (G_4) each evaluate to TRUE. Hence $G_1 \wedge G_2 \wedge G_3 \wedge G_4$ evaluates to TRUE.

5.1.2. Example 2

Suppose that the selected requirements are

$$(R1, R1.1, R1.2, R2, R2.1, R3, R3.1)$$

The product line logical expression becomes

$$(T \wedge (T \wedge T \wedge F)) \wedge...........................(G_1)$$
$$(T \wedge (T \oplus F)) \wedge..............................(G_2)$$
$$(T \wedge (T \vee F \vee F \vee F)) \wedge....................(G_3)$$
$$(F \bullet (F \wedge (F \vee F \vee F)))....................(G_4)$$

(G_2), (G_3) and (G_4) each evaluate to TRUE, but (G_1) evaluates to FALSE because the directly reusable requirement R1.3 was not selected. Hence, $G_1 \wedge G_2 \wedge G_3 \wedge G_4$ evaluates to FALSE.

5.1.3. Example 3

Suppose that the selected requirements are

$$(R1, R1.1, R1.2, R1.3, R2, R2.1, R3, R3.1, R3.2, R4, R5.1, R5.3)$$

The product line logical expression becomes

$$(T \wedge (T \wedge T \wedge T)) \wedge...........................(G_1)$$
$$(T \wedge (T \oplus F)) \wedge..............................(G_2)$$
$$(T \wedge (T \vee T \vee F \vee F)) \wedge....................(G_3)$$
$$(T \bullet (F \wedge (T \vee F \vee T)))....................(G_4)$$

(G_1), (G_2) and (G_3) each evaluate to TRUE. However, (G_4) is FALSE because R5, the multiple adaptor, was not selected. Hence, $G_1 \wedge G_2 \wedge G_3 \wedge G_4$ evaluates to FALSE.

5.2. Discriminant-Based Selection

If a discriminant-based selection method is used, then *prior* to selection, TRUE is assigned to all directly reusable requirements. The selection algorithm permits decisions to be made only at discriminant points. During selection, TRUE is assigned to those discriminants selected and FALSE to those not selected. These values are substituted into the product line logical expression. Under this approach, examples 2 and 3 can not occur because the values of R1.3 and R5, respectively, will always be TRUE.

6   Computational Considerations

We constructed the mobile phone worked example as a simple text file that formed the input file to a Prolog programme. The Prolog programme constructed the product line model as a logical expression. Prolog predicates were written to find answers to questions 1-4. We relied on Prolog's built-in depth-first search algorithm to traverse the search space.

An affirmative answer to Q1 arises when the first set of single-system requirements that cause the product line model logical expression to evaluate to TRUE is found.

Examples 1 and 3 are two example single systems that provide an answer to Q2.

The answer to Q3 is the set of combination selections for which the logical expression will evaluate to TRUE. For a product line model with N requirements, (since each requirement can assume possible values of TRUE or FALSE), this can mean computing 2^N different possible values of the product line logical expression.

In Figure1, N=17, that is, 131072 possible single systems can be generated from the mobile-phone product line model. This is a small number that is computationally tractable on the modern desktop PCs that are available to engineers. A more realistic but small product line model with 400 requirements will yield a search space of 2.6E+120, which is computationally intractable. However, the search space can be pruned by exploiting the dependency links and adopting a depth-first search. For example, in Figure 1 when R4 is FALSE, there is no need to consider the values of the requirements dependent on R4 (i.e., R5, R5.1, R5.2, R5.3). Hence the number of computations is reduced to $2^{13} = 8192$.

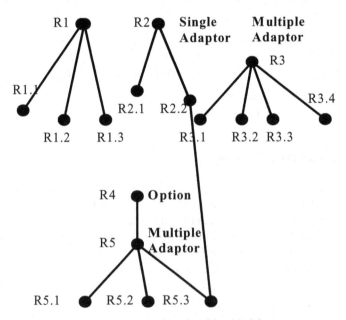

Fig. 3. Revised Product Line Model

Alternatively, we can prune the search space by assigning the value TRUE to the directly reusable requirements and permit variations in value only for discriminants. In Figure 1, R1, R1.1, R1.2, R1.3, R2, R3 and R5 can be set to TRUE, which reduces the number of computations to $2^{10}=1024$.

The number of valid single systems that can be built using a product line model (Q4) can be found by assuming that the value TRUE has been assigned to all directly reusable requirements and then by computing the number of variation points and the dependencies between these variation points. Consider subgraphs G_2 (single-adaptor) and G_3 (multiple adaptor) in Figure 1. The number of possible valid selection combinations is $(2 * 2^3-1) = 14$. If, however, G_3 had been joined to R2.2, then the number of possible valid selection combinations would be $(1 + 2^3-1)= 8$.

7   Discussion

The size and complexity of a product line model makes it very difficult and time-consuming to know whether a model is valid through inspection. This technique allows a product line engineer to know whether a product line model is valid or not (i.e., whether any valid single system can be selected). It is readily understandable, easy to automate and, by assigning TRUE to directly reusable requirements, runs quickly.

The technique does not prevent model constructions that may be unusual, but may help draw attention to them and encourage revisiting their design.

7.1.   Example 4

Suppose that a dependency link was introduced between R2.2 and R5.3 (Figure 3), the intention being to express that the SMPT protocol is available only from Carrier B. If this were written as R2.2∧R5.3, the product line logical expression would be

$$((R1 \wedge (R1.1 \wedge R1.2 \wedge R1.3)) \wedge \dots\dots\dots\dots(G_1)$$
$$(R2 \wedge (R2.1 \oplus (R2.2 \wedge R5.3))) \wedge \dots\dots\dots\dots(G_2)$$
$$(R3 \wedge (R3.1 \vee R3.2 \vee R3.3 \vee R3.4)) \wedge \dots\dots\dots(G_3)$$
$$(R4 \cdot (R5 \wedge (R5.1 \vee R5.2 \vee R5.3)))\dots\dots\dots\dots(G_4)$$

Suppose that the selected requirements are

(R1, R1.1, R1.2, R1.3, R2, R2.1, R3, R3.1, R3.2, R4, R5, R5.1, R5.3)

Then, the product line logical expression becomes

$$(T \wedge (T \wedge T \wedge F)) \wedge \dots\dots\dots\dots\dots\dots(G_1)$$
$$(T \wedge (T \oplus (F \wedge T))) \wedge \dots\dots\dots\dots\dots(G_2)$$
$$(T \wedge (T \vee T \vee F \vee F)) \wedge \dots\dots\dots\dots\dots(G_3)$$
$$(T \cdot (T \wedge (T \vee T \vee T))) \dots\dots\dots\dots(G_4)$$

(G_1), (G_2) (G_3) and (G_4) each evaluate to TRUE; hence, $(G_1 \wedge G_1 \wedge G_1 \wedge G_1)$ evaluates to TRUE. If the engineer's intention was to make the selected single system invalid, because R2.2 and R5.3 must go together, then the intention failed because R5.3's other parent R5, permits it to be selected without R2.2 being selected. However, this failure will at least invite the engineer to consider reworking the model.

For the user of any debugging tool, it is not enough to know if the input data is valid or not but rather when and where it is not valid. Product line engineers do not just want to understand if a product line model is invalid; they want to know what might be added, removed, or changed to make the set valid. We are currently exploring how to identify and best present this information. It is not as easy as identifying and presenting those parts of the expression that have evaluated to FALSE. In the course of identifying all the single systems that can be selected, it is necessary to deliberately make some decision points FALSE to explore different branches of the lattice.

Further work in the form of a detailed case study with a product line model containing several hundred requirements is needed to examine in more detail how to manage the computational difficulties brought on by the size and structure of the model.

8   Conclusion

We have developed a technique for product line model validation that uses propositional logic connectives and calculus. We have explained how a product line model can be represented as a logical expression. This expression can be instantiated by the requirements selected for a single system and used to establish whether the selected set is valid or not.

Techniques for product line model validation are important because such models are large, complex and prone to error during construction. We have demonstrated the technique by generating a set of requirements for a detailed worked example of a mobile phone.

References

1. Cohen, S., Hess, J., Kang, K., Novak, W., and Peterson, A.: Feature-Oriented Domain Analysis (FODA) Feasibility Study, Special Report CMU/SEI-90-TR-21, Carnegie Mellon University (1990).
2. Jacobson, I., Griss, M., and Jonsson, P.: Software Reuse: Architecture, Process and Organization for Business Success, Addison-Wesley, ISBN 0-201-92476-5 (1997).
3. Organization Domain Modeling (ODM) Guidebook Version 2.0, STARS-VC-A025/001/00, June 14 (1996), Electronic Systems Center, Air Force Systems Command, USAF, MA 01731-2816.

4. Bayer, J., Gacek, C., Muthig, D., Widen T., PuLSE-I: Deriving Instances From A Product Line Infrastructure, 7th IEEE International Conference on Engineering Conference on Computer-Based Systems, 3-7 April 2000, Edinburgh, ISBN 0-7695-0604-6.
5. Griss, M., Favaro, J., and d'Alessandro, M.: Integrating Feature Modelling with the RSEB, in Proc. of the IEEE Int'l Conf. on Software Reuse (ICSR5), Vancouver, June (1998) 76-85.
6. Coplien, J., Hoffman, D., and Weiss, D.: Commonality and Variability in Software Engineering, IEEE Software, 15, 6, November/December (1998) 37-45.
7. Mannion, M., Keepence, B., Kaindl, H., Wheadon, J.: Reusing Single System Requirements From Application Family Requirements, in Proc. of the 21st IEEE International Conference on Software Engineering (ICSE99), May (1999) 453-462.
8. Mannion, M., Lewis, O., Kaindl, H., Montroni, G., Wheadon, J., Representing Requirements of Generic Software in an Application Family Model, Lecture Notes in Computer Science (LNCS 1844), Software Reuse: Advances in Software Reusability, ed W Frakes, 6th Int'l Conference, ICSR-6, Vienna, Austria, 27-29 June 2000, ISSN 0302-9743, 153-169.

Product Line Annotations with UML-F

Wolfgang Pree[1], Marcus Fontoura[2], and Bernhard Rumpe[3]

[1] Department of Computer Sciences (guest), Univ. of California, Berkeley,
pree@eecs.berkeley.edu
[2] IBM Almaden Research Center, 650 Harry Road,
95120 San Jose, CA, U.S.A
fontoura@almaden.ibm.com
[3] Software and Systems Engineering, Munich University of Technology,
D-80290 Munich, Germany,
rumpe@acm.org
Internet: http://uml-f.net/

Abstract. The Unified Modeling Language (UML) community has started to define so-called profiles in order to better suit the needs of specific domains or settings. Product lines[1] represent a special breed of systems—they are extensible semi-finished pieces of software. Completing the semi-finished software leads to various software pieces, typically specific applications, which share the same core. Though product lines have been developed for a wide range of domains, they apply common construction principles. The intention of the UML-F profile (for framework architectures) is the definition of a UML subset, enriched with a few UML-compliant extensions, which allows the annotation of such artifacts. This paper presents aspects of the profile with a focus on patterns and exemplifies the profile's usage.

1 What Is a UML Profile?

The UML is a large and regrettably complex language. Still, there are many requests to explicitly represent additional features that cannot be described comfortably using the current version of the UML. Therefore, the UML provides mechanisms, in particular *stereotypes* and *tagged values*, which allow extensions. These extensions may be defined and grouped in so-called *profiles*.

Thus, a UML profile is defined as an extension of the standard UML with specific elements. A profile provides new notational elements and specializes the semantics of some elements. It may also restrict the use of UML elements. For example, [2] describes in further detail the profiling mechanism and a useful extension of it, called *prefaces*.

A UML profile may target a specific application domain. UML-RT, the real-time profile, is one prominent example. Other profiles may provide tool-specific exten-

---

[1] We use the terms product line and framework synonymously.

G. Chastek (Ed.): SPLC2 2002, LNCS 2379, pp. 188–197, 2002.

sions. For example, these might shape the UML so that it is better suited for modeling Web-based systems, as the one described in [1]. A Java™ profile would restrict the UML to single-class inheritance. The UML-F profile, which is described in detail in [4], supports product line annotations.

2   A Selection of Basic UML-F Tags

Though the UML version 1.3 already lists 47 stereotypes and 7 tagged values [6] and version 1.4 increased these numbers considerably, only a small number of them are particularly useful for product line annotations. This section picks out some of the tags[2] introduced by the UML-F profile for that purpose.

2.1   Product Line and Application Classes

Many product lines come together with prefabricated application classes that do not belong to the product line itself. These additional classes can be studied in order to understand the standard usage of a framework by examining and adapting their code, whereas the product line classes themselves are usually not subject to change.

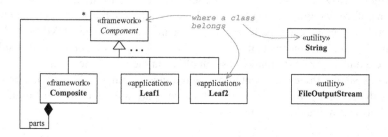

Fig. 1. «framework», «application» and «utility» Tags

The «application» tag marks application-specific classes. During the product line adaptation process, this tag may mark newly introduced classes as well. The «framework» tag marks classes and interfaces belonging to the product line. A third category of classes belongs to the utility level, as these classes are provided as basic classes by utility libraries or the runtime system. These may be tagged by «utility». Figure 1 exemplifies their usage. If a package is marked with one of these tags, then all of its classes and interfaces are implicitly marked as such. Table 1 summarizes the meaning of these UML-F tags.

™ Java and all Java-based marks are trademarks of Sun Microsystems, INC. in the U.S. and other countries.

[2] UML-F provides a slightly simplified mechanism that unifies standard UML stereotypes and tagged values to UML-F *tags* [4].

Table 1. UML-F Class Tags for Discerning Between Framework and Application Components

Tag-name	Applies to	Value type	Description
«application»	Class, Package Interface	Bool	The class/interface/package does not belong to a framework, but to an application.
«framework»	Class, Package Interface	Bool	The class/interface/package belongs to the framework.
«utility»	Class, Package Interface	Bool	The class/interface/package belongs to a utility library or the runtime system.

2.2   Completeness and Abstraction

The following UML-F tags deal only with the visual representation of elements; they do not define any properties of the annotated modeling elements.

The standard UML provides the ellipsis (…) to mark the omissions of attributes and methods. However, we also find it useful to be able to mark elements as complete. Therefore, we propose the UML-F © tag to mark completeness and the ellipsis tag to explicitly mark incompleteness. In accordance with standard UML, the ellipsis tag is the default. This means that class diagrams and all their elements are considered incomplete unless explicitly marked as complete via the use of the © tag.

Figure 2 shows three representations of the class Human. The first is complete, whereas the second partly omits the attribute compartment, and the third omits both the attribute and method compartments.

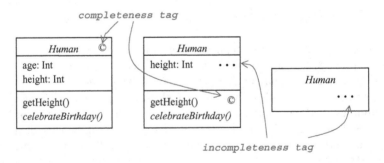

Fig. 2. Three Representations of the Same Class

3   UML-F Pattern Tags

Many patterns written up in the pioneering pattern catalog [5] by the *Gang-of-Four* (GoF—the four authors Gamma, Helm, Johnson and Vlissides) are product lines that rely on a few framework construction principles. This section discusses the relationship between the construction principles and the GoF catalog patterns, and introduces the UML-F tags for annotating both the framework construction principles as well as design patterns. Instead of listing the UML-F tags for each of the construction principles and patterns, we explain and exemplify how to derive the UML-F tags in a straightforward manner from their static structure.

3.1   Unification Principle – Adaptation by Inheritance

Hook methods can be viewed as placeholders that are invoked by more complex methods that are usually termed *template methods*[3] [3, 5, 7, 8]. The simple idea behind hook methods is that overriding hooks allows changes of the corresponding template method's behavior without having to touch the source code of the class to which the template method belongs.

The essential set of framework construction principles can be derived from considering all possible combinations between template and hook methods within one class or in two classes. The reason why this becomes feasible is that the abstract concepts of templates and hooks fade out domain-specific semantics to show the clear means of achieving extensibility in object-oriented technology. The UML-F tags for explicitly marking templates and hooks are «template» and «hook». In the sample UML-F diagram in Figure 3, the convert () method in the class CurrencyConverter is a template method invoking round () as its hook.

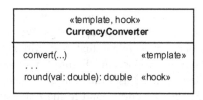

Fig. 3. UML-F Tags Annotating Template and Hook Methods

These UML-F tags can be used not only to mark methods, but also to mark classes and interfaces. Attaching the «hook» tag to a class or interface means that it contains a hook method. The «template» tag has the analogous meaning, though it only makes sense to attach it to classes and not to interfaces, since interfaces cannot provide method implementations. Figure 3 attaches both tags to the CurrencyConverter class, applying the UML-F tag rule that allows the listing of multiple tags.

---

[3] Template methods must not be confused with the C++ template construct, which has a completely different meaning.

The template-hook combination in which the template method and its corresponding hook methods reside in the same class, (as in the case of Figure 3) corresponds to the Unification construction principle. The general description of that principle calls the class TH (see Figure 4). The recipe for deriving the tags is to concatenate the construction principle name with each of the elements of the general structure of the construction principle. Thus, three UML-F tags annotate the Unification construction principle in a framework:

- «Unification–TH» marks the class
- «Unification–t» marks the template method
- «Unification–h» marks the hook method(s)

As a short cut, we suggest using the tags «Unif–TH», «Unif–t» and «Unif–h». Compared to the bare-bones template and hook tags, the explicit stating that the Unification construction principle underlies a certain aspect of the framework provides more semantic information. In particular, one who is familiar with the Unification construction principle might, for example, infer the degree of flexibility associated with that construction principle: Adaptations have to be accomplished in subclasses and thus require an application restart. This illustrates the layered structure of the UML-F tags – more "semantic-rich" tags can be defined in terms of more basic ones. This layered structure of the UML-F profile is further described in section 3.2.

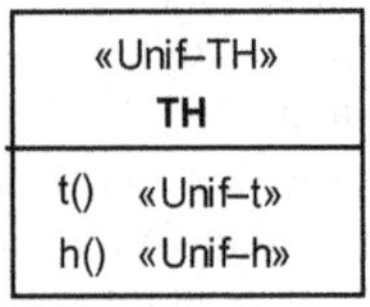

| «Unif–TH» |
| **TH** |
| t() «Unif–t»
h() «Unif–h» |

Fig. 4. Static Structure of the Unification Construction Principle

Figure 5 applies the Unification tags to annotate the CurrencyConverter class. In UML-F, any name can be defined for a group of tags. We chose the name Rounding for the Unification construction principle in that case. Although Figure 5 and Figure 3 represent the same aspect of the product line, Figure 5 makes the underlying construction principle explicit, while Figure 3 uses the more basic template-hook tags.

Conceptually, UML-F tags that correspond to the static structure of a framework construction principle provide a means for pinpointing the methods and classes in a product line that apply a particular design. Figure 6 illustrates that aspect. The arrows express the mapping of the structural components of the Unification construction principle to their manifestation in a certain part of a framework.

The Separation construction principle derives from the Unification construction principle by moving the hook method to a separate class H. The class T containing the template method has an association to H. The template method in T invokes the hook method in H through this association. The difference to the Unification construction principle is that the behavior of T can be changed at runtime by plugging in a specific H instance. The UML-F annotation is analogous to the Unification principle and discussed in detail in [4].

«Unif–TH: Rounding»	
CurrencyConverter	
convert(...)	«Unif–t: Rounding»
round(val: double): double	«Unif–h: Rounding»

Fig. 5. UML-F Annotation of a Sample Application of the Unification Construction Principle

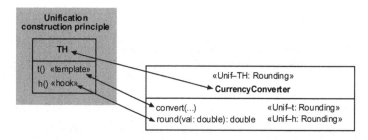

Fig. 6. Rationale Behind the Unification UML-F tags

3.2   UML-F Tags for Design Patterns

Analogous to the Unification and Separation construction principles, the structure of a design pattern determines the particular set of UML-F tags. In the case of the GoF patterns, each pattern description has a section labeled Structure that shows a class diagram. The class and method names in such a diagram, together with the pattern name, form the set of UML-F tags: «PatternName–methodName», «PatternName–ClassName» and for potential future Java- or C#-based versions of the GoF catalog or other pattern catalogs: «PatternName–InterfaceName». In occasions where associations and attributes play a role, tags of the form «PatternName-associationLabel» and «PatternName-attributeName» are present as well. This section illustrates that description scheme for the GoF pattern Factory Method.

Consider the layered relationship between the UML-F tags sets[4] for the design patterns, construction principles, and the template and hook tags (see Figure 7). The essential framework construction principles Unification, Separation, Composite, Decorator and Chain-Of-Responsibility represent the possible combinations of templates and hooks in one or two classes/interfaces. The patterns Composite, Decorator and Chain-Of-Responsibility are identical to those core framework construction principles that result from combinations of templates and hooks via inheritance. We suggest the names and structure of these three patterns as the basis from which to derive the UML-F tag sets.

---

[4] The tags of a construction principle or pattern form one tag set. For example, the three tags of the Unification principle form the Unification tag set (<<Unif-TH>>, <<Unif-t>>, and <<Unif-h>>).

Though the other GoF framework patterns and domain-specific patterns rely on either the Unification or Separation of templates and hooks, product line developers who need to express the richer semantic information inherent in these patterns, annotate a product line by means of the corresponding UML-F tag sets. The application of one of these patterns expresses the intended use and adaptation possibilities beyond the static structure to which a pattern is often reduced. The semantics of a pattern tag are defined through its structural and behavioral constraints, as well as its intended use.

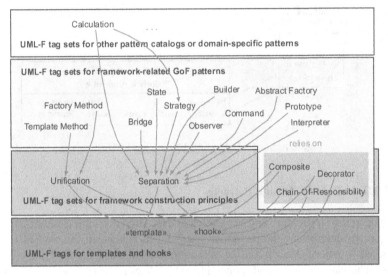

Fig. 7. Layers of UML-F Tag Sets

3.2.1   UML-F Tags for the Factory Method Pattern.

Figure 8 shows the static structure of the Factory Method pattern according to the GoF catalog [5]. Note that the diagrams in the GoF catalog adhere to the Object Modeling Technique (OMT) [8] notation which significantly influenced the UML, but which is no longer used in its original form. All the diagrams in this paper adhere to the UML notation.

According to the static structure of the Factory Method pattern[5], the UML-F tag set consists of these tags[6]:

- «FacM–Creator»
- «FacM–facM»
- «FacM–anOp»
- «FacM–Product»
- «FacM–ConcreteProduct»

---

[5] The tags adopt the Java convention of using uppercase first letters in class/interface names and lowercase first letters in method names. The use of the *italics* style indicates an abstract class, an interface or an abstract method.

[6] We suggest the abbreviations FacM for Factory Method and anOp for anOperation.

- «FacM– ConcreteCreator»
- «FacM–facM»

One could argue that the subclasses of Creator and Product are in some cases not relevant to documenting that pattern. So an alternative, shorter list of UML-F tags would be: «FacM–Creator», «FacM–*facM*», «FacM–anOp», «FacM–Product».

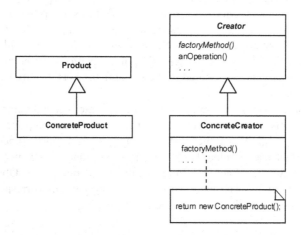

Fig. 8. Structure of the Factory Method Pattern (adapted from [5])

Figure 9 attaches the UML-F template and hook tags to the methods of the Creator class. This illustrates in detail the relationship between the tag sets of the Factory Method Pattern and the Unification construction principle. It also demonstrates the additional semantic information provided by the Factory Method pattern. For example, the Unification construction principle does not deal with a Product class.

3.3 Hooks as Name Designators of Pattern Catalog Entries

Hook methods form the points of predefined refinement that we call variation points or hot spots [7]. Product line adaptation takes place at these variation points. Depending on the hook placement and template-hook method combination used, more or less flexibility can be achieved.

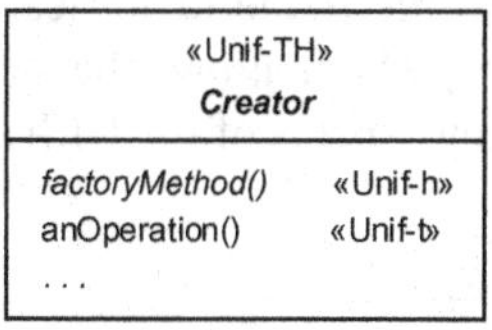

Fig. 9. Application of the Unification Construction Principle in the Factory Method Pattern

Every product line incorporates the two essential construction principles Unification and Separation, no matter how simple or how complex the particular template and hook methods are. Fine-grained classes apply the same construction principles as complex classes in order to introduce flexibility. They differ only in the granularity, the hook's semantics (often expressed in a hook's name), the number of defaults provided for a hook, and the number of template-hook pairs. Thus, we can take a fresh look at the design pattern catalog, that is, the 23 patterns published in [5].

Many entries in the pattern catalog can be regarded as small product lines[7], consisting of a few classes, which apply the essential construction principles in various more or less domain-independent situations. These catalog entries are helpful when designing product lines, and they illustrate typical hook semantics. In general, the names of the catalog entries are closely related to the semantic aspects that are kept flexible by the provided hooks.

A significant portion of the framework-centered pattern catalog entries relies on a separation of template and hooks, that is, on the basic Separation principle. The catalog pattern Bridge discusses the abstract-coupling mechanism generically. Other catalog entries that use template-hook separation introduce more specific semantics for their hooks: Abstract Factory, Builder, Command, Interpreter, Observer, Prototype, State and Strategy. The names of these catalog patterns correspond to the semantics of a particular hook method or the corresponding class.

3.4   UML-F Tags for Domain-Specific Patterns

Product lines contain numerous patterns that are not general enough to be published in pattern catalogs, but that rely on one of the essential framework construction principles. In many situations, it might be useful to introduce UML-F tag sets that explicitly refer to these domain-specific patterns. The definitions of these domain-specific UML-F tag sets work in the same way as for the pattern tags. The structure of a domain-specific pattern defines the tags. The structure of a domain-specific pattern should also be annotated, either by GoF pattern tags or the tags of the core construction principles. This ensures an explanation of the domain-specific pattern in terms of already understood designs.

4   Conclusions

The intention of the UML-F profile is the identification of a UML subset, enriched with UML-compliant extensions, which allows the annotation of product lines. Overall, the presented selection of key aspects of the UML-F profile pursues the following goals:

---

[7] These include Template Method, Factory Method; Bridge, Abstract Factory, Builder, Command, Interpreter, Observer, Prototype, State, Strategy; and Composite, Decorator, Chain-of-Responsibility.

1. UML-F provides the notational elements to precisely annotate and document well-known design patterns. Only a rather limited UML support currently exists for that purpose.
2. UML-F is itself in the spirit of frameworks—straightforward extensibility is the key to providing a suitable means for documenting any framework pattern including the future ones.
3. UML-F comprises a lean, mnemonic set of notational elements.
4. UML-F relies on the UML standard, that is, the extensions should be defined on the basis of the existing UML extension mechanisms.
5. The notational elements are adequate for being integrated in UML tool environments. For example, tools should be able to create hyperlinks between annotated framework patterns and the corresponding online pattern documentation.

More profiles will be standardized by the OMG in the future; sound proposals from various communities will get the process of defining and standardizing UML profiles started. In that sense, UML-F sets the stage for the UML profile for product lines.

References

1. Conallen, J.: Building Web Applications with UML. Addison-Wesley, Object Technology Series (1999)
2. Cook, S., Kleppe, A., Mitchell, R., Rumpe B., Warmer, J., Wills, A.: Defining UML Family Members Using Prefaces. In: Mingins, C., Meyer, B. (eds): TOOLS 32 Conference Proceedings. IEEE Computer Society (1999)
3. Fayad, M., Johnson, R. and Schmidt, D.: Building Application Frameworks: Object-Oriented Foundations of Framework Design. Wiley & Sons (1999)
4. Fontoura, M., Pree, W., Rumpe, B.: The UML Profile for Framework Architectures. Pearson Education/Addison-Wesley (2002)
5. Gamma, E., Helm, R., Johnson, R. Vlissides, J.: Design Patterns—Elements of Reusable Object-Oriented Software. Reading, Massachusetts: Addison-Wesley (1995)
6. OMG: Unified Modeling Language Specification. Version 1.3 R9 (1999)
7. Pree, W.: Design Patterns for Object-Oriented Software Development. Wokingham: Addison-Wesley/ACM Press (1995)
8. Rumbaugh, J., Blaha, M., Premerlani, W., Eddy, F., Lorensen, W.: Object-Oriented Modeling and Design, Prentice Hall, Englewood Clifs (1994)
9. Wirfs-Brock, R., Johnson R.: Surveying Current Research in Object-Oriented Design. Communications of the ACM, 33:9 (1990)

Feature Modeling:
A Meta-Model to Enhance Usability and Usefulness

Dániel Fey, Róbert Fajta, and András Boros

Nokia Research Center, Köztelek u. 6., H-1092 Budapest, Hungary
{Daniel.Fey, Robert.Fajta, Andras.Boros}@nokia.com

Abstract. A feature model captures the stakeholder-visible aspects and characteristics of a product line. By revealing a product line's inherent commonalities and variabilities, it acts as a key driver in the creation of core assets. Usability and usefulness, however, are important qualities for a feature model to possess in order to fulfill its role. In our opinion, these qualities can be ensured by building upon an adequate meta-model. The purpose of this article is to describe an extended meta-model for feature modeling. Meta-model elements, such as features and inter-feature relations, are presented in detail. We propose automated model analysis as the way of extracting information encapsulated in a feature model: algorithms are suggested for the identification of the commonality and variability in the modeled product line and for the automated consistency checking of products.

1 Introduction

In an increasingly competitive mobile terminal market, Nokia is under continuous pressure to widen its product range and to deliver products in a shorter time. As the general trend is that software has growing importance in product development, effective software reuse is an important success factor in withstanding that pressure. Software reuse is certainly not new to product development in Nokia. But is enough being done? Are all the possibilities being exploited? In repeated attempts to find the answers to these questions, attention has been drawn to product line oriented approaches to software development.

Assessments conducted within Nokia's development teams in charge of mobile terminal software development have hinted that there is room for improvement in the early stages of product line development. Hence, we have chosen to look at the applicability of a product line analysis method to the mobile terminal's user interface domain. The user interface domain has an infamous reputation for unstable requirements and a high level of variance, and, as such, is a good candidate for challenging any method.

1.1. The Context of Feature Modeling

A product line oriented approach examines software-intensive systems, and its objective is to organize them into a product line. We construe the term *product line* as

G. Chastek (Ed.): SPLC2 2002, LNCS 2379, p. 198–216, 2002.

defined by [1]. In the conceptual framework of [3], *product line analysis* is the product line engineering phase during which the elicitation, specification, analysis and verification of the product line requirements are performed. Requirements are gathered from the relevant stakeholders [4], namely people or systems that are, or might be, affected by the product line development. Characteristically to all similar approaches, product line analysis is performed to identify opportunities for reuse and to restructure requirements accordingly. The analysis results are represented formally in a model, the *requirements model*.

The *feature model* lies at the core of the requirements model as a composing work product. It captures the features of the systems included in the product line along with their relationships [2]. The model must include both functional and quality features. The features are typically organized in a hierarchy, with the most general features occupying the top and the most specific ones being located at the bottom. This hierarchy represents a static view on inter-feature relations; therefore, dynamic aspects of these relations are to be captured in a separate model. Tuovinen [5] describes an alternative technique to model feature interactions.

Most importantly, a feature model encapsulates information on the commonality and variability existing in the product line. Commonality and variability revealed during analysis is the key driver in the creation of product line assets in subsequent development steps.

1.2. The Meta-Model of the Feature Model

The requirements model may prove the initial decision of applying a product line oriented approach and may predict the consequences of the modeled requirements. Therefore, [3] argues, usability and usefulness must be the essential qualities of a requirements model. In the case of the feature model, these qualities are strongly related to the meta-model upon which the model is based.

1.2.1. Elements and Relations in the FODA Feature Model

In Feature-oriented Domain Analysis (FODA) [2], the feature model represents the features of a product line and their relationships. The structural relationship *consists-of*, which represents a logical grouping of features, is the basic element in forming the backbone of the model.

Of course, not all product line features are assumed to be present in every product. This type of differentiation is expressed by categorizing features as being *mandatory*, *optional* or *alternative*. The definition of the *mandatory* and the *optional* term is not clear enough in the FODA method [2], and this ambiguity has induced slightly different interpretations. For example, [8] assumes the *mandatory* category to be absolute, in that a mandatory feature is present in all products derived from a product line. In contrast, [9] sees the same category as being relative, in that a mandatory feature is included in a product if and only if its parent is included as well. *Alternative* features can be thought of as specializations of a more general feature, and only a single specialization can be included in a product.

Features can be connected using certain composition rules to express additional semantics existing between them. All optional and alternative features that cannot be selected when the named feature is selected (in a particular product) must be stated using the MUTUALLY EXCLUSIVE WITH statement. All optional and alternative features that must be selected when the named feature is selected must be defined using the REQUIRES statement.

1.2.2.   Limitations of the FODA Feature Model

DeBaud [7] notes – coinciding with our experience – that the FODA approach to feature modeling has some limitations that hinder its applicability in an industrial environment. Briefly, such limitations are

- Although the FODA method informally mentions the concept of feature attributes, it does not explicitly define any relevant relationships between them. In this paper, we demonstrate that such relations are indispensable (see Section 2.4.2 for further details). Therefore, we propose the modify relation to formulate dependencies between feature attributes.
- The studied product lines have revealed some examples for rather complex logical rules describing the selection of features into products. These rules cannot be described using only the set of relations provided by FODA. For example, the FODA method does not have the ability to express specialization with non-exclusive alternatives. We have found, however, many examples that can only be modeled by including arbitrary specialization variants in a product. To overcome this problem, we defined the concepts of *pseudo-features* and *provided-by* relations (see Section 2.3.2). Moreover, Section 4 is dedicated to the brief discussion of those rare cases that are not covered by the proposed meta-model.

In addition to the aforementioned limitations, we have also found that the analysis, especially automated analysis, of a FODA feature model is problematic.

- The FODA representation of the feature hierarchy is a well-formed tree. In Section 2.3.1, we argue that this structure is redundant, and thus it makes the development of an efficient analysis algorithm difficult.
- The *mandatory* and *optional* categories are easy to express using one inter-feature relation (the *require* relation, see Section 2.4.1). There is no need to use these categories explicitly. This solution increases the orthogonality of the relations in the meta-model, and thus it helps the application of analysis algorithms.

1.3.   Requirements Shaping Our Work

Having detected the aforementioned deficiencies, the extension of the FODA method's meta-model of the feature model was necessary. The following requirements have shaped our work:

- The meta-model must facilitate the creation of a feature model with minimum information loss. Information on requirements, gathered from various sources, should be represented as precisely as possible. The work of extracting information from a barely structured textual representation, for example, is tedious and time consuming enough to deter us from doing it more times than is absolutely necessary.

- The relations between features defined in the meta-model must ensure the consistency of individual products. For instance, the semantics of a feature may require the exclusion of another feature from a particular product.
- The ability of performing automated model analysis has been considered to be an important quality from the beginning. We see automated model analysis as a key criteria in determining the usefulness of a feature model. The purpose of the extended meta-model is to reduce the task of consistency checking and of performing commonality and variability analysis of the design and implementation of proper element selection algorithms.

This article is dedicated to the presentation of a meta-model that satisfies the requirements outlined above.

1.4.   The Mobile Handset Phonebook Domain

The meta-model elements and their roles are illustrated through examples taken from the phonebook domain, a typical subdomain of a Nokia mobile terminal's user-interface software.

The phonebook is a common database application that gives the user the ability to manipulate contact data, such as names, phone numbers, e-mail addresses, and notes. Entries of the phonebook can be stored, deleted, retrieved and edited. A typical entry is composed of a name field and one or more number fields. If more than one number can be stored, then one of them must be marked as the default one. The entries can be stored on either a SIM (Subscriber Identity Module) card – if present – or the mobile equipment's internal memory. Depending on the selected storage media (i.e., the SIM card or the internal memory), there are different limitations on certain parameters of the entries (for instance, only the mobile terminal's memory is able to store more phone numbers for a single-name entry). The data stored in each storage media can be transferred to the other, using the Memory Copy functionality. Access to the phonebook can be restricted, and the use of its resources may require some sort of product-specific authentication.

2   Meta-Model Elements and Relations

2.1.   Meta-Model Elements

We begin by covering the terms and concepts that are essential in understanding the proposed meta-model. These concepts become the first elements of the meta-model at the same time. The basic building block of any feature model is the *feature* itself. Using the FODA method's [2] definition,

> *A feature is a prominent or distinctive user-visible aspect, quality, or characteristic of a software system or systems.*

The feature model captures the aforementioned user-visible aspects, qualities and characteristics for the entire product line. An individual product, however, is described by a selected subset of features.

A product is a consistent set of features of a product line.

In this context, *consistency* ensures that all the product-definition-related constraints – if any are defined in the feature model – are satisfied. Section 2.4.1 will discuss in depth the representation of static consistency constraints using specific inter-feature relations.

Properties are feature attributes that represent any kind of measurable and variable aspect. Dependencies may exist between properties and other features or other features' properties. These dependencies constitute some kind of information flow between features; this information flow will be modeled through another category of inter-feature relations, as described in Section 2.4.1 Additionally, properties have an important role in the commonality and variability analysis, as explained in Section 3. Consider the following example:

- Feature A: the phonebook can store entries.
- Property P_A: the maximum number of entries that can be stored in the phonebook.

Figure 1 introduces a possible notation for a feature and its property.

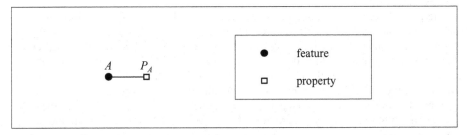

Fig. 1. Property of a Feature

In contrast with normal features, *pseudo-features* express abstract functionality, quality or characteristics. Pseudo-features alter the product selection: a pseudo-feature cannot be selected into a product without selecting at least one other realizing feature at the same time. The details of its use will be discussed thoroughly in Section 2.3.2.

Here's an example to illustrate the typical case when a pseudo-feature is needed:

- Pseudo-feature *A*: functionality of authentication to access the phonebook.
- Realizing feature *B*: PIN-code authentication.
- Realizing feature *C*: some kind of biometrics (for example, voice-based) authentication.

A product cannot simply have an abstract authentication functionality; it must be realized by a specific type of authentication. Figure 2 proposes a notation for pseudo-features; the *provided-by* relation, which expresses the realization of an abstraction, is discussed in Section 2.3.2.

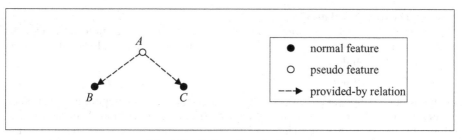

Fig. 2. Realizing a Pseudo-Feature

2.2. Feature Model Views

A typical feature model is expected to contain hundreds – if not thousands – of features. Many relations would be added to build the hierarchy, to ensure consistency, and so forth. Representing all this information to the user in a single view would have an obvious negative effect on the usability of the model. Therefore, it is a natural decision to define different views – or *planes* – to reflect different aspects. We have found that the following views are needed to effectively represent information in the model: the *hierarchy plane*, the *dependency plane* and the *feature sets plane*. In the subsequent sections, the inter-feature relations will be discussed in the context of these three planes.

The model elements – features and relations – shown in the hierarchy plane form the backbone of our whole model. This plane reflects the structure of the product line, in the way that people most likely would think of the logical organization of features. It incorporates the knowledge and experience of domain experts who build the model.

The dependency plane shows various kinds of dependency relations, classified into two major categories: the consistency relations and the feature property relations. Those that belong to the first one guard the consistency within products. In contrast with the "soft" relations of the hierarchy plane, these relations represent "hard" constraints that stem from the semantics of the described features. These constraints should be fully satisfied when products are built. Relations in the second category concentrate on feature properties and their dependencies on other features or other features' properties.

In the context of the feature sets plane, we have the possibility of grouping features from various points of view. This helps the domain experts to organize the features in the way that best fits their needs.

2.3. The Feature Hierarchy Plane

As already mentioned, the model elements shown in the hierarchy plane form the underlying structure of the feature model. The hierarchy is spawned by two meta-model elements, namely the *refine* and the *provided-by* relations.

2.3.1.   The *Refine* Relation

The purpose of the *refine* relation, similarly to the *consists-of* relation in the FODA method [2], is to describe the features of a product line stepwise at a lower abstraction level with additional details.

Refinement is a more detailed description of (the services of) a feature.

One or more top-level features start the hierarchy. As an important constraint, circularity in *refine* relations is prohibited. At the same time, more features can be refined by the same feature. Thus, *refine* relations – as edges – and features – as vertices – constitute a directed acyclic graph (DAG). Unlike in the FODA method [2], the resulting graph is not a tree. Therefore, we refer to this graph as a tree-like hierarchy, because there are potentially only a few locations where the tree structure is broken. The tree structure is typically broken when a subfeature has more than one parent. The next example (Figure 3) illustrates this case:

– Feature *A*: SMS sending.
– Feature *B*: Call initiation.
– Subfeature *C*: We can select a phone number.

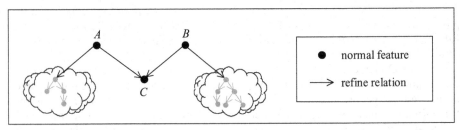

Fig. 3. Breaking the Tree Structure: Feature C has Two Refine-Parents

If the model would not permit a feature to have multiple parents, it would appear in several subhierarchies. As a result, the model will not only contain redundant information, but, more importantly, the commonality and variability analysis (see Section 3) performed on it will yield inaccurate results.

2.3.2.   The *Provided-by* Relation and Pseudo-Features

The concept of the pseudo-feature was already introduced in Section 2.1. The *provided-by* relation binds the features, which realize a pseudo-feature, into the hierarchy. A feature or pseudo-feature can have more than one provided-by parent. Having more provided-by parents breaks the tree structure, as the *refine* relation did. The main rule in connection with a pseudo-feature, is that it cannot be selected in a product on its own, but rather must be selected with at least one of the provided-by children (if this child is also a pseudo-feature, this rule should be applied recursively). Note, that the *provided-by* relation and pseudo-features together express the "requires at least one" semantics.

Since the *provided-by* relation helps to form the hierarchy and also sets up dependency constraints among features, it can be considered as a relation that is part of both the *hierarchy* and the *dependency plane*. Figure 2 has already proposed notation for the relation in question.

2.3.2.1. The Pseudo-Features and the Refine Children

A pseudo-feature – as any other feature – can have children linked by using the *refine* relation. These children can be the starting points of hierarchies spawned by both the *refine* and *provided-by* relations. For easier identification, let us call the refine-children[1] and their subhierarchies "refine-linked descendants". All provided-by children of a pseudo-feature implicitly inherit its refine-linked descendants (see Figure 4). The provided-by descendants also inherit all the properties of the particular pseudo-feature.

In order to keep the model clear, this implicit inheritance does not appear when the model is built and visualized.

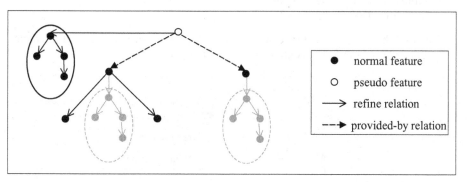

Fig. 4. Implicit Inheritance of Refine-Linked Descendants (marked gray)

2.4.   The Feature Dependency Plane

2.4.1.   Consistency Relations

As pointed out in Section 1.3, the meta-model must ensure the consistent nature of the model from the point of view of individual product definitions. Two additional meta-model elements, the *require* and the *conflict* relations, together with the *provided-by* relation guarantees this quality.

2.4.1.1.   The Require Relation

Many features in a product line are closely connected to each other. The *require* relation expresses a dependency between two features: one of them needs the presence of the other one in the same product, for its correct operation (or other relevant reason). There are no constraints concerning the two features' locations in the hierarchy; they can be, in fact, members of completely distinct hierarchies. A typical use case of the *require* relation is marking the mandatory subfeatures of a feature, but there can be *require* relations that cross the feature hierarchy. Figure 5 and Figure 6 propose a notation for the *require* relation.

---

[1] The term refine-child is a feature that is linked with a refine relation to another, the parent feature.

This is a non-symmetric relation (for example, this relation can be represented using directed edges in a graph). There are two special cases illustrating the asymmetric nature that are worth mentioning:

- The *require* relation between a parent and its refine-child does not imply that the child cannot be selected into a product without its parent. Despite the fact that it corresponds to the common case, this has to be explicitly marked with another, oppositely directed *require* relation. Consider the following example (Figure 5):

  – Feature *A*: Change existing phone number.
  – Subfeature *B*: Retrieve the number.
  – Subfeature *C*: Edit the number.
  – Subfeature *D*: Store the number.

  The "Edit the number" feature can surely be selected in a product without selecting the others. For example, it could be used to edit a new number.

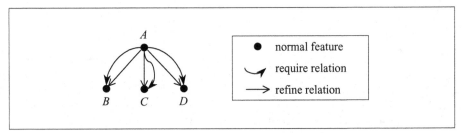

Fig. 5. Independent Subfeatures

- In contrast with the previous example, a refine-child may require its parent; it cannot exist independently in the product. Here's an example (Figure 6):

  – Feature *A*: There can be multiple phone numbers per phonebook name entry.
  – Subfeature *B*: There is a default phone number.

  Of course, it makes no sense to include "There is a default phone number" in a handset that is not capable of storing multiple phone numbers per name.

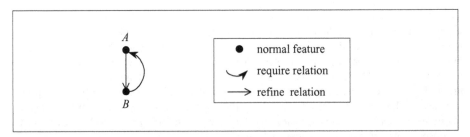

Fig. 6. Dependent Subfeature

In the FODA [2] approach, the optional or mandatory characteristics of a feature are explicitly stated in the model. Our meta-model contains the same information in an implicit manner, expressed using the *require* relation linking the parent feature to refine-children.

2.4.1.2.   The Conflict Relation

The *conflict* relation declares the incompatibility of two features: features that are in *conflict* relation cannot be selected in the same product.

At this point, it is worth recalling that the *provided-by* relation is able to express the "requires at least one" semantics. Therefore, the combination of the two can be used to express the "requires exactly one" semantics. This is achieved by marking the children of a pseudo-feature that conflict with each other.

Conflict is obviously a symmetric relation.

As previously presented, the FODA method [2] defines the term of *alternative features* and requires them to be explicitly shown in the feature model. As described above, the combination of the *provided-by* and the *conflict* relations can be used to represent the same configuration, as demonstrated on Figure 7, where features *B*, *C* and *D* are the alternatives.

We found our solution to be a more flexible way to express specialization, since, in contrast with the FODA approach we are not restricted to selecting only one child from the provided-by children. The desired set of the valid combinations can be produced with the help of *conflict* and *require* relations.

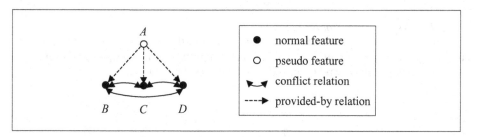

Fig. 7. Representing Alternative Features using the *Provided-By* and *Conflict* Relations

2.4.1.3.   Product Consistency

To conclude the discussion of the consistency relations, the conditions of product consistency should be established. A product is consistent, if

- with the selection of a particular feature for a product, all features that are in a *require* relation with this feature are also selected;
- with the selection of a pseudo-feature for a product, at least one feature that is in a *provided-by* relation with the given feature is also selected;
- there are no *conflict* relations between any of the features selected for a product.

2.4.2.   The *Modify* Relation and Feature Property Types

The motivation behind the introduction of the *modify* relation described in this section is best shown through two examples.

- Let feature *A* denote the handset's capability of storing names in the phonebook. As the storage capacity is limited, feature *A* must be parameterized with the maximum length of the name. The maximum length becomes *A*'s property P_A. Let feature *B* represent the handset's ability to place the phonebook in the handset's own memory, whereas feature *C* shows that the phonebook can be stored on the SIM card as well. The phonebook stored on the SIM card must comply with stricter length limitations than the one stored in the handset's own memory. The selection of *B* or *C* into the product clearly affects the value of P_A; therefore P_A depends on the existence of *B* or *C*.
- Let features *A* and *B* have the same meaning as in the previous example. *A*'s property P_A denotes the total number of entries, whereas *B*'s property P_B reflects the size of the memory reserved for the phonebook. Property P_B modifies property P_A, since the number of the storable entries depends on the capacity of the memory where we store them.

Information on the dependencies of properties is not ignorable. Both examples justify the introduction of a new dependency relation, which enables the modeling of the situations outlined above. The first example calls for a dependency relation between (the existence of) a feature and a property; meanwhile, the second example requires a dependency relation involving two properties. We propose the introduction of the *modify* relation.

2.4.2.1.   Types of the Modify Relation

The first example requires a type of *modify* relation that shows the direct effect that the selection/deselection of a feature has on a property. For this purpose, it is referred to as an *existence modify* relation. Figure 8 proposes the notation.

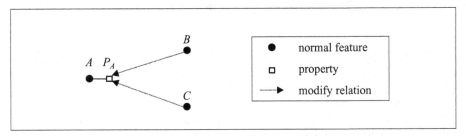

Fig. 8. The *Existence Modify* Relation

The second example implies a *modify* relation, which captures the effect that the change of a property value has on another property value. To reflect the nature of the dependency, it will be referred to as *value modify* relation. Figure 9 shows the notation.

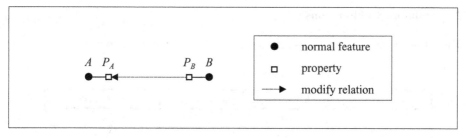

Fig. 9. The *Value Modify* Relation

2.4.2.2.   The Types of Properties
A careful look at feature properties can reveal further useful information for the product line engineers. Establishing the degree to which the property's value is likely to change is valuable configuration information in creating software assets. We have found the following three categories to be relevant:

- A property can have a fixed value throughout all products in the product line. These properties are typically determined by the hardware's characteristics, for example the dimensions/resolution of the handset's display. The property becomes a constant and can be treated accordingly in subsequent development phases. In this case, we regard this property as "fixed".
- A property's value could vary from product to product. A typical case is the phonebook capacity. These properties are called "family-variable".
- Finally, a property's value can vary within a product. For example, the length of the text buffer that holds the user input varies depending on the type of the edited information: a note attached to a phonebook entry is allowed to contain more characters than a name does. We call these properties "variable".

As *modify* relations express dependencies between properties and other features, or other features' properties, an examination of modify-relation chains leading to a particular property may reveal that the initial categorization of the property's type was incorrect. Such analysis is the object of Section 3.2.

2.4.2.3.   The Transitiveness of the Modify Relation
The *modify* relation is not transitive in the exact sense. In light of the previous section, we are, however, very interested in how the following are spread along the *modify* relations:

- how the effects of selecting/deselecting a feature in a product, and
- how the changes in values of properties

For example, if variable property P_A modifies family-variable property P_B, then P_B must become variable as well. Assuming that the modify chain is closed by family-variable property P_C modified by P_B, P_C becomes variable too because of the change in type of P_B. In this sense, change in type propagates over the chain of *modify* relations, and this fact attaches quasi-transitive characteristics to the relation. Section 3.2 discusses this problem in detail.

2.5. Summary of Relations

The following table summarizes the relations defined in the first two planes.

Table 1 Properties of Inter-Feature Relations

	Reflexive	Symmetric	Transitive
Refine	No	No	No
Provided-by	No	No	Yes
Require	No	No	Yes
Conflict	No	Yes	No
Modify	No	No	Quasi-transitive

2.6. Feature Sets

The last element of the meta-model is the *feature set*. These sets are the means for grouping features from an arbitrary point of view, such as market segment, mission, quality, and importance. The overall driving factor behind the introduction of feature sets is to reflect stakeholder-specific views and to help the orientation among features. In addition, feature sets may prove to be a useful tool in the hands of a product line engineer in reducing the complexity of feature models that contain a large number of features. Feature sets do not share any characteristics with features and they do not participate in any previously defined meta-model relation.

The rules of forming sets are rather simple. Feature sets can only contain features, but not other feature sets. If a feature belongs to a particular set, the descendants of this feature (reachable by *refine* and *provided-by* relations) will also be included.

2.7. Bringing the Meta-Model Elements Together

The Unified Modeling Language (UML) class diagram presented in Figure 10 shows the meta-model elements defined so far. Figure 11 presents a breakdown to planes of a simple feature model.

According to [10], our meta-model can be easily transformed into a Prolog program. Such a conversion is an important step towards automated consistency checking and commonality and variability analysis.

3   Commonality and Variability Analysis

The proposed meta-model enables a different approach to feature modeling, and to commonality and variability analysis in particular. Established approaches, such as the FODA method [2], would identify the variance during model creation and represent it explicitly in the model. More precisely, when using the FODA method in a particular domain, features are typically categorized on the surface as mandatory, optional or alternative (see [2]). In contrast, our approach incorporates variance

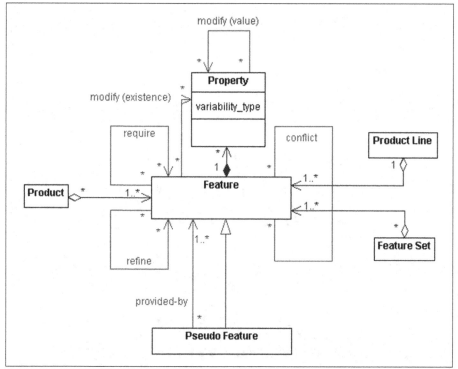

Fig. 10. UML Representation of the Meta-Model

information into the model implicitly using relations. Explicit information on commonality and variability is extracted from the model with the help of automated analysis.

What is commonality or variability? The feature model built using the proposed meta-model structures the features of a product line into a hierarchy (see Section 2.3). Features are cross-linked with *require* and *modify* relations (see Section 2.4). Commonality is the set of features that is obtained by selecting certain features of the feature model using a particular algorithm; the selection algorithm relies on the previously enumerated dependency relations. Variabilities are all the features that remain unselected. Subsequent sections will describe the algorithm in detail.

3.1.   Commonality Detection Using *Require* and *Refine* Relations

3.1.1.   The Set of Required Features

An important step in the commonality and variability analysis is to find the features that are selected into any product as a result of another feature being selected. These features are referred to as *the set of required features*. In the definition of the algorithm that creates the set of required features, we rely upon the term of transitive closure:

> *The transitive closure of a vertex in a directed graph is the set of vertices reachable by a directed path from the given vertex.*

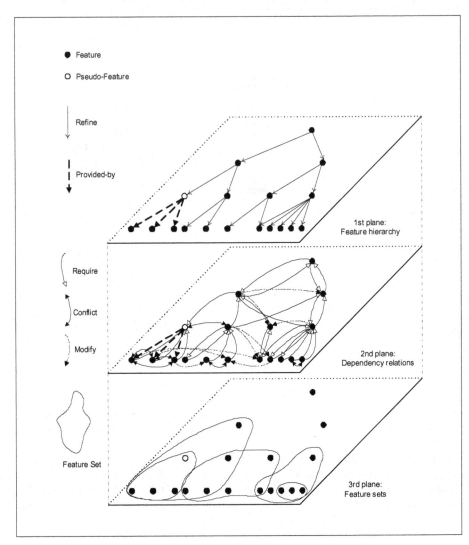

Fig. 11. The Three Planes of the Model

Let us consider the graph formed by the features together with *refine* and *provided-by* relations. At first glance, one would expect that the transitive closure of a feature using solely the *require* relation identifies the set of required features. Unfortunately, the situation is not as straightforward as it seems, as the *provided-by* relations must be also considered. As stated in Section 2.3.2, the features that are in *provided-by* relation with a particular pseudo-feature implicitly inherit the refine-linked descendants. Consequently, when a provided-by child is included in the set of required features, the refine-linked descendants of its provided-by parents must also be included. To summarize:

the set of required features (of a particular feature) can be obtained by creating the transitive closure of the given feature, using both the require and the oppositely directed provided-by relations.

Figure 12 visualizes the concept of the set of required features.

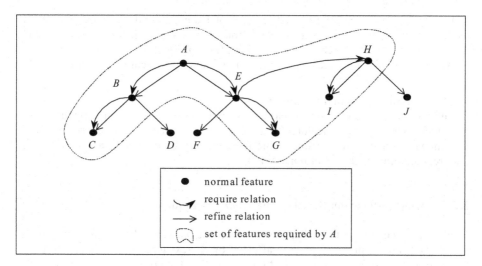

Fig. 12. The Set of Required Features

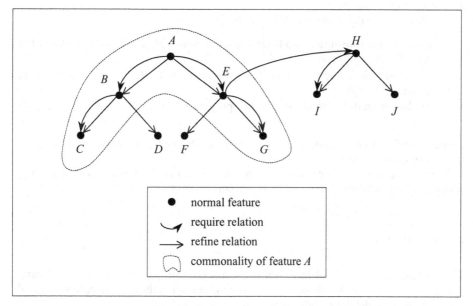

Fig. 13. Commonality of a Feature

3.1.2.   The Commonality of a Feature
The commonality of a feature is formed by those descendants, which are always selected into a product when their parent is selected. More precisely:

> *The commonality of a feature is the intersection of the set of its required features and its descendants in the feature hierarchy.*

Let R_A denote the set of required features of feature A, and H_A denote the set of features that are in the hierarchy starting from A. The commonality is $H_A \cap R_A$, and the variability of A is the remaining part of H_A, (i.e., $H_A \setminus R_A$).

An example of finding the commonality of a feature is presented in Figure 13.

3.1.3.   Commonality in a Product Line
Let us introduce a new top-level feature that requires, and it is refined by, all those (now) former top-level features that are surely selected for every product. Commonality in the product line is the commonality of the newly added top-level feature; variability is the set of remaining features.

3.2.   Variance Detection Based on the *Modify* Relation

Due to the quasi-transitive characteristics of the *modify* relation, the type of a particular feature's property may be affected by the existence of another feature, or the type of another property (see Section 2.4.2). This type of dependency may cause the initial perception of a property's type to be inaccurate. Since inaccuracies affect the usefulness of the feature model, the goal is to establish for each property its precise type of variance.

Variance can be detected by relying on the following rules:

- If the existence of feature A modifies feature B's property P_B, then P_B must be of at least family-variable type.
- If family-variable property P_A modifies another property P_B, then P_B must be of at least family-variable type.
- If variable property P_A modifies another property P_B, then P_B must be of variable type.

Using the rules above, property types should be checked repeatedly, until no more type changes are induced.

Note that the analyses presented in Section 3 can be implemented easily using simple Depth or Breadth First Search algorithms.

4   Further Work

The proposed feature model has been tried in a pilot project. Besides the promising results, the assessment has also revealed some cases when the defined relations could not accurately model the feature dependencies.

Let us take the following example from the phonebook domain. First, a quick reminder on the phonebook features: the mobile terminal phonebook domain contains the capability of storing multiple phone numbers per name (Feature A) and the functionality of Memory Copy (Feature B) too. When phonebook entries are transferred from the mobile terminal's memory (which can store multiple phone numbers per name) to the SIM card's memory (which is not able to store multiple phone numbers per name), a single number should be selected to be copied to the destination memory. A straightforward solution for this is to copy the default number. Let us call this feature Copy Default Number (Feature C). It is clear that if a particular product is able to store multiple phone numbers per name *AND* it has the Memory Copy functionality too, the CopyDefaultNumber feature should be also selected in the product. In other cases this feature is not needed. This dependency is different from the previously discussed ones. In this case, the selection of a feature is required when two other features are *simultaneously* present in a product. It is obvious that we are unable to express relationships of this type using the relations defined in our meta-model proposal.

The examples in which the expressiveness of the model is not satisfactory are rare, but of various sorts. Therefore, it is not a viable option to create a meta-model element to cover each particular exception. It seems much more rational to adopt a generic solution for the problem: to enhance the expressiveness, besides the relations, arbitrary sentential (zero-order) logic expressions should be employed to constrain the validity of products. Each product formed using the features of the product line must satisfy all of these constraints. The sentential variables in the expressions denote the existence of a feature in a product: for example, A in such an expression is true, if feature A is selected in the particular product.

Using this method in the example above, we would denote the discussed dependency as

$$A \wedge B \mapsto C$$

The consistency relations of the meta-model could be transformed very easily in such formulas:

A *require* B becomes $A \mapsto B$

A *conflict* B becomes $\neg(A \wedge B)$

A *provided-by* (B, C, D) becomes $A \mapsto (B \vee C \vee D)$

The question arises: why do we need the consistency relations defined in Section 2.4.1 at all, when we are able to express all the needed constraints using the logical expressions? The answer is relatively simple. Although more powerful, a model based only on logical expression to formulate dependencies would totally lack the visual expressiveness, and without a predefined set of relations to rely on, the model building would be considerably more difficult.

As a topic of further research, we would like to investigate the feasibility of integrating the elements of this idea in the proposed meta-model and the related algorithms[2].

---

[2] We should note, that the application of arbitrary complex logical expressions also has a serious impact on the algorithms designed for commonality and variability analysis.

5   Conclusions

The aim of this paper was to propose a meta-model extension that overcomes the deficiencies that the FODA method [2] has in its feature-modeling approach. To put the theory into practice and validate the results, we have created a feature model for the phonebook domain using the meta-model in question. The resulting formal model was well structured and consistent, despite handling a rather large number of features. The idea of automated analysis proved to be helpful in eliciting commonality and variability in this domain. As an additional benefit of the straightforward set of relations and expressiveness of the meta-model, many hidden inconsistencies in the specifications could also be revealed.

Acknowledgements

We would like to thank to Egmont Koblinger, Tuomo Vehkomäki, Dániel Varró and József Bíró for their helpful and valuable comments.

References

1. Clements, Paul; Northrop, Linda. Software Product Lines: Practices and Patterns. Addison-Wesley, 2001.
2. Kang, Kyo C.; Cohen, Sholom G.; Hess, James A.; Novak, William E. & Peterson, A. Spencer. Feature-Oriented Domain Analysis (FODA) Feasibility Study. (CMU/SEI-90-TR-21, ADA235785). Pittsburgh, PA: Software Engineering Institute, Carnegie Mellon University, 1990.
3. Chastek, Gary; Donohoe, Patrick; Kang, Kyo Chul; & Thiel, Steffen. Product Line Analysis: A Practical Introduction (CMU/ SEI-2001-TR-001). Pittsburgh, PA: Software Engineering Institute, Carnegie Mellon University, 2001.
4. Kuusela, Juha; Savolainen, Juha. Requirements Engineering for Product Families. ICSE 2000, Limeric, Ireland, 4-11 June 2000.
5. Tuovinen, Antti-Pekka; Xu, Jianli. Experiences in Modeling Feature Interactions with Coloured Petri Nets. 7th Symposium on Programming Languages and Software Tools, Szeged, Hungary, June 15-16, 2001.
6. CMU Software Engineering Institute. A Framework for Software Product Line Practice – version 3. http://www.sei.cmu.edu/plp/framework.html.
7. DeBaud, Jean-Marc; Schmid, Klaus. A Practical Comparison of Major Domain Analysis Approaches – Towards a Customizable Domain Analysis Framework. 10th International Conference on Software Engineering and Knowledge Engineering, San Francisco, June 18-20, 1998.
8. Savolainen, Juha; Schmid, Klaus; Tosch, Siegfried; Tuovinen, Antti-Pekka; Vehkomäki, Tuomo. Feature Analysis. ESAPS project (http://www.esi.es/esaps) document, 2001.
9. Czarnecki, Krzysztof. Generative Programming: Principles and Techniques of Software Engineering Based on Automated Configuration and Fragment Based Component Models. Ph.D. thesis, Technische Universität Ilmenau, 1988.

Feature-Based Product Line Instantiation
Using Source-Level Packages*

Arie van Deursen[1], Merijn de Jonge[1], and Tobias Kuipers[2]

[1] Centrum voor Wiskunde en Informatica(CWI)
P.O. Box 94079, 1090 GB Amsterdam, The Netherlands
Arie.van.Deursen@cwi.nl, http://www.cwi.nl/~arie
Merijn.de.Jonge@cwi.nl, http://www.cwi.nl/~mdejonge
[2] Software Improvement Group
Kruislaan 419, 1098 VA Amsterdam, The Netherlands
tk@software-improvers.com, http://www.software-improvers.com/

Abstract. In this paper, we discuss the construction of software products from customer-specific feature selections. We address variability management with the Feature Description Language (FDL) to capture variation points of product line architectures. We describe feature packaging, which covers selecting and packaging implementation components according to feature selections using the autobundle tool. Finally, we discuss a generic approach, based on the abstract factory design pattern, to make instantiated (customer-specific) variability accessible in applications.

The solutions and techniques presented in this paper are based on our experience with the product line architecture of the commercial documentation generator DocGen.

1 Introduction

This paper deals with three key issues in software product lines: variability management, feature packaging, and product line instantiation. It covers these topics based on our experience in the design, implementation, and deployment of DocGen, a commercial product line in the area of documentation generation for legacy systems.

Like many product lines, DocGen started out as a single product dedicated to a particular customer. It was followed by modifications to this product for a series of subsequent customers, who all wanted a similar documentation generator that was specialized to their specific needs. Gradually, a kernel generator evolved, which could be instantiated to dedicated documentation requirements. DocGen is still evolving, and each new customer may introduce functionality that affects the kernel generator. This may involve the need for additional variation points in DocGen, or the introduction of functionality that is useful to a broad range of customers meriting inclusion in the standard DocGen setup.

The business model we use to accommodate such an evolving product line specialized to the needs of many different customers is based on subscription: on a regular basis,

---

* This research was sponsored in part by the Dutch Telematica Instituut, project DSL.

G. Chastek (Ed.): SPLC2 2002, LNCS 2379, pp. 217–234, 2002.

customers can install a new DocGen version that is guaranteed to be compatible with that customer's specializations. For the customer, this has the advantage of access to benefits from DocGen extensions; For the supplier, it has the advantage of a continuous revenue flow instead of harder-to-predict large lump sums when selling a particular product.

The technological challenges of this business model and its corresponding evolutionary product line development are significant. In particular, product line evolution must be organized such that it can deal with many different customers. In this paper, we cover three related issues that are very helpful in addressing this problem.

Our first topic is managing the variation points, which are likely to change at each release. When discussing the use of DocGen with a potential customer, it must be clear what the variability of the current system is. The new customer may have additional wishes which may require the creation of new variation points, extending or modifying the existing interfaces. Moreover, marketing, customer support, or the product manager may come up with ideas for new functionality, which will also affect the variability. In Section 3, we study the use of the Feature Description Language (FDL) described in [8] to capture such a changing variability.

The second issue we cover is managing the source-code components implementing the variability. The features selected by a customer should be mapped to appropriately configured software components. In Section 4, we describe our approach, which emphasizes developing product line components separately, using internally released software *packages*. Assembling a product from these packages consists of merging the sources of these packages, as well as the corresponding build processes – a technique called *source tree composition* [15]. Packages can implement either a feature or functionality shared by other packages.

The third topic we address is managing customer code, that is, the instantiated variability. The same feature can be implemented slightly differently for different customers. In Section 5, we propose an extension of the abstract factory to achieve the appropriate packaging and configuration of customer code.

In Section 6, we summarize our approach, contrast it with related work, and describe future directions. Before we dive into that, we provide a short introduction to the DocGen product line in Section 2.

2   A Documentation Generation Product Line

In this section, we introduce the product line DocGen [9,10], which we will use as our case study throughout the paper. Our discussion of DocGen follows the format used by Bosch to present his software product line case studies [5].

2.1   Company Background

DocGen is the flagship product of the Software Improvement Group (SIG), a company based in Amsterdam, The Netherlands that offers solutions to businesses facing problems with the maintenance and evolution of software systems. The SIG was founded in 2000 and is a spin-off of academic research in the area of reverse and reengineering conducted at CWI from 1996 to 1999. On result of this research was a prototype documentation generator described by [9], which was the starting point for the DocGen product family now offered by the SIG.

2.2 Product Family

The SIG delivers a range of documentation generation products. These products vary in the source languages analyzed (such as SQL, Cobol, JCL, 4GL's, proprietary languages, and so on) as well as the way in which the derived documentation is to be presented.

Each DocGen product operates by populating a repository with a series of facts derived from legacy sources. These facts are used to derive web-based documentation for the systems analyzed. This documentation includes textual summaries, overviews, various forms of control-flow graphs, architectural information, and so on. Information is available at different levels of abstraction, which are connected through hyperlinks.

DocGen customers have different wishes regarding the languages to be analyzed, the specific set of analyses to be performed, and the way in which the collected information should be retrieved. Thus, DocGen is a software product line, providing a set of reusable assets well-suited to express and implement different customized documentation generation systems.

2.3 Technology

At present, DocGen is an object-oriented application framework written in Java.[1] It uses a relational database to store facts derived from legacy sources and provides a range of core classes for analysis and presentation purposes. In order to instantiate family members, a Java package specific to a given customer is created, containing specializations of core classes where needed, including methods called by the DocGen factory for producing the actual DocGen instantiation. DocGen consists of approximately 850 Java classes, 750 Java classes generated from language definitions, 250 Java classes used for continuous testing, and roughly 50 shell and Perl scripts.

In addition to the key classes, DocGen makes use of external packages, for example for graph-drawing purposes.

2.4 Organization

Since the SIG is a relatively small company, the development team tries to work as closely together as possible. For that reason, there is no explicit separation between a core product line development team and project teams responsible for building bespoke customer products. Instead, these are roles that are rotated throughout the entire team.

A dedicated person is assigned for each product instantiation, in order to fulfill the customer role. This person is responsible for accepting or rejecting the product derived from DocGen for a particular customer.

---

[1] Java and all Java-based marks are trademarks of Sun Microsystems, Inc. in the U.S. and other countries.

2.5 Process

The construction of DocGen is characterized by evolutionary design and is being developed following the principles of extreme programming [4]. DocGen started as a research prototype described by [9]. This prototype was not implemented as a reusable framework; instead it just produced documentation as desired by one particular customer. As the commercial interest in applications of DocGen grew, more and more variation points were introduced, evolving DocGen into a system suitable for deriving many different documentation generation systems.

With the number of customer configurations growing, it is time to rethink the way in which DocGen product instantiations are created, and what sort of variability the DocGen product line should offer.

3 Analyzing Variability

3.1 Feature Descriptions

To explore the variability of software product lines, we use the FDL discussed by [8]. This is essentially a textual representation for the feature diagrams of the Feature-Oriented Domain Analysis method (FODA) [16].

A feature can be *atomic* or *composite*. We will use the convention that names of atomic features start with a lowercase letter, and names of composite features start with an uppercase letter. Note that atomic and composite features are called features and subconcepts, respectively, in [7].

An FDL definition consists of a number of *feature definitions*: a feature name followed by a colon (:) and a *feature expression*. A feature expression can consist of

- an atomic feature;
- a composite feature: a named feature whose definition appears elsewhere;
- an optional feature: a feature expression followed by "?";
- mandatory features: a list of feature expressions enclosed in `all ( )`;
- alternative features: a list of feature expressions enclosed in `one-of ( )`;
- selection of features:[2] a list of feature expressions enclosed in `more-of ( )`;
- features of the form . . ., indicating that a given set is not completely specified.

An FDL definition generates all possible feature configurations, also called *product instances*. Feature configurations are flat sets of features of the form $all(a_1, \ldots, a_n)$, where each a_i denotes an atomic feature. In [8], a series of FDL manipulations is described, to convert any FDL definition into a *disjunctive normal form* defined as

$$\texttt{one-of}(\ \texttt{all}(a_{11}, \ldots, a_{1n_1}), \ldots, \ \texttt{all}(a_{m1}, \ldots, a_{mn_m}))$$

By converting an FDL definition into disjunctive normal form, a feature expression is obtained that lists all possible configurations.

Feature combinations can be further restricted via *constraints*. We will adopt the following constraints:

---

[2] Called "or-features" in [7].

– A1 requires A2: if feature A1 is present, then feature A2 should also be present
– A1 excludes A2: if feature A1 is present, then feature A2 should not be present

Such constraints are called *diagram constraints* since they express fixed, inherent dependencies between features in a diagram.

DocGen :
  all(Analysis, Presentation, Database)
Analysis :
  all(LanguageAnalysis, *versionManagement?*, *subsystems?*)
LanguageAnalysis :
  more-of(Cobol, *jcl*, *sql*, *delphi*, *progress*, **...**)
Cobol :
  one-of(*ibm-cobol*, *microfocus-cobol*, **...**)
Presentation :
  all(Localization, Interaction, MainPages, Visualizations?)
Localization :
  more-of(*english*, *dutch*)
Interaction :
  one-of(*static*, *dynamic*)
MainPages :
  more-of(ProgramPage, *copybookPage*, StatisticsPage, *indexes*, *searchPage*,
          subsystemPage, *sourcePage*, *sourceDifference*, **...**)
ProgramPage :
  more-of(*annotationSection*, *activationSection*, *entitiesSection*, *parametersSection*, **...**)
StatisticsPage :
  one-of(*statsWithHistory*, *statsNoHistory*)
Visualizations :
  more-of(*performGraph*, *conditionalPerformGraph*, *jclGraph*, *subsystemGraph*,
          overviewGraph, **...**)
Database :
  one-of(*db2*, *oracle*, *mysql*, **...**)

Fig. 1. Some Configurable Features of the DocGen Product Line Expressed in the Feature Description Language (FDL)

3.2 DocGen Features

A selection of the variable features of DocGen and some of their constraints are shown in Figures 1 and 2. The features listed describe the variation points in the current version of DocGen. One of the goals of constructing the FDL specification of these features is to search for alternative ways in which to organize the variable features, in order to optimize the configuration process of DocGen family members. Another goal of the FDL specification is to help structure/restructure the implementation of product lines.

The features listed focus on just the Analysis and Presentation configuration of DocGen, as specified by the first dependency of Figure 1. The Database feature in that dependency will not be discussed here.

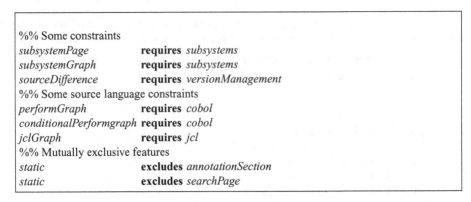

Fig. 2. Constraints on Variable DocGen Features

The Analysis features show how the DocGen analysis can be influenced by specifying source languages that DocGen should be able to process. The per-language parsing will actually populate a data base, which can then be used for further analysis.

Other features are optional. For example, *versionManagement* can be switched on, so that differences between documented sources can be seen over time. When a system to be documented contains subsystems that need to be taken into account, the *subsystems* feature can be set.

The Presentation features affect the way in which the facts contained in the repository are presented to DocGen end users. For example, the Localization feature indicates which languages are supported, such as English and Dutch. At compile time, one or more supported languages can be selected; at runtime, the end user can use a web browser's localization scheme to actually select a language.

The Interaction feature determines the moment the HTML pages are generated. In *dynamic* interaction, a page is created whenever the end user requests a page. This has two advantages: the pages always use the most up-to-date information from the repository, and interactive browsing is possible. In *static* mode, all pages are generated in advance. This also has two advantages: no web server is needed to inspect the data, and the data can be viewed easily on a disconnected laptop. As we will see, the Interaction feature puts constraints on other presentation features.

The MainPages feature indicates the contents of the root page of the derived documentation. It is a list of standard pages that can be reused and implemented as a many-to-one association to subclasses of an abstract "Page" class. Of these, ProgramPage consists of one or more sections.

In addition to pages, the presentation features include various Visualizations. These are all optional, allowing a customer to choose either plain (HTML) documentation (which requires less software to be installed at the client side) or graphically enhanced documentation (which requires plug-ins to be installed).

3.3   DocGen Feature Constraints

Figure 2 lists several constraints restricting the number of valid DocGen configurations of the features listed in Figure 1.

The pages that can be presented depend on the analyses that are conducted. If we want to show a *subsystemGraph*, we need to have selected *subsystems*. Some features are language specific: a *jclGraph* can only be shown when *jcl* is one of the analyzed languages.

Last but not least, certain features are in conflict with each other. In particular, the *annotationSection* can be used to let the end user interactively add annotations to pages, which are then stored in the repository. This is only possible in the dynamic version and cannot be done if the Interaction is set to *static*. The same holds true for the dynamic *searchPage*.

3.4   Evaluation

Developing and maintaining a feature description for an existing application, gives a clear understanding of the application's variability. It can be used not only during product instantiation, but also when discussing the design of the product line. For example, discussions about the DocGen feature description have resulted in the discovery of several potential inconsistencies, as well as suggestions for resolving them.

One of the problems with using feature descriptions is that feature dependencies can be defined in multiple ways, for instance as a composite feature definition or as a combination of a feature definition and constraints. We are still experimenting with these different constructs to develop heuristics about when to use each one.

4   Software Assembly

4.1   Source-Tree Composition

Source-tree composition is the process of assembling software systems by merging reusable source-code components. A *source tree* is defined as a collection of source files, together with *build instructions*, divided in a directory hierarchy [15]. We call the source tree of a particular part of a product line architecture a *source-code component*. Source-code components can be developed, maintained, tested, and released individually.

Source-tree *composition* involves merging source trees, build processes, and configuration processes. It results in a single source tree with centralized build and configuration processes [15].

Source-tree composition requires abstractions over source-code components, which are called *package definitions* (see Figure 3). They capture information about the component such as its dependencies on other components and its configuration parameters. Package definitions as the one in Figure 3 are called *concrete* package definitions because they correspond directly to an implementing source-code component. *Abstract* package definitions, on the other hand, do not correspond to implementing source-code components. They only combine existing packages and set configuration options. Abstract package definitions are distinguished from concrete package definitions by having an empty location field (see Figure 5).

```
package
identification
        name=docgen
        version=2.4
        location=http://www.software-improvers.com/packages
            info=http://www.software-improvers.com
    description='DocGen, documentation generation tool.'
    keywords=docgen, documentation generation, core
configuration interface
customer'name identifying customer-specific issues'
requires
    html-lib     1.5    with xml-support=on
    gnuregexp 1.1.4
    junit        3.5
```

Fig. 3. Example of a package definition for the DocGen core package. The 'configuration interface' section lists configurable items together with corresponding short descriptions. The 'requires' section defines package dependencies and their configuration.

After selecting the components of need, a software *bundle* (containing all corresponding source trees) is obtained through a process called *package normalization*. This process includes package dependency and version resolution, build order arrangement, configuration distribution, and bundle interface construction. We refer to [15] for a complete description of source-tree composition.

Package definitions are stored centrally in *package repositories* which can be accessed by developers to search for reusable packages. They are also accessed by the autobundle tool (see below) to resolve package dependencies automatically when assembling product instances.

Source-tree composition is supported and automated by autobundle[3] [15]. Given a set of package names, autobundle (i) obtains their package definitions from package repositories; (ii) calculates the transitive closure of all required packages; (iii) calculates a (partial) configuration of the individual packages; (iv) generates a self-contained source tree by merging the source trees of all required packages; and (v) integrates the configuration and build processes of all bundled packages.

4.2   Source-Tree Composition in Product Lines

With the help of autobundle, assembling products on a product line can become as simple as selecting the necessary packages. Autobundle is used to bundle them together with required packages into self-contained customer-specific source distributions.

Package selection can be performed by developers by accessing (online) package repositories (see Figure 4) and selecting the packages of need. By pressing the "bundle" button, autobundle is instructed to generate the desired software bundle.

---

[3] The   autobundle   tool   is   free   and   available   for   download   at
http://www.cwi.nl/~mdejonge/autobundle.

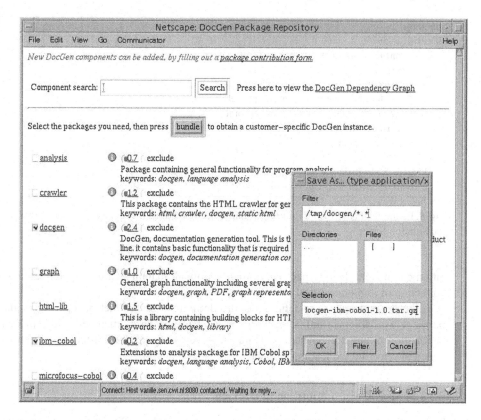

Fig. 4. Screenshot of an Experimental Online Package Repository From Which Implementing DocGen Packages Can Be Selected to Assemble DocGen Product Instances

By manually selecting concrete packages from an online package repository, a developer maps a selection of features to a corresponding selection of implementing source-code components. This is called product configuration. The manual selection of packages forms an implicit relation between features (in the problem space) and implementation (in the solution space).

This relation between problem and solution space is a many-to-many relation: a single feature can be implemented in more than one source-code package; a single source-code package can implement multiple features. Selecting a feature therefore may yield a configuration of a single source-code package that implements multiple features (to turn the selected feature on), or it may result in bundling a collection of packages that implement the feature together.

The relation between problem and solution space can be defined more explicitly in abstract package definitions. Abstract package definitions then correspond directly to features according to the feature description of a product line architecture (see Figure 5). The 'requires' section of abstract packages defines dependencies upon abstract and/or concrete packages. The latter define how to map (part of) a feature to an implemen-

```
package
identification
        name=c3-project
      version=1.7
      location=
          info=http://www.software-improvers.com/c3
   description='DocGen instance for customer C3.'
    keywords=customers, c3
configuration interface
requires
   docgen  2.4 with customer=c3
   analysis 1.2 with language=cobol
```

Fig. 5. Example of an *Abstract* Package Definition Which Forms a Mapping From the Problem to the Solution Space.

tation component. During package normalization, all mappings are applied, yielding a collection of implementation components.

Like concrete package definitions, the definitions of abstract packages can also be made available via online package bases. Package bases then serve to represent application-oriented concepts and features. Assembling product instances is then reduced to selecting the features of need.

4.3 Source-Tree Composition in DocGen

To benefit from source-tree composition to easily assemble different product instances, the source tree of the DocGen product line needs to be split up. Different parts of the product line then become separate source-code components. Every feature as described in the FDLs should be contained in a single package. This package can be either abstract or concrete. These packages may depend on other core or library packages that do not implement an externally perceivable feature, but implement general functionality.

Implementing each feature as a separate package promises a clean separation of features in the source code. Whether one feature (implementation) depends on another can be easily seen in the feature description. Currently, the coupling between the *feature* selection and the selected *packages* is an informal one. More experience is needed to know whether this scheme will always work.

The source-code components that implement a feature or general functionality are released internally as *source-code packages* (i.e., versioned distributions of source-code components as discussed in Section 4.1). These packages are subjected to an explicit release policy. The reuse of software in different product instances is based only on released source-code components. This release and reuse policy allows different versions of a component to coexist seamlessly. Furthermore, it allows developers to control when to upgrade to a new version of a component.

Apart from the packages that implement the individual features, there are several packages implementing general functionality. Of these, the docgen package implements the user interface of the software analysis side of DocGen, as well as things like the infrastructure to process files and read them from disk. It also implements the Application Service Provider interface where customers offer their sources over the Internet.

In order to generate the final presentation of DocGen in HTML, the `html-lib` package provides us with the grammar of HTML and a number of interfaces to generate files in HTML. The various graphical representations used in DocGen are bundled in the `graph` package which knows how to present generic graphs as PDF files.

The DocGen source-code components are stored in the DocGen package repository (see Figure 4) from which customer-specific source trees are assembled. The compilation of such assembled source trees is performed at the SIG to obtain customer products in binary form. The so-obtained products are then packaged and delivered to our customers.

4.4   Evaluation

Source-tree composition applied to a product line, such as DocGen, results in a number of benefits. Probably the most important one is that when using source-tree composition, it is much easier to exclude functionality from the product line. This may be necessary if customers only want to use a "low-budget" edition. Moreover, it can be crucial for code developed specifically for a particular customer: such code may contain essential knowledge of a customer's business, which should not be shared with other customers.

A second benefit of using packages for managing variation points is that it simplifies product instantiation. By using a package repository as derived by `autobundle`, features can be selected easily, resulting in the correct composition of appropriately configured packages.

Another benefit is that by putting variable features into separate packages, the source tree is split into a series of separate source-code components that can be maintained individually and independently. This solves various problems involved in monolithic source trees, such as: i) long development/test/integration cycles; ii) limited possibilities for safe simultaneous development due to undocumented dependencies between parts of the source tree; and iii) no version management and release policy for individual components. Explicitly released packages that have explicitly documented dependencies help to resolve these issues.

Special attention should be paid to so-called *crosscutting* features. An example is the aforementioned localization feature, which potentially affects any presentation package. Such features result in a (global) configuration switch indicating that the feature is switched on. Observe that the implementation of these features can make use of existing mechanisms to deal with crosscutting behavior, such as aspect-oriented programming [17]: the use of source-tree composition does not prescribe or exclude any implementation technique.

5   Managing Customer Code

5.1   Customer Packages

Instantiating the DocGen product line for a particular customer amounts to

- Selecting the variable features that should be included;

```
package docgen;
public class Layout
{
  ...
  String backgroundColor = "white";
  ...
}
```

Fig. 6. Part of the default Layout class

- Selecting the corresponding packages and setting the appropriate configuration switches;
- Writing the customer-specific code for those features that cannot be expressed as simple switches.

As the number of different customers increases, it becomes more and more important to manage such product instantiations in a controlled and predictable way. The first step is to adopt the source-tree composition approach discussed in Section 4 and create a separate *package* for each customer. First of all, this package contains customer-specific Java code. Moreover, it includes a package definition indicating precisely which (versions of) other DocGen packages it relies on and how they should be configured.

5.2 Customer Factories

Customer package definitions capture the package dependencies and configuration switches. In addition to this, the Java code implementing the packages should be organized in such a way that it can easily deal with many different variants and specializations for different customers. This involves the following challenges:

- DocGen core functionality must be able to create customer-specific *objects*, without becoming dependent on them;
- The overhead in instantiating DocGen for a new customer should be minimal;
- It must be simple to keep the existing customer code running when new DocGen variation points are created.

A partial solution is to adopt the *abstract factory* design pattern in order to deal with a range of different customers in a unified way [11]. Abstract factory "provides an interface for creating families of related or dependent objects without specifying their concrete classes". The participants of this pattern include

- An *abstract factory* interface for creating abstract products;
- Several *concrete factories*, one for each customer, for implementing the operations to create customer-specific objects;
- A range of *abstract products*, one for each type of product that needs to be extended with customer-specific behavior;
- Several *concrete products*: per abstract product, there can be different concrete products for each customer.

```
package docgen.customers.greenbank;
public class Layout extends docgen.Layout
{
  String backgroundColor = "green";
}
```

Fig. 7. The Layout class for customer Green Bank

- The *client* uses only the interfaces declared by the abstract factory and abstract products. In our case, this is the customer-independent DocGen kernel package.

The abstract factory solves the problem of creating customer-specific objects. Adopting the pattern as-is to a product line, however, is problematic if there are many different customers. Each customer will require a separate concrete factory. This can typically lead to code duplication, since many of these concrete factories will be similar.

To deal with this, we propose *customer factories* as an extension of the abstract factory design pattern. Instead of creating a concrete factory for each customer, we have one customer factory that uses a customer *name* to find customer-specific classes. Reflection is then used to create an instance of the appropriate customer-specific class.

As an example, consider the Layout class in Figure 6, in which the default background color of the user interface is set to "white". This class represents one of the *abstract products* of the factory pattern. The specialized version for customer green-bank is shown in Figure 7. The name of this class is the same, but it occurs in the specific greenbank package. Note that this is a Java package, which in turn can be part of an autobundle package.

Since the Layout class represents an abstract product, we offer a static getInstance factory method, which creates a layout object of the suitable type. We do this for every constructor of Layout.

As shown in Figure 8, this getInstance method is implemented using a static method located in a class called CustomerFactory. A key task of this method is to find the actual class that needs to be instantiated. For this, it uses the customer's name, which is read from a centralized property file. It first tries to locate the class:

```
docgen.customers.<current-customer-name>.Layout
```

If this class does not exist (e.g., because no customization is needed for this customer), the Layout class in the specified package is identified.

Once the class is determined, Java's reflection mechanism is used to invoke the actual constructor. For this, an array of objects representing the arguments needed for object instantiation is used. In the example, this array is empty.

5.3   Evaluation

The overall effect of customer packages and customer factories is that

- One autobundle package is created for each customer, which indicates exactly which packages are needed for this customer and how they should be configured;

```
package docgen;
public class Layout
{
  ...
  public static Layout getInstance()
  {
    return (Layout)CustomerFactory.getProductInstance(
                   docgen.Layout.class, new Object[]{});
  }
  ...
}
```

Fig. 8. Factory code for the `Layout` class.

- All customer-specific Java code is put in a separate Java package, which in turn is part of the customer's `autobundle` package;
- Adding new customers does *not* involve the creation of additional concrete factories: instead, the customer package is automatically searched for relevant class specializations;
- Turning an existing class into a variation point permitting customer-specific overriding is a *local* change: instead of an adaptation to the abstract factory used by all customers, it amounts to adding the appropriate `getInstance` method to the variation class.

A potential problem of using the *customer factory* pattern is that the heavy use of reflection may involve an efficiency penalty. For DocGen, this has not proven be a problem. If it is, *prototype instances* for each class can be put in a hash table and cloned whenever a new instance is needed. In that case, the use of reflection is limited to the construction of the hash table.

6   Concluding Remarks

6.1   Contributions

In this paper, we combined three techniques to develop and build a product line architecture. We used these techniques in practice for the DocGen application, but they might be of general interest when building other product lines.

Feature Descriptions. Feature descriptions live at the design level of the product line and serve to explore and capture the variability of a product line. They define features, feature interactions, and feature constraints declaratively. A feature description thus defines all possible instances of a product line architecture. A product instance is defined by making a feature selection that is valid with respect to the feature description.

Feature descriptions are also helpful in understanding the variability of a product during the development of a product line architecture. For instance, when migrating an existing software system into a product line architecture, they can help to (re)structure the system into source-code components, as we discussed in Section 4.3.

To assist the developer in making product instances, an interactive graphical representation of feature descriptions (for instance, based on feature diagrams or Customization Decision Trees (CDT) [14]) would be of great help. Ideally, constructing product instances from feature selections should be automated. The use of `autobundle` to automatically assemble source trees (see below) is a first step in this direction. Other approaches are described in [14,7].

Automated Source-Tree Composition. At the implementation level, we propose component-based software development and structuring of applications in separate source-code components. This helps to keep source trees small and manageable. Source-code components can be developed, maintained, and tested separately. An explicit release policy gives great control over which version of a component to use. It also helps to prevent a system from breaking down when components are being used and developed simultaneously. To assist developers in building product instances by assembling applications from different sets of source-code components, we propose automated source-tree composition. The `autobundle` tool can be used for this. Needed components can be selected easily and bundled automatically via online package repositories.

Package definitions can be made to represent features of a product on a product line. By making such (abstract) packages available via online package repositories, product instantiation becomes as easy as selecting the necessary features. After selecting the features, a self-contained source tree with an integrated build and configuration process is generated automatically.

Customer Configuration. When two customers want the same feature, but require slightly different functionality, we propose the notion of customer specializations. We developed a mechanism based on Java's reflection mechanism to manage such customer-specific functionality.

This mechanism allows an application to consist of a core set of classes, after source-tree composition, that implement the features as selected for this particular product instance. Customer specificity is accomplished by specializing the classes that are deemed customer specific based on a global customer setting. When no particular specialization is needed for a customer, the system will fall back on the default implementation. This allows us to implement only the actual differences between each customer and allows for the maximal reuse of code.

We implemented the customer-specific mechanism in Java. It could easily be implemented in other languages.

6.2   Related Work

The Reuse-driven Software Engineering Business (RSEB) covers many organizational and technical issues of software product lines [13]. It emphasizes an iterative process, in which an application family evolves. *Variation points* are distinguished both at the use-case and at the source-component level. Components are grouped into *component systems*, which are similar to our *abstract packages*. In certain cases, component systems implement the *facade* design pattern, which corresponds to a facade package in our setting that contains just the code to provide an integrated interface to the constituent packages.

FeatuRSEB is an extension of the RSEB with an explicit domain analysis phase [12] based on the FODA model [16]. The feature model is used as a *catalog* of feature commonality and variability. Moreover, it acts as a *configuration roadmap*, providing an understanding of what can be combined, selected, and customized in a system.

Generative programming aims at automating the mapping from feature combinations to implementation components through the use of generator technology [7], such as C++ template meta-programming or GenVoca [3]. They emphasize features that "crosscut" the existing modularization, affecting many different components. Source-tree composition could be used to steer such generative compositions, making use of partially shared configuration interfaces for constituent components.

Customization Decision Trees are an extension of feature diagrams proposed by Jarzabek et al. [14]. Features can be annotated with *scripts* that specify the architecture modifications needed to realizing the variant in question. In our setting, this could correspond to annotating FDL descriptions with package names that implement the given features.

Bosch analyzes the use of object-oriented frameworks as building blocks for implementing software product lines [5]. One of his observations is that industrial-strength component reuse is almost always realized at the source-code level. "Components are primarily developed internally and include functionality relevant for the products or applications in which it is used. Externally developed components are generally subject to considerable (source code) adaptation to match, e.g., product line architecture requirements" [5, p. 240]. *Source-tree composition* as proposed in our paper provides the support required to deal with this product line issue in a systematic and controlled way.

In another paper, Bosch et al. list a number of problems related to product instantiation [6] and recognize that it is hard to exclude component features. Our proposed solution is to address this by focusing on source-level component integration. Moreover, they observe that the initialization code is scattered and hidden. Our approach addresses this problem by putting all initialization code in the abstract factory, so that concrete factories can refine it as needed. Finally, they note the importance of design patterns, including the abstract factory pattern for product instantiation.

The use of design patterns in software product lines is discussed by Sharp and Roll [18]. Our paper deals with one design pattern in full detail, and proposes an extension of this abstract factory pattern for the case in which there are many different customers and product instantiations.

The abstract factory is also discussed in detail by Vlissides, who proposes *pluggable factories* as an alternative [19,20]. The pluggable factory relies on the *prototype* pattern (creating an object by copying a prototypical instance) in order to modify the behavior of abstract factories dynamically. It is suitable when many different, but similar, concrete factories are needed.

Anastasopoulos and Gacek discuss various techniques for implementing variability, such as delegation, property files, reflection and design patterns [1]. Our abstract factory proposal can be used for any of their techniques and addresses the issue of *packaging* the variability in the most suitable way.

The use of *attributed* features to describe configured and versioned sets of components is covered by Zeller and Snelting [21]. They deal with configuration management only: an interesting area of future research is to integrate their feature logic with the feature descriptions of the FODA model and FDLs.

6.3   Discussion and Future Work

There is a relation between the features as selected for a particular product instance and the corresponding composition (and configuration) of implementing source code components. We are still investigating how abstract packages can be used to define this relation and how `autobundle` can be used to perform product configuration automatically.

Also, the use of online package repositories to assist a developer in assembling product instances is subject to research. From online package repositories containing only abstract packages (which directly correspond to features), developers can select the features of need. With automated source-tree composition, the corresponding implementing components are determined and bundled in the intended product instance. It is not clear yet how to handle feature interactions and feature constraints.

The techniques we used in this paper cover customization by means of static and dynamic configuration. Customization can also be based on generative techniques [2,14,7]. Incorporating generative techniques (such as frame technology [2,14]) in the build process of DocGen for customer-specific customization would be interesting future work.

References

1. M. Anastasopoulos and C. Gacek. Implementing product line variabilities. In *Proceedings of the 2001 Symposium on Software Reusability*, pages 109–117. ACM, 2001. SIGSOFT Software Engineering Notes 26(3).
2. P. Bassett. *Framing Software Reuse. Lessons From the Real World*. Yourdon Press (ISBN 0-13327-859-X), 1997.
3. D. Batory, C. Johnson, B. MacDonald, and D. von Heeder. Achieving extensibility through product-lines and domain-specific languages: A case study. In *International Conference on Software Reuse*, volume 1844 of *LNCS*, pages 117–136. Springer-Verlag, 2000.
4. K. Beck. *Extreme Programming Explained. Embrace Change*. Addison Wesley, 1999.
5. J. Bosch. *Design and Use of Software Architectures: Adopting and Evolving a Product-Line Approach*. Addison-Wesley, 2000.
6. J. Bosch and M. Högström. Product instantiation in software product lines: A case study. In *Proceedings of the Second International Symposium on Generative and Component-Based Software Engineering (GCSE 2000)*, volume 2177 of *Lecture Notes in Computer Science*. Springer-Verlag, 2000.
7. K. Czarnecki and U. W. Eisenecker. *Generative Programming. Methods, Tools, and Applications*. Addison-Wesley, 2000.
8. A. van Deursen and P. Klint. Domain-specific language design requires feature descriptions. *Journal of Computing and Information Technology*, 2001.

9. A. van Deursen and T. Kuipers. Building documentation generators. In *Proceedings; IEEE International Conference on Software Maintenance*, pages 40–49. IEEE Computer Society Press, 1999.

10. Automatic Documentation Generation; White Paper. Software Improvement Group, 2001. http://www.software-improvers.com/PDF/DocGenWhitePaper.pdf.

11. E. Gamma, R. Helm, R. Johnson, and J. Vlissides. *Design Patterns: Elements of Reusable Object-Oriented Software*. Addison-Wesley, 1994.

12. M. Griss, J. Favaro, and M. d' Alessandro. Integrating feature modeling with the RSEB. In *Proceedings of the Fifth International Conference on Software Reuse*, pages 76–85. IEEE Computer Society, 1998.

13. I. Jacobson, M. Griss, and P. Jonsson. *Software Reuse: Architecture, Process and Organization for Business Success*. Addison-Wesley, 1997.

14. S. Jarzabek and R. Seviora. Engineering components for ease of customization and evolution. *IEE Proceedings – Software*, 147(6):237–248, December 2000. A special issue on Component-based Software Engineering.

15. M. de Jonge. Source tree composition. In *Proceedings: Seventh International Conference on Software Reuse*, LNCS. Springer-Verlag, 2002. To appear.

16. K. Kang, S. Cohen, J. Hess, W. Novak, and A. Peterson. Feature-oriented domain analysis (FODA) feasibility study. Technical Report CMU/SEI-90-TR-21, Software Engineering Institute, Carnegie Mellon University, Pittsburgh, Pennsylvania, november 1990.

17. G. Kiczales, J. Lamping, A. Mendhekar, C. Maeda, C. Videira Lopes, J.-M Loingtier, and J. Irwin. Aspect-oriented programming. In *Proceedings of the European Conference on Object-Oriented Programming (ECOOP)*, Lecture Notes in Computer Science. Springer-Verlag, 1997.

18. D. Sharp and W. Roll. Pattern usage in an avionics mission processing product line. In *Proceedings of the OOPSLA 2001 Workshop on Patterns and Pattern Languages for OO Distributed Real-time and Embedded Systems*, 2001. See http://www.cs.wustl.edu/~mk1/RealTimePatterns/.

19. J. Vlissides. Pluggable factory, part I. *C++ Report*, November/December 1998.

20. J. Vlissides. Pluggable factory, part II. *C++ Report*, February 1999.

21. A. Zeller and G. Snelting. Unified versioning through feature logic. *ACM Transactions on Software Engineering and Methodology*, 6(4):398–441, 1997.

Feature Interaction and Dependencies: Modeling Features for Reengineering a Legacy Product Line

Stefan Ferber[1], Jürgen Haag[2], and Juha Savolainen[3]

[1] Robert Bosch GmbH, Corporate Research and Development FV/SLD
Eschborner Landstraße 130–132, D-60489 Frankfurt, Germany
Stefan.Ferber@de.bosch.com
[2] Robert Bosch GmbH, Gasoline Systems GS/ESK
P.O. Box 30 02 40, D-70442 Stuttgart, Germany
Juergen.Haag2@de.bosch.com
[3] Nokia Research Center
P.O. Box 407, FIN-00045 NOKIA GROUP, Finland
Juha.Savolainen@nokia.com

Abstract. Reengineering a legacy product line has been addressed very little by current product line research activities. This paper introduces a method to investigate feature dependencies and interactions, which restricts the variants that can be derived from the legacy product line assets. Reorganizing the product line assets with respect to new requirements requires more knowledge than what is easily provided by the classical feature-modeling approaches. Hence, adding all the feature dependencies and interactions into the feature tree results in unreadable and unmanageable feature models that fail to achieve their original goals.

We therefore propose two complementary views to represent the feature model. One view shows the hierarchical refinement of features similar to common feature-modeling approaches in a feature tree. The second view describes what kind of dependencies and interactions there are between various features.

We show two examples of feature dependencies and interactions in the context of an engine-control software product line, and we demonstrate how our approach helps to define correct product configurations from product line variants.

1 Introduction

Automotive products are rich with variants to meet the special needs of different customers. Applying the Product Line Approach (PLA) for the embedded systems in automotive products is therefore quite natural. A product line is an important system development paradigm in the automotive industry to amortize costs beyond a single product. The paradigm is well established in the mechanical and electrical engineering practice in automotive companies like Bosch. To make the car more secure, economical, clean, and comfortable, more functionality is moving from mechanical to electrical, and from electrical to software solutions. Therefore, today's automotive products are software-intensive systems that are developed with the PLA paradigm [6,9,17,29,31].

Feature modeling provides an industrial strength method for managing the inherent variability of product lines. The variability modeling is often done using two techniques:

G. Chastek (Ed.): SPLC2 2002, LNCS 2379, pp. 235–256, 2002.
© Springer-Verlag Berlin Heidelberg 2002

tables and graphical models. In this paper, we concentrate on graphical modeling using feature trees and interaction diagrams. Based on our experience, graphical representation allows the easy understanding of complex structures and their dependencies, which is especially important in the reengineering context. On the other hand, using tables does not require any special tools, and it provides easy processing of information by automatic tools. In fact, these methods are complementary. We often model the first version of variability by listing all entries into a table. Later, we collect the variability information into a feature tree and use the graphical representation as a basis for creating the dependency and interaction models. Structuring features in trees allows to model requirements in different granularities. In practice, it is difficult to model features with all their implications and dependencies with current feature-oriented methods. In the real-life context, relations between features often become very complex without a clear way to model features with different dimensions or aspects, leading to a very complex graph of features. These graphs have nodes that represent the features and different types of edges between the nodes where the edges connect nodes in other parts of the feature hierarchy. The feature-oriented domain analysis (FODA) method [19] and successors of FODA [7] require a tree-like structure of the feature model which may be very difficult to generate, as there are no clear criteria to align the structure to a tree-like form. Moreover, you cannot capture all of the information contained in a (general) graph in a tree, leaving you with the possibility of omitting dependencies or losing control of the model[17].

Feature dependencies and interactions play an important part in complex software-intensive systems, since features often need other features to fulfill their tasks. There are feature dependencies, which are imposed by the domain, and other dependencies that exist due only to a certain design decision made during development or to the way that features are realized in the solution. Categorizing types of interactions by distinguishing all possible feature dependencies in a domain greatly helps to reengineer product line assets. This is because some domain-enforced dependencies among features are difficult if not impossible to change while dependencies that are based on design decisions can often be removed during the reengineering process. The feature-dependency analysis is a crucial part of the product line development, where the features are used to distinguish between product line variants. In this context, feature interaction can have very strong implications on the possible configurations of product line members. Knowing and managing the dependencies becomes very important, especially in highly configurable product lines.

We suggest different views on the feature model like architectural views on the architecture to represent the desired information. In this paper, we show two examples of feature views. One view captures the FODA-like concept of hierarchical refinement of features and their variability assumptions. In the second view, we present (static and dynamic) feature interactions and dependencies. This dependency and interaction view was used to reengineer features from legacy specifications and implementations of a product line.

The next section of this paper reviews current feature-modeling methods and motivates our extension, which is described in detail in Section 3. In Section 4, we apply our method to two examples. Our findings are related to other research in this area as described in Section 5. Finally, in Section 6, we conclude our experience and give an outlook on the future.

2   Feature Modeling

Features bridge the marketing view to the development view. On the marketing, side features define properties that the customer wants from the system. On the development side features are used as increments of implementation. Typically, features are defined in terms that the customer can understand. The customer focus also supports the use of features for configuration purposes, where the customer can choose which features are included in a product variant. The configuration aspect of the feature-based development is even more important when the product line techniques are used.

In the product line context, features are used to differentiate product line members. The high-end products tend to have more features than inexpensive product variants. Additionally, some features for more complex products may have more complex behavior. To handle this variation in features, a number of different approaches have been proposed. Currently, one of the most successful approaches in variability modeling is to use feature trees. The feature tree is a feature-refinement hierarchy that explicitly shows the variability among the product line members by attaching different symbols that communicate the related variability assumptions.

However, modeling variations among features is not enough to make the feature model an efficient tool for product derivation. The features are not independent from each other. All the features work together to achieve a common goal: the purpose of the system. In the gasoline engine-control domain, this is realizing a pleasant, economical driving experience that also addresses environmental values. The features cannot achieve this without interchanging information interacting among each other. The traditional justification of modeling software features is to see them as independent entities that can be specified and hopefully developed in isolation. But often, the crucial part of specifying a complex software system is actually based on the interactions of the features. This revelation justifies the clear need to model dependencies and interactions among software features. The interaction-modeling community has produced a lot of high-quality research on how the combined behavior of features can be specified and validated [33]. Specifying behavioral aspects of the software is beyond the scope of this paper, since we only address feature relationships as they affect the configuration and derivation of product variants. In this context, a key aspect of understanding the various relationships between two features is to realize how they are dependent on each other. To support this, some feature-modeling methods suggest a way to model dependencies among features. Most notably, in the FODA method, various rules are formulated to represent the dependencies. These rules, for example, set and require conditions between two features. Unfortunately, these rules make it very difficult to get the big picture of the overall dependencies. The other option is to add dependency links directly into the feature trees making them into more complex graphs. Modeling dependencies in this way as a part of the feature tree greatly reduces the understandability of the feature model, and degrades their usefulness. Even though some methods explicitly address the feature dependency problem, a surprisingly large number of feature-modeling methods do not provide any way to model dependencies among features. In the real-life context, feature trees may become very large. Any attempt to model dependencies among features as a part of the feature tree is doomed to failure in industrial use because of the lack of mechanisms to handle scalability. We solve these problems by providing another view on features: the feature-dependency view. For more discussion on approaches for modeling dependencies see Section 5.

The feature-dependency model describes all possible dependencies among features within the current scope. It shows how the functionality of features is dependent on the implementation of pieces of other features' functionality. In this paper, we use feature dependency for two main purposes. First, we record the feature dependencies to better understand the legacy product line by identifying how the various features are interrelated. This insight assists us in our reengineering efforts to create a new product line architecture. The feature dependencies are key information that can be used when a new reference architecture is created. In many systems, well-known functionality-related criteria, such as cohesion and coupling, are used to determine the correct system decomposition. Identifying the types of relationships seems to be a crucially important aspect, while identifying possible transformations of the existing architecture.

Second, dependency modeling is used to allow the easy derivation of product instances from the reference architecture. In the real-life product lines that we have experience with, the architecture is not driven only by the desired properties of the products; an equally important aspect is to identify what is possible based on the solution domain. Often, certain features are cheaper to implement using services from other features. Sharing common components may be appropriate even when some of the components' services are not needed for the low-end product. This kind of sharing of common assets may create dependencies between features that, from the customer's viewpoint, are not needed at all. Yet, the product derivation clearly requires this information while creating the low-end product. We solve this problem by expressing these kinds of relationships between features in the feature-dependency view.

In this paper, we show these techniques in the context of reengineering. But the models are also useful when creating new systems. However, then the engineers should guarantee that they do not prematurely commit on the specific designing choices while analyzing dependencies among features. These considerations are out of the scope of this paper, and all the recommendations of this paper are targeted on using the approach for reengineering existing product lines.

3   Two Views of the Feature Model

This paper assumes that a feature model describes complex interactions and dependencies between features in a product line context, which involves a lot of variability issues. Moreover, features have additional attributes like a detailed description, current state of development (e.g., specified, coded, tested, released), delivery information, needed memory and processor resources, traces to software components, and many more. Therefore, the complete feature model can hardly be described in one diagram or in one table. There are three possible ways to deal with the complexity in such models:

1. Split the model into multiple diagrams with different features in each diagram.

2. Use a hierarchy in which features can be described in more detail with subfeatures.
3. Employ different views with each view dealing with a certain aspect of the model.

We are using all three approaches to analyze the features in the software of a control system for gasoline engines, as we have to cover several hundred features with complex relationships (see Section 4). This paper covers only two views: one showing variability, the other expressing dependencies. But, we can think of additional views in this application: feature road maps and feature resource consumption. Probably, other domains require their own views.

3.1   Used Terminology

A feature is "a prominent or distinctive user-visible aspect, quality, or characteristic of a software system or systems" [19]. A domain model is "a definition of the functions, objects, data, and relationships in a domain" [19]. And a feature model is a specific domain model covering the features and their relationships within a domain. The domain in this case is the product line scope of the engine-control software for gasoline engines called motronic.

A hierarchy of features with semantic edges as relationships is called a feature tree. The edges can represent alternative, multiple, optional, and mandatory features. Two features, B and C, interact if the responsibility of feature B is to change the behavior of feature C. Usually, these features have a runtime relationship to fulfill their responsibility. Feature B depends on feature C, if feature B can fulfill its responsibility only if feature C is present (i.e., B requires C), or if feature C is not present (i.e., B excludes C).

The feature model consists of all features and relationships among them. The feature-tree view shows the variability assumption. The feature interaction and dependency view shows all feature interaction and dependency relationship. Note that some information is present in both views. For example, if feature B excludes feature C, one can represent this in the tree with an alternative relationship and in the dependency and interaction view with a relationship called "excludes".

The feature-tree view is the appropriate tool to structure features of a product line. Moreover, it can be used to select features for a product that is derived out of the product line even by non-expert users of a software system (e.g., salespeople, customer). The feature interaction and dependency view helps software integrators and developers to identify valid feature configurations in the product line. We used both views to mine and document the assets of the motronic product line.

3.2   Syntax and Semantics in the Feature Interaction and Dependency View

In this section, we describe how feature interactions and dependencies can be modeled and recorded for documentation and derivation use. In our model, we connect the features that participate to the interaction by using arrows that represent the types of the interactions. For the motronic domain, we have chosen five main types of feature interactions: usage, intentional, resource usage, environment induced, and excluded relation.

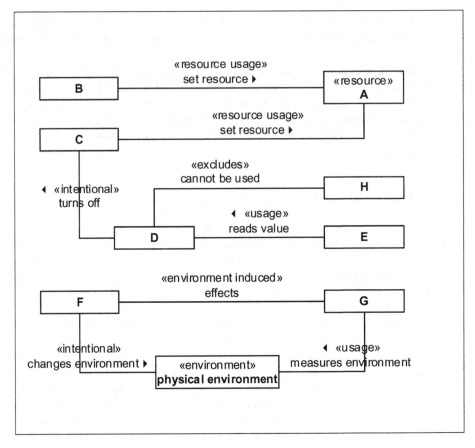

Fig. 1. Feature Interaction and Dependency Representational Model

Intentional Interaction. For some features, a large part of their functionality is based on the nature of the interaction, that is, they encapsulate a piece of interaction-oriented functionality. These features typically change the behavior of other features. For example, in the engine control software, the "limp-home" features influence the synchronization of the crankshaft and camshaft angles in certain degraded mode conditions (see the example in Figure 5).

Resource-Usage Interaction. Some resources are limited in the sense that only a subset of all features can simultaneously use them. Typically, this kind of relationship also presents itself in the timing-dependency-relationship dimension. Often this interaction is taken care of by another feature or service that manages the interaction between a potentially large number of features. For example, the driver requests high torque to accelerate the car, but the automatic transmission requests a low torque to shift down. A feature called Torque Coordinator schedules the torque demands from different sources.

Environment Induced Interaction. There are also other kinds of indirect, often very implicit, connections between features. These occur when a set of features monitor some properties of the physical environment on which some other features have some influence. In the concrete instances of this kind of relationship, it is important to specify how the features affect the environment. This means that features that are not directly connected together are affected by the changes in the environment. We record it as an implicit, environment-induced interaction between the corresponding features. These kinds of dependencies are difficult to notice, since most of the time there is no direct connection between the features. For example, the fuel-purge control adds gasoline into the intake manifold, which is observed much later by the exhaust lambda sensors.

Usage Dependency. The most common form of feature dependency is the usage relationship. This can be a simple "requires" relationship. Data-exchange relationships are normally based on the usage dependency. If a feature uses data from another feature, it creates a one-directional usage dependency from the data consumer to the data producer. Quite naturally, if we have multiple features, we can easily end up with cyclic relationships between the corresponding features. For example, sensor diagnostics for the camshaft sensor reads values provided by the Sense Camshaft Angle and Sense Crankshaft Angle features to detect inconsistent sensor values (see the example in Figure 5).

Excluded Dependency. Some features cannot be in the same family variant after the binding time. The excluded relation is heavily dependent on the binding time of the features: for example, if the binding time and the run time can both be present in the actual implementation of the family variant, they cannot operate at the same time. E.g. At one time there can be only either camshaft limp-home mode or the crankshaft limp-home mode active, since either one sensor is needed for the engine speed calculation. This definition means that the limp-home feature is excluded at runtime. Thus both features can exist in one family variant, but only one of them can be active at the same time. There is a natural reason for this kind of behavior, since either the crankshaft or camshaft sensor must be operational to guarantee speed calculations. If neither of these sensors functions correctly, no limp-home features can be activated (see the example in Figure 5).

Out-of-Scope Stereotype. Feature interaction and dependency, which crosscut views, are modeled in detail in only one view. Other views refer to these features with the "out-of-scope" stereotype.

3.3 Syntax and Semantics of the Feature-Tree View

Domain assumptions reveal the knowledge that a developer has on the operating domain. Domain assumptions constrain how product family members may vary within the current scope. The possible domain assumptions are mandatory, optional, alternative, and multiple.

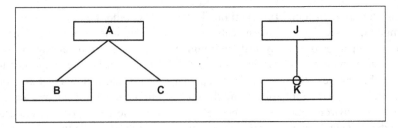

Fig. 2. Feature Variability Representational Model in the Feature Tree: The subfeature relationship is shown on the left and the optional feature is shown on the right.

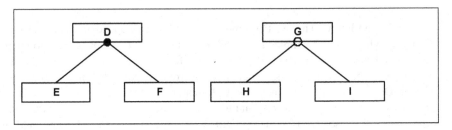

Fig. 3. Feature Variability Representational Model in the Feature Tree: The multiple relationship is shown on the left and the alternative relationship is shown on the right.

In Figures 2 and 3 we show all possible variability types and their corresponding representations. A solid line between features defines a subfeature relationship where child features are mandatory, if their parent is chosen. This is the case between features A, B, and C. Features E and F are part of a multiple relationship where one or both of the features can be chosen. On the other hand, H and I are alternative features, one of which must be chosen. Finally, K is an optional feature.

Mandatory: If, for a set of features, we have a mandatory domain assumption, then these features have to be present in all the products that belong to the current scope. For example, every family variant has an ignition system.

Optional: Optional domain assumption describes a feature that may or may not be included into the family variant. An optional domain assumption does not constrain the available options in any way it merely specifies that it is likely that, within the current scope, there will be systems that have this particular feature and those that do not. For example, an engine may have a turbo-charger.

Alternative: An alternative domain assumption represents a choice between a set of features. One and only one feature has to be chosen from the alternative set of features. For example, throttle-valve control is either by air-bypass actuator, throttle-valve actuator, or electronic throttle control.

Multiple: Multiple domain assumption captures a possibility to choose many features from a set of features, but the user has to choose at least one. For example, an engine can have an intake manifold pressure sensor, an air mass flow meter, or both.

3.4   Consistency of Views

Showing one model in two views raises a question of their consistency. We use very simple rules to achieve practical consistency in our models. Rules for the feature-tree view are

1. All features of the feature model are presented in the tree view (completeness).
2. Variability assumptions in the tree view are a subset of all dependencies (incomplete but free of contradiction).

Rules for the feature interaction and dependency view are

1. Only a subset of features are presented in the interaction and dependency view (incomplete).
2. All dependencies and interactions are shown in the interaction and dependency view (completeness).

These rules satisfy the practical needs for consistency, since in our process, we first create a feature tree, which has all the features that reside in the current domain. After that, we analyze dependencies. In the dependency view, we have a subset of all features, but we cannot have any features that are not part of a feature tree. If the feature is not in the feature tree of the related domain, then it is tagged with the stereotype "out of scope". That is, there cannot be any feature that is not defined in a feature tree. The dependency view adds information on how those features interact, but it cannot add new features without also adding them into the feature trees.

4   Feature Modeling for Engine Control Software

The feature-modeling method introduced earlier in this paper was used to analyze the functionality of the software of the Motronic control system for gasoline engines [13,14].

The Motronic system contains all of the actuators (servo units, final-control elements) required for intervening in spark-ignition engine management, while monitoring devices (sensors) register current operating data for engines and vehicles. Some of these sensor signals are

- Accelerator-pedal travel,
- Engine position,
- Cylinder charge factor (air mass),
- Engine and intake-air temperatures, and
- Mixture composition (air-fuel ratio, called "Lambda").

The system, consisting of a microprocessor and software, employs these data as the basis for quantifying driver demand, and responds by calculating the engine torque required for compliance with the driver's wishes. Out of the required engine torque, the actuator signals for

- electronic throttle device (and therefore for the air mass),
- injection (fuel mass),
- ignition,

and other devices are calculated. By ensuring the provision of the required cylinder charge together with the corresponding injected fuel quantity, and the correct ignition timing, the system furnishes the optimal mixture formation and combustion to fulfill the driver's wishes as well as emission laws.

Subsequently, two examples of the feature analysis are shown. The first example is the engine position management (EPM) of the motronic. In this example, the feature tree was created first to identify the current features and its variations. The feature interaction diagram was developed afterwards to identify the dependencies between the features.

The second example shows the feature analysis of the control system for the air-fuel ratio of the gasoline engine's exhaust gas (Lambda feedback control). In this example, the interaction diagram was used to rearrange the tree view of the feature model.

4.1   Example 1: Engine Position Management

The Engine Position Management (EPM) of the control system for gasoline engines has different responsibilities. A feature tree of the control system gives an overview of the functionality in the EPM domain.

Figure 4 shows the main features of the EPM. First of all, the engine speed and the crankshaft angle have to be sensed. But also the camshaft angle sensing and the synchronization are major parts of the EPM. A reliable synchronization in the whole speed range of the engine is necessary for the right ignition and injection timing and therefore to fulfill the strict emission laws. The optional limp-home modes (in case of sensor failure) and the start-up functionality are subfeatures of the synchronization. The start-up of the engine can be realized in different ways: fast, fast with history, or reliable. These subfeatures have a "multiple" relationship because a combination of them is required by some customers.

The "back-rotation detection" feature is optional because only some engine types could be destroyed if the engine runs in the wrong direction. This feature has two "alternative" subfeatures: it can either use the camshaft or the crankshaft sensor for detection.

There are more dependencies between the features of the EPM than shown in the feature tree. Of course these dependencies have to be known to reengineer features when implementing the EPM for a new product line. To describe all the dependencies, the interaction diagram (introduced in Section 3) was developed for the EPM (see Figure 5).

Though there are many dependencies and interactions between features in this case, they do not restrict the selection in the tree view to derive a valid product out of the product line features. You can see in Figure 6 that, for example, minimal feature selection does not contradict the feature interaction and dependency view.

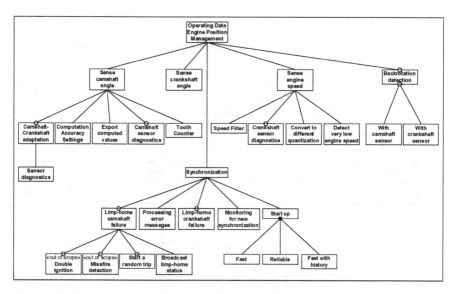

Fig. 4. Feature Tree View of the Engine Position Management (EPM).

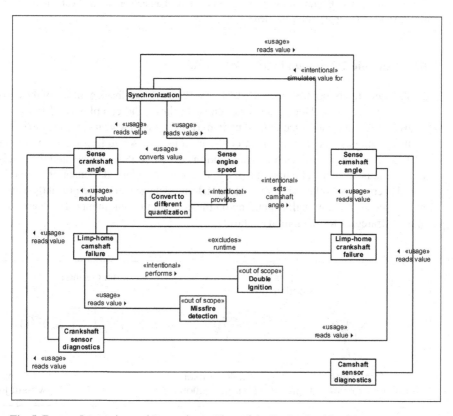

Fig. 5. Feature Interaction and Dependency View of the Engine Position Management (EPM)

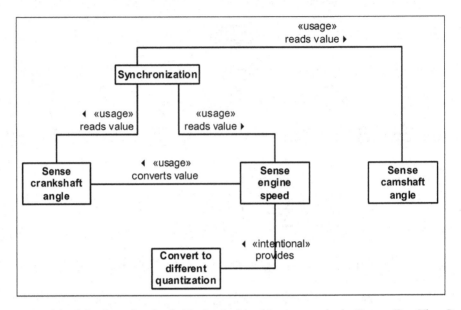

Fig. 6. Minimal Configuration for the Engine Position Management in the Feature-Tree View. It is also valid in the interaction and dependency view.

4.2 Example 2: Lambda Feedback Control

In this example, the control of the air-fuel ratio (Lambda feedback control) of the exhaust gas was investigated. Due to the strict emission laws, the complexity of the Lambda control system has increased dramatically during the last few years. Therefore, different control strategies and several sensor configurations are used to fulfill the requirements.

Figure 7 shows the possible configurations of the lambda sensors and the catalysts in the exhaust system. The first sensor can be a two-state lambda sensor or a wide-band lambda sensor. All other sensors are two-state lambda sensors. The precatalyst and the middle sensor are optional, depending on the emission requirements. There are several control strategies for the lambda control:

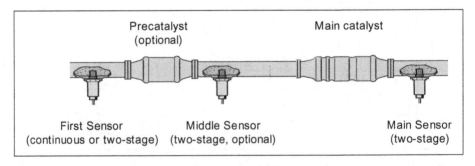

Fig. 7. Naming of Sensors and Catalysts in the Exhaust System

- continuous or two-state lambda feedback control first sensor
- continuous lambda feedback control middle sensor
- continuous lambda feedback control main sensor
- natural frequency feedback control
- catalyst outcome feedback control

Even for the domain expert, it was difficult to get an overview of the possible sensor configurations in combination with these different control strategies and their dependencies. Mixing features with the current implementation of these features made things even more difficult. This was probably due to the history of the functionality. As you can see, this feature tree (Figure 8) has two main disadvantages. First, the structure of the

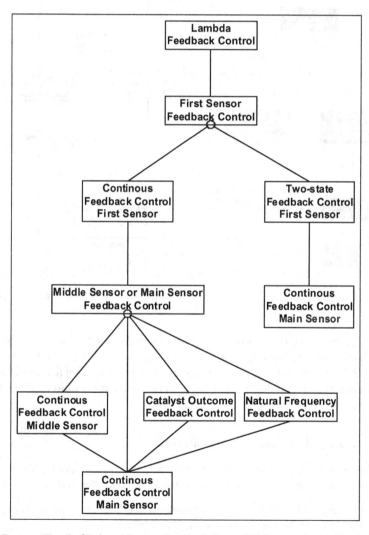

Fig. 8. Feature "Tree" of Exhaust System Feedback Control Before Analyzing Dependencies

tree isn't a proper tree structure, and second, it is necessary to represent the "continuous feedback control main sensor" feature twice.

To restructure the feature tree, the dependencies and interactions between the features were modeled. To express indirect dependencies, the related sensors were added in the same diagram (Figure 9). Due to the modeled dependencies (especially "exclude" and "requires") between features and sensors, it was possible to derive a very simple new feature tree containing most (except one) of the dependencies in Figure 10.

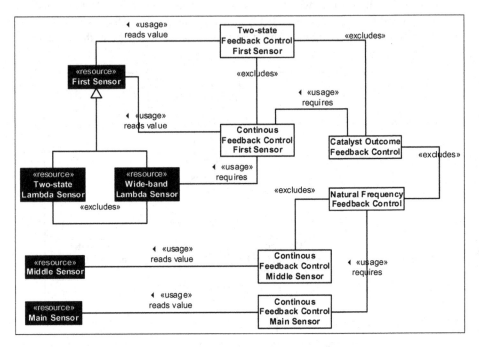

Fig. 9. Feature Dependency and Interaction View of the Lambda Feedback Control

Still, one needs the information in the interaction and dependency view for deriving products in the product line. Figure 11 shows a "valid" configuration of the feature-tree view in Figure 10. But, the exclude relationship of two selected features is only covered in the interaction and dependency view. In order to have a valid configuration, all the information in the feature model is needed.

4.3   Tracing the Realization of Features

In this feature analysis case, the software is already there. Capturing the traces for each feature is therefore quite easy. We collected additional information for each feature:

1. The variability mechanism for alternative, multiple, or optional features
2. The name of the variability point in the software
3. The software function that provides the feature

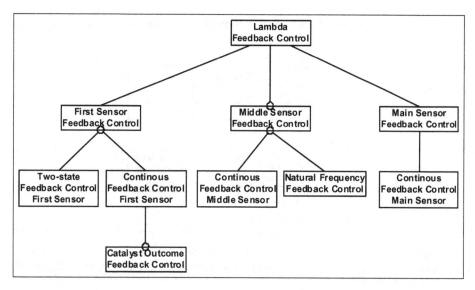

Fig. 10. Rearranged Feature-Tree View After Analyzing Dependencies of the Lambda Feedback Control

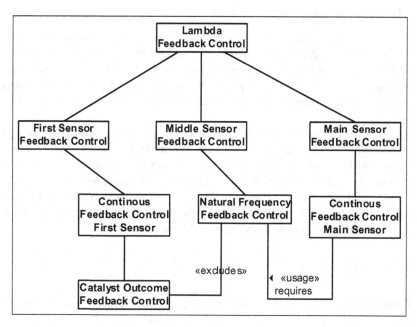

Fig. 11. An invalid configuration of lambda feedback control for one product in the product line.

This was captured in UML-like style as shown in Figure 12.

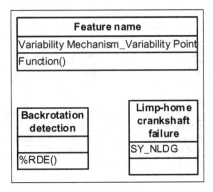

Fig. 12. Tracing Features to Variability Points in the Software and to the Software Function: The upper box describes the generic feature trace template, and the two lower boxes are examples of its usage for the EPM.

4.4   Modeling the Complete System

We used this approach to model the complete engine-control software. The feature model is shown in 40 different feature-tree views. We have shown only two simplified versions in this paper. Each feature-tree view has between 50 and 200 features and describes the functionality of a conceptual object in the domain. The depth of the hierarchy varies from three to nine whereas a depth of five seems to be a good tradeoff between overview and detail.

From this feature model, we were able to extract high-level and crosscutting features that describe the basic nature of the system. We call these features *system features*. There are nearly 300 system features which cover the most important feature dependencies.

Our experience indicates that this approach scales well. Maintaining the trees was the most difficult and time-consuming problem, as we had to rearrange the features by hand. Currently, an XML-based feature model with a set of supporting tools is under development and will (hopefully) resolve this problem.

5   Related Work

Feature-modeling research has been an integral part of product line research for many years. This has resulted in a natural tendency to explicitly target variability issues during the method development. Each of the methods has some way of representing the commonality and variability in the product family. However, surprisingly large number of feature-modeling methods do not provide equally powerful techniques to model dependencies between features. Especially, they do not provide any tools to manage the inherent complexity of the dependency models in any way that can support the scalability needed in the current industrial projects. In this section, we will focus on how existing feature-modeling methods model dependencies among features.

In the widely used feature-oriented domain analysis method, rules are created to represent the dependencies [7,19]. Composition rules define the semantics existing between features that are not expressed in the feature diagram. All optional and alternative features that cannot be selected when the named feature is selected must be stated using the mutually exclusive WITH statement. All optional and alternative features that must be selected when the named feature is selected must be defined using the REQUIRES statement. Unfortunately, these rules make it very difficult to get the big picture of the overall dependencies. The only way that approaches the solution of the scalability issues is the FODA approach, with its feature rules. However, we believe that there are major drawbacks to this approach. Separating the rules from the actual features that are affected by the rule makes it necessary in larger projects to search the whole set of rules to find those that have some effect on the current feature in question. This separation reduces understandability, hinders evolution, and complicates derivation.

On the variability management view, the FODA approach is quite similar to ours with its three kinds of structuring constructs. Mandatory features are those requirements of the system that have to be included in the product family. Alternative features are specializations of more general features that have multiple specialization features, one of which has to be chosen. Optional constructs model features that can be included into one product, but may be left out of another product. Our model shares these definitions on the three types of variability.

The Feature-Oriented Reuse Method (FORM) is an extension to the FODA approach [23]. FORM and FODA use similar notations for feature modeling. In the FORM method, feature diagrams support three kinds of relationships: a composed-of relation that represents a whole-part relationship between a feature and its children; a generalization/specialization relationship represented by the feature refinement structure; and an implemented-by relation where one feature is used to implement another feature. In addition to the feature relationships that conform to the feature-tree structure, the FORM method also supports composition rules that constrain the possible feature selection across feature-tree branches. The composition rules define mutual exclusion and mutual dependency among optional and alternative features in manner very similar to that used in FODA method.

Griss and colleagues have proposed integrating feature modeling as used in the FODA method into the Reuse-Driven Software Engineering Business (RSEB) method [15]. In the RSEB method, the domain is specified in the RSEB use-case model, which uses the standard methods for modeling relationships applying uses and extends relationships together with variation points among use cases[1]. The feature model is used to configure the use-case model, by expressing which use cases can be combined, selected, and customized for this system. The method also uses semantic constraints like REQUIRES and MUTUAL EXCLUSION. These rules constrain the selection of the optional and variant features much as the FODA method does. They suggest adding the constraints to

---

[1] Note that the current UML notation actually uses extend, include, and generalization relationships.

the UML diagrams as attributes or as UML constrains added to the classes or relationships (e.g., in the object constraint language (OCL)).

The generative programming framework by Czarnecki and Eisenecker also applies feature modeling for organizing knowledge of the product family structure [8]. They have extended the FODA feature models with OR features. They also provide methods and guidelines for normalizing feature diagrams, which basically means ways of transforming diagrams to another consistent model with the same set of features. Additionally, they indicate the need to identify constraints and dependency rules among features. The focus of their work concentrates on defining mutual-exclusion and REQUIRES constraints, as defined in the FODA method. In addition to previously published methods they also distinguish between horizontal and vertical constraints, which mainly define whether the features sharing a constraint belong to the same or different abstraction level. This work does not provide any explicit tools to define or mange constraints, but it implies that the OCL can be used to specify different constraints.

Feature modeling and analysis have been proved to be highly important aspects of modern industrial product line development. Thus, company-specific, feature-classification schemes have also emerged. The large-scale use of feature-modeling techniques lead to problems with feature dependencies, which do not fit into the chosen domain decomposition. The modeling of features' coupling crosses feature-tree branches and transforms feature trees into graphs that may become very complex with numerous dependencies between different parts of feature hierarchies. These kinds of hierarchies quickly change into structures that lose all of their initial benefits. These and many more issues discussed in the work by Hein and colleagues have greatly influenced our work [16,17,27].

The method for requirements authoring and management (MRAM) proposed by Keepance and Mannion uses discriminants to structure requirements [20]. Discriminants describe how one product is different from another product variant. Single and option discriminants correspond to mandatory and optional features in the FODA method, whereas multiple discriminants are not mutually exclusive as the alternative features are. We share the definition of multiple discriminants in our variability tree model. The MRAM approach also supports deriving concrete product instantiations from the reference architecture by binding the variation points. However, their MRAM method does not address the dependency problems of the related variations points.

The software productivity consortium has proposed a method to perform domain modeling [1]. During domain analysis, they use commonality and variability assumptions to describe what is common between different systems and how the systems vary. A related method, the family-oriented abstraction, specification and translation (FAST) method relies on the same ideas of commonality and variability assumptions as the SRC method [2]. The FAST method focuses on developing a domain-specific language that implements the assumptions, which were discovered during domain analysis. Domain-specific languages (DSLs) can be used to specify variability and eventually create all needed family variants. The semantic structure of the DSL is engineered for this particular domain, and it therefore specifies how the product family can vary within the current scope by holding all relevant domain assumptions. A correctly implemented DSL would also include the dependencies between decisions and could ensure that these rules are satisfied. Therefore, the created DSL includes all information on the relevant dependencies between features. However, using domain-specific languages hinders the ability to adapt and reengineer existing product families. In these environments, it is often impossible to propose completely new ways to handle variability and derive family variants. On the contrary, it is essential to carefully adapt the current way of working and use the existing design as the basis for reengineering. But the DSL can be created for a selected domain, as demonstrated by the FAST approach's application to the command and reports subsystem of the 5ESS telecommunications switch [32].

Viewpoint-oriented requirements management has become a commonly used paradigm among researchers [11,12,18,26]. Viewpoint-oriented methods concentrate on capturing separate descriptions that together form the complete specification. However, having these separate descriptions highlights the need for methods to identify and resolve possible overlaps and inconsistencies both within a viewpoint and across separate viewpoints. In our model, we preserve consistency by connecting dependency relation to the same features that are present in the feature tree. Checking the dependency view for any new features that don't exist in the feature tree occurs during the creation of the dependency model. If such features emerge, they must also be included in the feature model.

Many researchers have focused on studying the feature-interaction problem [24,25,33]. They have created methods to identify and resolve conflicts among features. The feature-interaction research targets studying the combined behavior features, whereas our work is interested mainly in the interactions as a tool to understand and configure the system better. Knowledge of the actual type of the dependency or interaction potentially helps us to refractor the system to remove those connections that prevent us from creating the optimal system structure.

6   Conclusion

We identified the main requirements of industrial-strength, feature-modeling methods. Then we explained why dependencies between features are a dominant problem in reengineering existing product lines. To support dependency analysis of existing product lines, we introduced a dependency analysis modeling technique and notation. We showed how our model can be applied in a concrete product family using two examples. Finally, we set the context by relating our work to other research about feature modeling.

The dependency modeling in the current feature-modeling methods belongs to two main categories. In the first category, there are methods that model dependencies between features using rules. Our method provides better tools to manage a large number of dependencies, and it supports the graphical modeling of key dependencies and thus improves the overall understanding of the system. The second category includes approaches that model dependency information directly to the feature trees that are normally used to represent variability. This approach has been validated to be impractical in large-scale use. Annotating feature diagrams with dependency information greatly decreases the usability of the feature models. By separating dependency information into another view greatly improved the understandability of the feature model.

The approach presented in this paper is based on our experience of feature modeling in multiple domains. In the future, we plan to create a feature dependency taxonomy that could be used in analyzing and communicating feature dependencies to all key stakeholders.

Acknowledgments

We would like to thank the engine-control domain experts Klaus Hirschmann, Magnus Labbé, and Elmar Pietsch for their patient support of our feature analysis.

References

1. Reuse-driven software processes guidebook. Technical Report Version 02.00.05, Software Productivity Consortium, November 1993.
2. M. Ardis and D. Weiss. Defining families: The commonality analysis. In *International Conference on Software Engineering ICSE1997*, pages 649–650. IEEE, 1997.
3. D. Batory, L. Goglianese, and M. Goodwin. Creating reference architectures: An example for avonics. In *Proceedings of the Symposium of Software Reuse*, pages 27–37. ACM, 1995.
4. J. Bayer, O. Flege, P. Knauber, R. Laqua, D. Methig, K. Schmid, T. Widen, and J. De-Baud. PuLSE: A methodology to develop software product lines. In *Symposium on Software Reusability (SSR'99)*, pages 122–131, 1999.
5. Paul Clements, Rick Kazman, and Mark Klein. *Evaluating Software Architectures: Methods and Case Studies*. SEI Series in Software Engineering. Addison-Wesley, Reading, MA, 2001.
6. Paul Clements and Linda Northrop. *Software Product Lines: Practices and Patterns*. SEI Series in Software Engineering. Addison-Wesley, Reading, MA, 2001.
7. S. Cohen, J. Stanley, W. Peterson, and R. Krut. Application of feature-oriented domain analysis to the army movement control domain. Technical Report CMU/SEI-91-TR-028, Software Engineering Institute, Carnegie Mellon University, Pittsburgh, PA, June 1992.
8. K. Czarnecki and U. Eisenecker. *Generative Programming — Methods Tools and Applications*. Addison-Wesley, Reading, MA, 2000.
9. James C. Dager. Cummin's experience in developing a software product line architecture for real-time embedded diesel engine controls. In Patrick Donohoe, editor, *Software Product Lines: Experience and Research Directions*, pages 23–45. Kluwer Academic Publishers, Boston, 2000.
10. Alan Michael Davis. *Software requirements: Analysis & specification*. Prentice-Hall, Englewood Cliffs, NJ, 1990.
11. S. Easterbrook and B. Nuseibeh. Using viewpoints for inconsistency management. *BCS/IEE Software Engineering Journal*, pages 31–43, January 1996.
12. A. Finkelstein, J. Kramer, B. Nuseibeh, L. Finkelstein, and M. Goedicke. Viewpoints: A framework for integrating multiple perspectives in system development. *International Journal of Software Engineering and Knowledge Engineering*, pages 31–58, March 1992.
13. J. Gerhardt, H. Hönninger, and H. Bischof. A new approach to functional and software structure for engine management systems — BOSCH ME7. In *SAE International Congress and Exposition, Session: Electronic Engine Controls, Detroit, MI, (February, 1998)*, pages 1–12, Warrendale, PA, 1998. Society of Automotive Engineers (SAE).
14. Jürgen Gerhardt. ME-motronic engine management. In *Gasoline-engine management*, pages 306–359. Robert Bosch GmbH, Stuttgart, Germany, 1999.
15. M. Griss, J. Favaro, and M d'Alessandro. Integrating feature modeling with the RSEB. In *Proceedings of Fifth International Conference on Software Reuse*, pages 76–85. IEEE, 1998.

16. A. Hein, J. MacGregor, and S. Thiel. Configuring software product line features. In *Workshop on Feature Interaction in Composed Systems 15th European Conference on Object-Oriented Programming (ECOOP 2001), Budapest, Hungary (June 18–22, 2001)*, 2001.

17. A. Hein, M. Schlick, and R. Vinga-Martins. Applying feature models in industrial setting. In P. Donohoe, editor, *Software Product Lines — Experience and Research Directions*, pages 47–70. Kluwer Academic Publishers, Boston, 2000.

18. A. Hunter and B. Nuseibeh. Managing inconsistent specifications: Reasoning analysis and action. *ACM Transactions on Software Engineering and Methodology*, pages 335–367, October 1998.

19. K. Kang, S. Cohen, J. Hess, W. Novak, and S Peterson. Feature-oriented domain analysis (FODA) feasibility study. Technical Report CMU/SEI-90-TR-021, Software Engineering Institute, Carnegie Mellon University, Pittsburgh, PA, 1990.

20. B. Keepance and M. Mannion. Using patterns to model variability in product families. *IEEE Software*, pages 102–108, July/August 1999.

21. M. Klein, R. Kazman, L. Bass, J. Carriere, M. Barbacci, and H. Lipson. Attribute-based architecture styles. In Patrick Donohoe, editor, *Software Architecture*, volume 140 of *International Federation for Information Processing*, pages 225–243. Kluwer Academic Publishers, Boston, 1999.

22. J. Kuusela and J. Savolainen. Requirements engineering for product lines. In *International Conference on Software Engineering (ICSE2000)*, pages 61–69, 2000.

23. K. Lee, K. Kang, W. Chae, and B. Choi. Feature-based approach to object-oriented engineering of applications for reuse. *Software Practise and Experience*, pages 1025–1046, 30 2000.

24. Louise Lorentsen, Antti-Pekka Tuovinen, and Jianli Xu. Experiences in modelling feature interactions with coloured petri nets. In Tibor Gyimothy, editor, *Proceedings of Seventh Symposium on Programming Languages and Software Tools SPLST 2001*, pages 221–230. University of Szeged, 2001.

25. Louise Lorentsen, Antti-Pekka Tuovinen, and Jianli Xu. Modelling feature interaction patterns in nokia mobile phones using coloured petri nets and Design/CPN. In *Proceedings of Third Workshop and Tutorial on Practical Use of Coloured Petri Nets and the CPN Tools, CPN'01, Aarhus, Denmark, August 29-3*, 2001.

26. N. Nuseibeh, J. Kramer, and A. Finkelstein. A framework for expressing the relationships between multiple views in requirement specification. *IEEE Transactions on Software Engineering*, pages 760–773, October 1994.

27. Michael Schlick and Andreas Hein. Knowledge engineering in software product lines. In *European Conference on Artificial Intelligence (ECAI 2000), Workshop on Knowledge-Based Systems for Model-Based Engineering, Berlin, Germany (August 22nd, 2000)*, 2000.

28. STARS. Organization domain modeling (ODM) guidebook, version 2.0. Technical Report STARS-VC-A025/001/00, Software Technology for Adaptable, Reliable Systems (STARS), June 1996.

29. Steffen Thiel, Stefan Ferber, Thomas Fischer, Andreas Hein, and Michael Schlick. A case study in applying a product line approach for car periphery supervision systems. In *In-Vehicle Software 2001, SAE 2001 World Congress, March 5-8, 2001, Cobo Center, Detroit, Michigan*, volume SP-1587, pages 43–55, Warrendale, PA, 2001. Society of Automotive Engineers (SAE).

30. A. D. Vici, N. Argentieri, A. Mansour, M. d'Alessandro, and J. Favaro. FODAcom: An experience with domain analysis in the italian telecom industry. In *Proceedings of the Fifth International Conference on Software Reuse*, pages 166–175, Los Alamitos, CA, 1998. IEEE Computer Society Press.

31. Jens Weber and Karlheinz Topp. Information technology — a challenge for automotive electronics. In *Embedded Software Session (PC34), SAE 2001 World Congress, March 5-8, 2001, Cobo Center, Detroit, Michigan*, number 2001-01-0029, Warrendale, PA, 2001. Society of Automotive Engineers (SAE).

32. D. Weiss and R. Lai. *Software Product-Line Engineering — A Family-Based Software Development Process*. Addison-Wesley, Reading, MA, 1999.

33. P. Zave. Feature interactions and formal specification in telecommunications. *IEEE Computer*, pages 20–29, August 1993.

Maturity and Evolution in Software Product Lines: Approaches, Artefacts and Organization

Jan Bosch

University of Groningen
Department of Computing Science
PO Box 800, 9700 AV, Groningen
The Netherlands
Jan.Bosch@cs.rug.nl
http://www.cs.rug.nl/~bosch

Abstract. Software product lines have received considerable adoption in the software industry and prove to be a very successful approach to intra-organizational software reuse. Existing literature, however, often presents only a single approach towards adopting and evolving a software product line. In this paper, we present an overview of different approaches to the architecture-centric, intra-organizational reuse of software artefacts. We relate these to maturity levels for product line artefacts and organizational models.

1 Introduction

Software product lines have achieved substantial adoption by the software industry. A wide variety of companies has substantially decreased the cost of software development and maintenance and time to market, and increased the quality of their software products. The software product line approach can be considered to be the first intra-organizational software reuse approach that has been proven to be successful.

Contemporary literature on product lines often presents one particular approach to adopting a product line, suggesting a particular process model, a particular organizational model, and a specific approach to adopting the product line approach. For instance, most existing literature assumes that the organization has adopted a domain-engineering unit model. This unit develops reusable artefacts, while the product or application-engineering units develop concrete products based on these reusable assets.

However, in our experiences with software companies that have adopted a product line approach, we have learned that the actually available alternatives are generally much more diverse than the particular approach presented in traditional literature. The adoption of a product line, the product line processes and the organization of software development have more freedom than one might expect.

Software product lines do not appear accidentally, but require a conscious and explicit effort from the organization interested in employing the product line

G. Chastek (Ed.): SPLC2 2002, LNCS 2379, p. 257–271, 2002.
© Springer-Verlag Berlin Heidelberg 2002

approach. Basically, one can identify two relevant dimensions with respect to the initiation process. First, the organization may take an evolutionary or a revolutionary approach to the adoption process. Secondly, the product line approach can be applied to an existing line of products or to a new system or product family which the organization intends to use to expand its market. Each case has an associated risk level and benefits. For instance, in general, the revolutionary approach involves more risk, but higher returns when compared to the evolutionary approach. In Table 1, the characteristics of each case are described briefly.

Table 1. Two Dimensions of Product Line Initiation

Project Type	Evolutionary	Revolutionary
Existing set of products	Develop vision for product line architecture based on the architectures of family members. Develop one product line component at a time (possibly for a subset of product line members) by evolving existing components	Product line architecture and components are developed based on super-set of product line member requirements and predicted future requirements.
New product line	Product line architecture and components evolve with the requirements posed by new product line members	Product line architecture and components developed to match requirements of all expected product line members

Independent of the adoption approach taken, the organization will evolve its approach to software development. Typically, the software product line developed by the organization typically evolves through a number of maturity levels[1]. As we will discuss later in this paper, these levels include standardized infrastructure, software platform, software product line, configurable product base, program of product lines, and product populations. For a given scope in terms of features and products containing a subset of these features, each of these approaches can be applied. Thus, these approaches present different solutions to the same problem.

The approach that is most appropriate for a particular situation is a function of the maturity of both the organization and the application domain. Organizations that are more mature in terms of domain understanding, project organization, and management and that have less geographical distribution will more easily adopt more mature product line approaches that typically focus more on domain engineering. A second influencing factor is the maturity of the application domain itself. For stable domains, it is easier to maximize domain engineering and minimize application engineering, because these investments have a high likelihood of providing an adequate return. It is important to stress that the economically optimal approach is a function of the maturity of the organization and the application domain. In highly

---

[1]Our use of the term maturity level has no relation to its use in the Capability Maturity Model (CMM) framework. CMM is registered in the U.S. Patent and Trademark Office.

volatile domains, it may, even for a very mature organization, be preferable to employ only a standardized infrastructure approach.

In addition to the maturity of the overall product line approach, one can also identify different maturity levels for the artefacts that are developed and used as part of the product line approach. These artefacts include the architecture, components, and products. For each of these, we discuss three maturity levels. Finally, different organizational models can be used for product line development.

The remainder of this paper is organized as follows. In the next section, we discuss the six maturity levels that we have identified for software product line approaches. In Section 3, we discuss the maturity levels for the main product line artefacts (i.e., the product line architecture, the shared product line components, and the products). The organizational models one may adopt are discussed in Section 4. In Section 5, we discuss the relationship between the product line approaches, the artefacts, and organizational models. Related work is discussed in Section 6 and the paper is concluded in Section 7.

2   Maturity Levels of Software Product Lines

As mentioned in the introduction, architecture-centric, intra-organizational reuse takes place in various forms. In our experience, these approaches can be organized in a number of levels. The approaches that we have identified are ranging from a standardized infrastructure based on which products are created to a configurable product base that can be used to derive a variety of products. Thus, for a set of products covering a defined scope and that exhibit some commonality, an organization has a number of alternatives for developing and evolving these products, in addition to developing each product from scratch.

In Figure 1, the different maturity levels are presented graphically. Starting from a situation in which each product or application is developed independently, the main maturity development path consists of a standardized infrastructure, a platform, a software product line, and finally, a configurable product base. Two additional developments can be identified: product populations and a program of product lines. A product population approach is chosen when the organization decides to increase the scope in terms of the number of products. The program of product lines is selected when the scope of the product line is extended in terms of the supported features. Typically, there is an overall architecture defining a set of components where each component is again a software product line. The approaches are described in more detail in the sections below.

2.1.   Standardized Infrastructure

Description. The first step that an organization takes when evolving towards exploiting commonality in its products is to standardize the infrastructure upon which the products to be developed will be based. This infrastructure typically consists of the operating system and the typical commercial components on top of it, such as a database management system and a graphical user interface. In addition, the organization may acquire some domain-specific components from external sources. These components are typically integrated through some proprietary glue code.

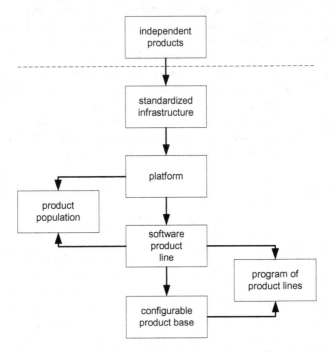

Fig. 1. Maturity Levels for Software Product Lines

Domain versus application engineering. Typical for this approach is that, although it provides a first step towards sharing software artefacts, it requires very little or no domain-engineering effort. Except for creating and maintaining the glue code, which is typically rather small compared to the size of the applications, all effort is directed to application (or product) engineering.

Variability management. The common infrastructure contains no domain-specific functionality, and therefore, no variability management is necessary. The infrastructure components may contain variations, but these need to be managed as in traditional software development.

Example. An example of a company exploiting this approach is Vertis Information Technology. This company develops administrative applications typically supporting some technical production systems. Vertis typically builds its applications on top of a Windows NT platform running the Oracle database system and associated tool set. It has bought a number of domain-specific components for the Dutch taxation system. These components have been integrated with the Oracle tool set and the operating system to form a rather advanced infrastructure on which newly constructed applications are based.

2.2. Platform

Description. The next level in achieving intra-organizational reuse is when the organization develops and maintains a platform on which the products or applications are based. A platform typically includes a standardized infrastructure as discussed in the previous section. On top of that, it captures all functionality that is common to all products or applications. The common functionality that is not provided by the infrastructure is implemented by the organisation itself. But typically the application development treats the platform as if it were an externally bought infrastructure.

Domain versus application engineering. This approach typically requires a certain amount of domain-engineering effort to create and maintain the platform. The main effort, however, is still assigned to application engineering. Although we discuss organizational issues later in this paper, one can typically observe that the organizational model typically is not changed when the platform is adopted. The platform is developed as a project by a team of persons from the different product units or by a separate organizational unit, but it typically captures the functionality that is obviously common to all products. Consequently, relatively little communication between the products units and the platform developers is required. Although product units are encouraged or even told to use the platform, this does not necessarily happen.

Variability management. Since the platform only captures the common functionality of the products, there typically are relatively few variation points. A possible exception may be provided by the variations that crosscut all products (e.g., different infrastructures, secure versus non-secure versions). Such variations that are common to all products can be captured in and supported by the platform. Such variations need to be managed explicitly.

Example. An example of a company employing the platform approach is Symbian Ltd. This company develops the Symbian OS (known earlier as EPOC), an operation system, application framework, and application suite for personal digital assistants and mobile phones. The Symbian OS is distributed in three device-family-requirement definitions (DFRDs), that is, a landscape display communicator (640 x 200 pixels and up), a portrait display communicator (approximately 320 x 240 pixels), and a smart phone family. Each of these DFRDs is distributed to the licensees as a platform that has to be extended with device-specific functionality and licensee-specific applications.

2.3. Software Product Line

Description. Once the benefits of exploiting the commonalities between the products become more accepted within the organization, a consequent development may be to increase the amount of functionality in the platform to the level where the functionality that is common to several but not all products becomes part of the shared artefacts. Now we have reached the stage of a software product line. Functionality specific to one or a few products is still developed as part of the product derivation. Functionality shared by a sufficient number of products is part of the shared product line artefacts, with the consequence that individual products may sacrifice resource efficiency or development effort for being part of the product line.

Domain versus application engineering. Typically, the amount of effort required for domain engineering is roughly equal to the amount of effort needed for product development or application engineering. Also, since the scoping of the features supported by the shared product line artefacts is much more intimately connected to the features supported by the products, explicit and periodic scoping and road-mapping processes are typically put in place.

Variability management. Once the product line stage has been reached, managing the variability supported by the shared artefacts becomes a real challenge. Depending on the stability of the domain, the supported variation points change frequently, both in binding time (typically to a later stage) and the set of variants (typically extended). In most cases that we have studied, however, there is no automated support for variability management.

Example. An example of an organization employing this approach is Axis Communication AB, Lund. It developed a range of network devices such as scanner servers, printer servers, storage servers, and camera servers. These products were developed by as many business units and based on a set of common software artefacts, that is, a product line architecture and a set of more than 10 object-oriented frameworks that were used as configurable product line components.

2.4.   Configurable Product Base

Description. Especially if the organization develops products in relatively stable domains and derives many product instances, there is a tendency to further develop the support for product derivation. The consequence is that the organization, rather than developing a number of different products, moves towards developing only one configurable product base that, either at the organization or at the customer site, is configured into the product bought by the customer. Some companies use, for instance, license-key-driven configuration, shipping the same code base to each and every customer. The code base configures itself based on the provided license key.

Domain versus application engineering. Once the configurable product approach has been fully adopted, all development effort has moved towards domain engineering. Little or no application engineering is provided because the product derivation typically is supported by automated tools or techniques. As presented in Figure 1, this approach represents the highest maturity level.

Variability management. Since product derivation typically is automated once this level is reached, all variation points have an explicit representation in the tool configuring the product for the particular instantiation. The variants for each variation point are part of the configurable product base, and adding new variants to variation points during product derivation is most often not supported. A common characteristic for companies applying this approach is that they understand the domain exceptionally well and, due to that, are able to provide almost all the variability that a customer wants as part of the delivered code base.

Example. An example of an organization applying this approach is Telelarm AB, selling fire alarm systems. After several years of developing and evolving an object-oriented framework for applications in the domain, the company reached the level where each customer basically received the same code base. The persons performing the installation at the customer site are supported by a configuration tool that manages the customer-specific configuration of the product.

As described in the introduction to this section, two additional directions of evolution can be identified. In these cases, the organization decides to extend the scope of the product line in terms of the features covered by the product line or the set of products. In the subsequent sections, these approaches are described in more detail.

2.5.   Programme of Product Lines

Description. Especially for very large systems, the program of product lines approach can be used. This approach consists of a software architecture that is defined for the overall system and that specifies the components that make up the system. Several or all of the components are software product lines. The result is a system that can be configured as the configurable product described above. However, because of the product's size, the configuration of the components is performed basically through product line-based product derivation or by using the configurable product-base approach.

Domain versus application engineering. The division of tasks between domain and application engineering is similar to the basic software product line approach or configurable product approach, depending on which approach is taken by the component developers. However, the actual work when deriving a system is of course greater in this approach. First the overall architecture needs to be derived for the specific system. In some cases, the architecture is constant for all derivations, but in others cases, deviations may occur (e.g., components are excluded). Subsequently, for each architectural component, a derivation from the associated software product line needs to take place. Finally, the system needs to be integrated and validated. These application engineering activities may take substantial effort, depending on the amount of derivation support that has been developed during domain engineering.

Variability management. Managing the complexity resulting from the amount of available variability is typically a real challenge, although it depends on the approach taken. The most complex cases often result from dependencies between variation points in different software product lines in the system. Also, customer-specific extensions to the system may create difficulties because these may crosscut the system's overall architecture.

Example. An illustrative example of this approach is provided by Nokia Networks. The main products of this division are telecom switches. Each system consists of several product families. These product families are developed on top of platforms that, in turn, consist of reusable design blocks consisting of reusable components. A system delivered to a customer requires the selection and configuration of each of the aforementioned elements. Change management in this context is a highly complex endeavour. Nokia Networks employs an approach that it refers to as System Feature Management.

2.6. Product Populations

Description. Whereas the programme of product line extends the set of features covered by a single system, the product population approach extends the set of products that can be derived from the shared product line artefacts. This does not refer to the situation where the same feature scope is populated with a more fine-grained set of products, but rather to the situation where the set of covered features is extended to allow for a more diverse set of products to be derived.

Domain versus application engineering. An interesting consequence of this approach is it diminishes the extent to which a predefined architecture can be imposed on each product. Instead, the components need to be combined in more diverse ways and prepared for this during domain engineering. The division between domain and application engineering is typically similar to that of software product lines.

Variability management. The main difference between this approach and the aforementioned approaches is the fact that variability is not just present within the components, but also in the different ways in which components can be composed. Different products may employ very different configurations. The component interfaces, consequently, need to be prepared for being bound to various interfaces and may need to be able to cope with smaller mismatches.

Example. Philips Consumer Electronics presents an excellent example of this approach. As discussed in [9], Philips has adopted an approach where a set of components can be used to derive a variety of different products, including analog televisions, digital televisions, video recorders, and digital set-top boxes. Many teams around the world develop components that adhere to the defined architecture and its underlying principles. Other teams create individual products by selecting, composing, and configuring components.

3   Product Line Artefacts

One can identify three types of artefacts that make up a software product line: the product line architecture, shared components, and the products derived from the shared artefacts. For each of these artefacts, one can identify three maturity levels, depending on the level of integration achieved in the product line. Below, we discuss each artefact in more detail.

The software architecture of the product line is the artefact that defines the overall decomposition of the products into the main components. In doing so, the architectures captures the commonalities between products and facilitates the variability. One can identify three levels of maturity:

1. **Under-specified architecture**: A first step in the evolutionary adoption of a software product line, especially when converging an existing set of products, is to define the common aspects between the products and to avoid the specification of the differences. This definition of the architecture gives existing and new products a basic frame of reference, but still allows for substantial freedom in product-specific architectural deviation.
2. **Specified architecture**: The next maturity level is to specify both the commonalities and the differences between the products in the software architecture. Now, the architecture captures most of the domain covered by the set of products, although individual products may exploit variation points for product-specific functionality. The products still derive a product-specific architecture from the product line architecture and may consequently make changes. However, the amount of freedom is substantially less than in the under-specified architecture.
3. **Enforced architecture**: The highest maturity level is the enforced architecture. The architecture captures all commonality and variability to the extent where no product needs, nor is allowed, to change the architecture in its implementation. All products use the architecture as-is and exploit the variation points to implement product-specific requirements.

The second type of artefact is the product line component, shared by some or all products in the product line. Whereas the product line architecture defines a way of thinking about the products and rationale for the structure chosen, the components contribute to the product line by providing reusable implementations that fit into the designed architecture. Again, one can identify three levels of maturity for product line components:

1. **Specified component**: The first step in converging a set of existing products towards a product line is to specify the interface of the components defined by the architecture. A component specification typically consists of a provided, a required, and a configuration interface. Based on the component specifications, the individual products can evolve their architecture and product-specific component implementations towards the product line, thereby simplifying further integration in the future.
2. **Multiple component implementations**: The second level of maturity is where, for an architectural component, multiple component implementations exist, but each implementation is shared by more than one product. Typically, closely related products have converged to the extent that component sharing has become feasible and, where necessary, variation points have been implemented in the shared components.
3. **Configurable component implementation**: The third level is where only one component implementation is used. This implementation is typically highly configurable since all required variability has been captured in the component imple-

mentation. Often, additional support is provided for configuring or deriving a product-specific instantiation of the component (e.g., through graphical tools or generators).

The third artefact type in a software product line is the products derived from the common product line artefacts. Again, three levels of maturity can be distinguished:

1. **Architecture conformance**: The first step in converging a product towards a product line is to conform to the architecture specified by the product line. A product can only be considered a member of the product line if it at least conforms to the under-specified architecture.
2. **Platform-based product**: The second level is the minimalist approach [1] where only those components that capture functionality common to all products are shared between products. Because the functionality is so common, typically little variability needs to be implemented.
3. **Configurable Product Base**: The third level of maturity is the maximalist approach [1], where all or almost all functionality implemented by any of the product line members is captured by the shared product line artefacts. Products are derived by configuring and selecting or deselecting elements. Often, automated support is provided to derive individual products.

4   Organizational Models

In this section, we discuss a number of organizational models that can be applied when adopting an approach that is based on a software product line. Below, we briefly introduce the models. For a more extensive discussion, we refer to [1].

- **Development department**: When all software development is concentrated in a single development department, no organizational specialization exists with either the assets or the products in the product line. Instead, the staff at the department is considered to be a resource that can be assigned to a variety of projects, including domain-engineering projects to develop and evolve the reusable assets that make up the product line.

- **Business units**: The second type of organizational model employs a specialization around the type of products. Each business unit is responsible for one or a subset of the products in the product line. The business units share the product line assets, and the evolution of these assets is performed by the unit that needs to incorporate new functionality in one of the assets to fulfill the requirements of the product or products for which it is responsible. On occasion, business units may initiate domain-engineering projects to either develop new shared assets or to perform major reorganizations of existing assets.

- **Domain-engineering unit**: This model is the suggested organization for software product lines as presented in the traditional literature (e.g., Dikel et al. [4] and Macala et al. [7]). In this model, the domain-engineering unit is responsible for the design, development, and evolution of the reusable assets (i.e., the product line architecture and shared components that make up the reusable part of the product line). In addition, business units, often referred to as product-engineering units, are responsible for developing and evolving the products based on the product line assets.

- **Hierarchical domain-engineering units**: In cases where an hierarchical product line has been necessary, a hierarchy of domain units may also be required. Often in this case, terms such as platforms are used to refer to the top-level product line. The domain-engineering units that work with specialized product lines use the top-level product line assets as a basis for their own product lines.

Some factors that influence the organizational model, but that we have not yet mentioned include the physical location of the staff involved in the software product line, the project management maturity, the organizational culture, and the type of products. In addition to the size of the product line in terms of the number of products and product variants, and the number of staff members, these factors are important for choosing the optimal model.

5   Relating Maturity Levels, Artefacts and Organization

In previous sections, we first discussed maturity levels of software product lines. Next, we discussed maturity levels for the product line artefacts (i.e., architecture, components, and products). Finally, we discussed the different organisational models that can be applied when employing software product lines. However, the various maturity levels and approaches cannot be combined arbitrarily. In our experience, certain combinations work well together where others do not. In Table 2, we relate the product line approaches[2] to the artefact maturity levels and organizational models that we have discussed. Although the absence of a '+' or '+/-' does not necessarily indicate an incompatibility, these combinations are, in our experience, less likely or require additional effort to achieve.

Below, we discuss the combinations in the table for each product line maturity level. The standard infrastructure approach cannot impose more than an underspecified architecture. Since the infrastructure typically only provides relatively generic behaviour, it cannot fully specify a software architecture for the product line. In addition, the standard infrastructure can only specify the part of component interfaces that is concerned with the functionality provided by the infrastructure. For instance, in the case of an object-oriented database being part of the standard infrastructure, persistent components need to support interfaces for persistence, queries, and transactions. Products based on the standard infrastructure only need to conform to the architectural restrictions imposed; they are free otherwise. Since the standard infrastructure requires little effort from the organization, there is no need for

---

[2] The previously listed approaches are abbreviated. Hence in Table 2, SI represents standardized interface, P represents platform, and so forth.

a separate organizational unit taking, maintaining, and evolving the shared artefacts. Consequently, the development department and business unit organizational models are primarily suited for this approach.

Table 2. Relating Maturity Levels to Software Product Line Artefacts and Organisation

Artefacts and Organisation	Product Line Approaches					
	SI	P	SPL	CPB	PP	PPL
Under-specified Architecture	+	+			+	
Specified Architecture			+		+	+
Enforced Architecture				+		
Specified Component	+/-	+			+/-	
Multiple Component Implementations.		+/-	+		+	+/-
Configurable Component			+/-	+		+
Architecture Conformance	+					
Platform-Based Product		+	+		+	
Configurable Product Base				+		+
Development Department	+	+	+			
Business Units	+	+	+			
Domain-engineering Unit			+	+	+	
Hierarchical Domain-Engineering Units					+	+

The platform approach typically employs an underspecified architecture, because it lacks the information about specific products constructed on top of the platform. Compared to the standardized infrastructure approach, the platform architecture typically demands more conformance from products in terms of architectural rules and constraints that have to be followed. Component interfaces are typically specified at least partially and for the common behaviour; component implementations may be provided by the platform. Products are constructed on top of the platform, as indicated in the table. Platforms are typically created through the efforts of a dedicated domain-engineering team, but do not necessarily require the existence of a domain-engineering unit during the usage and evolution of the platform.

The software product line approach specifies a product line architecture that captures the commonalities and variabilities of the products. For each architectural component, one or more component implementations are provided. For the more stable and well understood components, multiple implementations may have merged into one configurable component implementation. Products are based on the product line, but may deviate where necessary. We have worked with companies that employ widely different organizational models, including the development department, business units, and domain-engineering unit models.

The most domain-engineering-centric approach centres around a configurable product base. In this case, the architecture is enforced in that no product can deviate from the commonalities and variabilities specified in the architecture. Consequently, each architectural component typically has one associated configurable component implementation, and the products are derived from these artefacts by excluding those parts not needed. A configurable product base is typically developed by a domain-engineering unit, but since there are no associated application-engineering units, the organizational model is difficult to distinguish from the development department.

The product population approach increases the scope the product line in terms of features and products. Due to the wide variety of products, the architecture cannot be enforced. In addition, depending on the type of population, the architecture may even not be fully specified, because part of the variability is achieved by creative configurations of the components. There may be multiple component implementations, although some components may need to be specifically implemented for each product. Especially in the case where the product population is organized into smaller sets, a hierarchical domain-engineering-unit model may be applied. Otherwise, a domain-engineering-unit model is used.

The final approach (i.e., a program of product lines) extends the scope of individual products in terms of the features. The overall architecture is typically well specified as it defines the interaction between the component product lines. The architectural components are software product lines in themselves and, as such, are typically rather configurable. Products are derived by configuring the product line components for the specific context in which the products are used. Due to the size of the overall system, the hierarchical domain-engineering-unit model is typically employed.

6   Related Work

Software reuse is a long-standing ambition of the software engineering community, dating back to the late 1960s [9] and 1970s [11]. The increasing popularity of the object-oriented paradigm during the 1980s leads to the definition of object-oriented frameworks. As part of this work, for instance, the REBOOT project defined reuse maturity levels [7]. Also, Roberts and Johnson [12] discuss a number of maturity levels for object-oriented frameworks in the form of a pattern language.

During the 1990s, the notion of software product lines (or software system families) was adopted and achieved increasing attention as can be judged from the existence of several large european projects, including ARES, PRAISE, ESAPS and CAFE, the Software Product Line Initiative at the Software Engineering Institute (SEI) [2], and the first conferences in the field (e.g., [5]).

Several authors published work in related to this paper. Weiss and Lai [14] present an approach that relates to the maturity level that we refer to as a configurable product base. In their approach, a generator is developed that generates the specific product derivation that is required. Czarnecki and Eisenecker [3] also employ generative techniques to minimize the amount of application engineering needed.

Schmid [13] discusses the process of scoping during the adoption of software product lines.

7 Conclusions

Software product lines have received wide adoption in many software companies and have proven to be very successful in achieving intra-organizational reuse. Traditional literature for development based on software product lines typically takes one particular approach. However, in our experience with industry, we have identified that companies employ widely different approaches and that these approaches evolve over time. These approaches can be organized in a number of maturity levels. These maturity levels include standardized infrastructure, software platform, software product line, configurable product base, program of product lines, and product populations. For a given scope in terms of features and products, each of the approaches can be applied. The optimal approach for a company depends on the maturity of both the organization and the application domain.

Next to the different approaches to software product lines, we have also presented maturity levels for the product line artefacts (i.e., the architecture, components, and products). The product line architecture can be underspecified, fully specified, or enforced. The components can just consist of a component interface specification, multiple component implementations, and one configurable component implementation. Finally, a product can conform to the product line architecture, be a platform-based product, or be derived from a configurable product base. We discussed four alternative organizational models: the development department model, the business unit model, the domain-engineering-unit model, and the hierarchical domain-engineering-unit model.

In Section 5, we discussed the relations between the product line approaches, the artefacts, and the organizational models. We presented the more common and logical combinations of approaches, maturity levels of artefacts, and organizational models.

This paper is a first attempt to categorize the different approaches to software product lines. In the future, we intend to further validate, refine, and extend this taxonomy.

Acknowledgements

Many thanks to Osmo Vikman from Nokia who kindly provided information about the program of product lines approach as used within Nokia Networks and to Rob van Ommering from Philips Research for his information on the product populations approach.

References

1. J. Bosch, *Design and Use of Software Architectures: Adopting and Evolving a Product Line Approach*, Pearson Education (Addison-Wesley & ACM Press), ISBN 0-201-67494-7, May 2000.
2. P. Clements, L. Northrop, Software Product Lines - Practices and Patterns, Pearson Education (Addison-Wesley), ISBN 0-201-70332-7, 2001.
3. K. Czarnecki, U.W. Eisenecker, *Generative Programming - Methods, Tools and Applications*, Pearson Education (Addison-Wesley), ISBN 0-201-30977-7, 2000.
4. D. Dikel, D. Kane, S. Ornburn, W. Loftus, J. Wilson, 'Applying Software Product-Line Architecture,' *IEEE Computer*, pp. 49-55, August 1997.
5. P. Donohoe (ed.), Software Product Lines - Experience and Research Directions, Kluwer Academic Publishers, ISBN 0-7923-7940-3, 2000.
6. J. van Gurp, J. Bosch, M. Svahnberg, 'On the Notion of Variability in Software Product Lines,' Proceedings of the Working IEEE/IFIP Conference on Software Architecture (WICSA 2001), August 2001.
7. E-A. Karlsson, Editor, *Software Reuse - a Holistic Approach*, John Wiley & Sons, 1995.
8. R.R. Macala, L.D. Stuckey, D.C. Gross, 'Managing Domain-Specific Product-Line Development,' IEEE Software, pp. 57-67, 1996.
9. M. D. McIlroy, 'Mass Produced Software Components,' in 'Software Engineering,' *Report on A Conference Sponsored by the NATO Science Committee,* P. Naur, B. Randell (eds.), Garmisch, Germany, 7th to 11th October, 1968, NATO Science Committee, 1969.
10. R. van Ommering, 'Building Product Populations with Software Components,' *Proceedings of ICSE 2002* (to appear), 2002.
11. D.L. Parnas, 'On the Design and Development of Program Families', *IEEE Transactions on Software Engineering*, Vol. SE-2, No. 1, March 1976.
12. D. Roberts, R. Johnson, 'Evolving Frameworks: A Pattern Language for Developing Object-Oriented Frameworks,' Proceedings of the Third Conference on Pattern Languages and Programming, Montecillio, Illinois, 1996.
13. K. Schmid. 'Software Product Lines: Experience and Research Directions,' Proceedings of the First Software Product Line Conference (SPLC1), (Ed.) Patrick Donohoe, Kluwer Academic Publishers, Aug. 2000, pp. 513-532.
14. D.M. Weiss, C.T.R. Lai, *Software Product-Line Engineering - A Family-Based Software Development Process*, Addison-Wesley, ISBN 0-201-69438-7, 1999.

Evolutionary Introduction of Software Product Lines

Daniel Simon and Thomas Eisenbarth

Universität Stuttgart
Breitwiesenstrasse 20–22
70565 Stuttgart, Germany
{simon, eisenbarth}@informatik.uni-stuttgart.de

Abstract. Software product lines have proved to be a successful and efficient means for managing the development of software in industry. The significant benefits over traditional software architectures have the potential to convince software companies to adopt the product line approach for their existing products. In that case, the question arises how to best convert the existing products into a software product line. For several reasons, an evolutionary approach is desirable. But so far, there is little guidance on the evolutionary introduction of software product lines.

In this paper, we propose a lightweight iterative process supporting the incremental introduction of product line concepts for existing software products. Starting with the analysis of the legacy code, we assess what parts of the software can be restructured for product line needs at reasonable costs. For the analysis of the products, we use feature analysis, a reengineering technique tailored to the specific needs of the initiation of software product lines.

1 Introduction

Suppose a company C is developing and selling a software-intensive product P. Product P is very successful on the market; customers use P and pay for maintenance and support. Because of P's success, C's marketing division wants to develop variants of P that are tailored to customer-specific requirements. Being aware of anticipated future features of the software, the company's software engineers consider a software product line approach for P and its relatives. The general question now arises: is P product line ready? If so, how can a software product line be best introduced?

According to Bosch [1], the initiation of a software product line has two relevant dimensions. On one hand, the organization may either take an evolutionary or a revolutionary approach to introduce product line concepts. On the other hand, the introduction of a new product line is different from the application of the approach to an existing product (a set of products).

For the introduction of product line development, changes within the company's organization are due. These depend on several factors, such as the size and number of products, the staff involved, or the organizational culture. For a further discussion of organizational topics, we refer to [1] [2] and to the framework provided in [3].

In parallel to organizational changes in the company, the software development is subject to changes. In cases where there are existing products, the mining of legacy assets

G. Chastek (Ed.): SPLC2 2002, LNCS 2379, pp. 272–283, 2002.
© Springer-Verlag Berlin Heidelberg 2002

for product lines helps to protect investments and the domain competence encoded in the software. There are several frameworks addressing the migration and reengineering for product lines. The Option Analysis Reengineering (OAR) Method [4] provides a framework for the mining of components for a software product line. Similarly, the PuLSE [5] methodology for the development of product lines incorporates migration steps. Both the OAR and PuLSE methods provide a means for the revolutionary introduction of product lines but do not fully support incremental and gradual transitioning.

In the case of company C, there is a number of reasons *not* to take the revolutionary approach. Instead, an evolutionary introduction can bring strategic advantages for the business. Some reasons for the application of an evolutionary approach are the following:

- The software developers have detailed knowledge about the structure of the software and its current architecture, but it is not obvious whether the product line approach is feasible.
- The software developers have no experience with software product lines and they are not used to software product line concepts. A disruptive switch-over to the new technology bears a high risk of failure.
- The product is available and used by customers, and needs continuous maintenance and support. In contrast to a revolutionary approach, the evolutionary introduction allows the simultaneous maintenance with little overhead.
- By using an evolutionary migration process, developers can "learn on the job." They get used to product line concepts and have a better idea of how the product P can be seen from a product line perspective.
- The changes to the product are accessible immediately. The first results of migration efforts will take effect in a short time.
- High domain competence is encoded in the software. Therefore, investment protection [6] is necessary.

There is no doubt that there are some risks. Prominently, the product has been developed over a long period of time without product line concepts at hand, and therefore might not fit the needs of a product line. The migration is difficult, because the legacy code has to be reengineered. For the evolutionary transition, at least a complete reengineering (which would be too expensive) can be avoided by conducting partial reengineering of the legacy software. Because the transition to a product line is experimental, the cost should be as low as possible.

Overview The rest of this paper is organized as follows. Section 2 introduces a migration process that is suited for the incremental introduction of a product line architecture. In Section 3, we present a tailored reengineering method, called *feature analysis*, that can significantly contribute to the understanding of the legacy system from a product line perspective. In Section. 4, we compare our work to related research. Finally, in Section. 5, we summarize the results of this paper and give hints for future work.

2   Evolutionary Process

In this section, we propose a lightweight iterative process that assists the asset-mining-based evolutionary introduction of software product lines.

2.1   Prerequisites

The prerequisites for the application of the migration process are modest. For one thing, we assume that the features of the legacy system are, at least to some extent, known to the programmers and/or users of the system. The software itself is largely understood, but not necessarily suitable for product line development. The specific parts of the software that could be used for product line development are not known for sure.

Because the transition proceeds in several iterations that have some time in between, it is further not necessary that the needs of product lines are well understood right from the start. Instead, all participants will gain knowledge and experience throughout the gradual process towards the product line.

2.2   Participants

The process comprises the participation of several parties. We need an expert programmer and architect of the legacy software, a domain engineer, users and customers, a reengineer, and a product line expert. These people form different working groups during the process. However, for the development of the product line, the internal personnel of the company should always work closely together. That way, the participants get accustomed to the new technology more easily.

2.3   Process Steps

The evolutionary process iterates the following steps. As an illustration, the proceeding is depicted in Figure 1. The process as a whole can be iterated as well.

Identification of available and accessible features. The first step of the process uses the expert knowledge of programmers, software architects, users, and customers to obtain a list of existing features.

Priorization of identified features. The number of features a product provides is usually large. Because we do not want to perform a complete reengineering of the legacy code and because we want quick results, the domain engineer selects important features. With the involvement of customers, the features are ordered with respect to where the important variations for the customer are spotted.

Feature anticipation. The domain expert performs a market analysis to anticipate features of future versions and variants of the product.

Feature analysis. The reengineer and the product line expert analyze the legacy product(s) according to the selected number of features. Feature Analysis is described in detail in Section 3. The individual steps are

1. Feature location. Where are the features implemented in the legacy code?
2. Recognition of commonalities and variabilities. Where are the commonality and variability points in the legacy system?
3. Recognition of dependencies among features. Which features depend on which other features? Are there features not accessible for end users?
4. Metrics computation. The use of metrics facilitates the evaluation of the proposed changes. Is the intended architecture feasible for a product line approach?

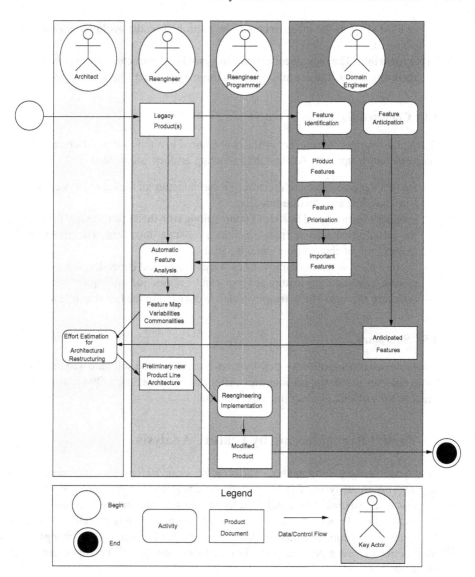

Fig. 1. One iteration step of the process for the evolutionary migration towards a product line architecture

Effort estimation. Based on the results of feature analysis, the product line expert and the reengineer decide if the restructuring is manageable and pays off. Further, the parts of the software where anticipated features can be hooked in are identified in the preliminary product line architecture. The product line expert and the architects of the old software perform an architecture analysis (e.g., the Software Architecture Analysis Method SAAM) [7] or the Architecture Tradeoff Anaylsys Method

(ATAM) [8]). If the effort seems to be unprofitable, the evolutionary migration is canceled.

Reengineering. The reengineer and the programmers restructure (parts) of the software according to its features and to the preliminary product line architecture.

2.4   Collected Data

During the process, all relevant artifacts are stored in a repository. After each iteration, the repository is updated. At least the following artifacts are needed:

– System's product line architecture. The architecture of the legacy system is used as a product line architecture initially.
– Product's feature list. The list of features along with their priorities and their potential for variations should be maintained as a separate document. The priorities of the features might change over some iterations.
– Feature map, feature commonalities, variabilities, and dependencies. All the information gained during feature analysis can be reused for subsequent iterations.
– Software sources. The software system is changed in the last step of each iteration.

2.5   Summary

The proposed process allows a step-by-step migration of the software without disrupting the maintenance and support activities. After each iteration, the software system is more suitable for software product line development.

3   Partial Reengineering by Feature Analysis

Traditional reengineering methods focus on the legacy software's components and usually require an analysis of the complete system at hand. Unfortunately, this kind of analysis is an expensive task and therefore is not feasible for experimental changes to the architecture. In our context, the cost for reengineering might well exceed the cost for reimplementation—because we know for sure that the architecture changes. Below, we describe the reengineering method called *feature analysis* that compensates for these shortcomings.

First, feature analysis is tailored to the needs of reengineering for product lines as it focuses on the features of a legacy software rather than on its components. Second, feature analysis allows for partial reengineering. The input for feature analysis is just the set of software features of interest. Starting from that, the rest of the software is inspected on a demand-driven basis. Third, feature analysis can be based on dynamic program behavior and can be implemented easily. It quickly yields results that can be combined and refined with conventional reengineering methods.

The remainder of this section explains feature analysis in detail. The first step (Section 3.1) of feature analysis is the location of a feature in the source code (or the components) of the legacy system. Second (Section 3.2), the dependencies of features are investigated. The feature's variabilities and commonalities are inspected. The last step of feature analysis (Section 3.3) consists of metric computation that indicates the feasibility and cost of the implementation of proposed results. Based on the results of feature analysis, restructuring proposals can be made along with an estimation of the cost of the proposed changes. Finally, an example for the application of feature analysis is given in Section 3.4.

3.1   Feature Location

To find the feature's implementation, there are either static or dynamic analyses, or the combination of both. A static approach is taken by Chen and Rajlich [9]. They propose a semi-automatic method for feature location that involves a human-guided search on the *Program Dependence Graph*. Their method takes into account documentation as well as domain knowledge and, as experiments in [10] show, can be quite time-consuming.

The general idea of dynamic feature location is founded in the observation that a feature exposed to a user can be invoked in a usage scenario. If we record the routines that were executed during the usage scenario, we know where to look for the feature's implementation. With source-code instrumentation, recording a usage scenario is simple. For further reduction of the search space, we compare different records for specific variants of the feature invocation.

Wilde and Scully [11] pioneered in taking a fully dynamic approach by analyzing *sequential traces* of program executions. After instrumenting the source code with the output of trace information, their *Software Reconnaissance* executes the program once, invoking the feature and once again not invoking the feature. By subtracting the trace results of the second from the first invocation, the parts of the source code implementing the feature can be identified. The software reconnaissance is implemented by the tool RECON [12].

For large programs, sequential traces grow voluminous and are difficult to handle. In those cases, execution profiles seem more suitable than sequential traces. The most simple code-instrumentation solution is using a profiler that is usually a part of the development environment. The profiler extracts the information about which and how often routines were executed during the program run (and various other information). We have presented a method for feature location based on execution profiles in previous papers [13] [14] [15].

Other than Wilde, we employ several program traces (program profiles) at a time. We collect the profiling result of a number of feature invocations and merge them into a relation table that contains the information *routine r is invoked in scenario s*.

Subsequently, we apply the mathematically founded method *concept analysis* to investigate the data. The result of concept analysis, the *concept lattice*, is interpreted manually, but guided by generally applicable interpretation hints. The concept lattice is represented graphically and provides useful means for the investigation of the software system.

3.2   Feature Dependencies, Variabilities, and Commonalities

For a product line architecture, it is important to understand the dependencies, variabilities, and commonalities of product features. To analyze relations between features, it is not sufficient to look at one feature at a time. Rather, it is essential to investigate a set of features. Because Wilde as well as Rajlich analyze only individual features, their approaches would have to be applied repeatedly, whereas our approach investigates sets of (more or less) related features.

The idea of our method is based on the following consideration: When we invoke a series of (related) features, and simultaneously record the execution profiles, we are interested in what routines are executed for all of the features (indicating commonalities) on one side. On the other side, the routines that are invoked exclusively for individual features indicate the variabilities. What we need is a useful grouping of routines. This grouping is achieved automatically by our method and can serve as a hint for the product line architecture of the involved features.

3.3   Restructuring Cost Assessment by Metrics

After we identified the features in code, we want to assess the complexity of a restructuring effort. Metrics are useful as a first indication in this regard.

One approach to quantify the relation between program components and features is studied by Wong et al. [16]. This work is based on Wilde's approach and tries to complement Wilde's results by providing a more complete picture of how the features are spread across the software source. Wong proposes three metrics: the disparity between features, the concentration of the feature implementation in components, and the dedication of components to features.

In the context of product lines, the disparity serves as an indicator for commonalities (the greater the disparity between features, the less they have in common). The concentration and the dedication allow for the assessment of the restructuring cost. However, the quantification does not take dependencies into account, as the feature-location technique it is based on does not. Currently, we are investigating metrics that are based on our concept lattices.

3.4   Example for Feature Analysis

In [13] [14] [15], we applied feature analysis to various software systems with promising results. In the following, we present a case study we performed in [15] with the drawing tool XFIG [17] for the purpose of program understanding. The results of the analysis are reinterpreted for product line goals.

XFIG is a menu-driven tool that enables the user to draw and manipulate graphical objects interactively under the X Window System. It is written in the C programming language and consists of about 75KLOC in 175 files containing over 1.900 C routines. Without a further look at the sources of XFIG, we compiled the program with profiling information.

We looked at the facilities to draw various shapes (e.g., *circles*, *ellipses*, *boxes*, *arcs*, and others). We executed the corresponding usage scenarios for creating the objects and collected the execution profiles. Then we applied our feature analysis tool. The resulting lattice is shown in Figure 2.

The boxes in Figure 2 represent *concepts*. They contain the features' names and the routines that were invoked during the features' invocation. A concept on the topmost level

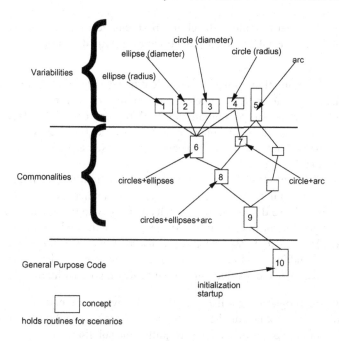

Fig. 2. Example lattice (excerpt) for an experiment with the drawing tool XFIG. The lattice reveals the variabilities and commonalities of selected features as found in the actual source code.

of the lattice corresponds to a single feature and contains the routines required specifically for that feature (e.g., Concepts #1–#5). Below the first level, the interdependencies of features are made explicit. The concept contain the routines that are jointly used for the atop feature. Concept #6, for example, lists the routines that are jointly used for the variants of ellipses and circles. The more we descend in the lattice, the more general the routines in the concepts are. At the bottom, Concept #10 lists the routines that are used in all scenarios (e.g., initialization code and the main start routine).

The lattice reveals the variabilities and commonalities for drawing circles and ellipses: the top-level concepts represent the variants for drawing round objects; Concept #6 below holds the common code. In the special case of XFIG, the following activities could be guided directly by our results.

Source Code Restructuring. XFIG's source files are not structured according to the concepts found by the analysis using shape features. If a file structure pursuant to the shape objects is desired, the concept lattice indicates how to restructure the sources.

Adding and Removing Features. New shape variants can be added easily using the structure of the other shapes as a template. For example, defining a circle object by three points can reuse the functionality as grouped in Concept #6. Existing variants can be removed easily by removing the routines of the variability concept of the corresponding shape. In order to remove the ellipse-by-radius feature, we remove the routines of Concept #1 and the GUI elements identified by a static dependency analysis [15].

Product Configuration. Since we have identified the groups of routines that implement the variants, we can try to parameterize the build process for XFIG (i.e., to introduce points for compile-time configurations). With respect to the variants, the routines that vary are included on demand. For example, all circles and ellipses depend on Concept #6, so if a product is configured to include circles or ellipses as product features, the routines in Concept #6 have to be included.

For XFIG, our technique leads us directly to the routines realizing the variabilities currently included in the system. But the system is not necessarily structured "configuration friendly." We do not get the knowledge of how to restructure the software to be more configurable for free, but it is fairly easy to spot the underlying structure of XFIG. For example, the manipulation features such as moving or resizing objects are organized as routines handling all kinds of shapes by a case statement. That leads to at least three options to organize the configuration of an evolving product line:

1. Give the programmer a list of all locations where the code has to be changed to add or remove kinds of shapes according to product configurations (i.e., a manual configuration of products, the least preferable solution).
2. Generate the case statements automatically according to product configurations (automatized configuration, higher effort for tool support).
3. When migrating from C to C++ (this decision in itself has a long-term strategic impact), the kinds of shapes correspond to classes, and the case statements would be replaced by virtual functions. Subsequently, the class hierarchy can be parameterized according to product configurations (use of modern implementation technology).

These options can be implemented such that the functionality of an accordingly configured product is exactly the same as that of the old product. That way, regression testing can be supported. Our method helps spotting potential variability points that can be restructured, so that the product line becomes more configurable.

4   Related Research

The need for mechanisms to develop software product lines starting from existing, successful products is generally recognized. The main research areas today are product line processes (i.e., frameworks for product line development and changes to a company's organization). Further, the support for the low-level modification of the legacy code itself is of vital interest, as this is a topic where investments can be leveraged.

Frameworks: The Software Engineering Institute promotes the software product line practice framework [3]. This framework collects information, including studies from various organizations and practitioners with the goal that the product line community can use the growing body of knowledge involving the development, acquisition, and evolution of a software product line. Bergey et al's framework [18] discusses software migration issues in general. The migration and mining efforts for the software product lines they propose are not evolutionary and incremental; they do not provide points to make a strategic withdrawal from product line technology when the migration is underway. Bosch [1] proposes methods for designing software architectures, in particular product line architectures. Bosch explores the concepts of product lines and discusses the pros and cons of the evolutionary and revolutionary instantiations of software product lines in the face of existing products. PuLSE [5] implements a complete framework for the introduction, scoping, evolution, and maintenance of software product lines.

Asset Mining for Product Lines: Bergey et al. [19] propose a method for mining assets for product line reuse at a high level of abstraction. Before the process can start, a product line architecture is required. Based on the Horseshoe Model and on the OAR method [4], they try to leverage components on a large scale. Reengineering techniques are used for architecture reconstruction to prepare the legacy software for modifications. The modification and restructuring of components according to product line needs is not considered. Within the PuLSE methodology for the development of product lines, RE-PLACE [20] is presented as an approach to support the transitioning of existing software assets towards a product line architecture. RE-PLACE uses architecture recovery for legacy systems. The main goal for reengineering is the identification of components that can be reused in the product line and the integration of components into the product line. Recovered components are treated as black boxes and are only reused as a whole. In the provided case study, the core of a legacy system is wrapped up for reuse. The transitioning process itself is not incremental and has no intermediate products. Instead, the software product line architecture is reached in one step.

5 Conclusion and Future Work

In the previous sections, we have introduced a process supporting the evolutionary introduction of software product line concepts. The process starts out from a legacy software system that supports no product line concepts. After each iterative step in the process, the legacy product is restructured so that parts of it conform to the needs of product lines. Throughout the process, there are dropout points (i.e., if restructuring the legacy code does not seem feasible, the migration process is canceled, and instead, a replacement of the software is indicated).

Our method avoids an expensive architectural reconstruction of the legacy system. Since the architecture will change anyway, we are interested in the features of the software rather than those of the architectural components. To restructure software according to the needs of software product lines, we use feature analysis. Feature analysis has proved to be a cheap and easy-to-implement yet powerful method to reinvestigate legacy code under a completely different paradigm.

Our future research goals include the further refinement of feature analysis and the evaluation of the iterative, incremental process in an industrial project that aims at the initiation of a software product line. The refinement of feature analysis is carried on in the context of the Bauhaus Project [21] at the Universität Stuttgart. We plan to improve that method by integrating further automatic source-code analyses.

References

1. Bosch, J.: Design & Use of Software Architectures. Addison-Wesley and ACM Press (2000)
2. Clements, P., Northrop, L.: Software Product Lines—Practices and Patterns. SEI Series in Software Engineering. Addison-Wesley (2001)
3. Northrop, L.M.: A Framework for Software Product Line Practice. Available at http://www.sei.cmu.edu/plp/framework.html (2001)
4. Bergey, J., O'Brien, L., Smith, D.: Options Analysis for Reengineering (OAR): A Method for Mining Legacy Assets. Technical Report CMU/SEI-2001-TN-013, SEI, Carnegie Mellon University (2001)
5. Bayer, J., Flege, O., Knauber, P., Laqua, R., Muthig, D., Schmid, K., Widen, T., DeBaud, J.M.: PuLSE: A Methodology to Develop Software Product Lines. In: Proceedings of the Fifth ACM SIGSOFT Symposium on Software Reusability (SSR'99), Los Angeles, CA, USA, ACM Press (1999) 122–131
6. Eisenbarth, T., Simon, D.: Guiding Feature Asset Mining for Software Product Line Development. In: Proceedings of the International Workshop on Product Line Engineering: The Early Steps: Planning, Modeling, and Managing, Erfurt, Germany, Fraunhofer IESE (2001) 1–4
7. Kazman, R., Bass, L., Abowd, G., Webb, M.: SAAM: A Method for Analyzing the Properties of Software Architectures. In: Proceedings of the 16th International Conference on Software Engineering, Sorrento, Italy, IEEE Computer Society Press (1994) 81–90
8. Kazman, R., Klein, M., Barbacci, M., Longstaff, T., Lipson, H., Carrière, S.J.: The Architecture Tradeoff Analysis Method. In: Proceedings of the 4th International Conference on Engineering of Complex Computer Systems, Monterey, CA, USA, IEEE Computer Society Press (1998) 68–78
9. Chen, K., Rajlich, V.: Case Study of Feature Location Using Dependence Graph. In: Proceedings of the 8th International Workshop on Program Comprehension, Limerick, Ireland, IEEE Computer Society Press (2000) 241–249
10. Wilde, N., Buckellew, M., Page, H., Rajlich, V.: A Case Study of Feature Location in Unstructured Legacy Fortran Code. In: Proceedings of the 5th European Conference on Software Maintenance and Reengineering, Lisbon, Portugal, IEEE Computer Society Press (2001) 68–75
11. Wilde, N., Scully, M.C.: Software Reconnaissance: Mapping Program Features to Code. Journal of Software Maintenance: Research and Practice **7** (1995) 49–62
12. Wilde, N.: RECON. Available at http://www.cs.uwf.edu/~recon/ (2001)
13. Eisenbarth, T., Koschke, R., Simon, D.: Derivation of Feature-Component Maps by Means of Concept Analysis. In: Proceedings of the 5th European Conference on Software Maintenance and Reengineering, Lisbon, Portugal, IEEE Computer Society Press (2001) 176–179
14. Eisenbarth, T., Koschke, R., Simon, D.: Feature-Driven Program Understanding Using Concept Analysis of Execution Traces. In: Proceedings of the 9th International Workshop on Program Comprehension, Toronto, Canada, IEEE Computer Society Press (2001) 300–309
15. Eisenbarth, T., Koschke, R., Simon, D.: Aiding Program Comprehension by Static and Dynamic Feature Analysis. In: Proceedings of the International Conference on Software Maintenance, Florence, Italy, IEEE Computer Society Press (2001) 602–611
16. Wong, W.E., Gokhale, S.S., Hogan, J.R.: Quantifying the Closeness between Program Components and Features. The Journal of Systems and Software **54** (2000) 87–98
17. The XFIG drawing tool, Version 3.2.3d. Available at http://www.xfig.org/ (2001)
18. Bergey, J.K., Northrop, L.M., Smith, D.B.: Enterprise Framework for the Disciplined Evolution of Legacy Systems. Technical Report CMU/SEI-97-TR-007, SEI, Carnegie Mellon University, Pittsburgh, PA, USA (1997)

19. Bergey, J., O'Brien, L., Smith, D.: Mining Existing Software Assets for Software Product Lines. Technical Report CMU/SEI-2000-TN-008, SEI, Carnegie Mellon University (2000)
20. Bayer, J., Girard, J.F., Würthner, M., DeBaud, J.M., Apel, M.: Transitioning Legacy Assets to a Product Line Architecture. In: Proceedings of the Seventh European Software Engineering Conference (ESEC'99). Lecture Notes in Computer Science 1687, Toulouse, France, Springer (1999) 446–463
21. The New Bauhaus Stuttgart. Available at http://www.bauhaus-stuttgart.de/ (2002)

Governance Polarities of Internal Product Lines

Truman M. Jolley, David J. Kasik, and Conrad E. Kimball

Boeing Commercial Airplanes
P.O. Box 3707
Seattle, WA 98124-3707 USA
truman.m.jolley@boeing.com
david.j.kasik@boeing.com
conrad.kimball@boeing.com

Abstract. Tension occurs when multiple organizations develop and deliver their own product lines to a single user community. We apply polarity management to the governance of shared architecture, products, and processes for the delivery and management of tens of product lines. These product lines contain hundreds of applications used by thousands of engineers in Boeing Commercial Airplanes. This paper focuses on the use of polarity management to construct extensible governance bodies and processes for the second phase of product line expansion. We define polarity to be "two principles which are both true but conflict." Polarities are often mistaken to be problems to be solved; however, polarities are *held*, not *solved*. Polarity management of the product line infrastructure, a complex customer-supplier network, identifies primary organizational tensions that require management; poorly held polarities cause chaos and failure.

1   Introduction

We describe an approach to constructing extensible governance bodies and governance processes for information technology (IT) product lines internal to a company. A previous paper [1] described the technology needed to develop the shared architecture needed for Boeing's Single Glass system. In this paper, we address "the organizational entity that has responsibility for the architecture and other core assets of the product line" [2].

Single Glass is a product line of engineering and manufacturing products supporting Boeing Commercial Airplanes. The product line contains tens of products with hundreds of applications for thousands of engineering users. Single Glass has been in production use for five years and has been credited with millions of dollars in savings in hardware costs alone.

We have begun a second, expanded development phase in response to engineering-business-process changes, key-vendor-product changes and host-platform changes. As we develop the complete infrastructure needed to sustain Single Glass, we discover that defining and integrating the people-based processes needed to sustain the product line are more difficult tasks than integrating the actual technologies. The area most fraught with peril is the clear definition of roles and responsibilities for the

G. Chastek (Ed.): SPLC2 2002, LNCS 2379, pp. 284–298, 2002.

governance of both technology and the IT processes needed to sustain an individual product line, let alone a collection of product lines.

Effective lines of authority and management are required to clearly define the roles and responsibilities needed to govern the shared products, shared processes and shared architecture within an individual product line. Similar problems occur when a collection of product lines must be jointly delivered and sustained. Figure 1 limits the scope of this paper to the governance of a collection of IT product lines and its relationship to the internal customers.

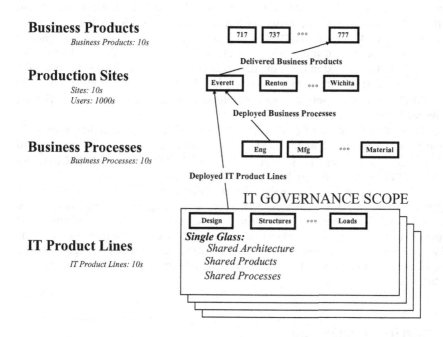

Fig. 1. The scope of this paper is IT governance. IT product lines, internal to the business, support business processes at production sites to build business products like airplanes.

As a system grows to include more products, product lines, platforms and sites, the team members increasingly do not report directly and administratively to the responsible product line managers. In addition, the system straddles several administrative, software development, asset management and funding cultures. Therefore, it is critical to be clear about who has a formal vote and who has a say, but not a vote, in directions for the architecture, components and processes that are shared across the constituent products. We discovered that polarity management [3] is useful to identify and respond to the stresses of product line organization that require infrastructure governance. We define polarity, identify key polarities, and discuss the approach we are using to manage Single Glass polarities. The concepts we describe are extensible to collections of product lines.

2   Polarity

A polarity is defined as "two principles which are both true but conflict." For example, a polarity of meeting comportment is RUTHLESS WITH TIME ↔ GRACIOUS WITH PEOPLE. In other words, meeting time stewardship can conflict with teaming efforts. Similarly, a polarity for preparation of this paper is LONG ENOUGH TO COVER THE SUBJECT ↔ SHORT ENOUGH TO BE READ.

More serious polarities are found in the U.S. Constitution. For example, the Federalist Papers [4] address the balance of power between the federal government and the state governments — a PART ↔ WHOLE polarity which we discuss in more detail in Section 3. Forrest McDonald [5] describes this division of government authority as "imperium in imperio" — governance within governance. The British Parliament's failure to extend its singular authority to manage the 13 colonies (the parts) led to the rebellion of the colonies. In addition to scope, Figure 1 depicts nested PART ↔ WHOLE polarities that require similar governance across the Boeing Commercial Airplanes business.

The BIG STATE ↔ SMALL STATE polarity receives much attention in the U.S. Constitution, as discussed in the next section. Also, our approach to project and product line governance is similar to the EXECUTIVE ↔ JUDICIAL ↔ LEGISLATIVE tri-pole polarity held by the Constitution.

Polarities provide a model to analyze organizational infrastructure in a way that is comparable to the structural analysis of an airplane. An airplane structure is analyzed recursively, and the strength of the resulting product is governed by the strength of the individual components, even when assembled in different configurations. The analogy between a structural analysis and an infrastructure analysis highlights the value of polarity management in identifying significant risks in the organization's structure.

3   Polarity Management

Polarities are often mistaken to be problems to be solved. However, polarities are *held*, not *solved*. Attempts to "solve a polarity" are fruitless and force us to honor the truth of the principles in conflict.

Hence, polarity management seeks mechanisms to *hold polarity*. For example, the U.S. Constitution holds the BIG STATE ↔ SMALL STATE polarity by definition of the bi-cameral legislature; the Senate favors small states, and the House of Representatives favors populous states. The two legislative bodies negotiate according to the rules of engagement defined in the Constitution. Further, the Electoral College continues to hold polarities by giving each state the number of electoral votes computed by adding the number of senators and representatives. Therefore, presidential elections also hold the BIG STATE ↔ SMALL STATE polarity. When individual states have a unicameral legislature, seat apportioning is made in a way that makes each electoral district approximately the same size, and a bi-cameral approach is not needed.

Polarity maps are used to analyze polarities. The top of the map describes the positive benefits of each true principle; the bottom of the map describes negative consequences of overemphasizing one pole at the expense of another. Figure 2 presents a polarity map for the PART ↔ WHOLE polarity adapted from Johnson [2]. In short, the "+" sections describe the upside of the pole's truth and the " –" sections describe the downside of the tilting balance toward that pole. The polarity map presentation acknowledges the truth of both principles and the expectation that they will conflict.

A constitutional example is contained in the 1781 Articles of Confederation. The Articles did not hold the PART ↔ WHOLE polarity. The overbalance to the states' (PARTs) rights left the country (WHOLE) with insufficient power to defend itself. The U.S. Constitution replaced the Articles in 1787 and has held this polarity for a remarkably long time.

PART		WHOLE	
+	**Uniqueness** • Freedom • Individual creativity • Individual initiative • Agility • Local optimization	**Connectedness** • Equality • Group synergy and creativity • Group cohesiveness and support • Clean integration of components • Global optimization	+
-	**Isolation** • Loss of equality 　• Loss of group cohesiveness and support 　• Globally inefficient	**Sameness** • Excessive conformity • Local inefficiency • Loss of individual creativity • Missed windows of opportunity	-
	Part CANARY	Whole CANARY	

Fig. 2. Polarity Map for PART ↔ WHOLE Polarity: A goal is to effectively put the "whole into the part" (i.e., put the product line architecture into the products).

The first step toward polarity management is to identify canaries for each pole. Borrowing from the historical practice of using canaries in coalmines to detect lethal levels of poisonous gases, the canary of a pole is the party most sensitive to the overbalance to the other pole. The canary helps to hold a polarity to harvest the benefits of the principles without the negative consequence of overemphasizing one of the poles. For example, in 1787, James Madison was a canary for federal rights and Thomas Jefferson was a canary for states, rights [2]. We continue working to hold this polarity today.

4   Polarities of a Product Line

In addition to the PART ↔ WHOLE polarity, the following are polarities of special interest in establishing a product line governance system.

4.1.   CUSTOMER-IN ↔ PRODUCT-OUT

CUSTOMER-IN ↔ PRODUCT-OUT (described in Figure 3) addresses realistic expectations with a realistic schedule. CUSTOMER-IN emphasizes a customer-centered approach to product development where the customer's voice is clearly heard; PRODUCT-OUT emphasizes a product-centered approach where delivery meets customer expectations of cost and schedule.

	CUSTOMER-IN	PRODUCT-OUT	
+	• Listen for defects • Respond to defects • Strong product support • Product well deployed	• Reliable • Predictable • On time • On cost	+
-	• Product requirements change too rapidly • Standard bearer: fail to harvest benefits of process improvement • Too few products	• Product does not match customer's needs • Technology push • Crusader: too much technology change	-
	CUSTOMER-IN Canary	PRODUCT-OUT Canary	

Fig. 3. Polarity Map for CUSTOMER-IN ↔ PRODUCT-OUT

This polarity must be held for IT projects, processes, and programs (a group of related projects). For example, the "software problem" is described as the inability to deliver software that meets the requestor's needs on time and within budget. Although not a "silver bullet" [6], this "problem" is organizationally addressed as a CUSTOMER-IN ↔ PRODUCT-OUT polarity that is not held. For example, requirements creep is a negative consequence of an overemphasis on CUSTOMER-IN.

To manage the polarity in IT projects, DMR Consulting's Productivity Plus (P+) [7] guides projects to assign a

- System Manager to broker requirements and deployment of the project's products
- Project Manager to broker commitment to construct the product according to a negotiated schedule

These two roles are canaries for the poles of this polarity. These canaries hold the polarity by negotiating deliverable definitions through the project's life cycle, collaborating and advocating their positions under the oversight of the System Owner, the funding source. This approach does not increase tension; it recognizes and formally addresses the tension with a forum, clear roles, and responsibilities rather than relying on informal, ad hoc means. We allow canaries to clearly speak and give every voter a "levels of agreement" scale from –3 to 2. This range lets the canaries identify "showstoppers" and allows them to invest energy in the most critical areas.

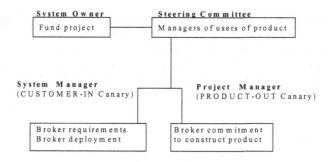

Fig. 4. DMR Consulting's Project organization chart as assigned canaries

We propose governance-process standards to extend the project-polarity management approach to products, processes, programs and product lines. For example, we accomplish "governance within governance" where

- Each product in the product line has a customer-in manager and product-out manager who hold the CUSTOMER-IN ↔ PRODUCT-OUT polarity at the product level.
- The product line's customer-in manager and product-out manager broker the aggregate positions of the two poles and engage to hold the polarity at the product line level.

4.1.1. Tri-Pole with Architect

The DMR [7] architect introduces a third pole to the CUSTOMER-IN ↔ PRODUCT-OUT polarity. Figure 5 depicts the constructive tension of the project manager and system manager with the architect. The architect role may cover system, technical, data, and functional architecture.

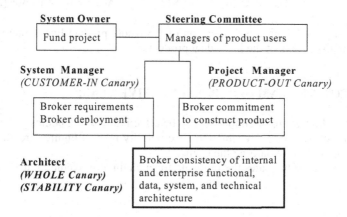

Fig. 5. Tri-pole including the architect-role extension.

The architect role is functionally at tension with the System Manager and the Project Manager in a manner similar to the EXECUTIVE ↔ LEGISLATIVE ↔ JUDICIAL approach of the U.S. Constitution.

The architect role is utilized at the product line, product and project levels. Charters for the architecture-governance bodies must carefully address the authority bounds of these levels of architects.

4.2. INNOVATION ↔ STABILITY

Project-specific needs often drive localized innovation; architects often seek stability for the enterprise. In addition, the Software Engineering Institute's (SEI's) maturity contributes to product line stability by insisting on reliable, predictable processes. However, technology and business changes can demand improved development cycle times to implement changes. Accommodating innovation and rapid change can be problematic for existing predictable processes. These examples of the INNOVATION↔STABILITY polarity are summarized in Figure 6.

	STABILITY		INNOVATION (CHANGE)	
+	**Continuity** • Avoid foolish risks • Know how to work with each other		**New energy** • New perspectives • New challenges – skills, knowledge, experiences • Willing to take risks	+
-	**Stagnation** • No new perspectives • No new challenges • Unwilling to take risks		**Chaos** • Take "foolish" risks • Constant readjustment to working relationships	-
	STABILITY Canary		INNOVATION Canary	

Fig. 6. Polarity Map INNOVATION ↔ STABILITY Adapted from Johnson [2]

This polarity communicates the tension of the whole product line's interoperation with the changing needs of the individual products.

4.3. EFFECTIVE TEAM ↔ REPRESENTATIVE TEAM

Representative bodies are often too large to be effective working bodies and add "one more person" to handle a new situation. The polarity map in Figure 7 reminds team sponsors of the risks of enlarging the team.

This polarity communicates the rationale for including or excluding team member candidates.

	EFFECTIVE TEAM	REPRESENTATIVE TEAM	
+	• 5 - 7 core contributors • Clear, concentric review audiences	• Complete participation aids buy-in and deployment	+
-	• Limited, incomplete perspectives	• Unwieldy decision-making • Unwieldy meeting participation	-
	EFFECTIVE TEAM Canary	REPRESENTATIVE TEAM Canary	

Fig. 7. Polarity Map EFFECTIVE TEAM ↔ REPRESENTATIVE TEAM

5   Governance Based on Polarities

We have used polarity management to design the governing bodies and governing processes for Single Glass. The goals of our analysis are

- Continue to hold the balanced polarities
- Address the unbalanced polarities.

Single Glass stresses the notion of "shared" entities (parts). Therefore, we use the PART ↔ WHOLE polarity as our starting point to address the governance of three key entities of the product line: architecture, products and processes.

5.1.   Shared Architecture

The two parts of the proposed architecture governance approach are

- Define the roles that bound the authority of architects as *define and monitor*.
- Define teams and team membership.

First, the product line architect authority is bounded as *define and monitor*. The products have authority to innovate within the constraints of the defined architecture:

- Vision, Direction and Strategic Development Plan
- Architecture Principles and Guidelines
- Data, Functional and Physical Architecture
- Performance Requirements

Clearly, the depth of the architecture deliverables is negotiated to hold the PART ↔ WHOLE polarity.

The product line architecture deliverables put the *whole into the part* (e.g., affect the architecture of each product integrated into Single Glass) without triggering the negative consequences of *whole* involvement shown in the PART ↔ WHOLE polarity map shown in Figure 2.

Another polarity-management goal is to harvest the benefits of stability from the enterprise architecture while avoiding the negative consequences of stability shown in the INNOVATION ↔ STABILITY polarity map of Figure 6.

The second part of the governance approach is to identify a technical architecture integration team (TAIT) as a representative body. The TAIT has one member from each product. The TAIT's authority is bounded as *define and monitor* over products.

In order to hold polarity with the 9 architects of the product PARTS, we selected the WHOLE members to be the 4 product line system architects and the 4 architects of the shared development, delivery and test environments to also be voting members of the TAIT. This results in a 17-member team that can be extended.

Since the TAIT is too large to be a working team, the EFFECTIVE TEAM ↔ REPRESENTATIVE TEAM polarity guided us to smaller technical teams called Technical Architecture Teams (TATs). TATs address key architecture issues and PARTS of the technical WHOLE, and have *define and monitor* authority. The TAIT has final approval authority over the technical team products. Membership of the TAIT (shown in Figure 8) holds two key polarities: INNOVATION ↔ STABILITY and PART ↔ WHOLE.

Approve	Canary type
5.2. Technical Architecture Integration Team (TAIT)	**REPRESENTATIVE**
Product *1* Architect	PART
Product *2* Architect	PART
...	...
Product *n* Architect	PART
Product Line System Architect (CHAIR)	WHOLE
Product Line Data Architect	WHOLE
Product Line Functional Architect	WHOLE
Product Line Development Environment Architect	WHOLE
Product Line Shared Product Architect	WHOLE
Product Line Test Environment Architect	WHOLE
Define and Monitor	
Technical Architecture Teams	EFFECTIVE
Issue 1 Team	PART
Issue 2 Team	PART
...	...
Issue m Team	PART

Fig. 8. Architecture Team Membership Summary

5.3.   Shared Products

The products of a deployed IT product line share the components of the computing delivery environment (e.g., operating system, network services, print services, and data management). This forces two proposed types of oversight.

First, the CUSTOMER-IN ↔ PRODUCT-OUT polarity is addressed by assigning a customer-in manager and a product-out manager for the shared components of the entire delivery environment.

Second, the change-management board of the delivery environment is a body of representatives from the product-out side of each product, the product architects

(TAIT). Originally, key technical opinion makers were selected for a separate board, but as their scope expanded to include architecture, the TAIT became the change board for the delivery environment.

Thus, the membership of the product-change board of the shared delivery environment is designed to hold the key polarities:

- Product architects weigh the technical and fiscal impact of changes (PART ↔ WHOLE).
- The delivery environment customer-in manager chairs the delivery-environment change board (CUSTOMER-IN ↔ PRODUCT-OUT).
- The delivery-environment customer-in and product-out managers vote at the same level as counterparts in other products (PART ↔ WHOLE).

5.4. Shared Processes

Because of the critical nature of IT processes to successful production, Single Glass has stressed shared processes since its inception. Process governance is proposed to be a TAIT counterpart, the Process Architecture Integration Team (PAIT).

Membership in the PAIT is a significant problem, because the local customs differ across geographic sites. We considered three alternate models: representatives from each product, representatives from each deployment site, or a combination of the two.

Figure 9 shows this as a polarity among products, sites, and processes. However, the number of products and deployment sites is so large that it becomes impossible to assign members from all the participant sites and products. We need an oversight scheme that is extensible and that honors the EFFECTIVE TEAM ↔ REPRESENTATIVE TEAM polarity.

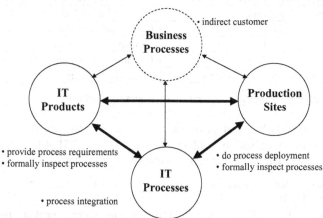

Process-Change Board: Customer-In Managers of IT Processes

Process Architecture Integration Team: Process Architects of IT Processes

Fig. 9. IT processes have users at multiple sites and multiple product line products.

Therefore, we first address the CUSTOMER-IN ↔ PRODUCT-OUT polarity. We propose a customer-in manager and product-out manager to provide stewardship for each process. The proposed process-change-board (PCB) members in Figure 10 are the customer-in managers, who broker the deployment of the process across the sites and products. As shown in Figure 11, there are 10 key IT processes identified as part of the Information Technology Infrastructure Library (ITIL) [8], so the member count of the process-management board is viable.

	Canary Type
Process Change Board Members	REPRESENTATIVE
Process *1* Customer-In Manager	PART
Process *2* Customer-In Manager	PART
...	...
Process *n* Customer-In Manager	PART
Product Line Process Customer-In Manager (CHAIR)	WHOLE
Product Line Process Architects	WHOLE
Formal Inspection Groups Members	
Sites:	
Process Customer-In Managers	PART
Products:	
Process Customer-In Managers	PART

Fig. 10. Members of the Process-Change Board

To insure formal participation by sites and products, the governance process includes formal inspections of the process changes.

Infrastructure Support Tools	**Service Delivery Tools**
Configuration Management	Service Level Management
Change Management	Cost Management for IT services
Problem Management	Contingency Planning
Help Desk	Capacity Management
Software Distribution and Control	Availability Management

Fig. 11. Baseline Processes from Information Technology Infrastructure Library (ITIL) [7]

Thus, the membership and governing processes of the product line's process change board are designed to hold the key PART ↔ WHOLE polarities as the product line grows. The attractive communication features are

- It clarifies who has a formal vote and who is assigned as customer-in manager, for each major IT process.
- It clarifies who has a say. Customer-in managers broker the common understanding and acceptance of process changes across products and sites, pos possibly through formal inspections conducted by designated product and site representatives who speak for their constituents.

6   Experience

In general, the first phase of the Single Glass product line was successful and met the requirements needed to give the users access to all the applications required to support a user's business process from a single workstation. This section lists the user and developer experiences of the first phase, as we begin our second expanded phase of product line development.

6.1.   Shared Products

Successful:

- We identified a system manager and project manager for the aggregate product line. Previously, the absence of the clear project manager and system manager caused fragmented, unfocused requirements. In addition, the product line was perceived as IT product-out and not appropriately responsive to users. This approach improved the stature of schedules and perception of value for users.
- We factored out the shared, tightly-coupled components (named Application Environment) of the product families and carefully identified neutral stewards and governance processes for these product line core assets: system owner, system manager, project manager, product change board, development team. Previously, this development team did not have a focused source of requirements and was perceived as a product-out organization that did not listen to individual product developers.
- We identified stewardship of the shared, loosely coupled services (named Delivery Environment) of the product families. A single system manager was identified for the Application Environment and Delivery Environment to improve coordination.

Unsuccessful:

- We did not extend the shared development environment to all product families.
- We did not identify formal project managers for each product family. This made integrated schedule management difficult.

6.2.   Shared Architecture

Successful:

- We performed architecture assessments (MONITOR) of product families based on evolving architecture principles (DEFINE).
- We established the product line architects as reviewers of change requests to minimize test time.
- The product line architects correctly exhibited special interest in the architecture of the core assets.
- We established the TAIT as a forum for architecture issues.

Unsuccessful:

- We did not identify formal architects for product families.
- The architects report administratively to the project manager, a situation that compromises the tri-pole relationship with the system manager. Historically, architects have been perceived as working behind the back of the project manager. We conclude that tri-poles are harder to hold than bi-poles.

6.3.   Shared Processes

Successful:

- We assessed cross-functional processes for usage and benefit recovery.
- We performed formal inspections and simulated walkthroughs of cross-functional processes.

Unsuccessful

- We did not identify clear stewards of cross-functional processes. As a consequence, process usage and benefit recovery is uneven.

7   Challenges

7.1.   Lean

The maturity[1] of the products of the product line varies significantly. We expect that the polarity management techniques proposed here appear over engineered and bureaucratic to many, especially to higher maturity organizations. The polarity management will yield leaner solutions as individual product lines mature.

7.2.   Extensible

The scope of the product line is increasing and changing. The governance structures must be extensible, easy to explain and straightforward to deploy.

7.3.   Product Line Customer Voices

We propose a customer-in manager for the product line. Our challenge is to broker requirements from the four points of view in Figure 10:

---

[1] Maturity as measured by the Software Engineering Institute's Capability Maturity Model (CMM). Capability Maturity Model and CMM are registered in the U.S. Patent and Trademark Office.

- Business products (e.g., newly funded projects assume the availability of new IT technology as part of their business case).
- Production sites (e.g.. size differences, the local users, and physical facilities make newer technology tractable for some sites).
- IT products (e.g., two essential commercial products are progressing at different paces).
- Business processes (e.g., a proposed business process demands product changes).

As chair of the product line change board, the customer-in manager will seek a board design to hold the balance between these legitimate, contesting positions for the company's benefit.

7.4. Holding the Whole ↔ Big State Polarity

One group of three product families has the largest user base and supports a critical engineering process. The idiosyncrasies of these dominant products can force significant, expensive concessions from other products and result in the negative consequence of failing to hold the Whole ↔ Big State polarity. We propose to hold this polarity architecturally by defining architecture principles (DEFINE) and assessing products (MONITOR) against the principles.

8   Conclusions

Polarity management formalizes our original Single Glass governance approaches and provides a consistent theoretical framework for product line organization design. We use polarity management to design governance bodies and processes for our expanded product line which

- Acknowledge and honor the primary points of governance business view.
- Address the tensions between the primary points of governance business view.
- Extend governance as the product line composition changes.
- Communicate the rationale for team roles and membership.

The resulting structure holds polarities instead of trying to solve them. Using polarity management offers an organized and extensible approach to governance rather than the more ad hoc approach we initially used.

Extensibility is essential as governance bodies address collections of product lines. Polarity management is directly applicable as a viable approach to determine the governance bodies and membership for an evolving collection of product lines.

Acknowledgements

We thank our DMR consultants, Eric Letourneau and David Sorrell, for their strong contributions to the architecture framework model.

We thank our polarity management consultant, Ahmed Yehia, for his advocacy and excellent instruction in polarity management.

References

1. Kasik, D., Kimball C., Felt, J., Frazier, K. A Flexible Approach to Alliances of Complex Applications. ICSE 99
2. Bass, L., Clements, P., and Kazman, R. Software Architecture in Practice. Addison Wesley Longman, 1998.
3. Johnson, B. Polarity Management. HRD Press, 1996.
    http://www.polaritymanagement.com/
4. Hamilton, A., Madison, J., Jay, J. Federalist Papers. 1787.
5. McDonald, F. States' Rights and the Union. Imperium in Imperio. 2000.
6. Brooks, F.P. Jr. No Silver Bullet. Essence and Accidents of Software Engineering. Computer Magazine. April 1987.
7. 7. DMR Consultants. http://www.dmr.com/macroscope
8. 8. Information Technology Infrastructure Library. http://www.itsmf.net/

Performance Analysis of Component-Based Applications

Sherif Yacoub

Hewlett-Packard Laboratories, MS 1126,
1501 Page Mill Rd.,
Palo Alto, CA 94304, USA
sherif_yacoub@hp.com

Abstract. Performance analysis is a software engineering activity that involves analyzing a software application with respect to performance quality attributes such as response and execution times. Performance analysis tools provide the necessary support for the analyst to monitor program execution, record and analyze performance data, and locate and understand areas of poor perform-ance. Performance analysis methods and techniques are highly dependent on the properties of the software system to be analyzed. Product line engineering applications possess some special properties that impose constraints on the selection of the performance analysis techniques to be applied and the tools to be used. The development of a component-based reference architecture is crucial to the success of a true product line. The component-based nature facilitates the integration of components and the replacement of a component with another to meet the requirements of an instance application of the product line. In this paper, we discuss performance analysis of component-based software systems and its automation. We discuss how component-based system properties influence the selection of methods and tools used to obtain and analyze performance measures. We use a case study of the document content remastering product line to illustrate the application of a performance analysis method to component-based applications.

Keywords: Component-based software engineering (CBSE), performance analysis, application and component profiling, and performance tools.

1   Introduction

Product Line Engineering (PLE) is a special software reuse paradigm that is con-cerned with the development of applications within the same domain. One objective of PLE is to facilitate the production of similar applications in the same domain through the composition of common domain components. A reference common architecture is often used because it embodies earlier design decisions for the product line and provides a framework within which reusable components can be developed and integrated [16]. Hence product line applications are mostly component based in nature.

G. Chastek (Ed.): SPLC2 2002, LNCS 2379, p. 299–315, 2002.

Performance of product line applications is an important concern to many product line engineers, especially when it comes to using the same reference architecture and plugging in and taking out components based on the application to be instantiated. Performance analysis methods and techniques are highly dependent on the properties of the software system to be analyzed. These properties include, among others, the choice of architecture, choice of programming paradigm, the underlying platform resources, parallelism, and distribution.

Product line applications are mainly component based. The application designers advocate a development life cycle that is based on the integration and assembly of software components. Ideal software components, as envisioned by researchers and practitioners, are self-contained, fairly independent concrete realizations that require little or no customization and provide well-defined services for the application in which they are integrated [7]. Components could be built in-house or acquired commercially (commercial off-the-shelf, COTS).

With the increasing popularity of this reuse paradigm, it has gained the interest of several researchers and practitioners. Research areas in this field include characterizing the nature of components, investigating the development life cycles, and unleashing issues related to component-based development [22, 5, 6, 11, 3]. Component integration has gained special attention. Many issues related to component packaging mismatches [8, 9] and architecture mismatch [13, 19] have been defined and acknowledged.

Though touted as an approach towards improving the application *quality* and maintainability, product line development is not a panacea. To be able to assess the quality of systems built out of integrating components in a reference architecture we need to define measurable quality attributes. *Performance* is usually one desirable quality attribute that is of concern for many application developers. Performance of components and applications can be measured using quantifiable attributes such as execution times, response times, and resource utilization. Traditional performance analysis steps include:

- *Instrumentation.* The program is instrumented and during execution the instrumentation hooks record performance data.
- *Data Extraction.* After performance data is recorded from one or more executions, data relevant to specific pieces (code fragments, routines, or objects) is extracted.
- *Data Analysis.* Data is analyzed to extract performance statistics such as average execution times or resource utilization.
- *Optimisation.* Areas of poor performance are identified and plans are made for improvements.

In this paper, we specifically address the problem of obtaining performance measures for component-based software applications and the process for automating those measures. Performance analysis is an important activity in component-based software development. We could assume that applications developed by integrating independently developed components (supplied by a third party) are not as optimized (in terms of performance) as their counterpart applications developed from scratch using traditional software development processes (such as waterfall, iterative, or prototype process models). Because we have no control over the method used in developing components that we acquire for component-based development, code and design optimization techniques as well as compiler optimization mechanisms are not applicable to the application as a whole. Moreover, component-based applications often experience performance degradation when compared to optimized systems developed from scratch as a result of using an underlying integration framework or architecture for component interactions or using wrappers and glue code for integration. Even when components interact directly through procedural call, the optimization of the performance of the application is not essentially a product of optimizing its individual components separately. For example, Optimize(Application) $\Leftrightarrow$ Optimize(C1) + Optimize(C2) + ... , where C1, C2 are the components composing the application. Therefore, performance analysis of components and applications built of components is an important activity in product line engineering in general and component-based software engineering in particular. Performance analysis activity will help us evaluate the tradeoff between gain in *productivity* as a result of component reuse and *degradation* in performance as a result of using wrappers, integration frameworks, or glue code.

Many performance analysis tools (sometimes called profiling tools) can be used at the code level. The profiling process helps the analyst to determine which functions or code snippets take the longest time to execute and which functions are called most often (e.g., the *prof* and *gprof* tools on the Solaris platform [21], the *DProf* for Perl [4], and several Java™ profiling tools [20]). For component-based applications, these tools are not useful because component-based applications are usually built by integrating black box component. Some of these components are developed in-house while others are COTS. Even when source code is available, the performance analyst has no control over the environment used to develop the component and hence components could be implemented using variety of languages. For instance, the system we describe in Section 4 has components developed in C, C++, Visual Basic, and Java programming languages. The heterogeneity of programming languages and the unavailability of source code make it more difficult to use off the shelf performance-analysis tools.

Component-based applications possess several properties that make it more difficult to conduct performance analysis: source code is not usually available, the application is often distributed in nature, there is heterogeneity in the underlying machine configurations, and the components may be acquired off the shelf. The work in this paper is motivated by the need to analyze the performance of component-based applications even when the source code of the components is not available (or should not be modified according to contract agreement with the component provider). Section 2 describes the performance analysis approach and the nature of applications for which it applies. Section 3 describes the automation process. We discuss the application of the approach to a case study in Section 4, and conclude the paper in Section 5.

™ Java and all Java-based marks are trademarks of Sun Microsystems, Inc. in the U.S. and other countries.

2   Performance Analysis Approach

For component-based performance evaluation, we identify two sets of performance metrics that the analyst could be interested in evaluating: application-specific metrics and system-specific metrics. Since the term "component" is usually overloaded with many meanings in different contexts, we first discuss the nature of component-based applications that we consider in this study.

2.1   Component-Based Applications

The performance analysis approach that we discuss in this paper is suitable for component-based applications that possess the characteristics discussed below.

2.1.1   Application = Components + Glue

We are mostly concerned here with applications built from components that are glued together using some integration mechanism. In this context, *components* provide the application-specific functionalities and the *glue* defines the workflow that integrates these functionalities to deliver some business logic (process) or satisfy some requirement scenario. Under this category, one can still consider several types of components and several techniques to glue these components together. To be more specific, we discuss the nature of these components and the nature of the glue in the sequel.

2.1.2   Components are Black Box

A component is an encapsulated, distributable software package with well-defined interfaces [5]. The encapsulation attribute implies the self-containment property of a component and its provision of some considerable functionality. The interface attribute implies the ability to compose components. A software component is a unit of composition with contractually specified interfaces and explicit context dependencies. A software component can be deployed independently and is subject to composition by third party [22]. D'Souza et. al. [11] define a component as a coherent package of software implementation that: (a) can be independently developed and delivered, (b) has explicit and well-specified interfaces for the services it provides, (c) has explicit and well-specified interfaces for the services it expects from others, and (d) can be composed with other components, perhaps customizing some of their properties, without modifying the components themselves.

The components that we consider here are *black box* components. The source code of these components is usually not available and if available is not modifiable. Components of that nature are usually binary executable components. Since these components are executables in one form or another, they might be dependent on specific operating system platform. For example, Executables (".exe") and Dynamic Link Libraries (".DLL") require *Windows* operating systems while Shared Objects or libraries (".so") require a *Unix* platform. However, other types of binary executable components will work on many platforms provided that an underlying interpreter exists on that platform. For example, Java Classes (".class") will run on *Windows* or *Unix* platforms provided that the Java Virtual Machine (JVM) is installed on that platform.

Another assumption that we make about components is that they are *stateless*. This means that once a component finishes the execution due to some specific input request, it is expected that on the next invocation the component has no memory of what it did in earlier invocations. This assumption is fairly suitable for applications built of components and glues because if we assume a component has memory then the glue has to keep track of the state of each component and synchronize the component invocations. This has two disadvantages. First the glue will be complicated since it keeps track of the workflow context as well as the context of each component. Second, this violates the encapsulation property of a component since its internal state will be disclosed to the glue.

2.1.3   The Glue Defines the Workflow

The ability to integrate components to compose applications is a key process in component-based software development. Integration issues influence our ability to select components, determine the development cost, and schedule the delivery of applications. Component integration is the process of gluing (integrating or composing) components together to develop applications. It is the main pillar of a component-based software development paradigm. In component-based applications, components are integrated together in a workflow (or scenario) whose execution delivers the output required from the application. There are several mechanisms to glue components:

a) One component knows about the other.

In this scenario, one component knows about the existence of another component in the system and calls it directly. This requires that: a) the two components are made accessible to one another (perhaps by making them available in the system search path), and b) the two components have exactly matching interfaces (see Figure 1).

Fig. 1. One Component Directly Invokes Another

b) Glue is used to integrate each two components

In this scenario, glue is developed to integrate each component pair. This has the advantage of relaxing the constraint that a component knows about another. The glue will be responsible for making the calls to one component, analyzing the results, and invoking the second component. This has the disadvantage of requiring the development of several glues for each component pair as illustrated in the following figure.

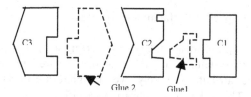

Fig. 2. A Schematic Diagram To Illustrate Using Glue For Each Component Pair

c) Using a glue infrastructure

In this scenario, we consider one gluing infrastructure into which components are plugged, as illustrated in the following figure. This scenario has the same advantages as the previous one and the additional advantage of having one controlled environment defining how components are integrated.

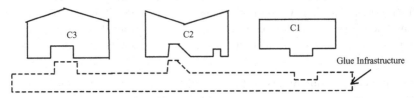

Fig. 3. A Schematic Diagram Illustrating Using Glue as an Infrastructure

d) Implementation of the Glue

The glue that integrates components together can be implemented in several ways. One solution is to use glue code written in some programming language. The coding approach has the advantage of achieving high performance as a result of using compiled code to integrate components, but also has the disadvantage of poor maintainability. Since the glue controls the sequence of execution of components, then each time we want to modify an existing sequence or generate a new sequence (which might happen during testing or maintenance), we have to regenerate (recompile) the glue component.

Scripting offers an elegant solution for developing glue infrastructures. Most scripting languages provide the necessary control flow capabilities required to construct scenarios of component execution. Application specific scripts can be developed to invoke black box components, process return results, make control flow decisions, and execute application-specific workflows. Scripts are easy to modify without recompilation and hence make them suitable for workflow construction.

2.1.4   Constraints on Component-based Applications

In summary, for the purpose of this study we consider component-based applications that are built of components glued together using a glue infrastructure. The components that we consider here are: 1) black box components (source code is not available), 2) binary executables, 3) developed either in-house or commercially with the assumption that we do not have access to their source code, and 4) stateless. The glue that we consider here is script-based glue infrastructure.

2.2   Application-Specific Performance Metrics

Application-specific performance metrics are performance measures taken for various functionalities in the system. Under this category, we are interested in the "*execution time*" performance attribute. Precisely, we are interested in the execution times of various functions. This is heavily application-specific; it depends on which functionalities we want to monitor.

For component-based applications, each component delivers a set of functionalities. Using the definition: component-based application = components + glue scripts; which execution times can we measure? Recall the constraints on the nature of components imposed in Section 2.1. Since source code is not available, it is not possible to collect statistics at the code statement level, procedure level, nor object level, because the gathering (collection) techniques for these statistics requires the execution of source code and the profiling of various statements, procedures, and objects. Hence, the performance evaluation of a component's internal content is not possible in component-based systems.

Using the assumption that a component provides an encapsulated considerable functionality, we can measure the execution time of the component itself. However, we do not have control over the way components are developed (they are usually provided from a third party, and the component user is not the same as the component provider). Thus, performance profiling of various components has to be done from outside the component (i.e., from the glue scripts - the application specific workflow-that uses the component).

Logging has been commonly used as a technique to analyze the control flow of programs, monitor the execution scenarios, and for debugging purposes. It is also used to analyze failures and guide performance tuning. Logging is usually simple to implement: we write some text message to a log location indicating that some event has occurred. It is a common task across applications. Because of this universal applicability, logging is a task that is ideally suited for component-based applications. In logging, applications are instrumented with various log statements to throw events (messages) to specific locations as they are executed. The logging location could be the standard output device (using some print statements), log files, log databases, email-messages, and so forth. There are several techniques for logging and various tradeoffs. It is not the purpose of this discussion to assess various logging techniques but instead we use logging as a means for performance analysis.

The following outlines a simple performance analysis approach:

- The glue scripts will be instrumented to log messages before each component call and after each return.
- Messages will be written to a persistent location like a file or a database.
- The log message should contain information about which component is being profiled, which particular function of the component (if the component provides many), the execution scenario specifics (if any), and time and date stamps of the event.
- The application is then executed and one or more workflows will be exercised.
- After some execution period (or after the application terminates), the log file (database) will be analyzed using a log parser / performance analysis tool.
- Results for the execution times of each component (or functions within components) will be made available for further statistical analysis such as obtaining mean execution times, level of confidence (variances), and other data statistics.

The above process is a simple, commonly used approach where various steps can be automated using off-the-shelf tools as discussed in Section 3.

2.3   System-Specific Performance Metrics

System-specific metrics are measures taken for the underlying system platform. While application specific metrics are used to obtain execution times for the various components and their functionalities, these measures are not often enough for component-based applications. This is because application-specific metrics do not take into consideration some other important aspects of component-based application. Component-based applications usually possess two important properties: parallelism and distribution.

- In component-based applications components can be executed in parallel on the same machine (hardware) if the underlying operating system supports parallelism[1]. Thus the metrics taken for one component execution not only depend on the underlying operating system and the underlying hardware but also on the number of processes running on the same machine at the same time (i.e. utilization of the underlying resources).
- Component-based applications are distributed in nature, hence components execute over a cluster of workstations and the underlying glue not only coordinates the operation between components on the same machine but components on other machines as well. As a result, the execution time of a component (or one of its functionalities) might depend on the execution of other components on a different machine. Hence, network delays and latency are important factors.

Therefore, in addition to obtaining application-specific performance metrics for components in a component-based application, it is essential to understand the utilization of the underlying resources on each machine in the cluster. Section 4 describes how application-specific metrics are insufficient for our case study and how system-specific performance metrics can help in identifying poor performance areas. System-specific performance metrics include, but are not limited to, the following metrics:

Physical Disk: For each physical storage device (disk) on each machine in the cluster, we can gather the following statistics:

- *% Disk time*: percentage of time the disk is performing tasks versus idle operation.
- *% Read Time*: percentage of time the disk is performing read operations.
- *% Write Time*: percentage of time the disk is performing write operations.
- *Disk Bytes / sec*: the rate by which bytes are read from or written to the disk.
- *Disk Read Bytes / sec*: the rate by which bytes are read from the disk.
- *Disk Write Bytes / sec*: the rate by which bytes are written to the disk.

Processor: *%Processor Time*: this percentage shows the utilization of the processing power. A 100% means we are utilizing the processors to their maximum capacity.

Memory: *Available Mbytes*: the size of the free megabytes available at given time on a machine.

---

[1] Executing concurrent processes is supported in most operating systems, even desktop operating system.

Network: We gather the following statistics for the network:

- *Bytes Total / sec:* the overall utilization of the network bandwidth
- *Bytes Received / sec* : the incoming traffic to a machine.
- *Bytes Sent/sec*: the outbound traffic from a machine to the others in the cluster.
- *Packet Outbound Errors.* an indication of collision on the network.
- *Output Queue Length.* an indication that the network is congested.

These metrics are *not specific* for component-based applications; in fact, they turn out to be a set of useful general-purpose metrics for application performance evaluation over any cluster of workstations. While these metrics are generally useful for many applications, we find them particularly important for component-based applications. Since components are used in this context as black boxes, we are *unable* to obtain specific measures for writing to disks, for sending a message across the network, or for allocating memory from the components themselves. Therefore, the alternative method to measure the average time the application used the resources (hard disk, memory, processor, or network) is to *monitor the resources themselves* and not the application execution.

3   Automation

In this section we discuss automating the process of gathering and analyzing data for application-specific and system-specific performance metrics.

3.1   Application-Specific Performance Metrics

The first step in obtaining the application specific metrics is to instrument the gluing scripts to log messages about the execution of components. The decisions involved in selecting the logger include the:

- Format of the message. To a minimum, the name of the component being logged, the time stamp, and a flag to distinguish the start and end of execution will be essential fields required to collect statistics about the execution time of a component.
- Location. Log locations include (but are not limited to) a database, a file, or an operating system specific repository. The log location should be persistent.

The second step is to stimulate the application to execute a certain workflow (scenario). At the end of the execution, the log file will contain the timed-stamped messages for component execution. The application can be executed for several workflows and results from each workflow will be recorded separately.

The third step is to analyze the log files and obtain measurements for the execution times for components and/or for the specific usage of components. The data required to obtain the application-specific performance metrics can be obtained from the log files. Usually log parser tools will have to be developed, acquired, or adapted to perform the data extraction and the data analysis operations.

The above three steps are general guidelines, and several tools can be used in each step. For the case study that we discuss in the following section, we have made some choices to simplify the process of quantifying the metrics using a combination of some easy-to-use COTS tools. These choices were based on the availability of tools for the platform and the operating system we are using for that particular application. We describe it below as an example for process automation.

Logging Messages

For message logging, we use a combination of an in-house logger component and *MS Windows EventLog* subsystem. We have developed a logger component that is used by the glue scripts whenever a message is to be logged. The logger runs as a binary executable component and takes parameters in command line to specify: the source of the message, the message body, and the criticality of the message. The logger component is developed using *MS Visual Basic*. It uses operating system specific APIs to log the message into application logs in the EventLog repository provided by the operating system. The day and time stamp is automatically logged by the APIs. As a result of using this simple combination, logging from the scripts has become a simple process of invoking a binary component with command line arguments. All the application logs are saved on log files on the physical storage. To simplify the logger component, we configure each machine in the cluster to host its own log files.

Analyzing Data

After the application execution terminates, the log files on each machine contain the log messages generated during the execution run. To be able to analyze the log and extract the metrics defined in Section 2, we need a log parser and a log analyzer. We use two off-the-shelf components: *MS Event Viewer* to parse the log files and *MS Excel* to process the files and extract metrics. The *Event Viewer* enables the analyst to filter messages from a specific source (component) and extract those messages in well-structured text format (such as tab or comma separated columns and rows). The extracted log files (in "csv" or "txt" format) are then parsed by *Excel* and presented in columns and rows where each row is a log message and each column is one particular field in a message.

The next step is to analyze the *Excel* files and produce quantifiable measures for performance data such as the average execution times, variances, execution times for various functions of a component, a workflow (scenario) execution time, etc. *Excel* provides the capabilities to run macros written in *Visual Basic Scripts,* which is an easy to used scripting language. We have developed the necessary processing macros that will run on spreadsheets of the log files and extract the application-specific metrics for our digital content processing application.

The simple procedure we use to quantify application-specific performance metrics is:

1. Use off-the-shelf (OTS) application to extract log files in a structured format. For example, for each machine in the cluster, we use *Event Viewer* to extract the "application" log files in a structured-text format.
2. Collect the log files from all machines into a central repository.
3. Using *Excel*, extract each log file and import the performance analysis modules.

4. Execute the application-specific performance analysis modules to extract the necessary performance measures.
5. Results are produced as charts and/or spreadsheets, which are created by the processing macros and contain all the required application specific performance statistics.

The first two steps (1 and 2) can be automated by using COTS tools such as *Event Achiever* [10]. The following figure describes the overall process. Components in **bold** fonts are off the shelf.

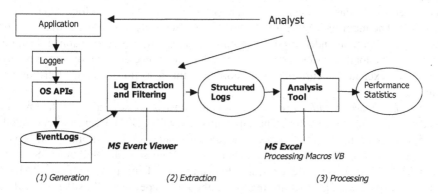

Fig. 4. A Process to Obtain Application-Specific Performance Metrics

3.2 System-Specific Performance Metrics

System specific performance metrics are low-level measures of the system resources. To quantify these metrics we use performance tools that are specifically developed for the platform being used. These performance analysis tools are independent of the application using the resources. They measure the usage of the resource and sometimes provide information about the usage profile of a resource and utilization by different application processes.

As an example of these tools, we use the OTS *Performance Monitoring* tool, which is provided as part of the *Windows* operating system[2]. The tool produces performance statistics in structured text file. This tool has plenty of performance counters that can be used to analyze the usage of various resources in the system such as the processor utilization, memory usage, disk IO, and network IO. The process includes selecting the performance counters, starting the performance tracing, executing the application scenarios, and obtaining the log files. We further use *Excel* to obtain performance charts for various resource counters[3].

---

[2] Other tools can be used, such as Eco Tools [12]

[3] Several other performance data analysis tools can be used such as Quantify by Rational [18]

4   Case Study

4.1   Description

The performance analysis approach outlined earlier evolved from the need to study the performance of a distributed component-based application that is implemented to process digital content. The main workflow of the application starts by loading scanned document images from an input source and producing information-rich documents in a format suitable for web delivery. In terms of input/output data, the input data is raster "tiff" images of books or journals pages and the output data is documents in Portable Document Format (PDF) for each book and for articles of each journal. The main requirement is to develop a system that fulfils the above functions and runs in an unattended mode. The input sources allow several scanned document images to be loaded into the system in parallel, and hence all components in the system must execute concurrently and coordinate the workflow without user intervention.

The *hardware architecture* of the system consists of several workstations connected via a network switch. The input media used is Digital Linear Tape (DLT); each carries up to 80GB of scanned document images. A DLT library with several DLT drives is used to allow simultaneous input from several DLT tapes. Since the system deals with large file sizes, a redundant array of inexpensive disks (RAID) is used to store input files that are read from the DLT tapes as well as the output files. The hardware architecture for the system is shown in the following figure:

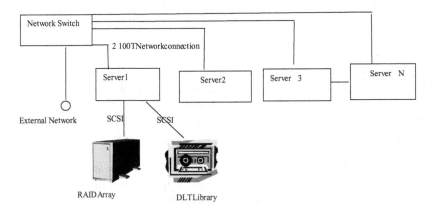

Fig. 5. The Hardware Architecture of the System

From a *software architecture* perspective, several components operate concurrently on each machine and all components on one machine operate concurrently with components on other machines. The various type of components include, but are not limited to: tape loading component, input quality assurance (QA) component, format conversion component, output verification component, logger component, page concatenation component, and Optical Character Recognition (OCR) components. Some of these components are acquired in-house or purchased from third parties. In all cases, the team gluing the components together and the term conducting the performance analysis have no control over the way the components are developed and hence the source code for most components is considered unavailable. At any time, several instances of these components should be running on any machine in the cluster.

The software architecture is designed as a shared repository (blackboard) that coordinates both the control flow and the data flow activities. Whereas control flow defines the possible workflows in the system, data flow defines how and where the data is organized. The workflow is controlled using a set of queue files that are made accessible from any machine on a shared file system. Each component reads from one queue and writes to the output queues (either a positive or negative queue) in a thread safe manner. Data required by any process is stored on the shared repository.

All components are stateless black box components that are glued together using shell scripts[4]. Glue scripts are developed to wrap executable components, perform component invocation, lock task queues to get or set a task, and monitor the execution of components among other system-wide functions. The current architecture makes it easy to add a new machine seamlessly to the cluster (hardware scalability). None of the components has knowledge of any other component of same or different type, which enables multiple component instances to run without inter-component communication constraints. The glue around the components make them work in a PULL mode as opposed to a PUSH mode; whenever a process is free the glue script reads a task from the input task queue and invokes the component to start execution.

4.2   Application-Specific Performance Metrics

For this content processing application, we are interested in profiling the execution times of various components. The following is a subset of mostly desired metrics that we consider for this application. The metrics are grouped into categories according to the various phases in the main workflow: loading data from input channels, QA of the input data, conversion, and QA of the output data.

Loading Data
We are interested in three performance metrics: *Scan Time (TL_s)*, the average execution time for scanning the content of a tape; *Actual Read Time (TL_r)*, the average execution time for reading data (document images) from the tape drive to the RAID Disk Array; and Total *Tape Reading Time (TL_tt)*, the total time required to load the content of a tape from the tape drive to the RAID Disk array.

Input Data Verification
Under this category we are interested in two performance metrics. The first is the *Time to Verify One page (TV_p)*, which is the time required to verify the integrity of one scanned document image (tiff) file. This includes reading the header, checking parameters, and checking the integrity of the file. The second is the *Time to Verify*

---

[4] Shell scripts (Korn Shell, awk, sed) are executed on Windows platform using MKS Toolkit [17]

One Book (TV_tb), which is the total time required to verify the integrity of all scanned document pages of a book.

Conversion

The following metrics are used to measure the processing time required to convert the scanned document images to information rich format (PDFs) and to generate intermediate metadata files.

- *Time to Convert one page (C_p)*. Time required to convert one document page.
- *Time used by OCR per book (C_ocr)*. Time required to produce the text output from an OCR engine.
- *Time to verify the sequence of scanned book pages (C_vsb)*. Time required to extract information about page insertion and page deletion within the tiff pages of a book.
- *Time to Concatenate Book Pages (C_cc)*. Time required to concatenate the PDF files for book pages into one file for the book.
- *Time to Convert a book (C_tb)*. The total time required to convert the book including all of the above processing times.

Output Data Verification

Time to verify one book (PV_b). This is the time required by the system to verify the output file for one book. This includes verification of the file format and verification that the file is printable using third party applications.

To automate the extraction of these metrics, we followed the outlines discussed in Section 3.1. All components used in the performance analysis were OTS, as explained in Section 3.1. In addition, the performance evaluation team developed some processing macros that are executed from within the *Excel* application (these include: conversionStatistics, tiffVerificationStatistics, pdfVerificationStatistics, and tapeStatistics macros). Below are some results obtained from applying the performance analysis approach to a sample workflow for our application.

The results illustrated in Figure 6 identify two main bottlenecks in the processing times. The first is loading input data from tapes and the second is the total time to process one book. The first is heavily an IO operation. To improve performance at this end, we can use tapes with larger block sizes. We can also replace the server to which the library is connected with another that has faster internal bus structure.

Metric	*Average Values (sample space)*
Scan Time, TL_s	3 hours (4 Tapes)
Actual Read Time, TL_r	6 hours (4 Tapes)
Total Tape Reading Time, TL_tt.	9 hours (4 Tapes)
Time to Verify One Tiff page, TV_p	< 1 second (21965 pages)
Time to Verify One Book, TV_tb	2 minutes 23 seconds (65 books)
Time to Convert one page, C_p	52 seconds (30321 pages)
Time used by OCR per book C_ocr	45 minutes (70 books)
Time to Verify the Scan of a book C_vsb	1 second (70 books)
Time to do PDF Concatenation C_cc	15 minutes (10 books)
Time to Convert a book, C_tb	4 hrs :50 minute (70 books)
Time to Verify the PDF of one book PV_b	8 minutes (331 books)

Fig. 6. Performance Analysis Examples from the Document Processing Application

The second bottleneck is a processing operation. To optimize performance at this end, further system analysis is required to determine whether the operation is memory-bound or CPU-bound. Hence, the role of system-specific metrics becomes important.

4.3   System-Specific Performance Metrics

As mentioned earlier, these metrics measure the utilization of the underlying system resources. The execution time of the components discussed in Section 4.2 is heavily dependent on the underlying system resources. For example, since the data to be processed is located in a shared repository, then the execution time of the conversion component includes data transfer across the network to store and retrieve the digital content.   Therefore it is important to identify any bottlenecks in the underlying resources (such as network, processor utilization, memory, and disk IOs) that affect the execution times of the components.

For each machine in the cluster we obtain the measures discussed in Section 2.3. We use the automation technique/tool mention in Section 3.2. Due to space limitations, we will mention a subset of the results as examples of how the performance analysis technique could be useful:

- The processors on all machines running the conversion component are 100% utilized most of the time. This explains that the conversion component bottleneck mentioned in the previous section is CPU bound.
- The memory utilization on machines running the conversion component is low. There is always 100 MB available when the components are running. This means that the memory for those machines is over-specified.
- The disk array transfer rate (reads and writes) is acceptable. They did not reach their maximum values (as tested and compared to running an exhaustive manual disk IO operation).
- The network is not a bottleneck; it is not 100% utilized. Thus, data transfer is not causing any overhead in component processing times.

The memory on the machine running the PDF concatenation component is fully utilized when the component is executed towards the end of the operation when many pages are added to the PDF tree in the memory. Usually this is a peak utilization point that occurs every 3-4 hours and lasts for 10 minutes.

5   Conclusion

Whereas performance analysis is a well-acknowledged software engineering activity, its application to specialized forms of software reuse paradigms (such as product line engineering and component-based software engineering) has not received thorough treatment from researchers and practitioners. In this paper we discuss a performance analysis approach for applications developed by the integration of components, which is often the norm in product line engineering practice. We investigate properties of component-based applications that impose constraints on the techniques and tools used in performance analysis. While the techniques and tools used are common to many software engineering disciplines, their application in performance analysis of component-based software is useful for assessing the quality claimed by product line development advocates. As a result of our study, we find that a combination of application-specific and system-specific metrics is useful. The analyst can use these metrics to understand areas of poor performance that require further optimization. These metrics can also be used to understand resource utilization and how that affects component execution. As concrete examples, these metrics help us identify: components that heavily utilize the processing capability of the machines, components that use memory mostly, when memory is fully utilized, and when over-specification of the underlying resources occurs. Another advantage of the approach is that we are able to profile the components execution in a runtime environment as opposed to using simulation techniques [15] or evaluating individual components independently.

This work discusses performance evaluation for specific type of component-based application as discussed in Section 2.1. Further studies are required for component-based application with different properties. This paper does not present a survey of performance analysis tools and does not deliver an assessment and comparison of these tools in the context of component based applications. This is a topic of future work. Additional research is also required to understand the effect of using reference architecture on the performance of product line applications.

References

1. Barton, J., and J. Whaley, "A Real-Time Performance Visualizer for Java." *Dr. Dobb's Journal* March 1998
2. D. Batory, Gang Chen, Eric Robertson, and Tao Wang, "Design Wizards and Visual Programming Environments for GenVoca Generators, *IEEE Transactions on Software Engineering*, May 2000, vol.26, no.5, pp441-452.
3. Bosch, J., C. Szyperski, and W. Weck. Report on the Second International Workshop on *Component-Oriented Programming* (WCOP'97) (in conjunction with ECOOP'97) Jyväskylä, Finland, 9 June, 1997
4. Brocard, L., "Graphing Perl" O'Reilly Open Source Convention Sheraton San Diego Hotel, San Diego, CA July 23-27, 2001 (also *Dprof Profiling tool.* http://www.engelschall.com/ar/perldoc/pages/module/Devel::DProf.html)
5. The 1999 International Workshop on *Component-Based Software Engineering*, in conjunction with the 21st *International Conference on Software Engineering*, Los Angeles, California, 1999, May16-22
6. The 2000 International Workshop on *Component-Based Software Engineering*, in conjunction with the 22nd International Conference on Software Engineering, Limerick, Ireland, June 4-11, 2000
7. Cox, B., J., "Planning the Software revolution", *IEEE Software* 7(6):25-35 Nov 1990
8. DeLine, R., "A Catalog of Techniques for Resolving Packaging Mismatch", In the *Proceedings of Symposium on Software Reusability*, SSR'99, Los Angeles, CA, May 1999

9.   DeLine, R., "Avoiding Packaging Mismatch with Flexible Packaging", In the *Proceedings of the 21ˢᵗ International Conference on Software Engineering 1999 (ICSE'99)*, Los Angeles, USA, May 1999, pp97-106

10. Domain Software Creations, "Event Archiver", http://www.eventarchiver.com

11. D'Souza, D. F., and Alan C. Wills "Objects, Components, and Frameworks with UML : The Catalysis Approach" , ISBN 0-201-31012-0 Addison-Wesley, 1998

12. CompuWare   Coorportation   EcoTools.   http://www.compuware.com/   products/ecosystems/ecotools/detail.htm

13. Garlan, D., R. Allen, and J. Ockerbloom, "Architecture Mismatch or Why it's Hard to Build Systems out of Existing Parts," Proc. 17th International Conference on Software Engineering, IEEE Computer Society Press, Los Alamitos, Ca., April 1995, pp179-185

14. Hill, J., P. Crumpton, and D. Burgess.,``The theory, practice, and a tool for BSP performance prediction" In *EuroPar'96*, Number 1124 in LNCS, pages 697-705. Springer-Verlag, August 1996

15. HyPerformix http://www.hyperformix.com/products/ products.htm

16. Mili, H., A. Mili, S. Yacoub, and E. Addy, "Reuse-based Software Engineering: Techniques, Organization, and Measurement", John Wiley, 2001.

17. The MKS Toolkit. http://www.mkssoftware.com

18. Rational   Software   Corporation.   *Visual   Quantify*.   Cupertino,   California. http://www.rational.com/products/quantify_nt/index.jsp

19. Shaw, M., "Architectural Issues in Software Reuse: It's not the Functionality, it's the Packaging", In the *Proceedings Symposium on Software Reusability*, SSR'95, 1995.

20. Shirazi, J., "Java Performance Tuning", Java Series O'Reilly, September 2000

21. Sun Microsystems Analyzing Program Performance With Sun WorkShop Part No. 806-3562-10 May 2000 (also available on the web: http://docs.sun.com/htmlcoll/coll.36.7/iso-8859-1/SWKSHPPERF/AnalyzingTOC.html)

22. Szyperski, C., "Component Software: Beyond Object Oriented Programming", Addison Wesley Longman, 1999.

Using the Options Analysis for Reengineering (OAR) Method for Mining Components for a Product Line

Dennis Smith, Liam O' Brien, and John Bergey

Software Engineering Institute,
4500 Fifth Avenue,
Pittsburgh, PA 15213
{dbs, lob, jkb}@sei.cmu.edu

Abstract. The Options Analysis for Reengineering (OAR) method is a systematic, architecture-centric means for mining existing components for a product line or new software architecture. The method incorporates a set of scalable techniques and exercises to collaboratively analyze existing components, determine viable mining options, and evaluate the most promising options. The OAR method has 5 activities that are followed in a systematic manner to identify components for mining and estimate the cost and risk of changes required to each legacy component to enable its reuse within a new software architecture. The OAR method provides visibility into this highly complex analysis activity. It also provides insights into implicit stakeholder assumptions, constraints, and other major drivers that impact the mining of components. Results from a pilot application of the OAR method are presented in this paper.

1 Introduction

Options Analysis for Reengineering (OAR) is a systematic, architecture-centric method for identifying and mining reusable software components within large and complex software systems [6], [7]. Mining involves rehabilitating parts of an old system for use in a new system. The OAR method identifies potential reusable components and analyzes the changes that would be needed to rehabilitate them for reuse within a software product line or new software architecture. The OAR method identifies mining options and the cost, effort and risks associated with each option.

1.1 Need for the OAR Method

Software product lines offer great promise in realizing economies of scale and developing software more efficiently [1].

Since most organizations have a substantial legacy base of existing software assets, few product lines or migrations to new software architectures start from "green fields." However, until now, there has been no systematic way to identify components for reuse, or to understand the types of changes that would be required for insertion

G. Chastek (Ed.): SPLC2 2002, LNCS 2379, p. 316–327, 2002.

into a product line architecture or a new software architecture [2]. In most cases, the only options available have been to either undergo the costly and high-risk process of reengineering an entire system (an ad hoc approach not focused on high-value components) or to simply build the new system from scratch.

Several researchers have outlined methods of rehabilitating components [3], [5]. Work has also been carried out in identifying risks in reengineering projects [4]. Identifying what components to mine and determining the effort, cost and risks involved has not been formalized in a thorough manner. Because of the difficulty of identifying potential components to mine, projects have often deferred mining decisions indefinitely. The OAR method addresses this need by establishing a more formalized approach to decision making for mining software assets.

Successful mining requires understanding what types of components are worth extracting and how to extract components. Once decisions are made on whether to extract, a set of problems often need to be addressed, including the fact that

- Existing components are often poorly structured and poorly documented
- Existing components differ in levels of granularity
- Clear guidance is not yet available on how to perform the salvaging.

The OAR method provides a systematic approach to making decisions on the mining of components from legacy systems for use in a product line.

This paper is structured as follows: Section 2 gives an outline of the OAR method. Section 3 gives details of the structure of each of the OAR activities. Sections 4 outlines the resources involved in applying the OAR method. Section 5 outlines a case study of the application of the OAR method. Section 6 concludes the paper.

2   Overview of OAR Activities

The OAR method consists of five major activities with scalable tasks. These are outlined in Figure 1.

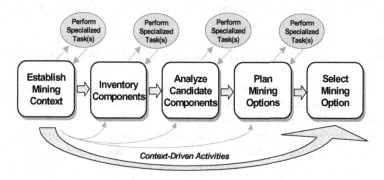

Fig. 1. Overview of OAR Activities

Each of these activities has a set of tasks and subtasks that enables it to meet its goals. Many tasks have data templates to provide a starting point for data items, as well as execution templates to guide the process. Each activity has a set of exit criteria. In addition, there is a feedback task at the end of each activity to analyze current progress and to determine if the method should be tailored based on the current context.

2.1 Establish the Mining Context

The Establish Mining Context (EMC) activity establishes an understanding of the organization's product line or new single-system needs, legacy base, and expectations for mining legacy components. It develops a baseline of the goals and expectations for the mining project and the component needs that mining is to address. It also determines the programmatic and technical drivers for making decisions and selects a set of potential candidate components for mining. These candidate components will be analyzed and evaluated in later OAR activities based on the drivers that are elicited during the EMC activity.

This first activity identifies product line needs that can potentially be filled by mining legacy components and selects about 10 to 20 of these needs to analyze in more detail. Next we identify candidate components from the legacy system that can potentially meet these needs.

Establish Mining Context has 10 tasks:

1. Review Goals and Objectives: determines stakeholders' goals and objectives for the mining effort.
2. Review Product Line Requirements: reviews the product line requirements.
3. Review and Select Component Needs: identifies the component needs that will be addressed through mining
4. Review Legacy Systems and Documentation: reviews the legacy systems and component documentation available.
5. Determine Mining Drivers: determines the programmatic and technical drivers for the mining effort.
6. Validate Goals and Objectives: evaluates compatibility between the mining drivers and the overall goals and objectives.
7. Identify Candidate Components: determines criteria for high-value legacy components and selects a set of components that are candidates to be mined to satisfy the selected needs.
8. Elicit Mining Issues: identifies any issues and concerns that may have arisen for example, identifying that the system the organization wants to mine is insufficiently documented to perform any analysis.
9. Evaluate Preparedness: determines the organization's level of preparedness. An example of preparedness factors would be that the organization has people committed to carrying out the mining effort. If not, there is little likelihood of success.
10. Review OAR Schedule: review and update the OAR schedule if necessary. The OAR schedule outlines the schedule for each activity and the tasks and effort involved in each.

2.2 Inventory Components

This activity identifies the legacy system components that can potentially be mined for use as product line components.

In this activity, the characteristics of the product line component needs are identified. Legacy components are evaluated based on these criteria, and those that don't meet the criteria are screened out. This activity results in an inventory of candidate legacy components that fulfill component needs.

The Inventory Components activity has six tasks:

1. Identify Characteristics of Component Needs: identifies characteristics that the legacy components should have
2. Identify Components Satisfying Characteristics: creates a Component Table of the legacy components with details of these characteristics and screens out those that do not meet the criteria
3. Match Components to Needs: matches legacy components to product line component needs
4. Inventory Candidate Components: updates the Component Table with the details about those candidate legacy components matched
5. Elicit Mining Issues: identifies any issues and concerns that may have arisen
6. Review OAR Schedule: reviews and updates the OAR schedule if necessary

2.3 Analyze Candidate Components

This activity analyzes the candidate set of legacy components to evaluate their potential for use as product line or new single-system components. We perform additional screening on the candidate components and identify the types of changes that are required to mine each one.

The Analyze Candidate Components activity has six tasks:

1. Select Desirable Components: determines desirability criteria for legacy components and screens out those that do not satisfy these criteria
2. Identify "As-Is" and Black-Box Components: identifies those components that can be used "as is" or wrapped
3. Identify White-Box Components: identifies those components that will need to be modified
4. Determine Required Changes: determines the types of changes that will need to be made to each component, the cost and effort involved, the level of difficulty and risk and the comparative cost and effort to developing the components from scratch.
5. Elicit Mining Issues: identifies any issues and concerns that may have arisen
6. Review OAR Schedule: reviews and updates the OAR schedule if necessary

2.4 Plan Mining Options

This activity develops alternative options for mining, based on schedule, cost, effort, risk, and resource considerations. We perform a final screening of candidate components and analyze the impacts of different aggregations of components.

The Plan Mining Options activity has eight tasks:

1. Select Favorable Components: develops criteria such as cost or effort levels and screens out components that do not satisfy these criteria
2. Perform Component Tradeoffs: identifies only one component (or combination) per product line component need
3. Form Component Options: develops criteria for aggregating components to form options
4. Determine Comparative Cost and Effort: for each option, determines the comparative cost of developing the components included from scratch
5. Analyze Difficulty and Risk: determines the level of difficulty and risk for each option
6. Validate Results: makes sure that information about each option has been captured
7. Elicit Mining Issues: identifies any issues and concerns that may have arisen
8. Review OAR Schedule: reviews and updates the OAR schedule if necessary

2.5 Select Mining Option

This activity select the mining option or combination of options that can best satisfy the organization's goals by balancing programmatic and technical considerations. Each mining option is evaluated. The optimal option or combination of options is selected. A summary report and justification for the selected option are prepared.

The Select Mining Option activity has five tasks:

1. Choose Best Option: determines the drivers for selecting the options and selects an option or a combination of them
2. Verify Option: makes sure that all the details about each of the chosen options have been recorded
3. Identify Component Needs Satisfied: completes the final list of component needs that were satisfied and not satisfied through the selection of the options
4. Present Findings: prepares findings briefing, giving details of the selected option(s)
5. Produce Summary Report: produces a final report detailing the chosen option(s) and the rationale for their selection

2.6 Specialized Tasks

Each activity also has a set of potential specialized tasks as a mechanism to address circumstances that may otherwise preclude completing the activity. These tasks may be applicable under the following conditions:

- The exit criteria for the prescribed activity are not satisfied.

- More work is required than can reasonably be accomplished in the activity wrap-up tasks.
- Additional data is needed to complete a particular task or address special customer needs.
- There is a need to supplement standard OAR tasks to enhance decision making and reduce risk.

Examples of specialized tasks for the Establish Mining Context activity are

- A focused effort to identify mining effort drivers and resolve programmatic and technical issues
- A focused effort to better define product line requirements and component needs in terms of required functionality and interfaces
- The isolation and identification of the functionality and interfaces of legacy components
- Development of the required level of documentation for legacy components

3 Structure of Activities

Each activity is composed of a set of tasks and subtasks. The tasks for each activity were outlined in Section 2, while the subtasks represent a lower level of detail.

3.1 Underlying Questions for an Activity

The tasks were designed to answer a set of activity-specific underlying questions. These questions also serve as a checklist to be included in the exit criteria for each activity.

An example of underlying questions for an activity is this subset of the questions for the Establish Mining Context activity:

- What are management's expectations for the mining effort?
- What are the requirements (e.g., quality attributes) and primary drivers (e.g., priorities and constraints) for mining components?
- What explicit (and implicit) constraints, ground rules, and assumptions apply?
- What specific product line component needs are going to be addressed?
- What legacy systems are relevant, and what documentation is available?
- What documentation is available describing legacy components (e.g., their functionality, granularity, and interfaces)?
- What is the level of preparedness of the organization in terms of experience, skills, available resources, and OAR timeframe?

3.2 EITVOX Structure of Activities

The activities are structured according to an EITVOX (Entry Criteria, Inputs, Tasks, Validation, Outputs, Exit Criteria) format. This structure is shown in Table 1.

Table 1. EITVOX Structure of OAR Activities

	E	Entry Criteria	Criteria for beginning activity
	I	Inputs	Artifacts required during execution of activity
Prescribed OAR Activity	T	Tasks	Tasks to carry out the prescribed activity
	V	Validation	Data collected to validate the activity
	O	Outputs	Artifacts produced during execution of activity
	X	Exit Criteria	Criteria defining completion of activity

The Entry Criteria are a set of criteria that must be met before undertaking any of the tasks in an activity. The Inputs are items that will be required during the execution of the tasks in the activity. The Tasks are the tasks and subtasks that are carried out within the activity. Validation lists the factors that determine that the activity has been completed satisfactorily. Outputs lists the output that is generated during the activity, and Exit Criteria lists the criteria that must be met upon completion of the activity.

3.2.1 Task Execution

Tasks and subtasks are executed in order. A set of task-execution templates and data templates are used to support performing the tasks and subtasks. Task-execution templates outline the steps, rationale, and assumptions for a task or subtask. Data templates provide example topics to be covered in support of the execution of a task. They often provide a starting point for eliciting information from a customer.

3.2.2 Example of Task-Execution and Data Templates

The task-execution template specifies how to perform the task or subtask. A task-execution template lists the task ID, name, description, steps, rationale, and assumptions.

For example, a task-execution template supports Task 4.2 of the EMC activity (Review Component Documentation). This task reviews what type of documentation is available at the component level of the legacy system.

The steps outlined in the task-execution template are

1. A representative of the customer organization conducts a walkthrough describing the type and level of documentation available on the legacy system(s) using the *EMC-4.2-DT* data template as a guide. Some key topics that should be addressed include
   - What is the level of granularity for legacy components?
   - How does this level of granularity compare to product line needs?

- What component documentation is typically available at that level of granularity?

2. Review and consider the information that is presented and ask questions to clarify and refine the type and level of documentation that is available to support the analyses that the mining team will be performing.

3. Identify any documentation deficiencies and their potential impact.

The *EMC-4.2-DT* data template suggests that the following types of data be collected:

- List of legacy components
- Component documentation (i.e., functionality and interface descriptions)
- Source code for legacy components
- Maintenance history for legacy components (e.g., cost, modification, timeframe, resource utilization)

4 Resources Required for the OAR Method

The OAR method can be tailored to suit an organization's mining needs. If there is a large number of product line needs and a large legacy base to mine, then the OAR method can be scaled accordingly. Ideally, an organization would want to examine whether it is worth doing a mining effort at all. In this case, they should focus on a smaller set of needs to determine if there are in fact legacy components to meet these needs. This could be followed by a larger effort.

When a set of about 15 to 30 product line needs is identified, the OAR method can be applied and completed in three sessions of 2 or 3 days each. Typically, each session is separated by several weeks. The OAR team consists of 2 or 3 OAR specialists, as well as a mining team of 3 people who have in-depth knowledge of the legacy system and the target product line system. Depending on the documentation of the legacy system, there may be specialized tasks between the OAR sessions.

5 An Example of an Application of the OAR Method

The OAR method was used to explore mining components for a Satellite-Tracking Agency (STA[1]). The STA provides analysis, system-level engineering, integration, and test and evaluation support for the development, acquisition, and deployment of satellite-tracking systems (STSs).

There is an urgent need to mine components from an existing STS for use in a new architecture that will be part of their Improved Satellite System (ISS). The ISS will integrate space assets in a variety of orbit configurations with a consolidated ground

---

[1] Because of the sensitive nature of the application, the organization's name and results have been disguised and abstracted.

segment. The ISS will require some of the capabilities of the STS. Because the STS has a set of reliable and validated models, a decision was made to mine the STS for selected components to insert into the ISS.

The OAR method was used to help identify relevant components and to provide estimates of the effort required to rehabilitate the STS components for use in the ISS. During the course of the EMC activity, a set of drivers for making decisions on candidate components was established, including the flexibility of interfaces, the satisfaction of real-time constraints, portability and interoperability, and a high level of code quality (high cohesion, low coupling).

Four types of new architecture component needs were identified:

1. Simulation Gateways
2. Message Gateways
3. Truth Model
4. Event Tracking Subsystem (ETS) and Message Generation

In the Inventory Components activity, six legacy system components were selected as mining candidates to satisfy these needs, including two simulation gateways (Sim1 and Sim2), a message gateway (C-Source), two truth-model components (Objects and Event), and an event-tracking subsystem (Event Track). Details for each component are shown in the Component Table, shown in Table 2.

Table 2. Component Table Identifying Component Characteristics

COMPONENT NEEDS	Legacy Components	Number of Modules	Size[1] Lines of Code (LOC)	Complexity	Coupling	Cohesiveness
1. Simulation Gateways						
	Sim1 Gateway	17	2,297	Low	Low	High
	Sim2 Gateway	57	4,877	Low	Low	High
2. Message Gateways						
	C-Source	45	4,186	High	Low	High
3. Truth Model						
	Objects	65	9,202	Med	High	High
	Event	39	4,412	Med	High	High
4. ETS & Message Generation						
	Event Track	89	5,417	Med / High	Low	Low

In the Analyze Candidate Components activity these components were analyzed to evaluate their potential for use in the new architecture. Of the potential legacy components, three were identified for wrapping (the two simulation gateways and the message gateway). These components would not require changes to their internal programs. The other three components (the two truth-model components and the event-tracking subsystem) were identified as potential white-box components where changes inside the programs would be required.

The basic types of changes required to rehabilitate these components were estimated. Estimates were also made of the effort and cost required for developing the candidate components from scratch as opposed to the cost of mining them. The details for each of the components are outlined in the expanded Component Table shown in Table 3.

Table 3. Expanded Component Table

Legacy System Software Components	Black Box / White Box Suitability	Level of Changes	Support Software Required	Level of Difficulty	Level of Risk	Mining Effort (mm)	Mining Cost	New Devel. Effort (mm)	New Devel. Cost	Comp. Mining Cost	Comp. Mining Effort
Sim1 Gateway	BB	None	S&D Files	1	Low	0.1	$1,000	7.7	$76,567	1%	1%
Sim2 Gateway	BB	None	S&D Files	1	Low	0.1	$1,000	16.3	$162,567	1%	1%
C-Source	BB	None	S&D Files	1	Low	0.1	$1,000	14.0	$139,533	1%	1%
Objects	WB	Minor (10%)	S&D Files	2	High	2.2	$22,000	30.7	$306,733	7%	7%
Event	WB	Minor (10%)	S&D Files	2	High	1.3	$13,000	14.7	$147,067	9%	9%
Event Track	WB	Major (50%)	S&D Files	4	Low	8	$80,000	18.1	$180,567	44%	44%
						12	$118,000	102	$1,013,034	12%	12%

TOTALs

Size estimates are based on the actual lines of code within each module. The S&D Files are the script and data files needed to run the components. An estimate of 6 man-months of effort and a cost of $60,000 were given for the conversion of the S&D Files. The level of difficulty is captured on a scale of 1 (minimal) to 5 (very high). Software engineering productivity information was provided by the STA with estimates of 300 SLOC per man-month at a labor burden rate of $10,000 per man-month.

The application of the OAR method surfaced the major issue that the interfaces for the new system had not yet been fully defined. Consequently, these cost estimates are preliminary and will need to be reviewed when the ISS interface specifics are fully defined.

In the Plan Mining Options activity, three options containing aggregations of components were developed. The simulation- and message-gateway components were aggregated as one option. However, since these components all depend on the interfaces that are still undefined, this aggregation may change.

The other two aggregations represent coarse-grained groupings of self-contained functionality. They were each treated as a separate option.

The comparative cost and effort of each aggregation was calculated based on the information captured in the Component Table. The aggregated level of difficulty and risks for each option were determined. These are presented in the Options Table shown in Table 4. The level of difficulty is calculated as a weighted average of the level of difficulty of the individual components in the aggregation. The level of risk for an aggregation is the highest level of risk for any of the individual components within the option.

Table 4. Options Table

Option No.	Legacy System Software Components	Support Software Required	Level of Risk	Level of Difficulty	Mining Effort[1] (mm)	Mining Cost[1]	New Development Effort (mm)	New Development Cost	Comparative Mining Cost	Comparative Mining Cost
1	Event Track	S&D Files	Low	4	8	$80,000	18.1	$180,567	44%	44%
	Option Summation		Low	4	8	$80,000	18.1	$180,567	44%	44%
2	Objects	S&D Files	High	2	2.2	$22,000	30.7	$306,733	7%	7%
	Event	S&D Files	High	2	1.3	$13,000	14.7	$147,067	9%	9%
	Option Summation		High	2	3.5	$35,000	45.4	$453,800	8%	8%
3	Sim1 Gateway	S&D Files	Low	1	0.1	$1,000	7.7	$76,567	1%	1%
	Sim2 Gateway	S&D Files	Low	1	0.1	$1,000	16.3	$162,567	1%	1%
	C-Source	S&D Files	Low	1	0.1	$1,000	14	$139,533	1%	1%
	Option Summation		Low	1	0.3	$3,000	38	$378,667	1%	1%

[1] Note: Mining Effort and Cost do not include effort and cost to convert scripts and data files that are part of the support software

In the Select Mining Option activity, these options were ordered in a possible sequence based upon when they will be undertaken by the STA. The ordering is shown in Table 4.

As part of the application of the OAR method, the STA learned how to carry out the various activities and will be able to apply the OAR method in the future. The STA is planning to choose a much larger group of components and apply the OAR method to that new grouping, so that it will have a better picture of the effort, cost, and difficulties involved in mining more of the STS for use in the ISS.

6 Conclusion

The OAR method is a systematic, architecture-centric method for mining existing components for a product line or new software architecture. It identifies product line component needs that can be satisfied through mining, as well as those that cannot be satisfied. Candidate components are screened based on criteria that are relevant for the organization. OAR provides management visibility into this highly complex analysis activity. It also provides insights into implicit stakeholder assumptions, constraints, and other major drivers that impact the mining of components.

As a first step, the OAR method establishes the component needs, identifies candidate legacy components and their related documentation, and determines other aspects that define the mining context. Next, it inventories the legacy components that can potentially fill identified product line needs and identifies their characteristics, the types of changes needed, and the estimated cost and effort. The OAR method reflects the elicited needs, priorities, and concerns of the organization. Its final outputs are a mining option or a combination of options that an organization may pursue and a list of the product line component needs that can and cannot be satisfied through mining.

Through the STA case study the OAR method has demonstrated its effectiveness in identifying components for reuse and analyzing the changes that need to be made to these components. The OAR method focuses on guiding the crucial decisions on which components to mine, and focuses on order-of-magnitude estimates of the amount of resources required to make the changes. The OAR method does not perform the actual changes to the components. Future work will include additional OAR pilots, as well as follow-up work on actual changes and a comparison of the actual costs to the estimated costs. In addition, the relationship between the OAR decisions and the follow-up factoring will be analyzed, together with the impact of different types of tool support.

References

1. Clements, P. and Northrop, L. M.: Software Product Lines: Practices and Patterns. Addison Wesley. New York, 2001.
2. Muller, H.; Jahnke, J.; Smith, D.; Storey, M.-A.; Tilley, S.; & Wong, K.: Reverse Engineering: A Roadmap,. The Future of Software Engineering. New York, NY: ACM2000, 47-60.
3. Sneed, H. and Majnar, R.: A Case Study in Software Wrapping, International Conference on Software Maintenance, 1998, 86-93.
4. Sneed, H.: Risks Involved in Reengineering Projects, Sixth Working Conference on Reverse Engineering, 1999, 204 –211.
5. De Lucia, A.; Di Lucca, G. A.; Fasolino, A. R.; Guerra, P.; Petruzzelli, S.: Migrating legacy systems towards object-oriented platforms, International Conference on Software Maintenance, 1997, 122 –129.
6. Bergey, J.; O'Brien, L. and Smith, D.: Options Analysis for Reengineering (OAR): A method for Mining Legacy Assets, Software Engineering Institute, 2001, CMU/SEI-2001-TN-013.
7. Smith, D.; O'Brien, L. and Bergey, J.: OAR: Options Analysis for Reengineering – Mining Components for a Product Line or New Software Architecture, International Conference on Software Engineering, Tutorial, 2001.

Widening the Scope of Software Product Lines –
From Variation to Composition

Rob van Ommering[1] and Jan Bosch[2]

[1]Philips Research Laboratories
Prof. Holstlaan 4, 5656 AA Eindhoven, The Netherlands
Rob.van.Ommering@philips.com
[2]University of Groningen, Department of Computing Science,
PO Box 800, 9700 AV Groningen, The Netherlands
Jan.Bosch@cs.rug.nl

Abstract. Architecture, components and reuse form the key elements to build a large variety of complex, high-quality products with a short lead-time. But the balance between an architecture-driven and a component-driven approach is influenced by the scope of the product line and the characteristics of the development organization. This paper discusses that balance and claims that a paradigm shift from variation to composition is necessary to cope with an increasing diversity of products created by an ever-larger part of an organization. We illustrate our claim with various examples.

Keywords: product population, software components, variation, composition.

1   Introduction

As a software engineering community, we have a long history of building software products: we have been doing this for half a century now. *Architecture* has always been an important success factor [7], though it has not received the attention that it deserves until the last decade. *Components* (or modules) serve as a means to cope with complexity (divide and conquer), and to streamline the evolution of systems [24]. We have been *reusing* software for a long time: operating systems, graphical and mathematical libraries, databases and compilers are rarely written from scratch for new products.

It is therefore not surprising that people developed the vision that the future of software engineering lies in the use of reusable components: new applications would be built by selecting from a set of existing components and then clicking or gluing them together. McIlroy was one of the first to advocate this idea [16], and many have followed since. We have indeed seen some successes in this area, for instance in the use of ActiveX controls (components) and Visual Basic (glue) to quickly build interactive applications for PCs. But we have also seen many failures, especially when reuse is applied *within* companies to create a diversity of products.

This is where software product lines enter. They provide proactive and systematic approaches for the development of software to create a variety of products. Again, software product lines have been around for decades, but have only recently begun to

G. Chastek (Ed.): SPLC2 2002, LNCS 2379, p. 328–347, 2002.
© Springer-Verlag Berlin Heidelberg 2002

receive the attention that they deserve. Note that product lines are not specific to software only: they are also commonplace in the car, the airplane and the food industry [8].

Most software product line research focuses on an early analysis of commonality and variation [1], followed by the creation of a variant-free architecture [25] with a sufficient number of variation points [13] to deal with diversity. While this works well for small product families in a small organization, we have experienced problems when applying this to larger ranges of products, especially when development crosses organizational boundaries.

This paper is about widening the scope of product lines to encompass a larger diversity of products (a *product population* [21]), where the development takes place in different organizational units but still within the same company. We believe that the successful building of product populations is the next hurdle to take in software engineering. Figure 1 illustrates this, showing on the one hand that the focus of our community shifts over time from products to components to families to populations, and on the other hand that we are seeking a balance between variation (as in product families) and composition (as in software components).

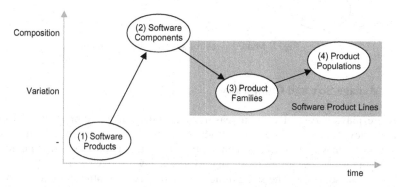

Fig. 1. Towards product populations

This paper is organized as follows. First we recapitulate the main drivers for software product lines. Then we discuss the influence of product scope and characteristics of the organization on software product lines. We proceed with introducing variation and composition as separate dimensions, and then explain variation and composition in more detail. We end with some concluding remarks. We take examples from the domain of one of the authors, the control software for consumer electronics products, but include examples from other domains as well.

2   Why Use Software Product Lines?

Let us first summarize *why* we want to create software product lines. In Figure 2, we show the main four drivers as we identified them within Philips at the left-hand side. We show three key solutions in the middle. But it's the combination of these three that forms the most promising solution to our problems: software product lines.

In the next subsections, we discuss each of the drivers and their relation to the solutions. Please note that arrows in Figure 2 show main dependencies only; arguments can be found for other dependencies as well, but adding them would obscure the main flow of the picture.

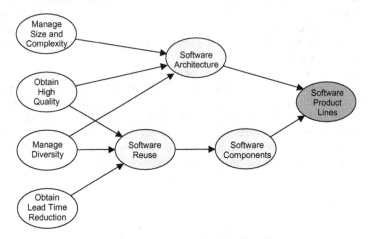

Fig. 2. Main drivers for software product lines

2.1.   Manage Size and Complexity

Software plays a role of ever-increasing importance in many products of today. In Philips televisions, software was introduced in the late 70s when a 1-kilobyte 8-bit microprocessor was first used to control the hardware signal processing devices. The size of the software grew following Moore's law: today, a TV typically has 2 megabytes of software. The same trend can be observed in other products, though the point in time when software starts to play a role differs. Typically, televisions run 10 years behind PCs, while shavers run 10 years behind televisions.

The best – perhaps only – way to manage size and complexity is to have a proper architecture. A software architecture defines, among other things, a decomposition of a system in terms of components or modules [12]. One common misconception (at least in our surroundings) is the assumption that components defined to manage size and complexity automatically help to satisfy the other drivers listed in Figure 2, most notably diversity. Experience has shown is not the case: defining components to manage diversity is an art per se.

2.2.   Obtain High Quality

The second driver in Figure 2 is quality: the more complex systems become, the more difficult it is to maintain a high quality. Yet for systems such as televisions, high quality of the software is imperative[1]. Television users do not think that they are communicating with a computer, so they will not accept crashes. Also, although lives may not seem to be involved, a TV catching fire can have disastrous effects, and it is partly the software that prevents this from happening.

Quality can be achieved by having a proper architecture that guarantees (or at least helps to satisfy) certain quality attributes. Quality can also be achieved by reusing software that has already been tested in the field.

2.3.   Manage Diversity

The third driver in Figure 2 is the first one specific to product lines: managing the efficient creation of a variety of products. For consumer products, we have 'small-scale' diversity within a family of televisions in areas such as the output device, the price setting, the region, the user interface, the supported standards, and interconnectivity. We have 'large-scale' diversity if we want televisions, VCRs, DVD/CD players/recorders, and so forth to be part of one product line approach. There is indeed sufficient commonality to justify the sharing of software between those products. We use the term *product population* to denote the large-scale diversity. Other examples of product populations can be found in the medical domain [14] and for printers and scanners [3].

There are actually two schools of thought for managing diversity, which we believe are two extremes in a spectrum of solutions. One is to build an architecture that expresses the commonality between products, with variation points to express the diversity. The other is to rely on reuse of software components for the commonality, but to use different compositions of these components to implement diversity. This paper is about balancing between these two solutions (variation and composition) depending on the scope of the products and the characteristics of the organization.

2.4.   Lead-Time Reduction

The fourth driver in Figure 2 is lead-time reduction. Although in principle this is also relevant for single product development, we think that it is especially relevant in product line contexts, since the goal of product lines is to produce a range of products quickly. The main way to obtain lead-time reduction is to reuse software. Experience has shown that higher level languages, modern development methods, better architectures, and advanced software development environments have indeed improved software productivity, but not with a factor that is sufficient to obtain the speed required in product lines.

2.5.   Does Software Reuse Imply Software Components?

Figure 2 may suggest that software reuse implies the deployment of reusable software components. Indeed the reuse of software components is one (compositional)

---

[1] Repairing software shipped in televisions sold to a million customers is as difficult as in a rocket sent a million miles into space.

approach to building product populations, and one that we will examine in this paper. But we should note that we can also have reuse *without* software components, for instance when using inheritance in an object-oriented (OO) framework. And, perhaps surprisingly, we can also build a product line that utilizes software component technology without actually reusing the components! An example of the latter is a framework with component plug-ins, where the plug-in components implement *diversity* rather than *commonality*. Figure 3 illustrates this: the left-hand side shows a reusable framework with product-specific plug-ins, while the right-hand side shows reusable components, composed in a product-specific way.

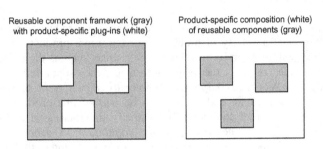

Fig. 3. Variation (left) and composition (right) are complementary approaches

2.6.   Finding the Balance

In the rest of this paper, we concentrate on the balance between the use of variation and composition in software product lines, depending on the scope of the product population and the characteristics of the organization building it.

3   The Influence of Scope on Software Product Lines

As we have said before, many software product line approaches advocate an early analysis of the commonality and variation of the products to be built, resulting in a variant-free architecture with variation points. This is indeed a valid approach, but there may be circumstances in which the preconditions for such an approach are not satisfied. We shall discuss two categories of these in the following sections: (1) product related and (2) organization related.

3.1.   From Product Family to Product Population

Traditional product lines cover families in which products have many commonalities and few differences. This enables the creation of a variant-free architecture with variation points to implement the differences. The variation points typically control the internals of a component, but they may also control the presence or absence of certain components, the selection of a concrete component to implement an abstract component (a place holder), or even the binding between components.

A typical product family in the consumer domain is the set of televisions (direct view, flat screen, projection) produced by a single company[2]. Let us now extend the product range to include video recorders, CD and DVD players, CD, DVD and hard disk recorders, audio amplifiers, MP3 players, tuners, cassette players, and so forth. These products still have enough in common to warrant reuse of software. But they are also sufficiently different to require different architectures.

The latter is actually not a fundamental problem. In principle, it seems perfectly possible to create a single architecture for a 'super consumer product', that would be the combination of all products mentioned above, and to strip this architecture for any subset to be sold. While this is certainly possible in hindsight, it is very difficult to predict which combinations of audio and video elements will actually be interesting next year, and to include that in the architecture in advance.

Instead, the market itself thrives on novel combinations of existing functions (for instance a mobile telephone with built-in digital photo camera). We believe that in such an evolving 'compositional' market, the software architectures must also be compositional. Put differently, variation can be used to implement diversity known ahead of time, while composition can be used for open-ended diversity.

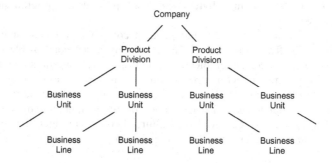

Fig. 4. Schematic Organization of a Large Company

3.2. From Business Line to Product Division and Beyond

The second argument in favor of composition has its roots in organization. A large company like Philips is typically organized in product divisions (Semiconductors, Consumer Electronics), which are split into business units (video, audio), which again are split into business lines (flat TV, projection TV). See Figure 4 for an illustration.

Within a business line, setting up a software product line is generally relatively easy. One person is in charge of the business, which has its own profit and loss calculation, and a product line is demonstrably an efficient way to create a variety of products. The products are reasonably alike (e.g.,all high-end Flat TVs). Moreover, the product roadmaps in a business line are usually carefully aligned, thus enabling the creation and use of shared software. A single architecture with variation points is very feasible.

---

[2] For technical reasons, low-end televisions usually belong to a different family than high-end televisions.

Compare this with a business unit. Although – of course –one person still is in charge, profit and loss responsibility is delegated to the business lines, making sharing software between business lines at least cumbersome. Each business line manager has his own agenda for planning software development. Protection of intellectual property (IP) is sometimes an issue, but more frequently the misalignment of roadmaps causes problems: one business line is changing software with its product release still far away, while another product line needs a mature version of the software for its immediate next release. A careful and explicit roadmapping is required here [22]. Products show more differences, but in general a single architecture with variation points is still be feasible.

Problems get worse at the level of a product division. Not only do the products become more different (e.g., TV versus set-top box), but the managers become more apt to look after themselves instead of after their common interest, the roadmaps become harder to align, and the cultures between organizations become different. In Philips, the TV business is a traditional and stable consumer business (low profit per product but high number of products, targeted directly at the person on the street), while the set-top box business is new and evolving (currently targeted at large providers who deliver the boxes free with their services). TVs are typically programmed in C in a few megabytes, while set-top boxes are programmed in C^{++} in many megabytes.

Finally, product divisions act as independent companies (at least at Philips), and while sharing of software between them is in many cases not feasible (as between medical systems and consumer electronics), it may in certain situations still be desirable. Philips Semiconductors produces for instance many of the chips for Philips Consumer Electronics, and it also sells the same chips to third parties, so certain software can be better leveraged if developed by the semiconductors division. This puts extra demands on protection of IP. Cultures between product divisions are even more different, and the levels of software engineering maturity may differ.

3.3.   How to Share Software in Large Organizations?

It should be obvious by now that the top-down creation of a single architecture with variation points to cover all consumer products within Philips is not feasible. Instead, we should find a way to let different business lines create the software components in which they are specialized (e.g., the business line DVD creates a DVD unit), and find ways to 'arbitrarily' compose them.

Should we then strive for a bottom-up approach as advocated by many believers in software component markets (i.e., (2) instead of (4) in Figure 1)? The answer is no: we still need a careful balance between top-down and bottom-up, because we need to make sure that components fit easily, as explained in the next section.

3.4.   Balancing between Architecture- and Component-Driven Development

Classical product and product line approaches ((1) and (3) in Figure 1) are architecture-driven, top-down, planned, intra-organization, with all software to be developed in the project. Component market evangelists ((2) in Figure 1) on the other hand, claim that software development should be component-driven, bottom-up,

	Component-driven	Bottom-up	Opportunistic	Available	Inter-organization
Architecture-driven	-	Extreme Programming		Design With Reuse	Domain Architectures
Top-down		-			
Planned	Roadmapping		-		Sub contracting
To be developed	Design For Reuse			-	
Intra-organization		Product Populations			-

Fig. 5. Balancing between Architecture- and Component-Driven Development

opportunistic, inter-organization and using components that are already available. Figure 5 shows both sets of these opposite characteristics along different axes. Note that they are not all dependent – we can make cross combinations:

Extreme programming could be seen as an opportunistic bottom-up yet architecture-driven method.

- Top-down, architecture-driven development deploying available software is sometimes called *design with reuse*, while on the other hand component-driven bottom-up development is sometimes called *design for reuse*.
- A top-down, architecture-driven development spanning multiple organizations is possible, but only if there is consensus on a *domain architecture*.
- The planned development across organizations of new software is often called *subcontracting*, and should not be confused with the development of reusable software[3].

Our vision is to achieve a component-driven, bottom-up, partly opportunistic software development using as much as possible available software to create products within our organization; we call this a *product population* approach. In reality, life is not so black and white. More specifically, we believe that such an approach should be:

- Component-driven (bottom-up) with a lightweight (top-down) architecture, since absence of the latter would result in architectural mismatches [10].
- Opportunistic in using available software but also planned when developing new software, with the latter carefully roadmapped [22].
- Intra-organizational but spanning a large part of the organization.

In a way, building product populations is more difficult than producing and utilizing software components on a component market. In the latter case, the laws of economics apply: component vendors can leverage development costs over many customers (as compared to a few in product populations), while component buyers can find second sources in case vendors do not live up to expectations. One would expect that the same economical model could be used *within* an organization, but in

---

[3] Within Philips, we have seen a single team that had as a mission the development of reusable software act in practice as two teams subcontracted for two different product projects.

practice this does not work: contracts within a company are always less binding than those between companies.

3.5. Third-Party Component Markets

Does this mean that we do not believe in third-party component markets [31]? Yes, we do, but not as the only solution.

First of all, most software components on the market tend to implement generic rather than domain-specific functionality. While this ensures a large customer base, it does not help companies like Philips to build consumer products. Put differently: of course we reuse generic components, such as a real-time kernel from third parties, but there is still a lot of software to be created ourselves. This situation may change with the arrival and general acceptance of TV middleware stacks.

Secondly, many companies distinguish between *core*, *key*, and *base* software. Base software can and should be bought on the open market. Key software can be bought but is made by the company itself for strategic reasons. Core software cannot be bought because the company is the only company – or one of the very few – actually capable of creating such software. But there may still be a need to share this software within the company.

Thirdly, many components out on the open market are still relatively small (e.g., buttons, sliders), while the actual need for reuse is for large components. Of course there are exceptions: underlying Microsoft's Internet Explorer is a powerful reusable HTML displaying *and* editing engine that can be used in different contexts (such as Front Page and HTML Help). But such examples are still exceptions rather than the rule.

Finally, to be accepted in an open market, functionality must be mature, so that there is consensus in the world on how to implement and use such functionality. This process may take well over 20 years. Consider operating systems and windowing systems as examples.

4   The Dimensions of Variation and Composition

Figure 6 shows variation and composition as two independent dimensions. The variation axis is marked with 'As is' (no variation), parameterization, inheritance, and plug-ins as subsequently more advanced techniques of variation. The composition axis is marked with no composition (yet reuse), and composition. The table is filled with some characteristic examples, which we discuss briefly below. We also zoom into variation and composition with more elaborate examples.

4.1. Plain 'Old-Fashioned' Libraries

The classical example of software reuse is through libraries. Examples include mathematical libraries, graphical libraries, and string-manipulation libraries. The functions in the library are either used 'as is' or can be fine-tuned for their specific application using a (procedural) parameter mechanism.

		COMPOSITION ➡	
		Reusable but not composable	Composable
V A R I A T I O N ⬇	'As is'	Libraries	LEGO
	Parameterization		Visual Basic
	Inheritance	OO Frameworks	Frameworks as Components
	Plug-ins	Component Frameworks	

Fig. 6. Variation and Composition as Two Independent Dimensions

Typically, the software deploying the library includes the header file(s) of the library, and thus becomes specifically dependent upon the library. It is possible to abstract from the library by defining a library-independent interface, for example, POSIX[4]. The build process may then select the actual library implementing this interface. However, in practice, most software built on top of libraries is still specifically dependent upon those libraries.

This is especially true for the library itself. Often, a library uses other libraries, but few of them allow the user to select which underlying libraries to use. Moreover, while some libraries are relatively safe to use (they define specific functions only, such as 'sin' and 'cos'), other libraries may introduce clashing names (e.g., String), or have clashing underlying assumptions (e.g., they both define the function 'main').

The conclusion is that while libraries are a perfect low-level technical mechanism, more advanced techniques are necessary to achieve the variation and composition required for product lines.

4.2. Object-Oriented Frameworks

An OO framework is a coherent set of classes from which one can create applications by specializing the classes using implementation inheritance. An example is the Microsoft Foundation Classes framework [26]. The power lies in the use of inheritance as a variation mechanism, allowing the framework to abstract from specific behavior and to be implemented by the derived classes. A base class usually has a very intricate coupling with its derived classes, with the base class calling functions implemented in the derived class and vice versa.

This intricate coupling is also one of the weaknesses of this approach. A new version of the framework, combined with old versions of the derived classes may fail due to subtle incompatibilities; this is known as the *fragile base class problem* (see 29 for a treatment). Also, since many frameworks are applications themselves, combining two or more frameworks becomes virtually impossible.

---

[4] POSIX stands for Portable Operating System Interface.

4.3.   Component Frameworks

A component framework is part of an application that allows plug-in components to specialize behavior. Component frameworks resemble OO frameworks; the main difference is the more precise definition of the dependencies between the framework and the plug-in components. The plug-ins can vary from quite simple to arbitrarily complex; the latter case enabling the creation of a large variety of applications.

Component frameworks share some of the disadvantages with OO frameworks. First of all, the plug-in components are usually framework dependent and cannot be used in isolation. Secondly, the framework often implements an entire application and therefore cannot be defined easily with other frameworks.

4.4.   LEGO

The archetype non-software example of composition is LEGO, the toy bricks with the standard 'click and play' interface. Indeed, LEGO bricks are very composable, but they support no variation at all! This results in two phenomena.

First of all, it *is* possible to create arbitrary shapes with standard LEGO bricks, but one must use thousands of bricks to make the shapes smooth (see Figure 7 for a pirate's head). As the components are then very small compared to the end product, there is effectively not much reuse (not more than reusing statements in a programming language).

Fig. 7. The pirate's head with ordinary LEGO® bricks[5]

To solve this, LEGO manufactures specialized bricks that can only be used for one purpose. This makes it possible to create smooth figures with only a few bricks. The down side is that specialized bricks can only be used in specialized cases. A solution could be parameterized bricks, which indeed is a mechanical challenge! Maybe a LEGO printer, a device that can spray plastic, could be an answer here![6]

[®] LEGO is a trademark of the LEGO Group.

[5] From http://www.lego.com

[6] Strictly speaking, a LEGO printer would be the equivalent of a code generator, which is a technique for building product lines that we do not tackle in this paper, although it can be very fruitful in certain domains (cf. compiler generators). See also [9].

4.5. Visual Basic

The archetype software example of composition is Visual Basic (VB). Actually, Basic is the non-reusable "glue" language, where ActiveX controls are the reusable components (later versions of VB also allow the creation of new ActiveX controls).

One of the success factors of Visual Basic is the parameterization mechanism. An ActiveX control can have dozens, even hundreds, of properties, with default values to alleviate the instantiation process. Another parameterization technique is the event mechanism, which allows the signaling of asynchronous conditions, where the application can take product-specific actions.

Still, ActiveX controls are usually quite small (the Internet Explorer excepted), and it is not easy to create application frameworks (e.g., supporting a document view control paradigm such as the Microsoft Foundation Classes do).

4.6. Frameworks as Components

The ultimate solution for variation *and* composition lies – we believe – in the use of OO or component frameworks as components. We have seen that frameworks provide powerful variation mechanisms. If a framework only covers part of an application domain, and if frameworks can be combined arbitrarily (making them *true* components), then we can create a multitude of products by selecting and combining them and then specializing them for a product.

There are some examples of OO frameworks used as components [4], but no examples of component frameworks used as components yet. The basic mechanism for achieving composition is to make every context dependency explicit and bindable by a third party, as we will see in a later section.

5   Variation Further Explained

Let us zoom into variation first, and then discuss composition in more detail.

5.1. Why Do We Need Variation?

The basic argument for variation is the one underlying all product line development: we need to implement diversity. We can achieve this with reusable components, but an interesting dilemma pops up. The more useful we make a component (read: larger), the less reusable it becomes. Conversely, the more reusable we make a component, the less useful it may become, the extreme case being the empty component: extremely reusable while not very useful! See also [29], Fig 1.1.

The solution for this dilemma is *variation* as a way to fine-tune components when instantiating them into a product. The archetype example is the Visual Basic ActiveX control, which usually comes with a long list of properties that can be modified at design-time and/or runtime. These properties also have default values to alleviate the effort of product creation; otherwise the burden on the designer may be too high.

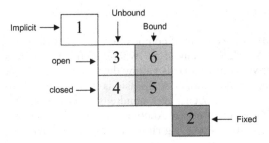

Fig. 8. A Life Cycle for Variation Points

5.2.   Types of Variation

A variation point can be implicit or explicit, open or closed, unbound or bound, and flexible or fixed [4]. Not all sixteen combinations are meaningful. See Figure 8 for an overview. When development starts, a variation point is implicit; it must be made explicit during analysis and design. An explicit variation point can be open if the set of possible values can still be extended, or closed otherwise. A variation point is unbound if a value has not been selected, and bound otherwise. A variation point is fixed if it's bound, and the value cannot be changed anymore.

Traditional single-product development starts at (1) in Figure 8 and then immediately jumps to (2). Classical product-family development proceeds through (3), (4) and (5) (identify a variation point, identify its values, and then choose a value) before ending in (2). There is a tendency to make (5) the end point of development, allowing the variation point still to change at the customer site. There is even a tendency to make (6) the end point of development, allowing the customer to extend the set of values.

5.3.   Example 1: Switches and Options

In our previous television software architecture, we distinguished between *switches* and *options*. A switch is a compile-time variation point (an #ifdef), closed, bound and fixed somewhere during development time. An option is a runtime variation point, a value stored in non-volatile memory and used in an if-statement, so closed yet unbound during development, and bound in the factory or at the user's home.

These variation points were used for adjustments of hardware, for the presence or absence of components, and in rare cases for selecting between components. The set of variation points was very specific for the product family and could not be used to achieve the large-scale structural variation that we needed to widen our family.

5.4.   Example 2: The Windows Explorer

The Windows Explorer is an example of an application with many explicit, open, unbound and flexible variation points. It can be tuned into almost any browsing application, though it cannot be used as a component in a larger application. In other words, it supports a lot of variation, but no composition.

The explorer can be tuned at a beginner's level and at an advanced level [18]. In the first case, simple additions to the windows registry suffice to change the file association (the application to be run for a certain type of file), the context menus or the icons. In the second case, handlers must be registered for specific shell extensions, and these handlers must be implemented as Component Object Model (COM) components. When such a handler crashes, Windows Explorer crashes, with all its windows including the desktop[7].

The folder view of Windows Explorer can be modified by name space extensions; some FTP clients use this to add favorite sites to the name space. The folder view is part of the Explorer bar, which can also host other views (search, favorites, history). The right pane normally hosts a standard list view control, but it can also host the Internet Explorer to view (folders as) web pages, or any other user-defined window.

5.5. Example 3: A Framework Architecture

Wijnstra [32] describes a software architecture in the medical domain that deploys component frameworks to manage diversity. Figure 9 provides a schematic overview of this architecture. It consists of a fixed structure of *units*, COM components (mostly executables) running on a Windows NT computer. Each unit is a component framework in which COM components can be plugged to implement the diversity of the product family. Plug-in components may talk to each other, but the initial contact is made through the main units.

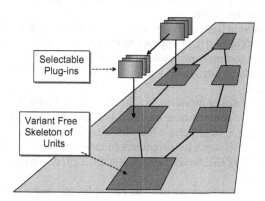

Fig. 9. Fusion

In this architecture, the fixed structure of units[8] implements the common part of the family, while the plug-ins take care of the differences between the products. It is therefore an example of variation rather than composition (see the left-hand side of Figure 3). Of course, this is true if the plug-ins are relatively small and specific for one product only. In real life, some plug-ins are rather large and shared between

---

[7] It is possible to run the desktop in a different process to prevent such crashes.

[8] Some units are optional.

multiple members of the family. In fact, if one can create products by taking arbitrary combinations of plug-ins, then this system exhibits signs of composition rather than variation.

6   Composition Further Explained

We shall now discuss composition as a technique for managing diversity.

6.1.   What Is Composition?

We speak of *composition* if two pieces of software that have been developed *without* direct knowledge of each other can be combined to create a working product. The components may have been developed in some common context, or they may share interfaces defined elsewhere. The essential element is that the first piece of software can be used without the second, and the second piece without the first.

The underlying argument for using composition to handle diversity is the large number of combinations that can be made if components are not directly dependent on one another. Note that composition excludes the notion of plug-ins, since these are directly dependent on the underlying framework, and cannot be used in isolation.

A nice analogy may be the problem of describing a language, where an infinite number of sentences must be produced with a finite (and hopefully small) set of 'components'. Typically, such components are production rules in a grammar, where the production rules function both as a composition hierarchy as well as a set of constraints on the composition.

Garlan has illustrated how difficult composition can be in his well-known paper on architectural mismatches [10]. It appears that two components being combined must at least share some common principles to work together efficiently. We call this a lightweight architecture, but leave it to another paper to elaborate on how to create such an architecture.

Szyperski [29] defines components as 'having explicit context dependencies only', and being 'subject to composition by third parties'. In Koala [20], the former are called (explicit) requires interfaces, while the latter is called third-party binding. Tony Williams recognized the same two elements in an early paper leading to open linking and embedding (OLE) [33], though an interface is called a 'base class' there, and the third party, a 'creator'.

In the following subsections we provide examples of compositional approaches.

6.2.   Example 1: The 'Pipes and Filters' Architectural Style

One of the oldest examples of the use of composition to create a diversity of applications with only few components is the pipes and filters architecture of Unix. With a minimum of common agreements (character based I/O, a standard input and output stream), and a new line as record separator, using a small set of tools such as *grep, sed, awk, find* and *sort* with essentially one simple composition operator, the

'|', one can program a large variety of tasks, including small databases, automatic mail handling and software build support.

Pipes and filters are considered an architectural style in [28], and indeed there are more examples with similar compositional value. Microsoft's DirectShow [17] is a streaming architecture that allows the creation of 'arbitrary' graphs of nodes that process audio and video signals. The nodes, called *codecs*[9], are implemented as COM servers and may be obtained from different vendors. The graph can be constructed manually with a program that acts as a COM client. A simple type mechanism allows the automatic creation of parts of such a graph, depending on the types of input and output signals. Other companies have similar architectures (e.g., Philips with the Trimedia Streaming Software Architecture (TSSA) [30]).

A third kind of pipes and filters architecture can be found in the domain of measurement and control. LabView [19] is an environment in which measurement, control and automation applications can be constructed as block diagrams and subsequently compiled into running systems. See also [5].

6.3.   Example 2: Relation Partition Algebra

Software architectures are normally defined *a priori*, after which an implementation is created. But it is also possible to 'reverse engineer' an implementation to extract a software architecture from it, if the architecture has been lost. Even if the architecture has not been lost, it is still possible to extract the architecture from the implementation and verify it against the original architecture. Discrepancies mean that either the implementation is wrong, or the original architecture is 'imperfect' (to say the least).

Tools can be built to support this process, but a large variety of queries would result in a large range of tools. As it turns out, mathematical set and relation algebra can be used to model 'use' and 'part-of' relations in software effectively; queries can be expressed mostly in one-liners. A compositional tool set for this algebra is described in [23]; a similar technique is also deployed by [11].

6.4.   Example 3: COM, OLE, and ActiveX

Microsoft's COM [27] is a successful example of a component technology, but this does not automatically imply that it supports *composition* from the ground up. COM can be seen as an object-oriented programming technique, its three main functions, *CoCreateInstance*, *QueryInterface* and *AddRef/Release*, being, respectively, the new operator, the dynamic type cast, and the delete operator. COM's main contribution is that it supports object orientation 'in the large': across language, process, and even processor boundaries.

If a COM client uses a COM service, the default design pattern is that it creates an instance of that service. It refers to the service by CLSID, a globally unique identifier that is nevertheless specific for that service, thus creating a fixed dependency between the client and the service. In other words, clients and services are (usually) not freely composable. To circumvent problems thus arising, some solutions have been found,

---

[9] For *cod*ing and *dec*oding streams of data.

most noteworthy the *CoTreatAs*, the *Category ID*, and the connectable interfaces. The latter provide a true solution, but in practice are only used for notifications.

Microsoft's OLE [6] *is* an example of an architecture that allows the free composition of document elements (texts, pictures, tables) rather than software components. An OLE *server* provides such elements, while an OLE *container* embeds them. An application may be an OLE server and container at the same time, allowing for arbitrarily nested document elements. An impressive machinery of interfaces is needed to accomplish this, as a consequence, there are not many different OLE containers around (though there are quite a few servers).

Microsoft ActiveX controls are software components that are intended for free composition. In general, they do not have matching interfaces, making it necessary to glue them together. The first language for this was Visual Basic; later it became possible to use other languages as well. An impressive market of third-party ActiveX controls has emerged.

6.5.   Example 4: GenVoca, Darwin, and Koala

GenVoca [2] is one of the few approaches that supports explicit *requires* interfaces to be bound by third parties. GenVoca uses a functional notation to combine components and is equipped with powerful code generation techniques. It has been applied to graph processing algorithms, where different combinations of the same set of components can be made to create a variety of applications.

Darwin [15] is a research language for the specification of distributed software architectures. It supports components with typed *provides* and *requires* interfaces, and it allows compound components to instantiate and bind other components. Darwin has been applied to the control and monitoring of coal mining, and - as Koala – to the control software for televisions (see below).

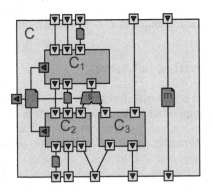

Fig. 10. The Koala component model

Koala [20] is an industrial architectural description language with a resource-friendly component model used for the creation of embedded control software for consumer products. Koala supports both composition and variation. Koala components can be instantiated and their (typed) interfaces can be bound by compound components as shown in Figure 10, thus forming a hierarchy of components. Variation is supported in the form of diversity interfaces, a special form of requires interfaces that resemble properties in ActiveX controls; and switches, a kind of pseudo-dynamic binding. Various products are already on the market, created from different combinations of different subsets of a repository of reusable components. Koala supports adaptation in the form of glue modules as a fundamental technique for binding components.

6.6.   Composability Is Actually a Form of Variation!

We have discussed variation and composition. We presented them as fundamentally different, but it is possible to unify the concepts. In all the examples that we have seen, components become 'freely composable' when context dependencies have been turned into explicit variation points. This may be in the form of an input stream or of connectable (requires) interfaces. Some approaches make every context dependency explicit (e.g., Koala), while others only make certain dependencies explicit (like in the pipes and filter architectures).

7   Concluding Remarks

Let us first recapitulate. Managing complexity and diversity while maintaining high quality and short lead times have become important software development issues. Reuse, architecture, and components are key solutions to achieve this. Originally, we envisaged reuse to happen 'automatically' once software components were available on the market. Later we discovered that sharing software actually requires a pro-active, systematic approach: that of software product lines. The first product lines rely heavily on (limited) *variation* in an otherwise variant-free architecture. With product scope increasing, and software development starting to cross organizational borders, we believe that more powerful techniques are required to handle diversity and discuss *composition* as one such a technique.

This does not mean that we're back to third-party component markets. Instead, a careful balance between architecture-driven top-down and component-driven bottom-up development is required, and we explain why and how. Also, composition does not replace variation, but rather they should be seen as two independent dimensions. We typify various points in the two-dimensional space with archetype examples, before explaining variation and composition individually in more detail. To make things as concrete as possible, we illustrate variation and composition with a rich set of well known examples.

Within Philips, we have moved from variation to composition in our architectures for certain sets of consumer products. We find that we can handle diversity better, and cover a larger range of products even though development is decoupled in time and space across organizations. We find that few other companies use composition, which originally surprised us. We then discovered that the few companies that do use composition also cover a wide product scope, cross organizational boundaries, or exhibit both phenomena.

Acknowledgements

We would like to thank attendants of the Software Architectures for Embedded Systems (ARES) workshops, the Software Product Line Conference, and the Philips 'Composable Architectures' project for many fruitful discussions on this topic.

8   References

1. Felix Bachmann, Len Bass, *Introduction to the Architecture Based Design Method*, Tutorial at the First Software Product Line Conference (SPLC1), August 28-31, 2000, Denver, Colorado, USA.
2. Don Batory, Sean O'Malley, *The Design and Implementation of Hierarchical Software Systems with Reusable Components*, ACM Transactions on Software Engineering and Methodology, 1 no. 4, pp. 355-398 (October 1992).
3. Joe Bauman, *The Perfect Architecture is non-optimal, Winning with Chaos*, Proceedings of the 4th international workshop on Product Family Engineering, Bilbao, Spain, October 2001.
4. Jan Bosch, *Organizing for Software Product Lines*, Proceedings of the 3rd international workshop on the development and evolution of software architectures of product families, Las Palmas, March 2000.
5. Klaas Brink, *Interfacing Control and Software Engineering: a formal approach*, PhD thesis, Technical University, Delft, The Netherlands, June 24, 1997.
6. Kraig Brockschmidt, Inside OLE Second Edition, 1995, Microsoft Press, ISBN 1-55615-843-2.
7. Frederick P. Brooks Jr, *The Mythical Man-Month, Essays on Software Engineering*, Addison-Wesley Publishing Company, ISBN 0-201-00650-2.
8. Paul Clements, Linda Northrop, *Software Product Lines, Practices and Patterns*, Addison-Wesley, 2002, ISBN 0-201-70332-7.
9. Krzysztof Czarnecki, Ulrich Eisenecker, *Generative Programming: Methods, Tools, and Applications*, Addison-Wesley Pub Co; ISBN: 0-201-30977-7.
10. David Garlan, Robert Allen, John Ockerbloom, *Architectural Mismatch, or: Why it's hard to build systems out of existing parts*, ICSE 95, Seattle, Washington USA.
11. Richard C. Holt, *Structural Manipulations of Software Architecture using Tarski Relational Algebra*, Proceedings of fifth Working Conference of Reverse Engineering, WCRE'98, IEEE Computer Society, 1998.
12. IEEE *Recommended Practice for Architectural Description of Software Incentive Systems*, http://standards.ieee.org/catalog/olis/se.html
13. Ivar Jacobson, Martin Griss, Patrick Jonsson, *Software Reuse – Architecture, Process and Organization for Business Success*, Addison Wesley, New York, 1997, ISBN 0-201-92476-5.
14. Frank van der Linden, Jan Gerben Wijnstra, *Platform Engineering for the Medical Domain*, Proceedings of the 4th international workshop on Product Family Engineering, Bilbao, Spain, October 2001.
15. Jeff Magee, Naranker Dulay, Susan Eisenbach, Jeff Kramer, *Specifying Distributed Software Architectures*, Proc. ESEC'95, Wilhelm Schafer, Pere Botella (Eds.) Springer LNCS 989 pp. 137-153 (1995).
16. M. D. McIlroy, *Mass produced software components*, Proc. Nato Software Eng. Conf., Garmisch, Germany (1968) 138-155.
17. Microsoft *DirectShow*, http://www.gdcl.co.uk/dshow.htm, part of DirectX.
18. Microsoft, *Shell Programmers Guide*, http://msdn.microsoft.com/library/
19. National Instruments, *LabView*, http://www.natinst.com/labview/

20. Rob van Ommering, Frank van der Linden, Jeff Kramer, Jeff Magee, The Koala Component Model for Consumer Electronics Software, IEEE Computer, March 2000, p78-85.
21. Rob van Ommering, *Beyond Product Families: Building a Product Population?*, Proceedings of the 3rd international workshop on the development and evolution of software architectures of product families, Las Palmas, March 2000.
22. Rob van Ommering, *Roadmapping a Product Population Architecture*, 4th International Workshop on Product Family Engineering, Bilbao, Spain, October 3-5, 2001.
23. Rob van Ommering, René Krikhaar, Loe Feijs, *Language for Formalizing, Visualizing and Verifying Software Architectures*, Computer Languages 27 (2001) p3-18.
24. David L. Parnas, *On the Criteria to Be Used in Decomposing Systems into Modules*, Communications of the ACM, Vol. 15, No. 12, December 1972, p1053-1058.
25. Dewayne E. Perry, *Generic Architecture Descriptions for Product Lines*, Proceedings of the Second International ESPRIT ARES Workshop, LNCS 1429, Springer Verlag, Berlin Heidelberg, 1998, p51-56.
26. Jeff Prosise, *Programming Windows 95 with MFC*, Microsoft Press, 1996, ISBN 1-55615-902-1.
27. Dale Rogerson, *Inside COM, Microsoft's Component Object Model*, Microsoft Press, ISBN 1-57231-349-8, 1997.
28. Mary Shaw, David Garlan, *Software Architecture, Perspectives on an Emerging Discipline*, Prentice Hall, 1996, ISBN 0-13-182957-2.
29. Clemens A. Szyperski, Component Software: Beyond Object-Oriented Programming. Addison-Wesley, Harlow, UK, 1998, ISBN 0-201-17888-5.
30. The Trimedia Streaming Software Architecture, http://www.trimedia.com/products/briefs/tssa.html
31. Kurt Wallnau, Scott Hissam, Robert Seacord, *Building Systems from Commercial Components*, Addison-Wesley Pub Co; ISBN: 0-201-70064-6
32. Jan Gerben Wijnstra, *Supporting Diversity with Component Frameworks as Architectural Elements*, Proceedings of the 22nd International Conference on Software Engineering, Limerick, June 4-11, 2000, p. 51-60.
33. Tony Williams, *On Inheritance, What It Means and How To Use It*, Microsoft Internal Report, 1990, http://research.microsoft.com/comapps/docs/Inherit.doc

A Method for Product Line Scoping
Based on a Decision-Making Framework

Tomoji Kishi[1], Natsuko Noda[1], and Takuya Katayama[2]

[1] NEC Corporation,
1753 Shimonumabe, Nakahara-ku, Kawasaki, Kanagawa, JAPAN, 211-8666,
+81 44 435 9460
{kishi@aj, n-noda@cw}.jp.nec.com
[2] School of Information Science,
JAIST-Japan Advanced Institute of Science and Technology
1-1, Asahidai, Tatsunokuchi, Noumi, Ishikawa, JAPAN 923-1292
+81 761 51 1111
katayama@jaist.ac.jp

Abstract. It is indispensable for strategic product line development to define the proper scope of the product line. Once the scope has been defined, we examine the corresponding product line architecture to realize systematic reuse for the product line. Therefore, in defining the scope, we have to decide whether or not it is appropriate to share the same architecture for the products in the product line. The appropriateness of sharing the same architecture among multiple products has to be examined from two points of view. One is from the point of view of the individual optimality (i.e., whether it is good for each product to use the shared architecture), and the other is from the point of view of the whole optimality (i.e., whether it is good for the product line as a whole to share the architecture). In this paper, we propose a method for product line scoping. We consider scoping as a decision-making activity in which we evaluate multiple candidates for the scope and then select the proper one after examining the appropriateness from the two points of view. In order to demonstrate its applicability, we applied the method to the actual problem picked up from Japanese ITS (Intelligent Transport Systems) projects.

1   Introduction

It is important to define the proper scope of product lines, as it is the very basis for the strategic development of product lines [3][10]. In developing product lines, we need to design the architecture for the product line, develop the reusable assets based on the architecture, and organize systematic ways to develop products [2]. If the scope of the product line is not appropriate, the systematic reuse does not work, and we cannot develop the product line efficiently and effectively. For example, if we include products that have entirely different characteristics in one scope, it would be difficult to design the common architecture shared by these products. Therefore,

G. Chastek (Ed.): SPLC2 2002, LNCS 2379, p. 348–365, 2002.

scoping product lines is one of the important activities in developing product lines. We have to carefully examine the nature of the domain, the product line and each product to determine the appropriate scope of the product lines.

The appropriateness of product line scoping has to be examined from two points of view. One is the point of view of the whole optimality, such as reducing the total development cost and increasing the reuse ratio. For example, we cannot benefit from designing the common architecture for products in the product line and develop reusable assets if we develop a small number of products, since it is expensive to develop reusable assets. We have to examine the overhead of developing reusable software and the expected cost reduction of developing products based on the reusable assets.

The other is the point of view to be examined is that of individual optimality. Even if we can reduce the development cost through reuse, it may not be best for each product to develop them based on the same architecture. For example, we can expect the performance of a product developed on the specialized architecture tuned for the product to be better than that of a product developed on the common platform. It is likely that a decision from the whole optimality point of view is inconsistent with that from the individual optimality point of view. This makes the product line scoping difficult.

In this paper, we propose a method for product line scoping in which we determine the appropriate scope of the product line, considering both the whole and the individual optimalities. Therefore we consider two types of requirements: those for a single product and those for the product line. The requirements for a single product consist of those requirements for the functionality and quality attributes [8]. The requirements on product lines are those for the ways in which the products are developed. For example, the order in which products in the product line are developed is a product lines requirement.

In our method, we list the candidates for product line scoping and then select the most appropriate one. As mentioned previously, the whole and the individual optimalities may conflict; in other words, a scoping candidate that is most suitable for the product line requirements on is not always the best answer in terms of single-product requirements. Therefore we apply a decision-making framework to the method to determine the most appropriate candidate. Namely, we regard product line scoping as decision making in which we select the most preferable scoping from options, using product line and single-product requirements as decision criteria.

Our research is motivated by our experience on the project "Study on ITS On-Board System Architecture" by the Association of Electronic Technology for Automobile Traffic and Driving. In this project we examine the development strategy of the Japanese ITS (Intelligent Transport Systems) on-board systems [1]. We examined 45 services that will be realized over the next 5 to 20 years. We were required to design a basic architecture for each service, considering the quality of each service and the sharing of the architecture among different services, as it is unrealistic for each service to have different on-board equipment. We were also required to make the examination objective and open, as the strategy has strong impacts on many stakeholders.

In Section 2, we formulate the product line scoping based on the decision-making framework. In Section 3, we propose a method for product line scoping. In Section 4, we apply the method to the actual problem picked up from the ITS project mentioned above. In Section 5, we discuss related technical issues.

2   Product Line Scoping as a Decision-Making Activity

This section describes product line scoping based on our decision-making framework.

2.1   Product Line Scoping

Product line scoping is used to define the product line. Namely, it determines the products that comprise the product line. Once a product line is defined, we design a product line architecture for it, and we examine the strategic development of the product line utilizing the reusable assets that are based on the architecture. Therefore, when we define the scope, we have to examine whether or not it is appropriate for the products in a product line to share the architecture. To examine the appropriateness of sharing the architecture, it is useful not only to determine a set of products in the product line, but also to examine what type of architecture those products would share. In this paper, we define product line scoping to be determining the member products as well as examining the architecture for the product line. In other words, scoping means to divide a given set of products into one or more product lines and to examine the architectures for those product lines.

We describe a scope as a set of product lines and a product line as a pair of members-list and architecture. For example, assume that we have a given set of products P1, P2, P3 and P4, and that A1 and A2 are architectural candidates for these products. Table 1 shows some examples of the scopes that we could define:

Table 1. Examples of Product Line Scopes

Name	Description
S1	{ <{P1, P2, P3, P4}, A1> }
S2	{ <{P1, P3}, A1>, <{P2, P4}, A2> }
S3	{ <{P1, P3, P4}, A2>, <{P2}, A1> }

S1 is a scope in which we define one product line that includes every product, and tall products share the A1 architecture. S2 is a scope in which we define two product lines, one includes P1 and P3, and the other includes P2 and P4. We do not prohibit a product line from containing only a single product.

2.2   Requirements on Products and Product Lines

As mentioned earlier, we consider two types of requirements: those for single products and those for product lines.

Single-product requirements consist of those for functionality and quality attributes. In our method, we examine the important services that the product has to provide and important requirements on quality attributes, such as performance and memory size. As we examine the architecture for each product line, we have to consider whether the selected architecture is suitable for single-product requirements. In this sense, the requirements for each product relate to the individual optimality.

Product line requirements are ways in which the products are developed. Even if the scoping is the same, the characteristics of the product line development may differ, for instance, the development cost. For example, consider two products P1 and P2, which are developed sequentially. If we want to develop P2 faster, it is a good idea to let P1 and P2 share the same architecture. Though there may be many complicated situations, there are typically two types of important situations in terms of determining the benefit of architecture sharing:

- Sequential: where products are developed sequentially. For example, develop the high-end model first, and then develop the cost-down model.
- Coexistence: where products are developed simultaneously or in parallel. For example, develop the products for different markets at the same time.

In the above cases, we can expect to develop the products efficiently, if they share the same architecture. On the other hand, if we have to change the architecture, it would take time and make the development expensive. We do not claim that every product that is developed sequentially or in parallel has to share the architecture with other products. There may be a situation where we want to release a product right after the previous product is released, or there may be another situation in which the quality of the product is more important than the release speed. Therefore, we should check the situation to determine the product line scope. In other words, if we are not sure which products are developed first, or which products are developed simultaneously, we cannot judge whether they should share the architecture. In this paper, we describe sequential and coexistence development as follows:

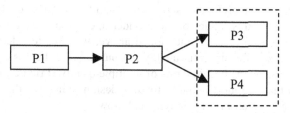

Fig. 1. Example of Description for Continuity and Coexistence

In Figure 1, an arrow denotes sequential developments, and a dotted square denotes coexistent developments. For example, P2 is developed right after P1, and P3 and P4 are developed simultaneously after developing P2. When we examine product line requirements we first identify these sequential products, which are developed subsequently and coexist. Next we evaluate whether a scope is good or bad in terms of the product line's quality. Consider the above example in Figure 1. Four sequential links and one coexistent link are defined. When all requirements are equally important we may define the scope to satisfy as many requirements as possible. If the requirements are prioritized, we define the scope to satisfy the most important ones. For example, assume that we want to develop P3 and P4 as fast as possible after developing P2. In such a case, Scope1 = { < {P1, P2, P3, P4}, A1 } and Scope2 = { < {P1}, A1 >, < {P2, P3, P4}, A2 > } are considered to be good scopes in terms of this requirement, since P2, P3 and P4 share the same architecture. However, Scope3 = { < {P1, P2}, A1 >, < {P3, P4}, A2 > } is not considered to be a good scope because the architecture for P3 and P4 are different from that of P2.

2.3   Design Policy

In determining the product line scope, using requirements for both single products and for the product line as a whole, we first have to judge whether the scope under consideration can fulfill the requirements. For example, assume that scope S = { < {P1, P2}, A1>, <{P3}, A2 > }. In order to fulfill the requirements on each product, A1 has to fulfill the requirements on P1 and P2, and A2 has to fulfill the requirements on P3.

Though we may restrict the number of scoping candidates by excluding those that do not satisfy the requirements, multiple candidates may remain. In product line scoping, we have to select one from these candidates. In such a case, we generally select the one that best matches the design policy of the product line. Each candidate that satisfies the requirements has different characteristics. The design policy should give us the way to select from different candidates. In this paper, we characterize the candidates by means of quality attributes, and the design policy is defined as the priority among those attributes.

2.4   Decision-Making Framework

During decision-making, we preferably select one candidate in terms of the decision criteria [4]. We can apply this framework to product line scoping, as it also requires many decisions. For example, as we mentioned above, we have to select the most appropriate scope that satisfies different quality attributes. Since there is no objective way to decide which one is the best in terms of multiple quality attributes, we have to make the decisions that are most suitable for our design policy. In this paper, we consider scoping as a decision-making activity as follows:

- Options: We assume that scoping means to preferably select one candidate for the product line scope in terms of the decision criteria.
- Decision criteria: There are two types of decision criteria. One type relates to requirements for each single product in terms of quality attributes, such as performance and reliability [4]. The other type relates to requirements for the product lines in terms of 'qualities' of the product line as a whole, such as total development cost and reuse ratio.

- Preference: In general, we have to consider multiple criteria, and it is difficult to select a single scope that is superior to other scopes in terms of multiple criteria. We have to prioritize criteria to reflect the policy of the product line development.

3   Method for Product Line Scoping

In this section, we propose a method for product line scoping.

3.1   Overview

The overview of our method is as follows:

- We first analyze the requirements for each product, and list the architectural candidates for each product. Then, we evaluate these candidates from two aspects: relative preference and applicability. This corresponds to examining product line scoping from the view of the individual optimality.
- Then, based on this result, we list the candidates for the product line scope. We evaluate the requirements on the product line, and examine the candidates. This corresponds to examining product line scoping from the view of the whole optimality.
- Finally, we examine the preferences of the scopes and of each product and determine the best scope, considering the quality of the product line and of each product. In this step, we have to consider the tradeoffs between the individual optimality and the whole optimality.
- In the above steps, the relative preference is determined using a decision-making method; in our case, we use the decision-making method AHP (Analytic Hierarchy Process) [9].

3.2   Procedure

In this section, we show how to determine the scope of the product line using the example of an information terminal and the four products listed in Table 2. Defining that product line's scope involves the eight steps described below.

Table 2. Given Set of Products

Name	Description
P1	Low-end model for the Japanese market.
P2	Standard model for the Japanese market.
P3	High-end model for the Japanese market.
P4	High-end model for the U.S. market.

3.2.1   Identify the Requirements

Identify the requirements for each product and for the product line. The requirements for each product are defined in terms of the products' quality attributes. The requirements for the product line are defined in terms of sequential and coexisting products.

Table 3 shows the requirements related to the following quality attributes of data retrieval for each product: the number of data elements in the search space, the response time and the required memory size. As P1 is a low-end model, it has a small number of data elements and is equipped with a small memory. On the other hand, P3 and P4 have a large number of data elements.

Table 3. Requirements for Single Products

Name	Number	Response time	Memory size
P1	100	< 2-3 sec	small
P2	1,000	< 2-3 sec	
P3	100,000	< 2-3 sec	
P4	100,000	< 2-3 sec	

Figure 2 shows the relations among products depicted using the notation introduced in the previous section.

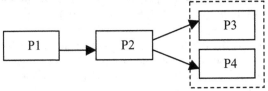

Fig. 2. Relations Among Products

Table 4 shows the requirements for the product line. As shown in Figure 2, we develop P1 first, then develop P2, and finally develop P3 and P4 in parallel. Among these requirements, developing P3 and P4 in parallel is the most critical factor in the products' development.

Table 4. Requirements for Product Lines

Product Type	Name	Description
Sequential	P1, P2	
	P2, P3	More important than Sequentially between P1 and P2.
	P2, P4	More important than Sequentially between P1 and P2.
Coexistence	P3, P4	Most critical requirement for development of the product line

3.2.2   Define Design Policy

Define the design policy in terms of priority among the requirements. The following is a design policy for this example:

- For the low-end model, a reduction of the memory size is the most important requirement.
- For the high-end model, performance is the most important requirement.
- If we can fulfill the above requirements, we would like to maximize the quality of each product.

3.2.3   List the Architectural Candidates

List the architectural candidates for the given products. For the data retrieval example, if the quality attribute requirements are not severe, we can fulfill them without considering any architectural technique. In such a case, we would design the architecture to reflect the structure of the analysis model that captures the nature of the target domain, because this is considered to be good for the extensibility. However, if the quality attribute requirements are severe, we may have to apply some architectural techniques to improve the quality attributes. In this example, we have three candidates; A0 does not have any architectural technique to improve quality attributes, A1 has a caching mechanism, and A2 loads index data of the storage onto memory at initialization time.

Table 5. Architectural Candidates

Name	Description
A0	Architecture that reflect the structure of the analysis model.
A1	Architecture that adopts the caching mechanism
A2	Architecture that loads index data onto the memory at initialization time. It also has cache.

3.2.4   Determine the Preference of Each Architectural Candidate

In this step, we examine each candidate and determine its relative preference among the other applicable architectural candidates, using the Analytic Hierarchy Process (AHP) [9].

In the AHP, the most preferable candidate is selected in terms of decision criteria. In this case, the alternatives are the architectural candidates listed above, and the criteria include the quality attributes on which requirements are imposed, such as performance and reliability. The AHP is based on a simple pair-wise comparison among criteria and alternatives. First, we decide the relative importance among the criteria, based on a pair-wise comparison. Second, for each criterion, we also make a pair-wise comparison among the architectural candidates.

Table 6 shows the preferences of the candidates for each product as determined using the AHP. (In the Appendix, we will show how to calculate the preference numbers).

Table 6. Preference of Architectural Candidates

	P1	P2	P3	P4
A0	0.367	0.26	0.193	0.193
A1	0.406	0.357	0.307	0.307
A2	0.228	0.364	0.501	0.501

3.2.5   Examine the Architectural Candidate's Applicability for Each Product

In this step, we determine whether each candidate can fulfill the requirements [6][7]. First, assess each architectural candidate in terms of each quality attribute and categorize the requirements is such a way that each requirement's category can be fulfilled by the same set of architectural candidates. For example, we can fulfill the performance requirements by any architectural candidate if the number of data elements is 100 to 1000, but only A1 and A2 can fulfill the performance requirement for 100,000 data elements. This leads to two types of requirements: performance and size, shown in Table 7.

Table 7. Category of Requirements

performance	number	response	architectural techniques
CP1	100 – 1,000	< 2-3 sec	A0, A1, A2
CP2	100,000	< 2-3 sec	A1, A2

size	memory size	architectural techniques
CS1	small	A0, A1
CS2	N/A	A0, A1, A2

Second, examine the requirements for each product within the categories above. Determine the applicability of each architectural candidate to the products. For example, for the performance aspect, A0 can be used for P1 and P2. For the size aspect, A0 can be used for every product. Thus, we determine that A0 can be used for P1 and P2, because both the performance and size requirements can be fulfilled. The applicability of candidates A0, A1, and A2 are shown in Table 8.

Table 8. Examine Applicability

	A0	A1	A2
performance	P1, P2	P1, P2, P3, P4	P1, P2, P3, P4
size	P1, P2, P3, P4	P1, P2, P3, P4	P2, P3, P4
merged result	P1, P2	P1, P2, P3, P4	P2, P3, P4

Table 9 shows another view of the results obtained by the above examination. In this table, 'x' means "applicable," and 'N/A' means "non applicable".

Table 9. Another View of Applicability

	P1	P2	P3	P4
A0	x	x	N/A	N/A
A1	x	x	x	x
A2	N/A	x	x	x

3.2.6   Examine the Candidates for the Product Line Scope

Do not assign "non-applicable" architectural candidates to the products. For the data retrieval example, we prepare the candidates shown in Table 10. Note that we do not intend to exhaustively list all possible combinations. S1 is based on the idea to maximize the architectural sharing. S2 and S3 are based on the idea to develop the low-end and high-end models, respectively on a different architecture than the other models.

Table 10. Candidates of Scope

Name	Description
S1	{ < {P1, P2, P3, P4}, A1> }
S2	{ < {P1}, A1 >, < {P2, P3, P4}, A2 > }
S3	{ < {P1, P2}, A1 >, < {P3, P4}, A2 > }

3.2.7   Determine Preferences among the Candidates
for the Product Line Scope

To determine the preference of the candidates for the product line scope we again use the AHP. The decision-criteria for the product line scope are sequential and coexistence development. For sequential, S1 is the best, as there is no architectural change during the development sequence. S2 is better than S3, because the requirements say that the sequences between P2 and P3 and between P2 and P4 are important. S3 requires architectural change between them. For coexistence, S1 is also the best. S2 and S3 are the same, since the requirements say that coexistence of P3 and P4 is important, and in both scopes, P3 and P4 share the same architecture.

Based on these judgments, we have determined the following weight using the AHP. We also obtain the sum of each product's weights defined in Table 6. For example, as S2 adopts A1 for P1, and adopts A2 for P2, P3, P4, we got 0.406 + 0.364 + 0.501 + 0.501 = 1.772. This weight represents the relative preference in terms of individual optimality.

Table 11. Weight of Whole Optimality and Individual Optimality

	Whole Optimality	Individual Optimality
S1	0.619	1.377
S2	0.229	1.772
S3	0.153	1.765

3.2.8   Define Scope

Based on the examination so far, we determine the preferable scopes. We make the observation from the result that S1 is the best from the point of view of the whole optimality, as it shares a single architecture. However, sharing a single architecture does not maximize the quality of each product.

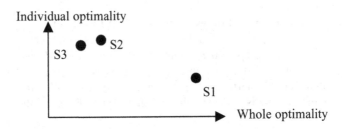

Fig. 3. Portfolio of Scopes S1, S2, and S3

Figure 3 shows the situation. Note that, though the scopes have different character-istics, they all satisfy the requirements on each product and the requirements on the product lines. Based on the design policy, we want to maximize the individual opti-mality while still fulfilling the requirements on the product line; we select S2 as our scope for this example.

4   Case Study

In this section we apply the method to the actual problem picked up from our past projects, in order to demonstrate the applicability of the method.

4.1   Overviews of the Project

The Association of Electronic Technology for Automobile Traffic and Driving com-pleted the project "Study on ITS On-Board System Architecture" in 1997. In the project, they investigated the required services and important technologies in the ITS (Intelligent Transport Systems) field, and examined the higher level architecture for an on-board system. In the project, there were 45 sub-services defined (corresponding to products), such as a route guidance, an assistance for economic driving, and a pro-visioning of road traffic control, and so on [1]. Using object-oriented (OO) analysis, they analyzed the 45 sub-services to identify the necessary information and functions. For each function, they have listed candidates for the architecture to realize the func-tion and qualitatively compared these candidates in terms of the quality attributes. As ITS is a long-term nationwide project, they picked up three years, 2003, 2008 and 2018, and examined the appropriate architecture for each year, considering the re-quirements and technologies expected for each.

4.2   Applying the Method

In this section, we pick up some products (sub-services) examined in the projects and determine the scope using the method. We pick up the following products: P02, P04 and P19. We have to develop each product in 2003 and 2008.

Table 12. Products

Name	Description
P02	Route guidance
P04	Provision of road traffic information
P19	Notification to emergency center

In this case, study we focus on the years 2002 and 2008. As the requirements on each product and technology may be different in these years, we distinguish the products in 2002 from those in 2008. In order to make a distinction, we attach the year behind the product name. For example, P02-2003 means product P02 in 2003. In this section, we focus on the architecture that realizes the function "detect the vehicle position" (one of the most important functions), and it has a strong impact on the entire architecture for these products.

4.2.1   Identify the Requirements

Table 13 shows the requirements for the products in 2003. For the 2008 version, the requirements are the same, except that the accuracy for P02 becomes higher. We consider the quality attributes defined in Table 14. Figure 4 shows the relations among the products. Finally, the product line requirements are shown in Table 15.

Table 13. Requirements on Products

	accuracy	Road coverage	Vehicle coverage	cost
P02	high	every-where		
P04	low	every-where		low
P19	high			

4.2.2   Define the Design Policy

The following is the design policy.

- For P02, the accuracy is the most important attribute. However, in 2003, the requirements will not be as severe, because we do not have enough services that require such accuracy.
- For P04, the cost is the most important attribute.

- For P19, the accuracy is the most important attribute, as this product relates to safety.
- If we can fulfill the above requirements, we would like to maximize the quality of each product.

Table 14. Quality Attributes to be Examined.

Attribute	Description
accuracy	The accuracy of the detected position.
Road coverage	The ratio of the area (road) where this function works. If the vehicle has the function, it may work everywhere, but if some equipment is required on the roadside, it may be difficult to cover the entire road, because we have to equip them everywhere.
Vehicle coverage	The ratio of the vehicle to which this function works. If the vehicle has to have some equipment, it may be difficult to detect every vehicle, because it may be difficult to equip them to all vehicles.
Cost	Cost of developing the infrastructure on the roadside.

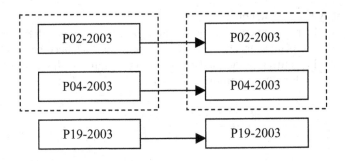

Fig. 4. Relations Among the Products

Table 15. Product Line Requirements

Type	Product	Priority
Sequential	P02-2003, P02-2008	same importance
	P04-2003, P04-2008	
	P19-2003, P04-2008	
Coexistence	P02-2003, P04-2003, P19-2003	same importance
	P02-2008, P04-2008, P19-2008	

4.2.3   List the Architectural Candidates

Table 16 shows the architectural candidates for "detect vehicle position."

Table 16. Architectural Candidates

(a)	Detect the position by the vehicle only. (no communication with the roadside or a center)
(b)	Detect the position by the vehicle and use the data from the roadside and the center to correct the error. (DGPS and KGPS are included in this).
(c)	Detect the position using the data from the roadside. Next, reflect the data of the database or the gyro in the vehicle.

4.2.4   Determine the Preference of the Architectural Candidate

Using the accuracy, road coverage, vehicle coverage and cost as criteria, we determine the following preference using the AHP.

Table 17. Preference of Architectural Candidates

	P02-2003	P02-2008	P04-2003	P04-2008	P19-2003	P19-2008
(a)	0.364	0.282	0.481	0.481	0.286	0.286
(b)	0.414	0.482	0.314	0.314	0.485	0.485
(c)	0.222	0.227	0.205	0.205	0.229	0.229

4.2.5   Examine Applicability of the Architectural Candidates for the Products

Using the procedure we discussed in the previous section, we determine the following applicability. There are no differences between 2003 and 2008 except for P02.

Table 18. Applicability of Architectural Candidates

	P02-2003	P02-2008	P04-2003	P04-2008	P19-2003	P19-2008
(a)	x		x	x		
(b)	x	x	x	x	x	x
(c)			x	x		

4.2.6   Examine the Candidates for the Product Line Scopes

We have examined the candidates shown in Table 19 for the product line scopes.

Table 19. Candidates for the Scope

Scope	Candidate Products
S0	{ < { P02-2003, P02-2008, P04-2003, P04-2008, P19-2003, P19-2008}, (b)>}
S1	{ < { P02-2003, P02-2008, P19-2002, P19-2008}, (b) >, < { P04-2003, P04-2008}, (a) > }
S2	{ < { P02-2003, P04-2003}, (a) >, < { P02-2008, P04-2008, P19-2003, P19-2008}, (b) > }

4.2.7   Determine the Preference Among the Candidates
for the Product Line Scope

The following shows the weights that represent the whole optimality and the individual optimality for each candidate of scope.

Table 20. Weight of the Whole Optimality and the Individual Optimality

	Whole Optimality	Individual Optimality
S1	0.644	2.494
S2	0.24	2.828
S3	0.116	2.611

4.2.8   Define Scope

Based on the design policy, we select S2 as the scope.

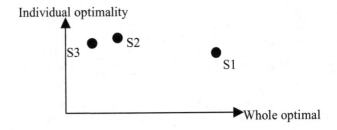

Fig. 5. Portfolio of Scopes

This decision means that in 2003, we develop P02 and P04 on a relatively inaccurate and low-cost architecture, as this service is for comfortable driving, but does not directly relate to safety. But for P19, we adopt an expensive but accurate technology as it relates to safety. In 2008, each product's functionality will be upgraded and will require an architecture that is more accurate. The result matches our value.

Through the case study, we demonstrated the following:

- We have a systematic procedure to determine the scope of the product line, considering the quality attributes of the single products and the quality of the product line.
- We can determine the scope of a product line in a systematic way to the resolution required by the actual projects.
- The methodology can be applied to real projects (more than 10 experts).

5   Conclusions

We have proposed a method to determine the scope of a product line and demonstrated the usefulness of the method using an actual problem. A software development involves many design decisions that are based on developers' intuition. However this is quite dangerous, because these decisions, especially those in the early phase of software development, have a serious impact on subsequent software developments. Furthermore, when we develop socially important systems, we have to demonstrate that these decisions are rational. We believe that our research contributes to the area as this method gives a systematic way to determine the scope of a product line.

References

1. Association of Electronic Technology for Automobile Traffic and Driving: Study on ITS On-board system architecture, http://www.jsk.org/jp/eindex.html, 1999.
2. Bass, L., et.al.: Software Architecture in Practice, Addison-Wesley, 1998.
3. DeBaud, J. and Schmid, K.: A Systematic Approach to Derive Scope of Software Product lines, Proc. of ICSE'99, 1999.
4. Jozwiak, L. and Ong, S.A.: Quality-Driven Decision Making Methodology for System-Level Design, Proc. of EUROMICO-22, 1996.
5. Kazman, R., et.al.: The Architectural Tradeoff Analysis Method, Proceedings of ICECCS, 1998.
6. Kishi, T. and Noda, N.: Aspect-Oriented Analysis for Product Line Architecture, SPLC1, 2000.
7. Kishi, T, Noda, N. and Katayama, T.: Architecture Design for Evolution by Analyzing Requirements on Quality Attributes, 8th Asia-Pacific Software Engineering Conference (APSEC 2001), 2001.
8. Ran, A., "Architectural Structures and Views", Proceedings of the Third International Software Architecture Workshop (ISAW3). 1998.
9. Saaty, T.L.: The Analytic Hierarchy Process, McGraw-Hill, 1980.
10. Software Engineering Institute: The Product Line Practice (PLP) Initiative, http://www.sei.cmu.edu/plp/plp_init.html.

Appendix: An Example of an AHP Calculation

The followings are the steps to determine the preference of the candidate using AHP [9]. In the example in Section 3, we determined the preference of the candidates for each product. Here we will show how to calculate the preference for P1. Other preferences are determined using the same steps.

1. Decide the relative importance among the criteria. We have focused on performance and size. We make pair-wise comparisons between criterions, using the following numbers.

Table A1. Numbers Used for Pair-Wise Comparisons

5	Strongly more important
3	Weakly more important
1	Equally important
1/3	Weakly less important
1/5	Strongly less important

The Table A2 shows the result of pair comparisons. The first row shows the relative importance of performance, and the second row shows that of size. P1 is the low-end model, so performance is less important than size.

Table A2. Comparison Between Criteria

	Performance	Size
Performance	1	1/3
Size	3	1

We obtain the priority vector by calculating and normalizing the principal eigenvector, yielding a value of 0.25 for performance and 0.75 for size.

2. For each criterion, decide the preference of the candidates. For each criterion, we compare three architectural candidates and calculate the relative preference.

Table A3. Comparisons Among Candidates in Terms of Performance

	A0	A1	A2	Preference
A0	1	1/3	1/5	0.105
A1	3	1	1/3	0.258
A2	5	3	1	0.637

Table A4. Comparison Among Candidates in Terms of Size

	A0	A1	A2	Preference
A0	1	1	5	0.455
A1	1	1	5	0.455
A2	1/5	1/5	1	0.091

3. Obtain the overall priorities. Based on the preference among criteria, and preference among candidates, we can calculate overall priorities as shown below:

$$0.25 \times \begin{bmatrix} 0.105 \\ 0.258 \\ 0.637 \end{bmatrix} + 0.75 \times \begin{bmatrix} 0.455 \\ 0.455 \\ 0.091 \end{bmatrix} = \begin{bmatrix} 0.367 \\ 0.406 \\ 0.228 \end{bmatrix}$$

The following table gives the preference among candidates for P1.

Table A5. Preference Among Candidates

	P1
A0	0.367
A1	0.406
A2	0.228

Using a Marketing and Product Plan
as a Key Driver for Product Line Asset Development[1]

Kyo C. Kang[1], Patrick Donohoe[2], Eunman Koh[1], Jaejoon Lee[1], and Kwanwoo Lee[1]

[1]Department of Computer Science and Engineering,
Pohang University of Science and Technology,
San 31 Hyoja-Dong, Pohang, 790-784, Korea
{kck, emkoh, gibman, kwlee}@postech.ac.kr
http://selab.postech.ac.kr/index.html
[2]Software Engineering Institute, Carnegie Mellon University
Pittsburgh, PA 15213
pd@sei.cmu.edu
http://www.sei.cmu.edu

Abstract. The product line engineering paradigm has emerged recently to address the need to minimize the development cost and the time to market in this highly competitive global market. Product line development consists of *product line asset development* and *product development* using the assets. Product line requirements are essential inputs to product line asset development. These inputs, although critical, are not sufficient to develop product line assets. A marketing and product plan, which includes plans on what features are to be packaged in products, how these features will be delivered to customers (e.g., feature binding time), and how the products will evolve in the future, also drives product line asset development; thus this paper explores design issues from the marketing perspective and presents key design drivers that are tightly coupled with the marketing strategy. An elevator control software example is used to illustrate how product line asset development is related to marketing and product plans.

1 Introduction

Developing reusable software requires an understanding of the application domain and, therefore, software reuse has been explored under the paradigm of domain analysis and engineering during the last decade or so [1], [2], [3], [4], [5], [6], [7]. When the application domain is not properly scoped, however, domain-engineering approaches have often suffered from schedule and cost overruns [8]. Also, reusability overdone with excessive layering and encapsulation often resulted in inefficient systems [9]. Deciding the right level of analysis in terms of the breadth and depth of a domain has always been a difficult task for analysts [10], and they tend to try to cover all possible products in the domain.

---

[1] The market-driven product line engineering concept was developed while Kyo C. Kang was at the Software Engineering Institute on sabbatical leave from Sept. through Aug. 2001 [11].

G. Chastek (Ed.): SPLC2 2002, LNCS 2379, p. 366–382, 2002.

The product line (PL) development paradigm [12], [13], [14], [15], which consists of *product line asset development* and *product development* using the assets, has emerged recently to address some of these problems. Domain analysis in the context of a PL has specific goals for reuse, and the scope of the analysis must take into account the scope of the PL, the PL future growth potentials, and technology evolution. The goals and analysis scope are manifested in *a marketing and product plan*, which is an output from a marketing analysis and business-case-planning activities. This plan sets the specific context for domain analysis and reuse exploration in the PL. With this paradigm, reuse is not opportunistic; it is carefully planned for a specific PL.

PL asset development also takes the marketing and product plan as a key driver. PL requirements are essential inputs to PL asset development, and these inputs, although critical, are not sufficient. A marketing and product plan describes what features are to be packaged in products, how these features will be delivered to customers, and how the products will evolve in the future. Thus this paper explores design issues from the marketing perspective and presents design drivers that are tightly coupled with the marketing strategy.

In this paper, we focus on PL asset development, taking a marketing and product plan as a key driver. We illustrate the importance of making explicit connections between marketing and asset development by showing how various design parameters can be derived from the marketing and product plan. As a starting point, Section 2 discusses elements of a PL's marketing and product plan in detail. PL asset development activities are explained in Section 3 and illustrated in Section 4 using an elevator control software example. Section 5 summarizes and concludes the paper.

2   Marketing and Product Plan as a Key Design Driver

The marketing and product plan is treated in this paper as a key design driver for the following reasons:

1. Requirements analysis typically focuses on the functionality of a product line, and design constraints and quality attributes are often not explored rigorously or communicated to designers. Also, while many design constraints or quality attributes are explored when developing a marketing and product plan, the information is often not utilized in the product development. For example, the cultural and technical background of potential users in a market segment is an important parameter in designing PL assets.
2. The multiproduct nature of a product line brings engineering challenges that are different from those in single-application development. A product line may be targeted for more than one market segment. For example, a security systems product line may be targeted for home as well as office or factory uses. Each market segment may have a unique set of needs and requirements or have users with different backgrounds from other market segments. PL assets must be designed with consideration of the commonalities and variabilities of these needs and user characteristics, which are manifested in the marketing and product plan.
3. A marketing and product plan includes what features will be included in the products, how they will be delivered to the customers in terms of installation and

adaptation, what extensions are allowed to the customers, and how the products can be extended. These decisions should be studied thoroughly and must be reflected in the design; they cannot be added *a posteriori.*

4. The product delivery method, which is detailed in the marketing plan, has business implications. For example, if the unit of sales and/or negotiation is features, products should be designed so that feature-based sales/negotiation and the composition of components becomes feasible. When the product delivery method is developed, engineering feasibility and associated costs must be explored and reflected in the design.

5. By tightly coupling asset development with marketing, design issues related to marketing can be explored early in the product development, and an evaluation of the technical feasibility and cost implications can be fed back to product planning and marketing.

Products developed without considering user's needs and capabilities and how the products will be marketed would not be "sold." Products must be configurable to meet the needs and capabilities of users. The marketing and product plan is a single plan consisting of two parts, the marketing plan and the product plan. Details of each part are described below.

2.1 Marketing Plan

A marketing plan includes a market analysis and a marketing strategy with a plan for realizing the business opportunities with products that meet the business needs. Figure 1 shows the elements of a marketing plan.

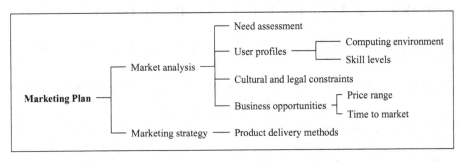

Fig. 1. Marketing Plan for Product Line Asset Development

A market analysis includes, for each market segment, a needs assessment and an analysis of computing environments, end-user skill levels, cultural and legal constraints, the price range, and the time to market.

The user profile provides important information for PL asset development. For example, if the target users do not have much experience with computers, the products for that market segment must have a set of user-interface features (e.g., a menu-driven interface instead of command interface) and quality attributes (e.g., understandability of messages) to address the needs of that segment. The cultural traits and the laws of each country must also be taken into consideration when designing the products. For example, different countries may have various ways to manage workflows, and particular colors used in the interface may have a special significance in certain cultures.

The marketing strategy initially includes an outline of how products will be delivered to customers. For example, one company's marketing strategy may be to allow budget-conscious customers to start with a "small" system with a few features and then grow to a bigger one by adding new features, without having to buy new products. Therefore, a product delivery method must be developed that considers the units of sales, methods of integration, installation, adaptation, and maintenance, and the skill level of persons (e.g., salesperson, customer, or user) who will perform these activities.

The marketing strategy for a PL may be flexible, and potential changes in this strategy should also be considered in the design. For example, if the strategy is to test the market with several products and adjust the marketing and product plan based on the results, this plan should also be communicated to the asset designer.

2.2 Product Plan

Once the marketing plan has been defined, it is important to identify the product features and develop a plan for incorporating them in products. A product plan includes product features and feature-delivery methods, each of which is described below. Figure 2 shows elements of a product plan.

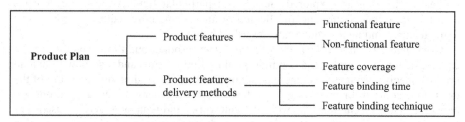

Fig. 2. Product Plan for Product Line Asset Development

Product features are distinctive characteristics of products in a PL. They are largely classified into functional and nonfunctional features. Functional features include services, which are often considered marketable units or units of increment in a PL, and operations, which are internal functions of products that are needed to provide services. Nonfunctional features include end-user-visible application characteristics that cannot be identified in terms of services or operations, but rather in terms of presentation, capacity, quality attribute, usage, cost, and so forth. These nonfunctional features are identified from the marketing plan. For example, in security systems, if the targeted market segment is household, usability may be one of the most important quality attributes. If the PL is for office buildings with many installation-specific requirements, reusability and adaptability may be important quality attributes. The ways product features are delivered to customers affect the PL asset design. Product delivery methods are refined to product-feature-delivery methods, which can be looked at in terms of what features are allowed (feature coverage), when they are incorporated into the product (feature-binding time), and how they are incorporated (feature binding techniques). Each of these issues is discussed below.

Feature coverage determines the scope of features for a product line. A product line may include closed sets of features, or it may include core features from which products can be built incorporating user-defined features before and/or after product delivery. For example, a security systems product line for home use may include a product with the fire- and intrusion-detection features and another product with the fire-, intrusion-, and flood-detection features. Asset development in this product line is based on a closed set of features targeted for a specific market. In contrast, a security systems product line for offices or factories may have critical installation-specific features, such as access control based on job functions or required special devices which may not be prepared for in advance. This product line requires asset components with a high degree of adaptability, which are assembled and extended for each installation.

Features may be incorporated into products during the product build time, product delivery/installation time, and product runtime [2], [6], [16]. Suppose, for example, that there are a number of ways in which the temperature of a building is managed (e.g., minimizing cost, maximizing comfort, or an optimal management strategy that is compromised of both). These management features may be made selectable while the system is running by encapsulating the strategies and binding a specific strategy at runtime. Alternatively, they may be made available as installation-time features, in which case only those selected at installation become available to the user. When to allow this binding is the marketing decision.

Once decisions are made about when to bind features, implementation techniques for feature binding are explored. Selecting a particular binding technique depends both on the binding time and the flexibility and adaptability required for features. Some feature-binding techniques are described below.

Asset and Product-Build-Time Binding: The product-build-time binding must explore how to implement the common product line features and also how to extend product-specific features from these common features. Depending on the nature of the extension required for product-specific features, code generation, encapsulation, and parameterization techniques, as well as frameworks and templates may be used. For example, if a component encapsulates other components or objects (e.g., devices) that do similar operations, common "operational structures" may be abstracted and defined as a framework [17], [18] or by using inheritance. If the differences between algorithms that implement different features (e.g., alternative features) can be parameterized, templates or other macro-processing mechanisms (e.g., frame technology [19]) may be used.

Product-Installation-Time Binding: Techniques include macro processing, load tables, and so forth. Macro-processing techniques may be used for product lines with closed sets of features (i.e., product lines in a mature, stable domain). Product lines with minor variations between products may be instantiated using a load table that contains parameter values for instantiation.

Product-Runtime Binding: The techniques for runtime binding include the dynamic binding of objects, plug-ins, and menus. Components must be designed to allow runtime binding.

The next section describes a method that incorporates information from a marketing and product plan into development activities for product line assets.

3   PL Asset Development Activities

Fielding products with features that the market demands in a timely manner and then evolving those products as the market evolves is the major driving force in the asset development for a PL. In this section, we provide an overview of the asset development aspect of the Feature-Oriented Reuse Method (FORM) [20], [21], [22], which has been extended in this paper to incorporate the marketing perspective (see Figure 3 for FORM activities and their relationships).

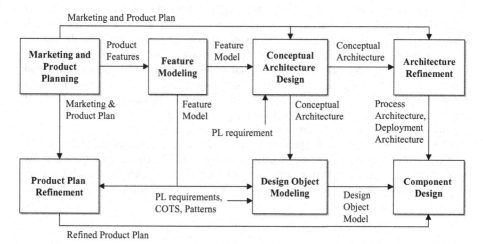

Fig. 3. Development Activities for Product Line Assets

The FORM starts with developing a marketing and product plan, which is the basis for the product line asset development. A marketing plan initially includes a market analysis and a marketing strategy. Based on this information, a product plan that includes product features and product-feature-delivery methods is developed.

In the feature modeling, product features, which include functional (e.g., service) and nonfunctional features (e.g., quality attributes), are organized into an initial feature model. This feature model is extended with the information on environments, domain technologies, and implementation techniques.

The conceptual architecture-design activity allocates features to conceptual architectural components and specifies the data and control dependencies between the architectural components. The result is a "conceptual architecture[2]." Then the conceptual architecture is refined into the process and deployment architectures[3] by allocating components to concurrent processes and network nodes, considering whether to replicate each process or not, and defining methods of interactions between processes. The marketing and product plan is used during architecture design

---

[2] The conceptual architecture describes a system in terms of abstract, high-level components and relationships between them [24].

[3] The process architecture represents a concurrency structure in terms of concurrent processes (or tasks) to which functional elements are allocated; the deployment architecture shows an allocation of processes to hardware resources.

and refinement. For example, the customer profile information in the marketing plan is useful in determining the quality attributes required for the products that are targeted for each market segment. This information is used in refining the conceptual architecture, as many quality attributes are manifested through architectural decisions [23].

For the component design, the product plan must first be refined with design features (i.e., environments, domain technologies, and implementation techniques). This information is used in exploring design alternatives in the component design activity. For example, once decisions are made about when to bind features, implementation techniques for feature binding are explored. Selecting a particular binding technique depends on both the binding time and the flexibility and adaptability required for features. Also, a design object model must be developed based on the conceptual architecture, the feature model, and other information, such as the product line requirements, commercial off-the-shelf (COTS) components, and design patterns [24] that are relevant to the product line. Using the design object model, the component design activity refines the process and deployment architectures into concrete components during component design. The results of this activity are product line architectures and asset components.

The FORM PL engineering processes are iterative and incremental, and repeated until the design has enough details for implementation. The arrows in Figure 3 show the data flow (i.e., the use of work products) of each activity. Details of each PL asset development activity are illustrated using an elevator control software example in the following section.

4   Method Application: Elevator Control Software (ECS)

The example selected in this paper is an elevator control software (ECS) product line that is targeted for two market segments: Asian and Western (US and European) markets. In this section, we illustrate how the marketing and product plan for the two market segments affects the engineering of assets for the ECS product line. For the purpose of illustration, we assume that the company's marketing strategy is to target the Asian market with high-end products and the Western market with low-end products, based on an analysis of market competitiveness.

4.1   Marketing Plan for ECS Product Line

The marketing plan is developed by analyzing each market segment in terms of market needs, user profiles, and legal constraints, as described in Section 2. Table 1 summarizes the market analysis results of the two market segments.

The Asian market is mostly targeted for high-rises such as business buildings or hotels that require elevators with a fast response and smooth ride. On the other hand, the Western market is for small buildings with customers who regard the adaptability and reliability of elevators as important.

Table 1. Market Analysis Results

		Asian Market	Western Market
Marketing Strategy		Construction boom; new large-scale office buildings and hotels need high -end products	Small buildings with low-end products
Market Needs		Highly responsive and comfortable elevator products with customer-selectable services as well as standard services	Adaptable and reliable elevator products with standard services
User Profile	**Computing Environment**	Stand-alone system	Network environment
	Installer's Skill Levels	Installers and maintainers have electronics or mechanics backgrounds and are familiar with the hardware configuration of the elevator products.	Installers and maintainers have computer science backgrounds and are accustomed to GUI -based application software.

Elevators in the Asian market are stand-alone systems, and maintainers upgrade a product by exchanging its ROM (read-only memory) chip. Elevators in the Western market are usually connected with supervisory systems through a network, and maintainers upgrade products online via remote access.

Installers in the Asian market usually have electronics or mechanics backgrounds and are familiar with text-based man-machine interface (MMI) systems. Those in the Western market, however, have computer science backgrounds and are accustomed to GUI-based application software.

With the information obtained from the above market analysis, the asset designer should consider the following issues related to product delivery methods:

1. To meet market needs, only the standard services that are common across the two market segments are pre-packaged in each product. Customer-selectable services needed in the Asian market should be separated from standard services.
2. At installation time, installers in the Asian market will configure customer-selectable services or product specific devices by using a low-level MMI, which displays and sets software and hardware parameters. Those in the Western market will use a high-level MMI (i.e., an installation wizard program), which downloads product-specific device drivers from a remote site and configures software automatically.
3. Because of the computing environment constraints, when new versions of software are released, maintainers in the Asian market replace existing ROM chips with new

ones, while those in the Western market upgrade software using remote online maintenance services.[4]

This marketing plan serves as a basis for developing a product plan, which is described in the next section.

4.2 Product Plan for ECS Product Line

The product plan consists of product features and product-feature-delivery methods, as discussed earlier. Each of these is summarized in the tables that follow.

Product features are identified based on the market analysis (see Table 2). *Automatic Driving* and *Maintenance Driving* are common standard services for the two market segments, while *VIP Driving* and *Each Floor Stop (EFS) Driving* are customer-selectable services for the Asian market. *Door Control, Run Control, Direction Control*, and *Call Handling* are common operations that are needed to provide the services. *Comfort* and *Response Time* were identified from an analysis of the Asian market, and *Adaptability* and *Reliability* are those from the Western market. *High-Level MMI* and *Low-Level MMI* are identified to support the product delivery methods described in the previous section.

Table 2. Product Features

		Product Features
Functional Features	**Services**	***Automatic Driving*** a normal driving service of an elevator
		Maintenance Driving : a driving for the maintenance of an elevator
		VIP Driving a special driving service for the exclusive use of VIPs
		EFS Driving a special driving service that stops at each floor
	Operations	***Door Control*** a control operation to open and close doors
		Run Control a control operation for the acceleration and deceleration of the elevator
		Direction Control a control operation to determine the moving direction of an elevator
		Call Handling a operation for handling passenger's button requests
Nonfunctional Features		***Comfort*** Smooth Ride, Regular Ride
		Response Time the time to respond to passenger's requests
		Reliability an ability to continue functions during a failure in a certain part of an elevator
		Adaptability an ability to adapt software to various types of external devi
		Usability High-Level MMI, LowLevel MMI

For these product features, delivery methods are explored in terms of feature coverage, feature-binding time, and feature-binding techniques (see Table 3). The common operational features (e.g., *Door Control*) may require different

---

[4] There are local safety codes specific to each country, but this issue is not addressed in this paper.

implementation techniques (e.g., door control techniques) for different market-specific operating environments (e.g., external door devices). To accommodate these differences, each of the operational features is designed as a framework, and market-specific components are integrated into the framework at product-build time. The load-table technique is used to support the negotiation and sales of customer-selectable services (i.e., *VIP Driving* and *EFS Driving*) at product installation time.

Selecting feature-binding techniques during product planning helps to explore the engineering feasibility, and that selection may change as we gain a deeper and better understanding of the PL later in the development process.

The above marketing and product plan provides a concrete basis on which a detailed feature analysis for the product line can start and from which architectures and asset components can be developed. The next section illustrates a feature-oriented domain analysis (i.e., feature modeling) for the ECS product line asset development.

Table 3. Product Feature Delivery Methods

| Product Features | Feature Coverage | | Feature-Binding Time | Feature-Binding Technique |
	Functional product features: O (required), X (not required) Nonfunctional product features: VC (very critical), C (critical)			
	Asian Market	**Western Market**		
Automatic Driving	O	O	Build Time	Framework
Maintenance Driving	O	O	Build Time	
VIP Driving	O	X	Installation Time	Load Table
EFS Driving	O	X	Installation Time	
Door Control	O	O	Build Time	Framework
Run Control	O	O	Build Time	
Direction Control	O	O	Build Time	
Call Handling	O	O	Build Time	
Comfort	Smooth Ride	Regular Ride	Build Time	Macro Processing
Response Time	VC	C	Build Time	
Adaptability	C	VC	Build Time	
Reliability	VC	VC	Build Time	
Usability	Low-Level MMI	High-Level MMI	Build Time	

4.3   ECS Feature Modeling

Feature modeling analyzes the commonalities and variabilities of a product line and organizes them into a feature model. Product features identified in the product plan are organized into an initial feature model (see the Capability features at the top of Figure 4). The ECS product line consists of functional features (e.g., *Driving Services*) and nonfunctional features (e.g., *Comfort* and *Reliability*). *Driving Services* is a generalization of *Automatic Driving, Maintenance Driving, VIP Driving,* and *EFS*

Driving, each of which consists of four common operational features: *Call Handling,*
Run Control, Direction Control, and *Door Control.*

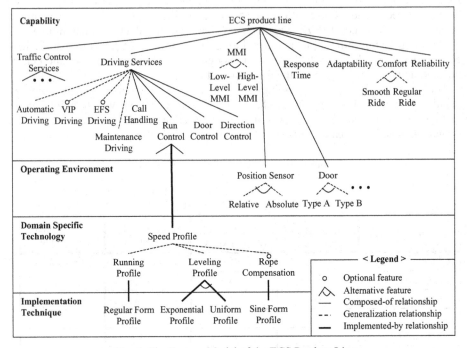

Fig. 4. The Feature Model of the ECS Product Line

The initial feature model is refined and extended by incorporating the operating
environment, domain-specific technology, implementation technique features, and
any capability features that are missing from the initial model. When incorporating
these features, analysts must investigate potential changes in the environments and
technologies (see [20], [22] for details on feature modeling).

Once the feature model is refined with design features that cover the environments,
domain technologies, and implementation techniques, this information is used to
refine the product plan, as shown in Figure 7. Since the initial marketing and product
plan may only contain delivery methods for functional and nonfunctional features,
product-feature-delivery methods for design features should also be explored. This
detailed plan is used for architecture and component design for the ECS product line,
which is described below.

4.4 ECS Architecture Design and Refinement

Architecture design starts with identifying high-level conceptual components and
specifying data and control dependencies among them. During the architecture design
activity, the marketing and product plan is used as a key design driver.

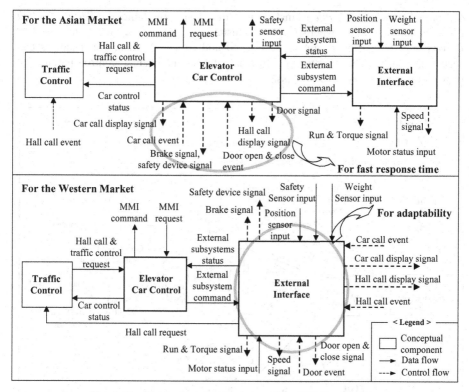

Fig. 5. The Conceptual Architectures of the ECS Product Line

The conceptual architecture of the ECS product line, shown in Figure 5, consists of three major conceptual components: *Traffic Control, Elevator Car Control,* and *External Interface.* As discussed in Section 4.1, the Asian market considers fast response times as important. Thus, the ECS architecture for the products targeted at the Asian market is designed with minimum layering. For example, as shown in the top half of Figure 5, the data and control flows in the circle are directed to the *Elevator Car Control* component without mediation by the *External Interface* component. Products in the Western market must be easily adaptable to product-specific external devices at installation time. To support this, the ECS architecture must be designed so that different types of devices can be configured easily without affecting the core part of ECS software. Thus, as shown in the bottom half of Figure 5, the *External Interface* component encapsulates the information on product-specific external devices and provides a common interface to the *Elevator Car Control* component.

The next step is to refine the conceptual architecture into process and deployment architectures. Figure 6 shows the process architecture for the *Elevator Car Control* component of the conceptual architecture for the Asian market shown in Figure 5. During the refinement, the product-feature-delivery methods (see Table 3) from the marketing and product plan are taken into consideration. The *Low-Level MMI* process, which implements the *Low-Level MMI* feature, is designed to configure the

Optional Service Spec Table at installation time. Using the table, the *Service Switch* process can determine whether or not customer-selectable services such as *VIP Driving* and *EFS Driving* are to be created and executed. Also, the installers can access the system to monitor the internal states and change control parameters through the *Low-Level MMI* process.

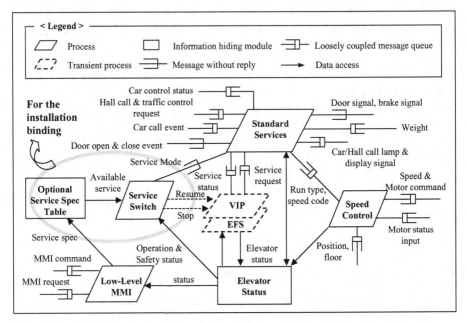

Fig. 6. The Process Architecture of the ECS Product Line for the Asian Market

As illustrated in the above examples, the marketing and product plan must be reflected in the architecture design; it is not easy to incorporate these design features after the fact. Once conceptual architectures are refined into process and deployment architectures, the architectural components are then refined into concrete components for implementation. The component design is illustrated in the next section.

4.5   ECS Component Design

As discussed in Section 3, component design starts with information from the marketing and product plan on how design features will be packaged into products and how they will be delivered to customers. Figure 7 shows a part of the product plan that is refined based on the feature model developed in Section 4.3. As the Asian market requires elevators with the *Smooth Ride* feature, two design features, *Exponential Profile* and *Rope Compensation*, are used to provide a smooth speed control. On the other hand, the Western market requires the *Regular Ride* feature and, therefore, the *Uniform Profile* feature is used. As the *Smooth Ride* and *Regular Ride* features are incorporated into products at product-build time (see Table 3), their related design features are also packaged into products at product-build time.

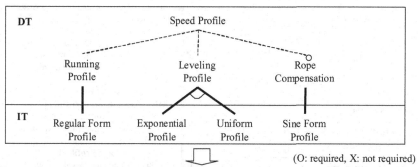

Product Features	Feature Coverage		Feature-Binding Time	Feature-Binding Technique
	Asian Market	Western Market		
Regular Form Profile	O	O	Build Time	
Exponential Profile	O	X	Build Time	
Uniform Profile	X	O	Build Time	Macro Processing
Rope Compensation	O	X	Build Time	

Product-Feature-Delivery Methods

Fig. 7. The Refined Product Plan

For the component design, candidate objects are also identified from the feature model and then incorporated into the design object model using necessary information such as product line requirements, COTS components, and design patterns that are relevant to the product line. The bottom left-hand box in Figure 8 shows the design object model developed from the feature model in Figure 7 and the Strategy Pattern [24]. Note that the design object model is not the design for the product line; no consideration of the product-feature-delivery methods has been made in structuring the model. It merely identifies objects that may be used for implementing architectural components.

Then, the component design activity refines the process and deployment architectures into concrete components using the design object model with considerations of the product-feature-delivery methods in the product plan. As shown in Figure 8, design objects are prepackaged into the *SpeedController* component, in which features are used to parameterize the component; this component will be instantiated at product-build time for the selected feature using a macro-processing mechanism. For example (see the right-hand box in Figure 8), if the variant features (i.e., *Exponential Profile, Rope Compensation*, and so on) are selected for the Asian market, the code segments related to the selected features are included in the product at product-build time. Otherwise, the code segments are excluded.

As another example of component design, the *Standard Services* process in Figure 6 is refined into a "framework" that defines a generic structure for the implementation of *Automatic Driving* and *Maintenance Driving* features. At product-build time, product-specific components for the *Automatic Driving* and *Maintenance Driving* features are instantiated using the framework.

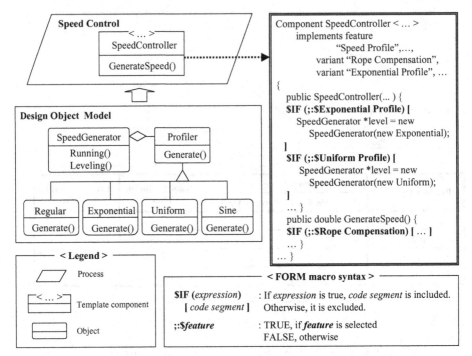

Fig. 8. A Design Object Model and Component Specification

We have illustrated how to develop product line assets (i.e., architectures and components) from a marketing perspective. The marketing issues must be studied thoroughly, and the engineering feasibility of the envisioned products must be analyzed carefully before the product line assets are developed. Without doing this, it will be very difficult to rectify these issues after components are implemented.

5   Conclusion

The reuse focus has shifted over the years from code reuse to design reuse, then from design reuse to domain engineering. Domain-engineering approaches, however, have often been found to be inefficient in discovering commonalities and engineering reusable architectures and components. Thus a new paradigm, called PL development, has emerged to remedy problems with the domain-engineering approaches that do not have a PL focus. The key element that differentiates the PL approach from others is the specific focus given to a family of products, *which is manifested as a marketing and product plan. This marketing and product plan sets the unambiguous context for PL asset development.*

This paper has introduced a method for PL asset development that uses the marketing and product plan of a PL as a key design driver. By demonstrating how the plan is used in PL asset development, this paper has (1) shifted the reuse perspective one step further to the front end of the product life cycle (i.e., to marketing and product planning), and (2) identified the key elements to be included in a marketing and product plan to be useful for PL asset development.

This marketing-oriented perspective can be very effective in uncovering critical quality attributes required for PL architecture and component design. The market analysis, which includes an analysis of the needs of the potential customers and their profiles (e.g., skill level or computing environment), provides critical information for deriving quality attributes required for the PL. These attributes may be refined and used to design required architectures and components. There is, however, no systematic method for identifying quality attributes from this marketing-oriented perspective.

By tightly coupling the marketing with asset development, we can develop assets that will support the business goals and satisfy the customers' needs. Also, asset developers can give feedback on the feasibility of the product plan early in the development process.

References

1. J. Neighbors, The Draco Approach to Construction Software from Reusable Components, *IEEE Transactions on Software Engineering*, **SE-10**(5), 564-573, September 1984.
2. K. Kang, S. Cohen, J. Hess, W. Nowak, and S. Peterson, Feature-Oriented Domain Analysis (FODA) Feasibility Study, *Technical Report CMU/SEI-90-TR-21*, Pittsburgh, PA, Software Engineering Institute, Carnegie Mellon University, November 1990.
3. R. Prieto-Diaz, Implementing Faceted Classification for Software Reuse, *Communications of the ACM*, **34**(5), 88-97, May 1991.
4. S. Bailin, Domain Analysis with KAPTUR, *Tutorials of TRI-Ada'93*, **I**, ACM, New York, NY, September 1993.
5. Software Productivity Consortium, Reuse-Driven Software Processes Guidebook, Version 02.00.03, *SPC-92019-CMC*, Herndon, VA, Software Productivity Consortium, 1993.
6. M. Simos et al, Software Technology for Adaptable Reliable Systems (STARS) Organization Domain Modeling (ODM) Guidebook Version 2.0, *STARS-VC-A025/001/00*, Manassas, VA, Lockheed Martin Tactical Defense Systems, 1996.
7. J. Coplien, D. Hoffman, and D. Weiss, Commonality and Variability in Software Engineering, *IEEE Software*, **15**(6), 37-45, November/December 1998.
8. K. Schmid, Scoping Software Product Lines, In Proceedings of the First Software Product Line Conference (SPLC), August 28-31, 2000, Denver, Colorado, USA, Patrick Donohoe (Ed.), *Software Product Lines: Experience and Research Directions*, 3-22, Norwell, Massachusetts: Kluwer Academic Publishers, 2000.
9. F. Buschmann, R. Meunier, H. Rohnert, P. Sommerlad, and M. Stal, *Pattern-Oriented Software Architecture: A System of Patterns*, Chichester, England, John Wiley & Sons Ltd., 1996.
10. K. Schmid and C. Gacek, Implementation Issues in Product Line Scoping, In Proceedings of the 6th International Conference on Software Reuse (ICSR-6), Vienna, Austria, June 2000. W. Frakes (Ed.), *Software Reuse: Advances in Software Reusability*, New York, NY: Springer-Verlag, June 2000.
11. K. C. Kang, F. Bachmann, L. Bass, and P. Donohoe, Product Line Component Design: Marketing and Product Plan as a Key Design Driver, *Technical Report*, Pittsburgh, PA, Software Engineering Institute, Carnegie Mellon University (in progress).
12. D. M. Weiss and C. T. R. Lai, *Software Product-Line Engineering: A Family-Based Software Development Process*, Reading, MA: Addison Wesley Longman, Inc., 1999.

13. J. Bosch, *Design and Use of Software Architectures: Adopting and Evolving a Product-line Approach*, Addison Wesley, ACM Press, 2000.
14. P. Donohoe, (Ed.) *Software Product Lines: Experience and Research Directions*, Norwell, Massachusetts: Kluwer Academic Publishers, 2000.
15. P. Clements and L. Northrop, *Software Product Lines: Practices and Patterns*, Boston, MA: Addison Wesley Longman, Inc., 2001.
16. K. Czarnecki and U. Eisenecker, *Generative Programming: Methods, Tools, and Applications*, Reading, MA: Addison Wesley Longman, Inc., 2000.
17. L. P. Deutsch, Design Reuse and Frameworks in the Smalltalk-80 System, In T. J. Biggerstaff and A. J. Perlis (Eds.) *Software Reusability, Volume II: Applications and Experience*, pp.57-71, Reading, MA: Addison-Wesley, 1989.
18. R. E. Johnson, Documenting Frameworks Using Patterns, In Proceedings of Object-Oriented Programming Systems, Language, and Applications Conference, pp.63-76, Vancouver, British Columbia, Canada, October 1992.
19. P. G. Bassett, *Framing Software Reuse: Lessons From The Real World*, Prentice Hall, Yourdon Press, 1997.
20. K. Kang, S. Kim, J. Lee, K. Kim, E. Shin and M. Huh, FORM: A Feature-Oriented Reuse Method with Domain-Specific Reference Architectures, *Annals of Software Engineering*, **5**, 143-168, 1998.
21. K. Lee, K. C. Kang, W. Chae, and B. Choi, Feature-Based Approach to Object-Oriented Engineering of Applications for Reuse, *Software-Practice and Experience*, **30**(9), 1025-1046, 2000.
22. K. C. Kang, K. Lee, J. Lee, and S. Kim, Feature Oriented Product Line Software Engineering: Principles and Guidelines, to appear as a chapter in *Domain Oriented Systems Development – Practices and Perspectives*, UK, Taylor & Francis, 2002.
23. L. Bass, P. Clements, and R. Kazman, "Software Architecture in Practice", Reading, MA: Addison Wesley Longman, Inc., 1998.
24. E. Gamma, R. Helm, R. Johnson, and J. Vlissides, Design Patterns: Elements of Reusable Object-Oriented Software, Reading, MA: Addison Wesley Longman, Inc., 1995.
25. F. Bachmann, L. Bass, G. Chastek, P. Donohoe, and F. Peruzzi, The Architecture Based Design Method, *Technical Report CMU/SEI-2000-TR-001*, Pittsburgh, PA, Software Engineering Institute, Carnegie Mellon University, January 2000.

Engineering Software Architectures, Processes and Platforms for System Families – ESAPS Overview

Frank van der Linden

Philips Medical Systems N.V.
Veenpluis 4-6, 5684 PC Best, NL
Frank.van.der.linden@philips.com

Abstract. Between July 1999 and June 2001, 22 European companies and research institutes worked together in the ESAPS project to enhance their capabilities for engineering software for system families. This paper describes the main objectives of the project, and an overview of the results obtained in the project. Finally, the project is related to other projects and initiatives with similar goals.

1   Introduction

Between July 1999 and June 2001, a consortium of 22 companies and research institutes in 6 European countries performed the ESAPS project (Engineering Software Architectures Processes and Platforms for System families). This project is part of the Eureka Σ! 2023 Programme, ITEA [12], and is project no. 99005 in this program. ITEA is to promote the development of embedded and distributed software and related software engineering technologies. It is an industry-driven strategic research and development program supported by national governments within the Eureka framework. The purpose of ITEA aim is to coordinate European software development efforts. Europe's leadership in embedded software and software-intensive systems is crucial to securing future competitiveness in a wide range of industries.

Companies within ESAPS are working on a large variety of embedded systems including medical imaging, mobile phones, flight control software, power distribution control, and car electronics. These companies felt market pressure to come with a software family approach. This pressure originated from the diverse market. Our customers have diverse requirements and expectations for the products. For instance, this may be based upon differences in age, culture, geographic region, legislation and budgets. In addition, there are differences in equipment that have to act in cooperation with the products. No single system serves all.

Moreover, the market asks for more functionality in our systems, which should have a higher quality in safety, security, reliability, and speed. To serve these requests a variety of complex products has to be produced, and they have to be marketed. This has to be done in a short time frame. Therefore the partners are faced with a need to produce systems in families to be able to design and manage commonality and diversity for similar systems.

G. Chastek (Ed.): SPLC2 2002, LNCS 2379, p. 383–397, 2002.

The development organisation needs to improve its efficiency: we need more diverse and more complex products with the same number of people. This is an additional reason to introduce system families. Produce the common parts only once and provide variation in a managed way, even if the variation is initially not accounted for. In order to provide a large amount of diverse products in a short time a kind of mass customisation is needed. We have to move from custom-made to ready-made products and keep the diversity according to customers' requests. This means just-in-time diversity, or mass customisation.

In short, we have to plan, design, market, develop, and sell diversity. This is the main objective of system family development: produce many variants in a short time.

The project consisted of a diversity of partners (see Figure 1). The first group of main partners, Philips, Nokia, Siemens, Thales, and Telvent, were in the course of introducing system family developments in large software organisations. There was a need for sharing experience and best practices among them. There were seven other companies involved in the program. They introduced system family development within smaller development groups. Finally, there were 10 research institutions involved in parts of the program. They had a focus on special topics and acted as consultants for companies that were both in and outside ESAPS.

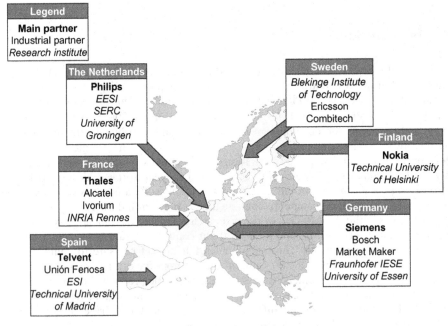

Fig. 1: ESAPS participants

This paper gives an overview of the highlights of ESAPS. Because ESAPS was a large project, the document is too short to present all results. The reader is referred to the complete set of results of the project, which can be found at [11]. At relevant parts of the text the reader is pointed towards more specific deliverables of ESAPS. In the next section the goals of ESAPS are presented. After that the main topics of ESAPS are introduced and achievements and main findings are presented. In many cases the arguments for the findings are not presented here. They can be found in the separate deliverables. After the findings, the relationship with other approaches is presented. We finish with conclusions and next steps.

2   ESAPS Goals

Figure 2 summarises the two main technical goals of ESAPS: to improve both in development paradigms and in reuse level. Improvement of the state of practice in software development is one way to improve the software productivity. In practice this means that we have to move towards component based development [9]. To improve the productivity even more, we need to improve our possibilities to reuse software parts and other software development assets for our diverse products [2]. In practice this means design not as a single product, but design diversity as a family: the *system family* approach. To move from bottom to top along this axis mean that more assets, not only software, become reusable, including designs, patterns, requirements, test specs, and test results, for instance. In addition, more planning and design of reuse becomes necessary. When ESAPS started, most software development for commercial embedded systems was located somewhere in the cloud. The aim was to move to state of practice to the northeast, to improve in both axes.

In addition to this set up, all ESAPS partners already have a collection of systems in the field that have to belong to the family, and for which maintenance is needed for several years onwards. Moreover, these systems contain assets that can be transformed into family assets, to be reusable in future family members. In short, incorporate the already existing (legacy) systems in the family, and treat them as family members henceforward.

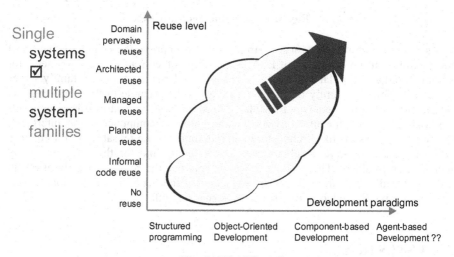

Fig. 2: ESAPS goals

2.1   ESAPS Reference Process

All activities in ESAPS are related to the family reference development process, depicted in Figure 3. This process is defined in the Praise project [13]. It is an abstract reference process for family development. At the bottom, we find a simple reference process for single system development. This process is augmented with a domain process producing family assets, to be reused by the product development process. In the middle repositories for family assets are shown. This process is instantiated in many different forms within the ESAPS companies.

The process classification of [2] can be mapped to this model as well. Application Family Engineering (AFE) is related to the activities in the top left-hand block, while Component System Engineering (CSE) is related to the other blocks in the top row and Application System Engineering (ASE) comprises the bottom row.

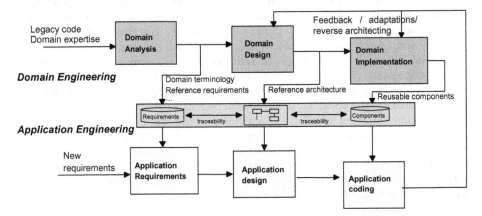

Fig. 3: ESAPS reference process

As discussed above, there was a strong force to improve the original situation of most partners at the beginning of ESAPS, which involved separate developments for separate products. Similar systems were grouped in domains. A system family serves a part of a domain. Family development involves the separate design, building and management of family assets in reusable entities. Since we move towards component-based development, the main assets are the software components and interfaces. However, other assets like architecture and requirements are reusable. Within the domain, there are separate developments for the family and for the different family members as products. The product developments use the reusable family assets in order to speed-up the production. The advantage of this set up is that the total development cost will be reduced after several systems are built.

3   ESAPS Results

Global attention points of ESAPS are:

- Analysis within the domain (top left of Figure 3)

- Specific topics: features, quality, scoping.
- Family development (top row of Figure 3)
  Specific topic: separate the common basis from the variation
- Manage the set of family assets (middle row of Figure 3)
- Requirements in a family context (left column of Figure 3)
- Development process (instantiations of Figure 3)
- Family evolution and product derivation (bottom row and feedback arrow, at the right of Figure 3)

For each of these subjects we have a separate section below.

3.1   Analysis within the Domain

Three different analysis issues were addressed: architecture analysis, domain analysis and aspect analysis.

3.1.1   Architecture Analysis

Various techniques are used for architecture analysis. Because of the importance of architectural decisions, the architecture has to be carefully modelled and analysed. If problems are found early in the software life cycle, they are easier to correct. Software quality cannot be appended late in a project. It must be inherent from the beginning. These arguments particularly hold for system family development, where the architecture has to be used in a variety of systems that all have to exhibit certain qualities. Moreover, certain qualities like variability and extensibility particularly hold for system families.

Architecture analysis is aimed to get confidence in the qualities of the architecture before a system is built. In the context of family development, architecture analysis also addresses the question whether the architecture is fit enough for being the basis of the complete family. Moreover, since the family architecture may be more generic, architecture analysis techniques may give rise to insufficient results. Within ESAPS we investigated whether additional techniques are necessary for family architectures, and whether existing analysis techniques are also useful for system families.

Architecture analysis is the process of measuring system properties based upon the architecture description. Architecture analysis in ESAPS concentrated itself to two topics: architecture assessment, which is mainly qualitative, and architecture verification, which is mainly quantitative. Assessment case studies within ESAPS resulted in some additions to traditional architecture assessment. However, we did not find enough difference with traditional architecture assessment. A specific case study resulted in an architecture mismatch assessment process.

Architecture assessment usually results in a qualitative validation. However, we did some experiments in a more quantitative direction. For instance, ESAPS introduced the application of assessment metrics for evolution analysis. This resulted in the determination of the priorities for architecture improvement. To support assessment, architecture extraction was considered.

Often legacy systems do not have a well-described architecture; it has to be extracted first. Architecture extraction techniques can also be used for automating the verification of implemented systems, to determine if they satisfy the defined architecture. Case studies were performed, and an extraction process is described. The results enforce our conviction that semi-automatic architecture extraction is possible and useful, both for the improvement the development process and for the ability to know where effort should be focussed.

3.1.2   Domain Analysis

Domain analysis is one of the basic activities in system family development. All systems in the family belong to the same domain, or a small set of domains, and the results of the domain analysis (the domain model), is usable for all these systems. Knowledge of the domain model is crucial for the family architecture, since the complete family architecture is described in terms of the domain model. ESAPS determined the main activities in a domain engineering process. We studied three parts of domain analysis: conceptual domain analysis, feature analysis, and scoping.

Conceptual domain analysis deals with the development of methods for identifying and modelling those assets that are common to all family members and those that are variable. Several case studies in conceptual domain analysis were performed. It was observed that conceptual domain model provides a shared framework for all systems in the family and is the basis for a common agreement amongst the developers.

Feature analysis deals with the modelling of commercial product features in domain entities. Relating the commercial features to architectural entities is crucial in determining which products have to be built, and in which order. Within ESAPS several feature models were built. Such a model is an important ingredient in the communication between the commercial and technical personnel. In addition, it helps to determine which features interact, and in which way. A feature model can be used to determine the relevant domains for the family, and it can be used as the basis for scoping.

Scoping deals with the determination of the border to the system family (i.e. determining which product do and which products don't belong to the family). The border is defined in terms of the domain model. Scoping activities resulted in a domains-taxonomy. ESAPS separated three distinct kinds of scoping: product line scoping, (determining the portfolio), domain scoping (determining domain boundaries), and asset scoping (determining what are the reusable assets in the family). A decision model for building reusable family assets, based on scoping the family, was determined. One of the findings is that scoping is a means to combine and provide decision support for the interaction between business objectives and domain modelling.

3.1.3   Aspect Analysis

Aspect analysis deals with the use of special system views for separate quality concerns. Like all architecture design, and more than in ordinary system development, the design of the system qualities should be done before the system is built. Aspects provide a secondary decomposition of the system [5], and when designed well, automatic code generation for many aspects may be supported [4]. This is especially important for system families, where the variation of the produced systems is also expressed in variable system qualities. The analysis and design for system quality aspects should be done in such a way that quality predictions could be made for all systems in the family before they are built. As the design for system qualities is not yet very mature, ESAPS had to set up an initial effort in this direction. This was directed towards aspect analysis, and aspect identification techniques were determined. It was found that in general, non-functional requirements are not expressed well enough. Case studies were performed to separate functional from non-functional aspects. It resulted in more useful views of the system, and it was found that the identification of the relevant aspects speeds up the requirements engineering process. The identification of aspects was found to be useful in focussing the architecture evaluation, and can be used as input for scoping activities.

More details on the analysis subjects can be found in the three deliverables "Architecture analysis and modelling," "Domain analysis," and "Aspect analysis and modelling" [11].

3.2   Family Development

Developing systems in families enable system and software developers to build systems through the binding of variability within the systems assets. Therefore ESAPS did an explicit investigation on the subject of variability. Designing system families requires finding a way of architecting the commonality and variability in order to exploit them during the tailoring phase. The system family architecture, or reference architecture, defines the components (mandatory, optional, and alternative), component interrelationships, constraints, and guidelines for use and evolution in building systems in the system family. Consequently, the reference architecture must support common capabilities identified in the specification, the commonality, and the potential variability within the system family. The reference architecture is then used to create an instance of a particular architecture for a new variant.

The modelling of product line architectures within ESAPS resulted in the separation of the concepts of *variability-in-the-large* and *variability-in-the-long-term*. This separates the cases where many variants exist at the same time from the cases where few variants exist concurrently, but a large number of variants will be built over time. This is a useful separation because it is connected to the type of equipment and to the market. The first case we usually find in consumer products, the latter in professional products. Note that there is no sharp border between these cases, and there are systems with many variants and a long history. ESAPS found that the family patterns differ for these categories. For instance, in the first case often a hierarchy of architectures (reference architecture, family architecture, product architecture, ...) will be present, in the second case often a single, but layered, architecture is used.

A specific study was performed on the representation of variability information in the architecture. This resulted in a list of variability mechanisms, guidelines for using them, and their representation in UML. It was found that neither UML nor any other commercial description technique has ready-to-use mechanisms for variability support. As a first step, ESAPS proposed the addition of variation points to all kinds of entities in UML.

In order to support the product selection process, a design decision model may be useful. Such a model captures the dependencies between variation points and provides guidelines in which order variant selections should be taken. Several experiments with such decision models were performed. Tool support is often crucial for dealing with design decision models; it should keep track of decisions already taken, and what are the consequences on the remaining decisions to be taken, and provide information about the resulting system properties. Such tool support may lead to the semi-automatic instantiation of the variability to derive product architectures.

Details can be found in the deliverable "Style, structures, and views for handling commonalities and variabilities" [11].

3.3   Manage the Set of Family Assets

System families can only be based upon platforms and components [9]. A platform is the common (software) basis upon which the complete family is built. Components are the most important reusable software assets within a system family. Platforms and components have to developed carefully in order to be able to build the systems right. In many cases, the platform itself is built from components. However, there are several ways this can be done. Therefore ESAPS investigated asset development, with a focus towards components and platforms.

ESAPS determined a list of relevant assets within system family development. Based upon this list a tool chain for asset management and product derivation was proposed. It was found that in a system family context each asset needs to carry much more of information than is practice presently for traditional software packages. Specific attention was paid to component interfaces as separate assets, since interfaces can be used to decouple variation points. The advantage of using separated information models as additional assets to components and interfaces was investigated. By putting frequent changing elements in the information models, the interfaces and components can remain stable for longer times and are therefore more reusable in a family context. In addition, explicit variability support for components was addressed.

ESAPS proposed a process to design, implement, and deliver components, including a component configuration management approach. This process covers the use of third party and legacy components within the family. A specific study was performed on wrapping legacy components. A model of relationships between entities representing the different layers of abstraction of specification and realisation was proposed to support the component development process. In addition, ESAPS addressed component description methods and techniques. In particular, investigations related to both formal and non-formal approaches were addressed. Issues were the relationships between properties of compositions and properties of constituting components. Specific attention was on quality requirements.

ESAPS addressed the supporting services of and variability within component-based platforms for system families. In addition, ESAPS investigated the problems of having several third-party, frameworks in a single platform. Examples of such problems are

- Bad cohesion between frameworks
- Gaps and overlaps in domain coverage
- Architecture design choices

ESAPS proposed a collection of solutions for dealing with these problems in several situations.

The complete set of diverse assets has to be managed in order to be able to produce new system variants within the family. In particular, it has to be clear which assets are available to produce new variant systems, which assets have to be adapted, and which have to be build anew. ESAPS investigated *change management* to address these questions. Change management should enable the prediction of properties of

- Assets before actually building or adapting them,
- Systems based upon the new or adapted assets

This is important for system families, because changes in one asset will have consequences to many products in several ways. We need to be very careful with changes. Guidelines and automated support are very essential for identifying the changes caused by the modification of a given asset, and vice versa (identifying the required changes to produce a given variant system). These guidelines may be accomplished with tradeoffs or constraints on specific products or product parts.

The change management process was introduced as a specific activity in the product engineering process. ESAPS separated evolution from change, based on the affected time frame. A specific investigation into architecture evolution resulted in the identification of several architecture evolution categories. These categories were used to estimate the change impact. Another study determined a process for dealing with change, taking into account the sources and the kinds of change. Guidelines for family evolution and a design hierarchy for change management were introduced.

Several additional aspects of the change management related to system family development were addressed. The consequences of parallel development for change management were studied. The propagation of change over family assets was studied, and related to a design decision model. ESAPS identified the activities and roles within a change request process, and also for working in parallel developments. In all cases, first attempts to deal with these complex matters were proposed and experimented with. Finally, change management was viewed from a logistic perspective, including the assembly, deployment, and support of the system.

Details can be found in the deliverables "Platform and Components" and "Change management and evolution support" [11].

3.4 Requirements in a Family Context

Within system families, the requirements come in several sorts. There are requirements that hold for the complete family, but there are also requirements that only hold for only one, or few systems. In addition, there are requirements dealing with functional and with nonfunctional properties. A clear classification of the diverse kinds of requirements is needed. In system families, requirements may have variation points that distinguish the different constituent systems. To be able to deal efficiently with requirements, it should be clear what kinds of requirements are necessary and useful in the family. It is also necessary to be able to select the requirements for a single member of the family and use that for fast selection of assets needed to build that member. ESAPS considered requirements management for addressing these issues.

In order to be able to derive a new variant system we should be able to identify all requirements for this variant. These are both those requirements that are common to all product variants, and those that belong to the specific variant. A clear distinction between family generic requirements and product specific requirements should be made. A product specific requirement may be a specific variant of a generic requirement, but it may also be a separate requirement for the variant.

Having determined the requirements for a specific system is just the first step. The requirements should lead to the selection of the assets to build the system. *Requirement traceability* addresses this aspect. Traceabilty deals both with the

- Relationships between requirements of different abstraction levels
- Relationships between requirements and other system assets

Traceabilty helps to select those parts of the system family architecture that can be reused in the new variant, and possibly be adjusted. We should be able to document and reuse the architectural decisions at the variation points. Traceability is necessary to know what should be part of actual systems, and what still has to be developed. It is also essential for change management. Therefore establishing and maintaining traceability between development artefacts is essential for an effective and error-free definition of product specific architecture.

Traceability was classified in several variants based upon its use: pre & post, horizontal & vertical. The classification was captured in a usable traceability model and led to explicit requirements for traceability tools. One of the main findings was that the traceability model is an excellent communication medium for the family stakeholders.

ESAPS attempted to find out how requirements should be described to support all actions discussed above. For instance, the description should allow for variation points. It should also allow the introduction of traceability links of several kinds. A conceptual model for system family requirements was built to be able to identify the separate kinds of requirements. Based on this, a design decision model was proposed.

Requirement models were constructed incorporating traceability of different kinds. The models are related via traceability to other system family models. The models and the traceability links were used to keep the set of requirements consistent with the architecture and the system produced. The requirement management process was described, and related to the software engineering process. In particular, it is related to change management activities. Several experiments on requirement description, traceability, and supporting tools were performed within the contributing companies. Details can be found in the deliverables "System family requirements classification and formalisms" and "Requirements modelling and traceability" [11].

3.5   Development Process

System family development processes are more complex than single system development processes. The development and management of reusable assets have to be performed, and should be related to the product development process. Because of the many possibilities in determining the family development process ESAPS addressed this topic. The existing approaches needed to be compared because there are many possible processes. The processes of domain, component, and application engineering may be synchronised and interlaced in several ways. There are many reasons to do it in one way or another. Moreover quality concerns are related to both family and single-product issues. This has to be reflected in the process as well.

Within ESAPS several process frameworks are in use. Many of these frameworks are proprietary, but some of them are derived from published frameworks, such as RUP or PuLSE. ESAPS presented all process frameworks used in the participating companies in the same template. In this way, ESAPS determined a clear set of necessary activities and work products for family development. The template was used to compare the different frameworks. In fact, all frameworks were compared with R-SPICE, a framework developed at the ESI. This was the most complete process of all.

Because no framework covered all identified activities, the comparison indicated room for improvements for all of them. In all cases there are separate processes for domain and application engineering, as already indicated in Figure 3. Since no existing framework exhibits all of the important activities, it was concluded that all existing process frameworks are insufficient for product line development. Details can be found in the deliverable "System family process frameworks" [11].

3.6   Family Evolution and Product Derivation

A system family evolves over time. One cause for evolution is that new products are built within the family. Another one is that existing assets are improved, split, or combined. Within a system family the latter kind of evolution has a large impact, since such adaptations may affect many existing systems in the family. ESAPS addressed both aspects of system evolution: the first one because system family development is introduced to make system development cheap and fast; the latter one because this aspect may make it expensive and slow.

Product derivation deals with the fast production of systems based upon the specific requirements. The components that form the application system have to be selected. A selection also has to be made for the parameters (properties, attributes) for instances of generic components. Based upon the selection, the executable system has to be built. In order to provide feedback, it has to be clear how a selection influence the functional and quality attributes and other constraints (e.g., time to market).

ESAPS investigated the use of family *asset management*, in order to be able to find the right assets to build the systems. This should help to support asset evolution, and keep track of which assets are used for which variant. Meta models were built to be able to better classify the different kinds of assets in the family. Methods for effective component and interface selection in an asset base were introduced. The derivation process covers the complete set of activities to derive a product in the family. The merits of a declarative approach towards configurability were investigated. Such an approach improves quality of the resulting system.

Specific attention was directed towards *variable resolution*, since this is an important step in the derivation of the products themselves. ESAPS determined a framework of the technology and the concepts that are related to variability. The framework helps to recognise where and when variability is needed, and to recognise which patterns often related to variability. A crucial factor here is the right choice of variable point representation. ESAPS studied development processes and tool support for product derivation based upon an asset base, using design decision models. One of the results is a clear set of requirements for supporting tools.

Depending on the situation, system configuration may be static or dynamic at initialisation and/or run-time. Any choice for the moment of configuration influences the possibilities of customising, upgrading, or adapting the components, architectures, and requirements. ESAPS investigated techniques for the configuration support that involve a configuration declaration language, a verifier, and a system generator. ESAPS also introduced a model relating features, variability resolution, and software logistics. This led to methods to support late variability selection. Details can be found in the deliverable "System family variant configuration and derivation" [11].

4   Relationship to Other Approaches

ESAPS is a project in a series of projects all dealing with a European approach towards software product family development. Figure 4 shows the ESAPS project in a
sequence of family development projects. The picture shows which of the main development concerns are addressed by ESAPS. These main development concerns are:

- Business – how to make your money
- Architecture – how to make your systems in a technical sense
- Process – what the responsibilities are in the creation of systems
- Organisation – how the responsibilities are distributed over the people

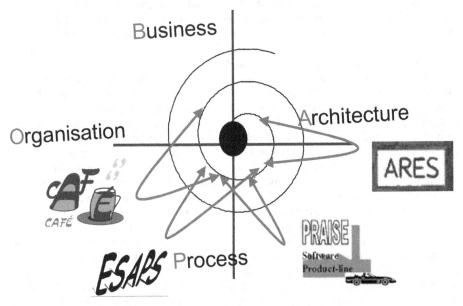

Fig. 4: ESAPS Concerns

The idea that system family development might be beneficial for business originated
in 1990. Within several companies there were already initial developments leading to
the introduction of system families. For instance, the Building Block approach of PKI
[5] was an initial system family approach within Philips. Based upon these initial efforts it was realised that such an approach is beneficial for other development departments. Several European companies with the same conviction that a system family
approach is beneficial initiated the ARES project (1995-1998) [3]. This project
mainly considered the architecture concerns for system families, because these were
considered to be the most important. Another group of companies formed the
PRAISE project (1998-1999) [13]. They considered process concerns for system family development. The companies involved in both projects joined forces, and initiated
the ESAPS project (1999-2001). As is described here, ESAPS has a focus on the
process issues. However, several architecture issues were also addressed, and certain
organisational concerns. It is based upon the results of ARES and PRAISE. The fol-

low-up project CAFÉ (2001-2003) [10] has more focus on organisation issues and more business concerns. The partners of CAFÉ are mainly the same as those from ESAPS On the organisational side, effort is directed towards asset development and management in distributed organisations, and the organisation of testing. On the business side, it wants to establish evidence in the cost reduction of system family development, and it wants to address issues of how and when a system family approach can be introduced in an organisation.

In all these projects, the involved companies were the initiators and determined the agenda. It was based upon their own experience and economic need for product families. The projects joined forces to learn from each other. Research institutes were selected according to their added value for the projects.

During the course of the projects we realised that architectural problems were not the most important ones in the introduction of system families. We recognised the importance of process, organisation and business drives for going towards product families. It is more important that the technical and architecture solutions that be used within the family. However, the right architecture is still crucial in families. The spiral that is shown in Figure 4 symbolises the order in which we envisage improvements. Based upon the intuitive ideas that a family approach is beneficial for the business, the architecture concerns are addressed (ARES). A process is put in place around the architecture (PRAISE, ESAPS). An organisation implements the process (ESAPS, CAFÉ). As soon as all is in place, the business may be addressed more clearly (CAFÉ), which in turn may lead to an improved architecture, process etc.

Within these projects we have organised a sequence of workshops on the topic of product family engineering [6][7][8]. Through these workshops we came in contact with others working on the same subject: most notably, with the people from the SEI Product Line Initiative [1], which started almost at the same time. This initiative had the same objectives in mind: Improving, and introducing, product families (product lines) in the industrial organisations.

The Product Line Initiative, founded at the SEI, became involved in product line programmes in their clients' businesses. Again, the driving force was the economic need of the involved companies. Because of their background, the SEI did more work in putting all (process) ingredients in a single framework [1], which extensively lists the main practices that are found to be important for system family development. The results of ESAPS, and CAFÉ, are not yet described in a framework and a collection of best practices. This may be a task of a follow-up project of CAFÉ. Until now, The main partners of ESAPS are industries and they do not want to spend their resources to put everything in a single framework. ESAPS is an ITEA project and thus is restricted to a two-year time frame. It was considered to be more important, in such a time frame, to produce an initial set of practices, which would have to be abstracted later. Moreover, we found a diversity of practices, and it is not always easy to merge practices of company borders. The main partners have different cultural backgrounds, and in Europe country borders often imply cultural borders. Therefore processes and organisations that work well in one company may work less well in other companies. This still has to be sorted out. In the mean time the way the ESAPS results are produced are good enough for our present purposes. The main industrial partners can benchmark themselves towards others, and take over practices of other companies that appear to be beneficial.

5   Conclusion and Next Steps

ESAPS is built around a collection of European industries that have an economic need to introduce system family development in their software development organisations. ESAPS resulted in a set of many different deliverables, each addressing a single topic within family development. The main reason for being active in ESAPS is to exchange information, and to speed-up software improvement. The conviction is that improvement may be based upon the comparison of benefits and drawbacks of the approaches taken by the different partners. The major focus of the project was around process issues, although there was also some attention to architecture and organisation issues. ESAPS was not meant to be a research project; instead it was aimed to introduce research solutions into the companies. Moreover it was aimed to spread knowledge available within the development organisation towards others, resulting in an improvement of all that are involved.

ESAPS was organised in a large (~20) set of working groups, each addressing a separate topic. Each deliverable of ESAPS is in fact a deliverable of such a working group. To keep coherence two measures were taken: first, people and companies were involved in more than one working group; second, on a regular basis internal workshops took place, which involved the complete project. A consequence of the setup was that not all deliverables were of the same quality and of comparable structure, but we got people together in the involved companies who really have to work with the material. We found that this setup was good for the involved people. Architects found that they were not the only ones with their problems. For most topics we addressed in ESAPS, improvements were obtained. We got a better insight in the real problems involved in family development, and where to put our attention for follow-up activities. Processes and organisations have been adapted, but most are still in the course of adaptation. In many cases experiments were performed, and the results are used in the companies. See also the deliverable "Experiment results" [11]. A drawback of the whole approach is that we still do not have a single overall picture of what is really achieved within ESAPS.

Because of our positive experiences, the European consortium that did the ESAPS work continues in roughly the same constitution in a follow-up project, CAFÉ [10]. This project takes some early and late process issues into account. Moreover, more attention is paid towards business and organisation needs. In fact, CAFÉ addresses the following main topics: adoption of system-family approach in the organisation, asset management, improvement of traceability and change impact analysis, product derivation, validation, and testing of the assets produced. As within ESAPS the main drive is to learn from each other, not to put a single framework in place.

Of course each of the ESAPS results cannot be seen as a final result on the topic. For that purpose most results are in a too rough shape. However, the involved partners trust that the results serve their needs for improvement. Others, especially research institutes, may build upon the ESAPS results to make more polished results, possibly within a single framework. In addition, most of the ESAPS results indicate additional work that still needs to be done. Some of these topics, but not all, are taken into account in CAFÉ. In many cases there is a lack of good tool support. The tool vendors are not used to make tools for product family development organisations, and their tools do not support the needs we have. In most cases the models ESAPS made were only initial models, and we have to improve upon them. A similar remark holds for the processes. A lot of work still has to be performed in asset management and change management. We need to keep control of all products that are and will be made within the family. The different approaches that are introduced within ESAPS do not always integrate well. Work has to be done to perform such integration.

References

1. Paul Clements, Linda Northrop, Software Product Lines, Addison Wesley 2001, ISBN 0-201-70332-7
2. Ivar Jacobson, Martin Griss, Patrik Jonsson, Software Reuse, Addison Wesley 1997, ISBN 0-201-92476-5
3. Mehdi Jazayeri, Alexander Ran, Frank van der Linden, Software Architecture for Product Families, Addison Wesley 2001, ISBN 0-201-69967-2
4. Gregor Kiczales, et. al., Aspect-Oriented Programming, Proceedings ECOOP '97, Object-Oriented Programming 11th European Conference, Springer Verlag 1997, LNCS 1241, pp. 220-242
5. Frank van der Linden, J.K. Müller, Creating Architectures with Building Blocks, IEEE Software 12 no. 6, 1995, pp. 51-60
6. Frank van der Linden (ed.), Development and Evolution of Software Architectures for Product Families, Springer Verlag 1998, LNCS 1429, ISBN 3-540-64916-6
7. Frank van der Linden (ed.), Software Architectures for Product Families, Springer Verlag 2000, LNCS 1951, ISBN 3-540-41480-0
8. Frank van der Linden (ed.), Product Family Engineering, to be published Springer Verlag 2002, LNCS 2290
9. Clemens Szyperski, Component Software, Addison Wesley 1997, ISBN 0-201-17888-5
10. CAFÉ Web-site at ESI: http://www.esi.es/cafe/
11. ESAPS Web-site at ESI: http://www.esi.es/esaps/
12. ITEA web-site: http://www.itea-office.org/
13. Praise Web-site at ESI: http://www.esi.es/Projects/Reuse/Praise/

Author Index

Lecture Notes in Computer Science

For information about Vols. 1–2312
please contact your bookseller or Springer-Verlag

Vol. 2353: A. Heyden, G. Sparr, M. Nielsen, P. Johansen (Eds.), Computer Vision – ECCV 2002. Proceedings, Part IV. XXVIII, 841 pages. 2002.

Vol. 2355: M. Matsui (Ed.), Fast Software Encryption. Proceedings, 2001. VIII, 169 pages. 2001.

Vol. 2358: T. Hendtlass, M. Ali (Eds.), Developments in Applied Artificial Intelligence. Proceedings, 2002 XIII, 833 pages. 2002. (Subseries LNAI).

Vol. 2359: M. Tistarelli, J. Bigun, A.K. Jain (Eds.), Biometric Authentication. Proceedings, 2002. X, 197 pages. 2002.

Vol. 2360: J. Esparza, C. Lakos (Eds.), Application and Theory of Petri Nets 2002. Proceedings, 2002. X, 445 pages. 2002.

Vol. 2361: J. Blieberger, A. Strohmeier (Eds.), Reliable Software Technologies – Ada-Europe 2002. Proceedings, 2002 XIII, 367 pages. 2002.

Vol. 2362: M. Tanabe, P. van den Besselaar, T. Ishida (Eds.), Digital Cities II. Proceedings, 2001. XI, 399 pages. 2002.

Vol. 2363: S.A. Cerri, G. Gouardères, F. Paraguaçu (Eds.), Intelligent Tutoring Systems. Proceedings, 2002. XXVIII, 1016 pages. 2002.

Vol. 2364: F. Roli, J. Kittler (Eds.), Multiple Classifier Systems. Proceedings, 2002. XI, 337 pages. 2002.

Vol. 2366: M.-S. Hacid, Z.W. Raś, D.A. Zighed, Y. Kodratoff (Eds.), Foundations of Intelligent Systems. Proceedings, 2002. XII, 614 pages. 2002. (Subseries LNAI).

Vol. 2367: J. Fagerholm, J. Haataja, J. Järvinen, M. Lyly. P. Råback, V. Savolainen (Eds.), Applied Parallel Computing. Proceedings, 2002. XIV, 612 pages. 2002.

Vol. 2368: M. Penttonen, E. Meineche Schmidt (Eds.), Algorithm Theory – SWAT 2002. Proceedings, 2002. XIV, 450 pages. 2002.

Vol. 2369: C. Fieker, D.R. Kohel (Eds.), Algebraic Number Theory. Proceedings, 2002. IX, 517 pages. 2002.

Vol. 2370: J. Bishop (Ed.), Component Deployment. Proceedings, 2002. XII, 269 pages. 2002.

Vol. 2371: S. Koenig, R. Holte (Eds.), Abstraction, Reformulation, and Approximation. Proceedings, 2002. XI, 349 pages. 2002. (Subseries LNAI).

Vol. 2372: A. Pettorossi (Ed.), Logic Based Program Synthesis and Transformation. Proceedings, 2001. VIII, 267 pages. 2002.

Vol. 2373: A. Apostolico, M. Takeda (Eds.), Combinatorial Pattern Matching. Proceedings, 2002. VIII, 289 pages. 2002.

Vol. 2374: B. Magnusson (Ed.), ECOOP 2002 – Object-Oriented Programming. XI, 637 pages. 2002.

Vol. 2375: J. Kivinen, R.H. Sloan (Eds.), Computational Learning Theory. Proceedings, 2002. XI, 397 pages. 2002. (Subseries LNAI).

Vol. 2377: A. Birk, S. Coradeschi, T. Satoshi (Eds.), RoboCup 2001: Robot Soccer World Cup V. XIX, 763 pages. 2002. (Subseries LNAI).

Vol. 2378: S. Tison (Ed.), Rewriting Techniques and Applications. Proceedings, 2002. XI, 387 pages. 2002.

Vol. 2379: G.J. Chastek (Ed.), Software Product Lines. Proceedings, 2002. X, 399 pages. 2002.

Vol. 2380: P. Widmayer, F. Triguero, R. Morales, M. Hennessy, S. Eidenbenz, R. Conejo (Eds.), Automata, Languages and Programming. Proceedings, 2002. XXI, 1069 pages. 2002.

Vol. 2381: U. Egly, C.G. Fermüller (Eds.), Automated Reasoning with Analytic Tableaux and Related Methods. Proceedings, 2002. X, 341 pages. 2002 .(Subseries LNAI).

Vol. 2382: A. Halevy, A. Gal (Eds.), Next Generation Information Technologies and Systems. Proceedings, 2002. VIII, 169 pages. 2002.

Vol. 2383: M.S. Lew, N. Sebe, J.P. Eakins (Eds.), Image and Video Retrieval. Proceedings, 2002. XII, 388 pages. 2002.

Vol. 2384: L. Batten, J. Seberry (Eds.), Information Security and Privacy. Proceedings, 2002. XII, 514 pages. 2002.

Vol. 2385: J. Calmet, B. Benhamou, O. Caprotti, L. Henocque, V. Sorge (Eds.), Artificial Intelligence, Automated Reasoning, and Symbolic Computation. Proceedings, 2002. XI, 343 pages. 2002. (Subseries LNAI).

Vol. 2386: E.A. Boiten, B. Möller (Eds.), Mathematics of Program Construction. Proceedings, 2002. X, 263 pages. 2002.

Vol. 2389: E. Ranchhod, N.J. Mamede (Eds.), Advances in Natural Language Processing. Proceedings, 2002. XII, 275 pages. 2002. (Subseries LNAI).

Vol. 2391: L.-H. Eriksson, P.A. Lindsay (Eds.), FME 2002: Formal Methods – Getting IT Right. Proceedings, 2002. XI, 625 pages. 2002.

Vol. 2392: A. Voronkov (Ed.), Automated Deduction – CADE-18. Proceedings, 2002. XII, 534 pages. 2002. (Subseries LNAI).

Vol. 2393: U. Priss, D. Corbett, G. Angelova (Eds.), Conceptual Structures: Integration and Interfaces. Proceedings, 2002. XI, 397 pages. 2002. (Subseries LNAI).

Vol. 2398: K. Miesenberger, J. Klaus, W. Zagler (Eds.), Computers Helping People with Special Needs. Proceedings, 2002. XXII, 794 pages. 2002.

Vol. 2399: H. Hermanns, R. Segala (Eds.), Process Algebra and Probabilistic Methods. Proceedings, 2002. X, 215 pages. 2002.

Vol. 2401: P.J. Stuckey (Ed.), Logic Programming. Proceedings, 2002. XI, 486 pages. 2002.

Vol. 2403: Mark d'Inverno, M. Luck, M. Fisher, C. Preist (Eds.), Foundations and Applications of Multi-Agent Systems. Proceedings, 1996-2000. X, 261 pages. 2002. (Subseries LNAI).

Vol. 2405: B. Eaglestone, S. North, A. Poulovassilis (Eds.), Advances in Databases. Proceedings, 2002. XII, 199 pages. 2002.

Vol. 2407: A.C. Kakas, F. Sadri (Eds.), Computational Logic: Logic Programming and Beyond. Part I. XII, 678 pages. 2002. (Subseries LNAI).

Vol. 2408: A.C. Kakas, F. Sadri (Eds.), Computational Logic: Logic Programming and Beyond. Part II. XII, 628 pages. 2002. (Subseries LNAI).

Vol. 2409: D. Mount, C. Stein (Eds.), Algorithm Engineering and Experiments. Proceedings, 2002. VIII, 207 pages. 2002.